Euripides: Four Plays

Medea
Hippolytus
Heracles
Bacchae

In memory of Adeline Veronica Aquilino
Angel of courage and of love
1952–2002

Cover: Brygos Painter (5th BCE). Maenad (Bacchant), Attic Wine Cup, 490 BCE. Staatliche Antikensammlung, Munich, Germany. Photo credit: Erich Lessing / Art Resource, NY

ISBN 10: 1-58510-048-X
ISBN 13: 978-1-58510-048-4

This book is published by Focus Publishing, R. Pullins & Company, Inc., PO Box 369, Newburyport MA 01950. All rights are reserved. No part of this publication may be reproduced, stored in a retrieval system, or transmitted in any form or by any means, electronic, mechanical, by photocopying, recording, or by any other means, without the prior written permission of the publisher.

Printed in the United States of America.

16 15 14 13 12 11 10 9 8 7 6

0911TS

EURIPIDES: FOUR PLAYS

MEDEA
HIPPOLYTUS
HERACLES
BACCHAE

TRANSLATION WITH NOTES
AND INTRODUCTION

STEPHEN ESPOSITO, EDITOR
BOSTON UNIVERSITY

Focus Classical Library
Focus Publishing
R. Pullins Company
Newburyport MA

In memory of Adeline Veronica Aquilino
Angel of courage and of love
1952-2002

Table of Contents

Preface

ACKNOWLEDGEMENTS

This anthology collects four of the greatest plays of the fifth-century Athenian dramatist Euripides. All four have been previously published as single volumes in the Focus Classical Library over the past fifteen years. For this volume they have been revised and updated. Such a large project requires the help and cooperation of many people. So I would like, at the outset, to recognize those friends who have stood beside me along the way.

I thank my friend Fran Hurley for her generous encouragement, kindness, and constructive criticism. My mother and father, Mary and Joseph Esposito, have also, as always, been wonderful in their moral support.

For sharing their vast knowledge of Greek history and literature and for steering me away from many errors I thank Jay Samons, Stephen Scully (my Classics colleagues at Boston University) and Charles Segal (of Harvard). Charlie had many useful comments on my original manuscript of the *Bacchae*. He is missed by all lovers of Greek literature. My friends Lewis Fried, Beni Kane Jaro, Norma Dancis, and Charlotte Gordon shared their love and wisdom of Judaism and for that I am most appreciative.

Colleagues at Boston University gave me the benefit of their various wisdoms and I thank especially Jeff Henderson, Frank Nisetich, Zsuzsanna Varhelyi, Stephanie Nelson, Peter Hawkins, Jonathan Klawans, Deeana Klepper, Diana Lobel, David Eckel, Bernard Prusak, and Richard Oxenberg.

My collaborators, Michael Halleran and Tony Podlecki, have been most generous with their time and energy as we reviewed the texts together. I am deeply appreciative for their stimulating discussions over the past year.

My publisher Ron Pullins has been a pillar of patience and I thank him for his encouragement in bringing this project to successful completion. Thanks also to Cindy Zawalich and Melissa Wood.

Lastly I remember Addie, to whom I dedicate this book. We enjoyed many wonderful years together and she is dearly missed.

NOTES ON REVISIONS TO THE TRANSLATIONS (2002)

All four translations in this anthology have been previously published as separate volumes in the Focus Classical Library: *Heracles* (1988, revised 1993), *Medea* (1989, revised 1998), *Bacchae* (1998), and *Hippolytus* (2001). Each translation has been updated for this volume. In revising the previous editions for this anthology, I have abridged (substantially) the notes to the *Medea* and *Bacchae*. The notes to the *Hippolytus* and *Heracles* have been altered very little. Virtually all those notes in the earlier editions which concerned the state of the Greek text have been removed in this volume.

A few brief remarks with regard to alterations made to each play: In A.J. Podlecki's *Medea* I have made substantial revisions throughout the translation, especially in the choral odes. I made these numerous changes in light of recent scholarship and in fruitful consultation with Tony Podlecki. Unfortunately the superb new commentary by Donald Mastronarde, *Euripides: Medea* (Cambridge, 2002) appeared too late, and is used only in my introduction.

The only changes made to Michael Halleran's *Hippolytus* 2001 edition are typographical.

In Halleran's *Heracles*, two changes were made, one of which is quite important. Both Halleran and I agree that line 1351 should be translated "I will brave death" rather than "I will endure life." In this we follow both the ancient manuscript tradition (which reads *thanaton*, "death" rather than *bioton*, "life") and also numerous modern scholars (e.g. W. Arrowsmith, J. Gibert). Another change, of less moment, has been made at line 1313, where Halleran has provided a supplemental translation to fill in a gap left in the Greek text.

In my own *Bacchae*, the only important textual change is in the translation of the controversial choral refrain at 877-81 (= 897-901). This passage has been retranslated in light of a discussion I had with Charles Segal. His argument can now be found in his commentary (pp. 121-22) in *Euripides: Bakkhai* (Oxford, 2001) trans. Reginald Gibbons, notes and introduction by C. Segal.

NOTES ON REVISIONS TO THE TRANSLATIONS (2004)

All four translations have been updated in one form or another for this corrected version of the 2002 edition. The revisions have involved correction of simple errors as well as substantial changes to the general introduction, translations, notes, and stage directions. The bibliography has also been updated to reflect recent scholarship on Euripides, the plays herein, and Athenian tragedy generally. The most numerous and significant alterations have been made to Esposito's *Bacchae*, especially in light of the recent splendid work of David Kovacs, namely the sixth and final volume of his Loeb series, *Euripides: Bacchae, Iphigeneia at Aulis, Rhesus* (Harvard UniversityPress: Cambridge, Ma. and London, 2002) as well as his philological studies of the Greek text in *Euripidea Tertia* (Brill: Leiden and Boston, 2003) with pages 111-136 on *Bacchae*.

I would like to thank Madeline McNeely for her moral support and Ron Pullins for his editorial assistance and continued passion for bringing the Greek and Roman Classics to the students of America through the Focus Classical Library.

Stephen Esposito, Boston University, June 2004

Introduction

by Stephen Esposito

"Has any nation ever produced a dramatist who would deserve to hand him his slippers?"

Goethe on Euripides (1831) [1]

The four plays collected in this anthology present four of the most powerful and provocative tragedies ever produced. Of the surviving 18 plays of Euripides, these are, arguably, the four best. In this opening essay I have five goals. First, to explain Greek polytheism and some of its significant implications for understanding Athenian tragedy. I will do this with a general cultural overview that contrasts the polytheistic world-view of the ancient Greeks with the monotheistic traditions of the early Israelites and Christians. Second, I present a brief biography of Euripides. Third, I discuss some major characteristics of Greek tragedy, and what, in particular, is specifically Athenian about tragedy since it is that city, and that Greek city alone, which has bequeathed this remarkable genre. Fourth, I offer an interpretation of two of the four plays, *Medea* (431 BCE) and *Bacchae* (406 BCE), which focuses upon the dramas in their historical context. These two plays, like bookends, frame the Peloponnesian War—the 27-year conflict (431-404 BCE) between Athens and Sparta which the Athenian historian Thucydides called "the greatest convulsion that ever shook the Greeks" (1.2). [2] I argue that the private tragedies of the *Medea* and *Bacchae* reflect the public tragedy which befell the city of Athens in the late fifth century. Finally I discuss the poet as prophet, by which I mean Euripides' role as a cultural critic trying to teach his city, to show her the dangers of a life, of an empire driven by fear, honor, daring, eros, and self-interest.

At the end of this introduction Michael Halleran presents a short essay on "Greek Tragedy in Performance"(pp. 24-27). There he discusses the nature of stage production in the Theater of Dionysus in Athens and the logistics of acting in that vast space, with its 15,000 spectators. At the end of the entire anthology Halleran also presents incisive literary interpretations of the other two plays included herein, namely the *Hippolytus* (428 BCE) and *Heracles* (c. 415 BCE).

PART I. THE POLYTHEISTIC WORLD-VIEW OF THE GREEKS
AND ITS SIGNIFICANCE [3]

The first segment of this introduction explores some of the ways in which the world of the ancient Greeks differed from the traditions of the early Israelites and Christians. The fundamental difference is that the Greeks believed in many gods (poly-theism) and inclined towards a more man-centered (anthropo-centric) perspective on the world than the Israelites and Christians, who focused their attention on one God (mono-theism). These biblical peoples worshipped this God as their omnipotent and loving Creator, and as such He occupied the center of their (theo-centric) world-view. By contrasting these traditions I hope to offer a partial explanation as to why the genre of tragedy looms so prominently in ancient Greek culture but is virtually absent in the Hebrew and Christian faith traditions. In this discussion I focus more on the Hebrew (than on the Christian) Bible because that world is more contemporaneous with the 350 years of Greek cultural history, namely the archaic and classical periods (c. 750-400 BCE), which provide the historical context for this anthology.

Judaism and Christianity originated in the ancient Middle East, the cradle of monotheism, and were inspired by God's self-revelation to Abraham and Moses. The Hebrews and Christians believed that God created "man" in His image (Genesis 1.26; 5.1; 9.6). The ancient Greeks had a different perspective. Their gods, to judge from their early poetry, were imagined as being modeled, in some fashion, after man. Herodotus, "the father of history" (c. 420 BCE), informs us about this tradition in his account of the birth of the gods: "It is Homer and Hesiod who created for the Greeks their theogony: it is they who gave to the gods the special names for their descent from their ancestors and divided among them their honors, their arts, and their shapes." [4] Herodotus' account aligns well with the general anthropocentric inclination of Hellenic culture. [5] The Greeks apparently thought about the gods beginning with or through man, whereas the Israelites thought about man beginning with or through God. [6] Rejecting the "mythological" gods of polytheism, the Israelites believed in a single Divine Creator who operated from outside space and time, brought the world into existence by His own volition, and used his omnipotence for two main purposes: to create and sustain the world, and to guide its moral progress.[7] In short, the Hebrew people saw the world from a theocentric perspective.

Unlike the transcendent God of the Israelites, the Greek gods operated within this world from their city atop Mt. Olympus on the north coast of Greece.[8] They operated within this world because they were born into this world, as the seventh-century poet Hesiod tells us: "First of all Chasm [formless void beneath the earth] came into being; and next wide-breasted Earth...and dark Tartaros [the lowest part of the underworld]...and Eros, the most handsome among the immortal gods, the loosener of limbs who conquers the reason and shrewd counsel in the breasts of all gods and all humans." [9] With the appearance of Eros (the creative principle of Desire within the cosmos), all creation becomes procreation. [10] The prominence of erotic desire in the Greek theogony (the origin of the gods) and cosmogony (the origin of the world) distinguishes the Greek from the Hebrew tradition. The Hellenic gods, especially Zeus, are fiercely driven by eros. In contrast, as Richard Oxenberg observes, "Yahweh cannot have eros in the common sense because there is nothing more perfect for him to strive for or desire. Yahweh begins as complete. Eros implies incompleteness striving for fulfillment." [11] Indeed God's conspicuous lack of a female partner can be seen as evidence of Israel's protest against polytheism which, especially in Cannan, Babylonia, and Egypt, frequently paired male gods and female (mother) goddesses. [12] The fact that the Greek gods were born into this world by virtue of Eros meant that they resembled humankind. For example, in the same way that successful mortal kings established their monarchies, so Zeus, king of the Olympian pantheon, established his by consolidating power (primarily) through political and intellectual savvy. [13] He was not omnipotent like the Hebrew God.

One of the cornerstones of the relationship of the Israelites to their God was their holy Covenant with Him. [14] This personal Covenant is exemplified by the *Shema*, the famous creedal prayer of Jewish piety: "Hear, O Israel: The Lord is our God, the Lord alone. You shall love the Lord your God with all your heart, and with all your soul, and with all your might." (Deuteronomy 6.4-5). [15] Greeks did not speak of loving their gods in this way, nor even (generally) of having this kind of personal relationship with divinity. "It would be absurd," says Aristotle, "if someone were to say that he loves Zeus." [16] The personal relationship between the Israelites and their God grounded itself in the Ten Commandments, spoken by God to His people at Mt. Sinai. This Decalogue set forth God's fundamental claim on the Hebrews and established the boundaries for inclusion in their special community of faith. [17] The breaking of that Covenant, such as happened with the idolatry of the golden calf (Exodus 32), was a sin, an act of spiritual betrayal which transformed the nearness of God into estrangement. Because the Greeks lacked this personal covenant with their gods, they did not think in terms of sin, repentance, and atonement but rather in terms of error (*hamartia*), staining pollution (*miasma*), and purification (*catharsis*). [18]

Why did the Hebrews believe in their God? Because, unlike Zeus and the Greek deities, the God of the Israelites exploded into their history by liberating them in their exodus from the oppressive Pharaoh, by revealing Himself at Mt. Sinai, and by making a sacred Covenant with His people. As Bernhard Anderson puts it, "no other nation of antiquity, as far as we know, viewed divine activity in history as central to the self-understanding of a people and God's relation to them." [19] Faith in this God was a cornerstone of ancient Judaism: "...the righteous live by their faith." (Habakkuk 2.4) [20] But there was much more to this faith than a belief system; righteousness and the doing of good deeds were crucial: "You shall love your neighbor as yourself: I am the Lord." (Leviticus 19.18).

These various observations lead to the main point, that, unlike the Israelites and Christians, the Greeks had no Bible or sacred book with a fixed truth (and so no religious fundamentalism, no "holy wars"), no Covenant with any deity, no Savior, no divine Revelation, no Prophets, no Decalogue, no dogma, no creed, and not much in the way of organized religion. [21] In short, the Greeks did not have the "safety-net"—if that is the right expression—of the possibility of deliverance/redemption by the grace of an eternal, all-powerful, all-knowing, holy, just, merciful God of steadfast love. [22] What I mean by this "safety-net" of deliverance/redemption can be seen in two examples. First, a national example—God's liberation of the Israelites from slavery in Egypt (Deuteronomy 9.26; 15.15) and the covenant relationship that allowed them to face the future knowing that their God would be with them. [23] Second, an individual example—the story of Job, "one who feared God and turned away from evil" (Job 1.1). Job's life seems, initially, to shatter the traditional belief that piety begot prosperity and sin brought suffering. Despite his disinterested righteousness Job loses his property and children because of God's wager with his adversarial son, the satan. In the end, however, out of respect for the sincerity of Job's challenge to Him—Why should a good man suffer such evils?—God comes "out of the whirlwind" to confront Job, who is, in turn, humbled by the experience and repents. Immediately thereafter God restores Job's fortunes and children by twofold (Job 42.5-10).

My point is that the Israelites, both as a nation and as individuals, have a "safety-net" that consists of the possibility of deliverance/redemption by virtue of a personal relationship with their loving God. [24] The Christians, too, have a "safety-net," indeed a double "safety-net": not only the comfort of a loving God but also, because of Jesus' miraculous resurrection from the dead, the promise of an afterlife in Heaven. By their very constitutions the ancient theologies of the Hebrews and Christians might be said to preclude the possibility of a tragic world-view. Indeed, "one might even go so far as to say that for the Hebrews a 'tragic' world-view would itself be a sin: a denial of God." [25] I do not mean to suggest the Israelites did not know tragedy. To take one example, the story of the first Hebrew king, Saul (and his suicide), shows otherwise (I Samuel 28-31). And the suffering of Christ animates the entire New Testament: "My God, my God, why have you forsaken me?" [26] But in both these traditions God, finally, does care.

In contrast, the Greeks, especially in the late fifth century, viewed the human condition as subject to huge reversals of fortune about which the gods, if they themselves did not cause those reversals, often cared little or not at all. [27] Examples of immoral or amoral behavior by the gods abound in this anthology. To give one instance: Euripides' Heracles, renowned hero and loving husband, returns home from Hades just in time to save his family from being slain by the tyrant Lycus. Then, for no reason except jealousy at her husband Zeus, the immortal Hera causes the mortal Heracles to go mad and murder his three sons and wife. As the shamed hero wonders why he should not commit suicide, he blasts Hera: "Let the famous wife of Zeus dance, striking Olympus' sparkling floor with her shoes. For she has achieved the purpose she wished, turning upside down the first man of Greece from the foundations. Who would pray to such a goddess?" [28] Here is the great reversal from good to bad fortune, the free-fall without any safety-net. Indeed it is the queen of the gods herself who pushes the blameless hero into the abyss. Such was the nature of reality for the Greeks. Higher powers stalked the world, powers who ferociously protected their own turf, powers often beyond good and evil, powers unlike God, who Himself created good and evil (Isaiah 45.7). In such a world, human responsibility is radicalized; no safety-net exists except courage and friendship.

One of the enduring legacies of the Greeks is their trust in the efficacy of rational investigation, of man's capacity to comprehend the macrocosm of the world and the microcosm of "man." It was the power of the word, of *logos*, that set humankind apart from all other animals and allowed for the differentiation of justice from injustice. [29] By means of this *logos* the Greeks came to analyze systematically many of the subjects we study in the Academy today. In light of the breadth of this intellectual legacy (in fields such as philosophy, logic, drama, rhetoric, literary criticism, political science, some of the natural sciences), one might well say, with Harold Bloom, that we in the West "have no ways of thinking that are not Greek and yet our morality and religion—outer and inner—find their ultimate source in the Hebrew Bible."[30] This distinction between Greek cognition and Biblical spirituality reminds us that, despite their poignant literatures of pathos, the monotheistic traditions of the Israelites and the Christians have not produced a genre of tragedy. In college, for example, a student does not typically take a course in Jewish or Christian tragedy. One possible reason is that these monotheistic traditions —buoyed by faith in an all-powerful, just, and benevolent God—appear to be essentially anti-tragic.[31]

For the Greeks, from Homer onwards, "man" is precariously poised between beast and god.[32] The reason for this precariousness resides in the very nature of being human, of being saturated to the core with explosive Eros, that mysterious force of nature that rages in the heart of everything.[33] The mutability of the human estate—perhaps the most persistent theme of Athenian tragedy—makes mortals susceptible to free-fall at a moment's notice. "Creatures of a day! What is anyone? What is he not? Man, the shadow of a dream." [34] Ephemeral, insubstantial, fleeting, finite, and always yearning—that is how the Greeks viewed man's lot in the world. Their competitive drive for fame, their fascination with the heroic temper—"ever to be bravest and pre-eminent over others" (*Iliad* 6.208)—can perhaps be partially explained by the fact that for them only collective memory, in the form of the poet's song about the hero's glorious deeds, could bring immortality. [35] For the Greeks there was no Redeemer, no Messiah, no Promised Land, no Second Coming, nor much in the way of an afterlife. [36] Once the curtain fell, the show was over.

PART II. EURIPIDES' LIFE

We know little about Euripides' life. He was probably born on the island of Salamis, near Athens, in 485 or 480 BCE and died in northern Greece (Macedonia) in early 406, a few months before his older contemporary and competitor, Sophocles. Euripides lived in the *deme* (village) of Phyla, north of Mt. Hymettus, part of the Athenian tribe of Cecropis. Unlike Sophocles, who held the offices of general, imperial treasurer, and special city counsellor, Euripides held no public office.

Euripides wrote some eighty-eight plays, of which eighteen survive. These dramas were produced as tetralogies—three tragedies, usually unrelated thematically, followed by a satyr play, an anti-tragic burlesque. The plays were performed in Athens at the city's two main dramatic festivals, the Lenaia (January) and the City Dionysia (March-April). Euripides competed some twenty-two times, though he won first prize only five times, whereas Aeschylus, Euripides' older contemporary (525-456 BCE), who wrote some eighty-two plays, won thirteen victories, and Sophocles (c. 496-406), who wrote some 124 plays, took eighteen first prizes (which means he won three out of every five times he competed). Aeschylus captured his first victory in 484, Sophocles in 468 (defeating Aeschylus), and Euripides in 441. In the year of Aeschylus' death (456) and three years after the production of his famous Oresteia trilogy, Euripides made his debut with a play about the story of Medea (*Daughters of Pelias*) and won third prize. Nearly twenty-five years later he returned to the same story with his famed *Medea* (431) and again won third prize. The dates of half of Euripides' surviving plays are known from ancient sources; the chronology for the others has been roughly surmised from metrical considerations. Of his five first prizes—and prizes were awarded not just for one play but for all four as a unit—we know the dates of only three: 441 (plays unknown), 428 (including the revised *Hippolytus*), and posthumously in 406/5 (including the *Bacchae* and *Iphigeneia at Aulis*). Euripides wrote these last two plays in Pella, the capital of Macedonia, where he had apparently moved, along with other notable Athenians (the tragedian Agathon and perhaps the historian Thucydides), at the invitation of King Archelaus, who was trying to make Macedonia a center of Greek culture (which it would become fifty years later under Philip II, father of Alexander the Great).

The intellectual and rhetorical bent of Euripides' plays reveals a dramatist clearly influenced by the "enlightenment" movement associated with the sophists (paid, itinerant professors, especially of rhetoric) in the second half of the fifth century. He had a reputation for being "bookish" (Aristophanes *Frogs* 943, 1409). His friends seem to have included men such as the philosophers Socrates, Anaxagoras, Protagoras and Prodicus as well as the politicians Alcibiades and Critias, and the lyric poet/musical innovator Timotheus. Euripides pioneered the complex sounds of the "new music" which clashed with traditional values; Aristophanes likened it to the noise of ants. [37]

Euripides' life coincided with the 75-year duration of the Athenian Empire. He seems to have written some sixty-six tragedies and twenty-two satyr plays (of which *Cyclops*, c. 412, is our only extant example in the tragic corpus). If Euripides was born c. 484 BCE, then he would have written *Medea* (431) at age 54, *Hippolytus* (428) at age 57, *Heracles* (c. 415) at age 70, and *Bacchae* at age 79. No plays survive from the first third of his career (455-439 BCE). Indeed, all but one of his eighteen plays (*Alcestis*, 438) come from the second half of Euripides' career and fall within the period of the Peloponnesian War (431-404 BCE). During this time, and especially in his last fifteen years, he was remarkably prolific. For several centuries after his death Euripides was the most popular of the fifth-century dramatists, far surpassing Aeschylus and Sophocles in revival performances.

PART III. WHAT IS GREEK TRAGEDY?

Greek tragedy is more properly called Athenian tragedy because it was performed almost exclusively in Athens by Athenian dramatists. Tragedy originated in Attica, the large county in which Athens was located, [38] in the late sixth century (c. 534 BCE) under the (benevolent) tyranny of Pisistratus (546-527). [39] Tragedy developed gradually [40] but exploded as a genre in fifth-century democratic Athens. [41] Aeschylus (c. 525-456), who produced his first play in c. 498, was the first to employ a second actor. [42] This suggests that the first 35 years of tragedy involved the interaction of a chorus and a single actor.[43] So one could reasonably claim that Aeschylus created tragedy;[44] certainly his use of two actors marks the beginning of Western drama as we know it. [45] But tragedy, although the only form of poetry native to Attica, is best understood as a continuation of a tradition of song and myth that stretched back to Homer (c. 750). [46]

In asking "What is Athenian tragedy?" we must inquire, however briefly, into the relationship between tragedy and Athenian democracy. Does democracy have anything substantial to do with the explosion of drama in Athens? To begin, we must situate that democracy in the larger context of the Greek political landscape, since other democracies existed in the fifth century.[47] Almost all Hellenic cities shared a similar tripartite institutional hierarchy: a small body of chief Magistrates, an advisory Council, and a large voting Assembly of citizens.[48] Within this general framework, what distinguished Athenian democracy? Four things: the lottery system (by which they selected randomly, rather than elected, most key public officials), the very low property qualification for citizenship (restricted to males), pay for public service (e.g. jury or military duty) and the high degree of free speech. These mechanisms put substantial power (*kratos*) in the hands of the people (*demos*) so that Pericles could call Athens a *demo-cracy*, "not in the interest of the few but of the many" (Thuc. 2.37.1). Two of these four hallmarks of Athenian democracy—the low property qualification and pay for public service—increased the participation of the poor and created something of a welfare state, especially after 450 BCE. [49] The Athenians prided themselves on *parrhesia*, the citizen's right "to speak out openly and frankly," especially in the voting Assembly. [50] *Parrhesia* gained currency as a political catchword in the late fifth century. [51] It occurs first in Euripides' *Hippolytus* (428 BCE) when Phaedra expresses the following wish (421-25): "But as free men with the freedom to speak openly (*parrhesia*), may my sons live in glorious Athens and enjoy a glorious reputation with regard to their mother." Fifteen years later Euripides' *Ion* (c. 413 BCE), in search of his mother, says to his father (670-75): "I pray that my mother is from Athens so that, as my inheritance from her, I may have the freedom to speak openly (*parrhesia*). For if a foreigner, even though he is a citizen in name, comes into a pure-bred city, still he possesses the mouth of a slave and has no freedom to speak openly (*parrhesia*)." These two passages serve to mark out *parrhesia* as a trademark of Athens, a privilege of her male citizens. I dwell on *parrhesia* (literally, "saying everything") because it appears that this trait, more than any other, marks out the genre of drama as a specifically Athenian institution. All other cities had assemblies but the extant evidence suggests that the Athenian Assembly surpassed the others by its enormous size and intensive nature.

The Athenians learned the art of rhetoric, of speaking frankly, in their Assembly, which was the city's most powerful political body. [52] Some 6,000 citizens met on the Pynx Hill, near the Acropolis, about forty times per year (at a minimum). In this place Athenians could participate directly in determining the major political issues of their city. [53] Here they learned to compete by means of *logos*, to give speeches, to persuade, to debate the day-to-day issues of war, justice, citizenship, empire. Given the aggressive character and insatiable appetite of Athenian imperialism and interventionism (*poly-pragmosyne*, Thuc. 6.87)—with the power of its imposing coinage decrees, tribute-lists, tax-collectors and triremes—the Athenians had countless issues to deliberate. Their Assembly was, by its nature, a theater of political ideas, emphatically contemporary and particular. The tragic performances at the Theater of Dionysus were, on the other hand, emphatically remote in time and more generic in their concerns, dealing with the larger-than-life heroes of the mythical past. [54] But the Theater of Dionysus could also be deeply political, not only in theme but in fact. Thucydides (8.93) informs us that the Theater of Dionysus in the Athenian harbor town of Piraeus, and even (and most unusually) the huge Theater of Dionysus in Athens, were used for political assemblies at the time of the oligarchic coup of 411 BCE. No dramatist explores the socio-political issues of his day more insistently than Euripides.[55] In play after play he focuses on the destructive impact of war, eros (both personal and political), and revenge - all set in a mythical past, like *Medea, Hecuba, Andromache, Trojan Women, Orestes, Iphigeneia at Aulis, Bacchae*, but all undeniably meditations on contemporary culture and (often) on the savagery of the Peloponnesian War.

So, does democracy have anything substantial to do with the explosion of drama in Athens? In this sense it does: that the Athenian democracy was so imperialistic and ever-expanding in nature that it forced the Athenians, in a qualitatively different way than other cities, to deliberate constantly on difficult issues of morality and justice. The Assembly was one place for intense debate (*parrhesia*) to occur. The stage of the theater was another. But in distancing itself, by way of myth, from the maddening crowd, the theater held up a mirror to the Assembly. It showed not only the debate (e.g. Jason vs. Medea), but also the suffering that resulted from the debate (e.g. Medea's infanticide) and the pity that such suffering evokes. Furthermore the theater, unlike the Assembly, was a place of pity, a place that gave voice to the silenced and marginalized of the city: women, the "barbarian" other, the common man, the slave. These characters, in particular, were favorites of Euripides. He took Athens to the other side, to the *under* side; he taught them how to read the sad faces of victims of war and revenge and eros. Athenian democracy, with its imperial money and power, gave Euripides a stage, a big one. On it he held high his mirror and tried to reflect what he saw. The face in the mirror was not handsome, though by holding up the mirror he tried to show how it could make itself so.

The Athenians considered the dramatist a teacher (*didaskalos*, whence our "didactic") whose job was not so much to inculcate moral lessons but, by his skill and good counsel, "to make people better members of their cities."[56] So what did tragedy teach? Using Aristotle as a springboard, I suggest that tragedy made the Athenians better citizens by teaching the following: that the ground of the human condition is one of constant change, conflict, and fragility in which man is not the measure of all things (i.e. not self-sufficient), in which reason and intellect, man's distinguishing trait, is often morally impotent against the forces of evil and darkness that are inherent in human nature (witness *Medea* 1078-80), and in which there is a frequent eruption of irrational, mysterious, and other-worldly forces (e.g. erotic passion, madness, chance, ancestral curses, oracles, Furies, gods). Despite the constraining yoke of these necessities tragedy teaches that men and women are still deeply responsible for their destinies (i.e. "man" makes morality), especially given that the Greeks did not have, as the early Israelites and Christians did, the "safety-net" of a benevolent and loving God . The plot of an Athenian tragedy arouses in the spectator particular emotions (pity, fear) and this is healthy because these emotions have tremendous cognitive value, because working through such emotions enhances our understanding of life's complexity. [57] Such understanding is essential to the moral, spiritual, and political education of good citizens. Or expressed somewhat differently, character (*ethos*, one's settled moral disposition) determines destiny (*daimon*), but that destiny (or the daimonic power controlling that destiny) simultaneously determines character. Thus, there is an unrelenting but productive tension between the two (*ethos* and *daimon*; cf. Heraclitus fragment 119). [58]

PART IV. EURIPIDES' *MEDEA*

IV. 1. The historical context of *Medea*

The cloud of the Peloponnesian War hung over the *Medea* of 431 BCE. The Athenians—a restless, impulsive, aggressive, and ambitious people, as Thucydides shows—had taken provocative action against several major Peloponnesian rivals in the immediately preceding years. [59] In 431 BCE Athens possessed a huge fleet of warships: 200 swift, sleek triremes, manned by 40,000 sailors skilled in the latest and most lethal naval tactics. [60] Several of Athens' provocations and entanglements are worth recounting in order to establish the historical context of Euripides' *Medea*.

Episode one: the battle of Sybota. In late August 433, Athens had intervened in a massive naval battle in the northwest Ionian Sea between her mighty enemy, Corinth (an ally of her arch-enemy Sparta) and Athens' own ally Corcyra, which had the second biggest navy in Greece (120 triremes). Athens did not want fertile Corcyra (modern Corfu), a strategic island link between Greece and Italy, to fall to Corinth. This battle of Sybota, off the coast of Epirus, involved 290 ships carrying over 45,000 men. One hundred of those ships were sunk, of which 70 were Corcyrean. The Corinthians sailed amidst the wreckage, "killing the men rather than taking them as prisoners, unwittingly slaying their own friends..." (Thuc. 1.50). This slaughter of some 1,000 sailors avenged the Corcyrean execution of prisoners at the battle of Leukimme (a northern cape of Corcyra) two years earlier, in 435. [61] Both these atrocities foreshadow the violence and suffering that would characterize the forthcoming Peloponnesian War. According to Thucydides (1.50) the battle at Sybota was "the greatest sea-battle of Greeks against Greeks up to this time." [62] Athens' intervention enabled Corcyra to proclaim herself pyrrhic victor but also gave Corinth "her first cause of war against Athens" (Thuc. 1. 55).

Episode two: the siege of Potitaea. In 432 Athens initiated a very expensive siege against the Corinthian colony of Potidaea in the Chalcidice peninsula (north-central Greece); among the dead that year were 150 Athenians and their general Callias (Thuc. 1. 63). [63]

Episode three: the Megarian decree. Later in 432 Athens imposed harsh trade sanctions against her neighbor Megara, another Spartan ally. These actions and the fierce anti-Spartan policy of Athens' senior statesman Pericles —whose first words in Thucydides are "Do not yield to the Peloponnesians!" (Thuc. 1.140; cf. 1. 127)—virtually compelled the usually sluggish Spartans to attack in order to halt the seemingly relentless march of Athenian imperialism throughout Greece. In an assembly debate at Sparta in 432 the Peloponnesian League (i.e. Sparta and her allies) voted to go to war against the "tyrant city" of Athens (Thuc. 1.122-124).

At this time Sparta had no treasury reserves or income from "tribute" (Thuc. 1.19). Athens, by means of an empire called "tyrannical" not only by the enemy but even by her own leading statesmen, [64] had built up, through the collection of "tribute" from some 150 allied/subject cities, a huge navy (200-300 triremes) and a massive war-chest. [65] To display her imperial power the Athenians had this annual tribute paraded through the *orchestra* at the front of the Theater of Dionysus before the plays began. [66] In 433 Athens had centralized funds from various temples across Attica (the "county" of which Athens was the center) creating another treasury (along with the Treasury of Athena) that could provide ready funds for war. Construction of various monuments (e.g. the Propylaia, the enormous marble "gateway" to the Acropolis) ceased so that money could be poured into the building of miles of city walls and docks. [67]

Euripides staged his *Medea* in late March 431 BCE. Only a few weeks later the Spartan army ravaged the Athenian countryside. Such despoiling had not occurred since the Persians ravaged Athens fifty years earlier (Thuc. 2. 18). This invasion began the Peloponnesian War between the land-power Sparta and sea-power Athens. The *Medea* was performed at a dramatic festival, the City Dionysia, which annually attracted the largest crowd of any event on the Athenian calendar. In that momentous spring of 431 Euripides' audience would have included the most famous Athenians of the day: Herodotus, Thucydides, Aeschylus' son Euphorion (who won first prize against Euripides), Sophocles (who won second prize), Aristophanes, Socrates, Alcibiades, Cleon, Pericles and his mistress Aspasia from Asia Minor. [68] Because this festival coincided with the beginning of the sailing/military campaigning season, the audience would have been included not only a large portion (15,000) of the citizen body (30,000 to 50,000) but also many foreigners. Given this enormous audience the dramatists could expect to influence, however obliquely, the debate about the nature and direction of Athenian policy. [69] In his *Medea*, Euripides appears deeply concerned about the unleashing of greed, ambition, and violence which the impending Peloponnesian War promised. I will suggest that he meant to express those concerns metaphorically on stage. Euripides, of course, could not have known that this war would last twenty-seven years and virtually destroy his city, but the aforementioned events (those preceding 431) must have signaled that serious trouble was, like the child-murdering Medea at the end of Euripides' play, winging its way to Athens. The writing was on the wall, so to speak; Euripides put it on the stage as well.

IV.2. The structure of *Medea*

Medea contains two main narratives: a rescue plot which features a damsel in distress who is saved, unexpectedly, by a prince in shining armor (Aigeus, king of Athens); then a revenge plot, full of action and violence, which sees the damsel become a ferocious semi-divine Fury. In the first half Medea is supported in her revenge plan by the chorus of Corinthian women (who serve as the play's internal audience); in the second half she is condemned by them for her new revenge plan. The crucial link between the rescue and revenge narratives is the scene (662-763) with Medea and the childless Aigeus, who has come to Corinth from Delphi where he had consulted Apollo's oracle about how to become a father. His *eros* for children (714) and obsession with fatherhood (722) remind Medea of just how important sons are to an aristocratic Greek male. This realization triggers two important consequences, both focused on the theme of children: firstly Medea's shift from plan #1 (murdering Creon, his daughter and Jason: 375) to plan #2 (murdering Creon, his daughter and Jason's two sons: 783-96); secondly it enables one man (Aigeus) to become a father (and thereby have sons who can inherit and perpetuate his kingship) and causes another (Jason) to be deprived of fatherhood through the murder of his sons. [70]

IV.3. *Medea's* tragedy

Medea's struggle begins as an external one against Jason, a fierce battle of the sexes which evolves into a struggle within the protagonist herself, a psychological war between a mother's loving instinct and a rejected wife's rage and passion for revenge. [71] The trajectories of both conflicts culminate in premeditated infanticide, the most shocking crime in Athenian tragedy.

Two unilateral decisions by two men create these conflicts. First is Jason's divorce of Medea, unique as the only divorce in the thirty-two extant tragedies.[72] Although not a legal union by Athenian standards (since Medea was neither Greek nor given in marriage by a father or brother), both Jason and Medea call their union a "marriage" (1341, 1388). Furthermore, that bond was sealed by oath with his right hand as a sign of trust (21, 496, 899). Jason has abandoned Medea and married the daughter of Creon, king of Corinth. From the perspectives of Medea, the nurse, the chorus and Aigeus, his action is one of dishonor (20, 33), insult (*hybris*: 256, 603, 1366), infidelity (412, 423), and injustice (580-82), Because Medea sacrificed so much to be with him, Jason's divorce has devastated her. Medea's passion for him (8, 432) had induced her not just to help him on his quest; she herself actually slayed the dragon that guarded the prized fleece of the golden ram (482). Then she foolishly murdered her brother and betrayed her father (167, 483, 1332-34) in order to elope with Jason. Immediately after the divorce Creon, fearing "incurable harm" (283) from Medea's "silent cleverness" (320), decreed exile for her and her two sons (272-76). So this proud woman, once highly regarded by her adopted city (11-12), suddenly finds herself deprived of any civic status (*apolis*, 255; cf. 386, 646).

Jason provokes Medea's fury not only by what he did but how he did it. He has already remarried before even telling her (586-87, 910) and already lives in the palace of his new father-in-law (378). Why has Jason jilted Medea? Two main reasons: his fear of the disrepute of growing old with a "barbarian" wife (591-2), and the political advantage of marrying the king's daughter (697-700; cf. 593-95, 914-21); such a marriage would enable Jason's new "legitimate" sons to succeed Creon as king. Jason's fear about his "mixed" marriage, in particular, would have resonated with the original audience because at the time of this play (431) Athenians would have been feeling the full impact of Pericles' famous Citizenship Law, passed in 451/50, which stated "that a man could not share in [the rights of the] city unless born from parents who were both [Athenian] citizens." [73] By prohibiting marriages such as Jason's with the "barbarian" Medea, Pericles' law guarded the ethnic purity as well as the political and economic privileges of the citizen body of the ever-expanding Athenian Empire. Pericles' law presumed the natural superiority of Greeks to "barbarians" (cf. *Medea* 1330-43). This presumption had three tacit justifications: "barbarians" had tyrannical rulers (cf. *Medea* 532-41), lived in immoderate luxury, and exhibited unrestrained emotionalism. On all three points the Greeks believed they embodied the opposite characteristics: rule of law (egalitarianism/democracy), austerity, and emotional self-discipline (hence the prominence of such virtues as *sophrosyne*, moderation; cf. *Medea* 824-45). [74]

Medea hates the "injustices" of Jason and Creon (117, 208, 578, 692) and part of the raw power of Euripides' play is that this private family dispute explodes into large public questions such as what it means to be a woman, a wife, a mother in Greek/Athenian society. In her first speech Medea foregrounds the female's vulnerability in the traditional marriage arrangement (230-34; cf. 443-45): "Of all creatures that have life and a sense of judgment, we women are the most wretched race; first, we must use an excess of cash to buy our husbands, and what we get are masters of our bodies—a second evil more painful still than the first!" In other words, the new wife not only has to buy her husband but he becomes her owner and she his physical slave. The irony that the slave has to buy her master only adds salt to the wound. [75]

Medea's nurse had earlier given voice to the conventional fifth-century

Athenian attitude toward marriage when she stated that for a wife not to dis-agree with her husband makes for "the greatest safety" (14). But now Jason, although having given his right hand as a sign of "the greatest trust" (22) and claiming the family's welfare as his "greatest concern" (559), has foresworn that oath. So marriage, for Medea, represents not "the greatest safety" but "the greatest struggle" (*megistos agon*) because "women have no means of divorce that brings good reputation (*eu-kleia*) nor is a wife able to refuse her husband...As for a man, whenever he becomes annoyed with the company of those inside, going outside he stops his heart's vexation. But we are forced (*ananke*) to look at one soul only."(235-7, 244-7) The spatial contrast between inside/outside and private/public reveals the culture's systemic sexual asym-metry. When a husband becomes vexed with those inside (i.e. his wife) he can get his sexual needs met by those outside (i.e. prostitutes). For the husband there are "other fields to plow" as Creon bitterly puts it to Haimon in Sophocles' *Antigone* (569). But not for the wife; once under the yoke (*zugon*: 242, 804; 623, 1366), always under the yoke. Medea hates this patriarchal subjugation and its degrading assumptions: "Men say that we women live without danger in the house, while they fight with the spear. What fools! I would rather stand three times behind a shield (in the battle-line) than bear a child once!" (248-51) For Medea birthing is like battle, only more dangerous. An infantryman, at least, has a shield to ward off the enemy. A mother, especially in a world before medicine, had no such defense; for her a "wicked, wretched helpless-ness" (*a-mechania*) and "loss of reason" (*a-phrosune*) accompanied pregnancy and the pangs of childbirth (*Hippolytus*, 161-4).

In this world of husbands as masters and wives as "slaves," where marriage was an exchange of women by men for the benefit of men, where the wife's "job" was to produce male heirs for the husband, it is not surpris-ing that Jason urges Medea "to bear lightly the plans of those who are more powerful" (449). One advantage of Medea's barbarian "otherness" is that she can, more directly than a Greek wife, question her husband's unthinking misogyny and ethnocentrism. Medea's "otherness" does not mean, however, we should not take seriously her critique of Jason's cultural assumptions. Euripides presents a complex protagonist; not only does she represent, with respect to Greek/Athenian women, "the Other" but she also embodies, in crucial respects, "the Same." Consider, for example, how closely the reflec-tions on marriage of this barbarian protagonist parallel those of Sophocles' Athenian princess Procne, wife of Tereus, the barbarian king of Thrace. Procne, who avenges her husband's rape of her sister Philomela by murdering their son Itys, articulates the female dilemma in this way: "But now, separated [from my family], I am nothing. Indeed often I have looked at women's nature in this way—that we are nothing. As young girls in our father's home we live, I think, the sweetest life of all human beings, for foolishness always nurtures children joyfully. But when we reach puberty and understanding, we are thrust outside, bought and sold away [in marriage] from our paternal gods and from our parents who gave us birth, some to foreign men, others to barbarians, some to houses where everything is strange, others to houses of abuse. And when a single night has yoked us [to our husband], we must praise this [lot] and make it seem that we are faring well." [76] The young bride is sold in the marketplace and then yoked to a life of pretense. In Sophocles' lost *Iphigeneia* (frag. 307) Clytemnestra advises her daughter, who, by a fraud of Agamemnon, is about to be betrothed to Achilles: "Be mindful to change the color of your true thought to [match] your man, as the octopus [adapts its color] to a rock." For purposes of survival—either avoiding a predator or ambushing a prey—the wily *polyp* must disguise its true self. So, too, must the wife skillfully adapt to her husband. But even when she does so, the results often spell disaster. Take, by way of further example, the case of Deianeira, the most un-Medea-like woman in tragedy, when she learns of her husband's philandering. While off on one of his "labors," Heracles is smitten with *eros* for Iole, a beautiful young maiden whom he has brought home for his pleasure. When the gentle Deianeira realizes the truth, she gives us one of the saddest moments in Greek tragedy: "I have taken on a girl—no, I reckon she's no longer that—but a yoked woman, like a ship captain takes on one piece of cargo too many, merchandise that outrages my heart. And now we wait, the two of us under one sheet, a single object of embrace for Heracles, whom I called so trustworthy and brave! This is the reward for my housekeeping, my compensation for his long absence... For I see Iole's youth blossoming while mine fades. A man's eye loves to pluck the young flower but from the others he runs away." [77] When Deianeira's naïve plan to ward off this invasion of her bed backfires, she ends up killing herself and, inadvertently, her "heroic" husband, thereby fulfilling, against all probability, the etymological meaning of her name, "Husband-slayer."

In the classical Greek world the female rite of passage from "girl" to "woman" was achieved by the domestication of eros through marriage/ childbirth. The analogous male rite of passage from "boy" to "man" was achieved through the organized violence of battle/killing. While men achieved glory and good reputation (*kleos* and *eu-kleia*) by martial skills in the public arena of war, women rarely earned the same honor for marital skills in the private quarters of the house. Why? Because raising a family was considered easier and less dangerous than being an infantryman or hoplite.

Part of Medea's tragedy is that she and Jason think so differently about the world and therefore speak practically different languages, not so much because of the ethnic difference (Greek/barbarian) as because of the gender gap and the dichotomies (public/private, master/slave, power/impotence) that reinforce that gap. Jason, for example, in his "debate" with Medea, tellingly calls the children "mine" (550), apparently blind to the pathetic irony of a father driving his young sons into exile. Medea immediately tries to protest his appropriation but Jason effectively silences her with his smug "Keep quiet!" (550; cf. 596; 793, 1045). He claims not only "ownership" but blithely asks "What need have you of children?" (565), as if children were "needs" rather than pledges of love. Indeed (more) children are, for him, just that, instruments for augmenting his power. Medea will counterattack savagely, using the boys as pawns of revenge to annihilate Jason's dynastic dream and his irrepressible lack of respect (569-75): "You women have gone so far that if things in bed go right, you think you have everything. But if some disaster strikes you in the bedroom you treat the best and happiest circumstances as the most vicious acts of war. Mortals ought to generate children from elsewhere and the female race ought not to exist. Then men would be free from trouble!" Medea does indeed view this "best and happiest circumstance" of unannounced divorce and immediate exile as an act of war not because her sex-life has disappeared but because her bed has been dishonored (696, 1354), her family destroyed. She loathes Jason's "false-face and slippery words" (584; cf. 1392) and the cowardice that took a new bride before even telling the old one (155-57, 584-87, 1366). His treachery becomes for her "a test of courage" (403-5). Jason had earlier told her to "keep quiet" when she tried to dispute his claim that the children were "his" (550). She will not be so dismissed (807-10): "Let no one consider me indifferent and lacking strength and quiet. I am just the opposite, harsh to my foes, kind to my friends. For such a life brings the most illustrious fame (eu-kleia)."

As a female and a foreigner in this patriarchal setting (410-445) Medea finds herself trapped. Since no paradigm except self-sacrifice existed for decisive feminine action against male injustice, the only way of striking back, of winning repute rather than ridicule, was to adopt the traditional Greek moral code of "helping friends, harming foes." [78] So husband and wife become enemies, their house a battleground, and the innocent boys weapons of war. Medea's famous "divided self" speech (1021-80) reveals the profundity of her tragedy: here the tragedy of the self embodies the tragedy of the city. [79] Despite knowing better, she feels compelled, even as she embraces her young sons, to murder her maternal instinct (symbolized by a mother's milk) and become a monster of revenge (symbolized by her own children's blood). Victim becomes victimizer; loving mother becomes cold warrior, encasing herself, like Agave in the Bacchae (hoplis-menai, 733), in the panoply of the front-line warrior: "They must die and since they must, we will kill them, the very ones who gave them birth. Up then! Arm yourself in steel (hopliz-ou, "become a hoplite"), my heart! Why delay doing the dreadful evil deeds that must be done?" (1240-43). The ferocity of her triple "must" here (cf. 1013-14, 1051) underscores Medea's huge fear of being mocked. Jason feels no gratitude, claiming that she chose to save him when the Argonauts sailed to fetch the Golden Fleece; rather Aphrodite and Eros forced (ananke, 530) her to rescue him. By denying her agency he insults her pride and "forces" her to respond in kind. So despite knowing the evils she is about to dare, as she says in her most famous lines (1079-80), "my seething spirit (thumos) dictates my (murder) plans, the same spirit which causes the greatest evils for mortals." [80] So it is that "necessity" (ananke) and anger become the mothers of tragic invention.

For Jason this "unholiest deed" (1328), which even Medea calls "unholy murder" (1383; cf. 796), has transformed her into a beast, "a lioness not a woman" (1342), "a child-killing lioness" (1407), more savage in her nature than the "Etruscan Scylla" (1343-45), the immortal six-headed female monster who ate six of Odysseus' best sailors on the voyage back to Ithaca. [81]

IV.4. The Ending of *Medea*

In the finale Jason pounds on the house doors, riveting our attention there, center-stage. We expect the stage-trolley to roll out the boys' bodies.[82] Suddenly the high priestess of revenge (1054, 1333) appears triumphantly above the house with her sons' bloody corpses in her arms. [83] There Euripides' diva hovers in the dragon-drawn chariot of the Sun (her grandfather) like some goddess out of the machine, proudly prophesying the pathetic death of the Argonautic hero (1386-87): "You'll be struck on the head by a remnant of your ship, Argo, seeing a bitter end and fulfilment of your marriage to me." The ship that began his story will end it as well; once epic hero, now tragic anti-hero. Jason begs to bury the corpses (1377) but Medea refuses, thereby denying him any closure on his loss. In her ferocity she has become "a wretched murderous Fury of Vengeance" (1260; cf. 1333), but Jason reminds her that she will be pursued by her sons' Furies (1371): "They live, alas, as demons of bloodstain (*miasma*) to take vengeance on your head."

At the end Medea is set to fly to the Athens of King Aigeus. But her coming cannot be propitious, both because of the vengeance she has exacted and the vengeance that will pursue her. As a polluting and polluted woman she is going to "a sacred, unravaged land" whose citizens "feed on a most renowned wisdom, always "stepping luxuriously (*bainontes habros*; 830; cf. 1164) through the brightest air where once, they say, the nine sacred Muses of Mt. Pieria created golden-haired Harmony." But shortly after the production of Medea the Peloponnesian War began and foreign (Spartan) invaders ravaged Athens for the first time since 480 (Thuc. 2.18). This is the same Athens about which the chorus had said that "Aphrodite, drawing water from the streams of the fair-flowing Cephisus River, breathes sweet, moderate (*metrios*) breezes down over the land. And always around her hair wrapping wreaths of scented roses she sends passionate desires (Erotes) to sit beside Wisdom (Sophia), companions in producing every kind of excellence (*arete*)" (835-45). But the Aphrodite blowing into Athens in the person of Medea from Corinth was anything but moderate. Indeed one of the saddest aspects of Euripides' play—which features no heroes—is the divorce of passion (*eros*) from wisdom (*sophia*) and the attendant absence of any kind of excellence (*arete*). This divorce of passion and wisdom might well represent the greatest tragedy of historical Athens during the Peloponnesian War. And Medea might likewise represent, at least in part , a warning to his city. The brave new world unleashed in this play's finale, where self-interest and retaliation obliterate every kind of excellence, where the lust for revenge leaves moderation in the dust, where mothers kill their children—this all foreshadows the omnivorous violence of the impending war where, as Thucydides tells us in his searing account of the civil war in Corcyra in 427: "Death thus raged in every shape; and, as usually happens at such times, there was no length to which violence did not go; sons were killed by their fathers... Reckless audacity came to be considered the courage of a loyal ally; prudent hesitation, specious cowardice; moderation was held to be a cloak for unmanliness... Fanatic violence became the attribute of manliness; cautious plotting, a justifiable means of self-defense.

The advocate of extreme measures was always trustworthy; his opponent a man to be suspected... Revenge also was held of more account than self-preservation." [84] Much of Thucydides' account of degeneration of human nature under extreme pressure parallels Euripides' account in *Medea*, especially his unsettling ending. The best account I have read (and one which has influenced mine) belongs to William Arrowsmith:

> And this is Euripides' point, that "one touch of nature" makes kin of Hellene and barbarian. In Medea's barbarism we have a concentrated image of human *physis* [nature] and a symbol of the terrible closeness of all human nature to barbarism. In her inadequate *sophrosune* [self-mastery] and her imperfect *sophia* [wisdom/cleverness] is represented the norm of Hellenic, and most human, society. Thus when Jason cries out, "No Greek woman would have [ever] dared this crime" [1339-40], we are meant, not to agree, but to wonder and doubt, and finally to disbelieve him.
>
> The validity of that doubt and disbelief is immediately confirmed by the appearance of the golden chariot of the Sun in which Medea makes her escape to Athens. In this chariot Euripides does two related things: he first restates, vividly and unmistakably, the triumph of Medea over Jason, and secondly he provides the whole action with a symbolic and cosmological framework which forces the private *agon* [struggle] of Jason and Medea to assume a larger public significance. And by showing Medea, murderess and infanticide, as rescued by the Sun himself—traditionally regarded as the epitome of purity, the unstained god who will not look upon pollution—he drives home his meaning with the shock of near sacrilege. As for the chariot of the Sun it is the visible cosmic force which blazes through Medea's motives and which her whole *pathos* [suffering] expresses: the blinding force of life itself, stripped of any mediating morality or humanizing screen; naked, unimpeded, elemental *eros*; intense, chaotic, and cruel; the primitive, premoral, precultural condition of man and the world. If that force vindicates Medea as against Jason, her ardor as against his icy self-interest, it is only because her *eros* is elemental and therefore invincible. But she is vindicated only vis-à-vis Jason; and she is not justified at all. Of justification there can be no question here, not only because *eros* is, like any elemental necessity, amoral and therefore unjustifiable, but also because Euripides clearly believes the loss of *sophia* [wisdom] to be a tragic defeat for man and human culture.
>
> In the *agon* of Jason and Medea, passion, vengeance, and self-interest expel *sophia*. That *agon* ... stands for the Peloponnesian War—the war which Euripides, like Thucydides, feared would expel *sophia* from civilized cities, thereby barbarizing and brutalizing human behavior. At any time, in both individuals and cities, *sophia* is a delicate and precarious virtue; if anywhere in the Hellenic world, *sophia* flourished in Athens, but even there it bloomed precariously (how precariously the plague which overtook the city in the following year proved). And with the coming of Medea to Athens, Euripides seems to imply, comes the spirit of vengeance and passion, endangering *sophia*, that *sophia* whose creation and growth made Athens, in Thucydides' phrase [2.41], "the education of Hellas." For Hellas and humanity a new and terrible day dawns at the close of the *Medea*." [85]

PART V. EURIPIDES' *BACCHAE*

V. 1. The formal elements and structural design of the *Bacchae*:

Paradoxically this most formally structured of Athenian tragedies is the most violent in content. Dionysus, the fierce but effeminate god of ecstasy, invades and explodes the palace, the mind, and finally the body of King Pentheus. This relentless progression from political to psychological to physical fragmentation (*sparagmos*) makes one wonder how a divinity could harbor such wrath, and against an opponent so clearly outmatched. [86] Euripides' plot apparently followed the traditional outline of the myth about Dionysus' return home and his revenge on Pentheus. [87] This story had already been set forth in a (lost) trilogy of Aeschylus. The plot's main components are Dionysus' arrival and introduction of his rites; resistance to the god; direct confrontation between Dionysus as "the Stranger" and Pentheus; and the king's madness and death. The parts - exposition, confrontation, aftermath—cohere into a powerful and logical unity.[88]

This linear progression is enhanced by another striking unity, namely the chronological presentation of characters, which proceeds in a circular or chiastic pattern.[89] This highly symmetrical 'ring structure' offers another perspective from which to comprehend the chaos of the action. Dionysus himself frames the play (as do Aphrodite and Artemis in *Hippolytus*) in the prologue as a mortal with disguise and in the epilogue as an immortal without disguise. Between these two poles the action plays itself out as Pentheus is transformed from hunter to hunted, spectator to spectacle, man to woman, authoritative king to sacrificial scapegoat. The three consecutive confrontations at the plot's center illustrate the ironic pattern of the narrative, proceeding from the apparent defeat of the Stranger when Pentheus jails him (Act 2), to the psychic capture of Pentheus when the Stranger coaxes him into cross-dressing (Act 3), to the decisive victory of the Stranger over Pentheus with his frenzied double vision (Act 4). Euripides has bracketed the major confrontation of Act 3 (286 lines) with the much shorter Acts 2 and 4 (75 and 65 lines respectively), thereby highlighting the crucial dramatic sequences. Even so brief an analysis suggests how Euripides has blocked his play structurally, steadily zeroing in on the fierce struggle between man and god. The stakes of this struggle are nothing less than control of the city, control of the women, control of Pentheus' psyche, and, indeed, control of the plot itself. [90]

V.2. Major Themes of the *Bacchae*

The *Bacchae* may be the darkest and most ferocious tragedy ever written. Its finale is one of those rare dramatic experiences that leaves the spectator so completely frozen in horror and sadness that one can only wonder if Gloucester was not right: "As flies to wanton boys are we to th' gods, They kill us for their sport." (*King Lear* 4.1.36-37). An earthquake, a shattered palace, fits of madness, the rending of animals by frenzied *maenads* ("mad women"), a hilariously tragic cross-dressing scene, surreal visions of bulls and double suns, the tearing apart of an adolescent son by a maddened mother who then plays a game of ball with his body parts, the coaxing of that mother out of her insanity by her father, a merciless god coming "out of the machine" to announce the undeserved fate of a loving grandfather who will be metamorphosed into a savage serpent: there are so many strange sequences, culminating in the destruction of the family (infanticide: Pentheus as son) and the city (regicide: Pentheus as king), that we are left groping for a stable center from which to understand this disturbing drama whose apocalyptic vision might well be said to symbolize the end of fifth-century Athens. [91] More than any other Greek drama this one takes us deep into the heart of darkness.

The *Bacchae* enacts two views of power colliding violently with one another. These differing perspectives are symbolized by the drama's two dominant physical spaces, the city and the mountain. The city embodies civilization in its most articulate shape, a place of culture whose walls fence off the outside world of nature, beasts, and barbarians. In the Greek imagination the city represents order, wisdom, sanity, culture, architecture, law, morality, religion, and politics. Certainly Pentheus' city does not embody all these things, but he thinks it does. Those mighty walls and palace prisons embody, most of all, the traditional male warrior code. Pentheus personifies that code and rules the city accordingly—with a fierce temper and an iron fist. When a problem arises, his customary response is to hunt, capture, arrest, bind with chains, and imprison the enemy.

Beyond the severe walls and tight-fisted regulations of Pentheus' seven-gated city lies the wilderness of the mountain, Cithaeron, where Dionysus has driven mad the women of Thebes, all of them. Euripides' schematization could not be more emphatic: the males occupy the city, the females the mountain. What happens in one arena reverses what happens in the other. [92] If Thebes represents city and law (*nomos*), Cithaeron represents anti-city and nature (*physis*). The mountain embodies that which is beyond human control; it is linked to the city only by boundary-crossing characters such as shepherds and herdsmen; and, of course, by Dionysus, the boundary transgressor *par excellence*. The mountain in the *Bacchae* pulses with the green energy of nature and with the song, dance, ecstasy, fawnskins, madness, disorder, and miracles of the *maenads*. The spectators never see this world of exotic otherness because it lies miles from Thebes. But Euripides brings that mountain energy to life in the huge *orchestra* where the Asian Bacchae, who are visible to the audience, dance to the Dionysian music, decked out in their animal costumes and ivy wreaths. The Asian Bacchae are mirror images of the Theban Bacchae on Mt. Cithaeron, who, though visible only to our imaginations, are similarly dressed. The choral song and dance of the Asian Bacchae, vigorously driven by the pounding rhythms of their oriental drums, transports to the city the mountain world of the Theban Bacchae. But the choral songs celebrate not only bacchic exuberance and Asian otherness; they celebrate, too, traditional Greek wisdom, with its attendant warnings about *hybris* and the transgression of divine law.[93]

This peculiar duality within the chorus—one part nature, another part culture; one part Asian, another part Greek; one part fierce and vengeful, another part peaceful and gentle—mingles the worlds of mountain and city.

This commingling finds an analogue not only in the duality of Dionysus but also in Pentheus. Despite his headstrong machismo he wants to participate in, or rather peer into, this other world represented by the frenzied women on the mountain. An *eros* (813), a strong desire, possesses him to see the maenads, and especially his mother, on Mt. Cithaeron. But that sexual passion collides with his masculine sense of honor and glory. He would not be "caught dead" dressed as a woman but only by doing just that can he spy on his mother. The vehemence with which he rejects the feminine suggests an insecurity about his own sexuality. But we must remember that Pentheus is probably only eighteen years old or so. He knows virtually nothing about sex and not much more about life. Why should he? His father Echion ("Snake-man"), born from the dragon's teeth sown by Cadmus and so bypassing birth from the female, is absent from his life (and, largely, from the play). His mother Agave, leader of the maenads, has become the enemy in that other place. Yes, Pentheus does have a surrogate father in his grandfather Cadmus, but the old man—all bedecked in his Bacchic dress and headed off to the mountain to dance—hardly exemplifies fatherhood or political authority. His advice to Pentheus: accept the new god Dionysus, even if it means lying, so that the house of Cadmus can accrue more honor.

The lack of parental paradigms means that Pentheus is unschooled in life and in one of its most baffling mysteries, sexuality. Some critics call him a Peeping Tom or perverted voyeur. But these labels do not resonate. Pentheus is what he is, an adolescent struggling to become a man and a king. His struggle must be read in context. Pentheus' suspicions about the nocturnal drunkenness and promiscuity of the maenads, based on reports delivered to him while he was out of the country, are not without some basis. He has, after all, returned home to a city out of control. The whole situation is sexually charged: women driven mad onto a mountain, at night, with wine, worshipping some exotic foreigner. Tiresias tells Pentheus that Dionysus will not force the maenads to be chaste, though the truly virtuous ones will be (317-18). This opens the possibility that those maenads who lack self-control might be corrupted. No wonder Pentheus is concerned. What inexperienced young Greek king would not be? In the context of late fifth-century Athenian culture, Pentheus' fear becomes even more understandable. Maenads, after all, had a reputation. Their sexual activity pervaded Greek vases; satyrs, the phallic followers of Dionysus, were forever pursuing them. In a fragment of Aeschylus (448), maenads are called "shameless [i.e. loose] women." And Euripides' Ion (c. 410 B.C.) speaks of them at the wine-god's torch-lit festival atop Mt. Parnassus in the context of drunkenness and sex.

A similar perspective can be taken on the issue of Pentheus as "a fighter against the gods" as he is called by the Stranger, Tiresias and Agave. For Pentheus does not stand alone in his opposition to the new so-called god. The entire city of Thebes, both women and men, rejected Dionysus, all except Cadmus and Tiresias (195), whose motives for believing are hardly theologically inspiring. Like maenads, "new gods" had a reputation. Late fifth-century Athens was teeming with foreigner mercenaries and slaves as a result of the Peloponnesian

War. This invasion of foreigners meant an influx of numerous new divinities and mystery cults; these were often the target of the comic poets. One of these new gods was Sabazius, an oriental version of Dionysus from the mountains of Phrygia (Asia Minor) and Thrace (northern Greece). His Dionysus-like cult included nocturnal rituals, ecstatic dances to the flute and kettledrum, along with animals (snakes, bulls, fawn) which served as vehicles of the god. Cicero tells us that "In one of his plays Aristophanes, the wittiest poet of Old Comedy, so satirized the new gods and the nightlong observances of their rites, that Sabazius and certain other gods, having been condemned as foreigners, were thrown out of the city." [94] Such evidence suggests that, in the context of Euripides' world, Pentheus' fears about the promiscuity of the maenads and his hostility to the cult of the "new god" do not seem so outlandish.

Pentheus, then, as he attempts to negotiate the rite of passage from adolescence to manhood, does the best he can with the little he has. To dramatize the perils of this rite of passage, Euripides uses initiation into the mysteries of Dionysus as his vehicle. Why Dionysus? Because he confounds all the rigid dichotomies of Pentheus' life. Dionysus straddles two worlds—mortal and immortal, god and beast, Greek and Asian, gentle and savage, playful and violent, calm and frenzied, comic and tragic, born of male and female wombs (Zeus' and Semele's), inhabitant of the city and of the mountain, initiator into the life of his mysteries and conductor into Hades of those who resist initiation. Dionysus contains all these polarities. From a perspective that looks outward rather than inward, Dionysus (god of theater, mask, madness, wine, and illusion) represents the antithesis of Apollo (god of rationality, restraint, consciousness, light, and order.) [95] Perhaps for this reason the Athenians situated the Theater of Dionysus at the center of their community. With all its rage for order, the city embodies the Apollonian. But beneath the cultural constructs (*nomos*) that constitute civilization abides that "subterranean something" which must be incorporated into the city; thus, at the end of Aeschylus' *Oresteia* trilogy (458 BCE), Athena, virgin goddess of the city, works mightily to persuade the ancient Furies, powers of the earth and defenders of the ghost of slain Clytemnestra, to become part of the *polis*. That "subterranean something" which pulses through both cities and individuals, "the force that through the green fuse drives the flower" (Dylan Thomas' phrase), that is Dionysus, at once most gentle and most terrifying for mankind. Like the intoxicating wine over which he presides as god, Bacchus is the liquid force of liberation that allows mortals to free themselves from the restrictions and boundaries that culture must inevitably create to sustain itself.

If Dionysus is the god of liberation, what does he liberate in the *Bacchae*? One eminent scholar has recently argued that Dionysus liberates Thebes politically from the oppressive autonomous rule of Pentheus and "the irredeemably self-destructive rejection of the god by the royal family," that the god, in his final epiphany, establishes himself and his cult as a vital and cohesive force for the benefit of the city. [96] But this thesis does not tally with the emotional experience of the final scene. Could a mother cradling her own son's head, a head that she severed, welcome this god's cult? Or could a grandfather re-assembling the corpse of his grandson? Speaking to Dionysus about this excessive punishment Cadmus complains (1248): "Gods ought not be like mortals in their passions (*orge*)." It is precisely this, the god's vindictive passion, that reverberates through the epilogue. His wrath and vengeance have shattered the city and her people. That is how Cadmus and Agave interpret the events.

Why, then, is Dionysus so vindictive and why does the *Bacchae* end so darkly? A more convincing thesis relates the play to its historical context and sees Euripides as presenting a radical critique of the city in which he produced tragedies for half a century.[97] Looking down from Macedonia in northern Greece, where he seems to have exiled himself around 408 BCE, Euripides saw an "Athenian tragedy" writ large. What kind of city would paint a teenager like Pentheus into a corner, or allow Pentheus to paint himself into a corner, where his choices were constrained by such narrow cultural constructions of right and wrong, where the dichotomies of gender had become so rigid and isolating as to invite fragmentation of community and of self, where *eros* had so divorced itself from *sophia* (wisdom) that young men like Pentheus, virtually devoid of role models, were bound to become misfits who knew neither themselves nor their world? [98]

Part VI. The Poet as Prophet

In his role as cultural critic the poet becomes his city's prophet.[99] Euripides' *Medea* (431 BCE), on the one hand, and his *Bacchae* (406 BCE) on the other, virtually frame the years of the Peloponnesian War (431-404) and present his response to the gradual escalation of violence during these war years. These plays bracket the tearing apart of a once magnificent culture, a city that had, in time past, harmoniously yoked passion and wisdom (see *Medea* 824-45).

To recapitulate some of our earlier ideas, Medea can be read as a premonition about passion gone crazy: a mother forced to choose between love for her children and lust for revenge on a husband who had abandoned her for a younger and politically more advantageous bride. The age-old Greek moral code of "help your friends, hurt your enemies" now faced a dilemma: what happens when the enemy lives in your own house? Since, by Greek cultural definition, revenge against the enemy provided the surest path to attaining glory, Medea, like a Greek hoplite warrior, armed her heart in steel (1242) and murdered her two boys. She would, by creating a brand new set of rules, prove to her husband who was more powerful. The outraged Jason confidently proclaims that "there is no Greek woman who would have dared such a deed" (1339). We are meant to doubt him; for he has failed to understand that "great suffering makes a stone of the heart" (W. B. Yeats). When, in the shocking finale, this mother-turned-monster flies off in the chariot of the Sun god, the personification of pollution being whisked off by the symbol of purity, we see Eros unbound headed for Athens. Thucydides, who chronicled so brilliantly the first two decades of the Athens-Sparta debacle, describes how the kind of *eros* personified by Medea arrived in Athens. In recounting the Athenian decision to sail on the ill-fated Sicilian expedition in 415-413 BCE, Thucydides says "All alike fell in love (*eros*) with the enterprise... With this enthusiasm of the majority, the few that liked it not, feared to appear unpatriotic by holding up their hands against it, and so kept quiet." [100] The casualty list of that naval extravaganza: 7,000 Athenians captured, thousands killed, and over 100 warships destroyed. Eros had indeed gone crazy. [101]

The *eros* that flew out of Corinth winging towards Athens, at the end of *Medea* all those years ago, has in the *Bacchae* finally reached its destination, further twisted and distorted by its 25-year journey through the intervening Peloponnesian War, the "violent teacher" that revealed to all Greece the many faces of atrocity (Thuc. 3.82).

The eros for revenge that once consumed Medea—the damsel in distress transformed into semi-divine Fury—has now consumed Dionysus: "Pentheus will come to the Bacchae and pay the penalty of death... Let us punish him! ... I want the Thebans to mock him" (848-54); "Take revenge on him!" (1081). It was this god who "gave special ease to her hands" as Agave, "foaming at the mouth..., held fast by the Bacchic god" ripped out her son's shoulder (1124-28).

Why does Euripides present such a conflict of divine and human "wills to power" as the crux of this play? In part to reveal Dionysus as a divine power, a natural force within the human psyche that must be honored, respected, and indeed celebrated. When denied, as in the case of Pentheus, this force will erupt with volcanic fury. That explains part of Dionysus' taurine ferocity. But Euripides meant to extend that private theme to the public, political arena as well. In other words, the tragedy of the self implied the tragedy of the city. And that meant exposing, through the theme of revenge, the brutal reality of power politics in the late fifth century. "Of gods we believe and men we know, that by a necessary law of their nature they rule wherever they can."[102] So the Athenians argued in 415 BCE before they massacred all the men of military age on the island of Melos (Thuc. 5. 105). Their argument left no room for compassion. The theater, however, does leave room for compassion. Indeed, being the stage of sudden reversals of fortune, the theater becomes, by natural extension, the place of pity. Indeed that may well constitute Athenian tragedy's most enduring legacy. In a world-view that holds no hope of divine redemption, humans must rely on one another, on their capacities for empathy and sympathy. Medea and Jason, Aphrodite and Artemis in *Hippolytus*, Hera in *Heracles*, Dionysus and Pentheus in *Bacchae*, they all seem to embody the anger of jealous city-states battling one another.[103] If no firm moral compass stands steady in the mythic world of these tragedies, that is because Euripides found no moral center in the world around him. The *Bacchae*, like so much of Euripides, presents fragments of characters. Medea, Jason, Phaedra, Hippolytus, Lycus, Agave, Pentheus: they are all just parts of a whole. The old Sophoclean protagonist, bound to a Promethean rock of moral certitude, had little purchase on Euripides because that kind of heroic temper had disappeared from his everyday world.

Euripides' earlier prophetic warnings were history now. The pathetic image of a Bacchic mother—driven mad by the god of theater himself—raising the impaled head/mask of her own son on a cultic *thyrsus* in honor of that god; this horrific image was Euripides' final vision. Night had come. The time for the remembrance of things past had passed. All he could summon was pity and fear. It was too late now for anything else; too late for Pentheus and Agave, too late for Athens, and even too late, it seems, for the disembodied mask of tragedy itself.[104]

PART VII. GREEK TRAGEDY IN PERFORMANCE
by Michael Halleran

Medea, Hippolytus, Heracles, and *Bacchae* were, like almost all ancient Greek tragedies, first performed in Athens at an annual religious festival in the Theater of Dionysus. This theater was very large, capable of seating some 15,000 spectators. Built on the southeastern slope of the acropolis, its rows of seats went up the hill. The viewing area was called the *theatron*, whence English "theater;" the performance itself took place below. The *orchestra*, a spacious circular dancing area, dominated the spectator's view. About 65 feet in diameter, it was the chief area of activity during the play. The other main focus of attention was the *skene*, an (originally) wooden building, with a roof strong enough to support more than one actor, located at the far side of the *orchestra*. It served as the backdrop for the action, being a palace in all four plays collected in this volume, or whatever the world of the play claimed. Some scene painting was employed, but our knowledge of this is meager. In addition to providing the backdrop for the action, the *skene* served as a stage building or changing room and helped in projecting the actors' voices in the large open-air theater. The *skene* had one central double door, and very possibly one or two side doors in this period. Certainly some scenes would have been much easier to stage if we assume more than one door was available for comings and goings.

The *skene* was the main place for entrances and exits. But characters could also enter into the orchestra and leave it along the two long entrance ramps, each one called an *eisodos* (often called today, less accurately, *parodos*), which led at angles on either side into the acting area. Most entrances and exits occurred along these long ramps. It is important to remember in this regard the great openness of the Greek theater, which could focus significant attention on the entrances and exits.

Characters usually entered and exited on the ground, but could also appear on high as does Medea at the end of her play. For divine appearances aloft a crane-like device called the *mechane* was available. The roof of the *skene* could also be used for divine appearances as well as for mortals' activities. Another device, the *ekkyklema* was a platform that could be rolled out into the acting area, permitting an interior scene to be shown to the audience. One of the stage conventions was that all the action takes place outdoors, so anything that occurs inside must be revealed through voices from offstage, an eye-witness account of the event, or the scene presented on the *ekkyklema*.

The existence of a raised stage in the fifth century is most unlikely. In subsequent centuries the stage became significantly elevated, furthering the distance and distinction between the worlds of the chorus and actors. This was not the case in the fifth century. As the plays themselves make amply clear, even if the actors are on a slightly raised platform, they and the chorus communicate freely with one another and can impinge on each other's acting area; no barrier is felt between the two groups. On balance it seems as if there was a slightly elevated platform extending from the *skene* used by the actors, while the chorus, the other members of the production, operated in the *orchestra* proper.

Two groups comprised the performers of a Greek tragedy: actors and chorus. All the participants seem to have worn the same basic outfit: an ankle-length robe or tunic (*chiton*) with an outer garment (*himation*) over it. Footwear consisted of a simple thin-soled shoe or boot; and occasionally actors or chorus would appear barefoot. Of course there would be variations in costume within a given production and differences from one production to another.

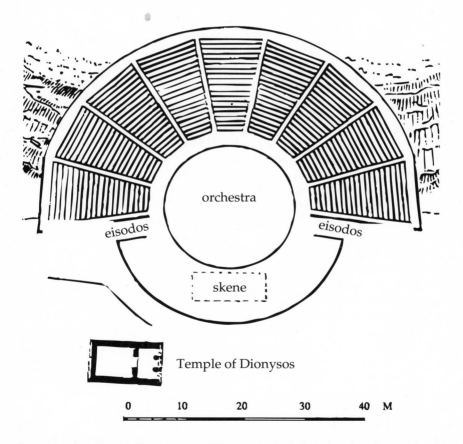

A reconstruction of the theater of Dionysos in Athens during the second half of the fifth century BCE. (Based on the sketch by J. Travlos, *Pictorial Dictrionary of Ancient Athens* [London 1971] 540.)

Men played all parts (compare the *onnagata* roles in Japan's Kabuki theater). This might tax our response as spectators, but for the original audience the playing of female roles by male actors both was conventional and was aided greatly by an important feature of these performances—the wearing of masks. The actors, as well as the members of the chorus, all wore full-face masks. Made probably of reinforced linen, they covered the front of the head and had wigs attached. Although no mask survives from this era, vase painting and the plays themselves suggest that an attempt was made at realism. The basic requirement of the mask was to identify a character in distinction from the other characters. The use of masks not only allowed this recognition of characters (the old man, the young woman, etc.), it also encouraged a close identification between the actor and the role. And, of course, the mask did not permit changes in facial expression, the type of nuance which we, accustomed to close-up shots in cinema, have come to expect. (Such fine touches in any case would have been lost to the great majority of spectators in the vast Theater of Dionysus.) The mask with its unchanging expression drew attention, as another critic has put it, "not to the unexpressed thought inside, but to the distant, heroic figures, whose constant *ethos* it portrays." [105]

Of the two constituent parts of a Greek tragedy the chorus is the more distant and difficult for a modern audience to appreciate. The members of the chorus, fifteen in number when the four plays in this volume were produced, acted usually as a group, singing and dancing their part, a continuous presence in the *orchestra* once they entered. (Their number included a chorus leader, *coryphaeus*, who would at times act independently of the larger group.) This is not what we are used to in modern drama. Music and dance were integral features of the choral elements of the drama. (In fact the Greek word *choros* has "dance" as its primary meaning.) Music from a reed instrument, the *aulos*, accompanied the performance of the dancing, but the precise nature of the music and of the dancing is impossible to determine from the ancient evidence, although we do know that in general Greek dancing was mimetic.

Even with little information about the music and dance, it is readily apparent that the choral lyrics are rich poetry and important to the drama. All parts of a Greek drama, both the dialogue and the songs, were composed in verse, but the poetry of the songs was different in kind: denser, more striking in its imagery, and more suggestive in its language. The chorus has been called the "ideal spectator" and the "voice of the poet." Neither is true. Although the chorus is generally less well defined and at times less integral to the action than the other characters in the play, it does have a specific personality and a definite role to play. The chorus responds to the action, reflecting on the events and often referring to past events as a context for the current ones. Owing to the nature of their poetry and their function, the choral songs are heard in, as it were, a different key. The typical choral song is strophic, that is to say it is written in paired stanzas, each member of the pair having the same metrical composition. The first member is called the strophe and the second the antistrophe. While the two members of the pair of stanzas are identical rhythmically, no two pairs are alike. After one, two, three or even more paired stanzas, the ode may conclude with a single stanza with no responding element; this is called an epode. The first song is called the *parodos*, the song usually delivered as the chorus entered into the orchestra; subsequent ones are each called a *stasimon*, a song delivered after the chorus had taken up their position in the *orchestra*.

Our traditions about Greek tragedy point to an origin in a song sung at a ritual. The name Thespis is attached to the first actor, and this man is often called the creator of tragedy: at a time of thoroughly choral presentations, he is said to be the first to break away from the chorus and give speeches and respond to the chorus. With this major innovation, tragedy ceased to be only a sung narrative and became enriched with a new dimension, that of actors and their spoken words. After the introduction of the first actor, others were later added: Aeschylus is said to have introduced the second actor and Sophocles the third. There the number of actors with speaking parts became fixed: each dramatist worked with only three actors. Of course a play could have more than three characters, but this would be handled by the "doubling" of roles: one actor would play more than one part. There were so-called "mute characters," "extras" who would have silent parts to play, such as attendants and children. The reason for this limit was perhaps aesthetic, or maybe it reflects an attempt at fairness so that all playwrights would be competing for the prizes under the same conditions. Whatever the reason, the effect is noteworthy: the Greek tragic stage, with the exception of the chorus, tended to be rather uncrowded. Dialogue among three characters, although possible, was in fact uncommon. The plays generally show conversations between two characters, or one character and the chorus, or one delivering a soliloquy. Even when the three actors with speaking parts are on stage together, they only infrequently carry on a three-way dialogue. The doubling of roles necessitated by the relatively small number of actors was also facilitated by the masks and the identification they created between the mask-wearing actor and the character he played. In a given drama an actor might play several roles, and with each mask that he donned he became that character and the audience could thereby readily make the adjustment.

As Aristotle long ago observed, the fundamental structure of tragedy is based on the alternation of speech and song, the dialogue of the actors and the songs of the chorus. Periodically the chorus leader will have a few lines to speak, and the actors will occasionally sing their lines, but the basic dynamic is the alternation of speech and song. This alternation gives tragedy much of its rich and varied texture. Tragedy's structure also involves not only the alternation of speech and song but also this alternation tied up with exits before the song and entrances after them. One should be alert to this basic pattern and variations on it.

ENDNOTES

[1] Quoted from B. Snell *The Discovery of the Mind: The Greek Origins of European Thought* (1953) 135.

[2] Translations from ancient Greek are my own unless otherwise indicated.

[3] Translations from the Bible come from *The Harper-Collins Study Bible: New Revised Standard Edition* ed. Wayne Meeks (1989).

[4] Herodotus *The History* 2.53, trans. David Grene (1987).

[5] It is not accidental that the first word of Homer's *Odyssey* (c. 700 BCE) is "man" (*andra*). For criticism of Homer's anthropomorphic theology see Xenophanes (570--478 BCE) in *The Presocratic Philosophers* eds. G. Kirk, J. Raven, M. Schofield (1983) 168-72.

[6] I owe this formulation to my colleague Bernard Prusak. Otherwise put, "the Hebrews had a top-down perspective, the Greeks a bottom-up perspective on reality. For the Greeks the gods are emergent in a way that God is certainly not for the Hebrews." This last is the formulation of another colleague, Richard Oxenberg.

[7] See M. Greenberg "Biblical Law: Establishing a Moral Order" *Bible Review* 7 (June 1991) 42.

[8] On the city (*polis*) of the gods on Mt. Olympus, with its market-place, city-gates, assembly place, and king, see S. Scully "The Nature of the Gods in Early Greek Poetic Thought" in *Philosophies of Nature: The Human Dimension* eds. R. Cohen and A. Tauber (1998) 163-76 and "Reflections of Olympus: Images of Order in Hesiod's Theogony and Plato's Republic" in *Acta: First Panhellenic and International Conference on Ancient Greek Literature* (Athens 1997) 75-91.

[9] Hesiod *Theogony* 116-22; these first four Greek gods were spontaneously generated without source or cause.

[10] See R. Caldwell *Hesiod's Theogony* (1987) 35-36 and 87-89.

[11] Private communication.

[12] B. Anderson *Understanding the Old Testament* (abridged fourth edn, assisted by K. Darr, 1998) 98.

[13] On Zeus' political savvy see *Hesiod Theogony* 501-6, 613-7, 881-900; cf. N. O. Brown *Hesiod: Theogony* (1953) 19-35; on Zeus' socialization of *eros* see Scully op. cit. (1998) 166-70.

[14] Martin Buber speaks felicitously of this Covenant in terms of an "I-Thou" relationship; *I and Thou* (1937; second edn. 1958).

[15] Jesus later called this cornerstone of monotheism "the greatest commandment" (Matthew 22.37; Mark 12.28-30).

[16] Aristotle *Magna Moralia* 1208 b30; quoted from W. Burkert *Greek Religion* (1985) 274.

[17] The Ten Commandments = Exodus 20. 1, 21-22, Deuteronomy 4.12, 5.4, 22; cf. M. Weinfeld "What Makes the Ten Commandments Different?" *Bible Review* 7 (April 1991) 35 ff.

[18] By "sin" I mean estrangement from God for violating His Law. The Homeric verb (*alitaino*), although sometimes translated as "I sin", is more properly rendered "I transgress." Cf. R. Parker *Miasma: Pollution and Purification in Early Greek Religion*

(1990); J. Klawans *Impurity and Sin in Ancient Judaism* (2000).

[19] Anderson op. cit. 98.

[20] As we learn in Numbers 13-14, lack of faith destroys most of the exodus generation.

[21] Cf. C. Seltman *The Twelve Olympians* (1952) 15-25.

[22] Examples of redemption: Isaiah 41.14; 54.8; Psalms 34.7; 107.1-2; Ezekiel 37.12-14; of God's steadfast love, Exodus 34. 6-7.

[23] Compare Psalms 130. 8 where God will redeem Israel of its sins.

[24] "The word 'redeemer' and its related terms 'redeem' and 'redemption' appear in the Bible some 130 times…" *The Encyclopaedia Judaica* vol. 14 (1971), "Redemption", p. 1.

[25] I owe this formulation to my colleague Richard Oxenberg.

[26] Jesus at Mark 15.34 and Matthew 27.46, quoting Psalm 22.1.

[27] See E. R. Dodds "Euripides the Irrationalist" in *The Ancient Concept of Progress* (1973) 78-91.

[28] Euripides, *Heracles* 1303-8, translated by M. Halleran.

[29] Aristotle *Politics* 1.1.10 (= 1253 a 8).

[30] H. Bloom (ed.) *Homer* (1986) 1 and *Ruin the Sacred Truths: Poetry and Belief from the Bible to the Present* (1989) 146-47; cf. 27.

[31] Cf. G. Steiner: "Tragedy is alien to the Judaic sense of the world… Christianity is an anti-tragic vision of the world. [It] offers to man an assurance of final certitude and repose in God. This leads the soul toward justice and resurrection… Real tragedy can occur only where the tormented soul believes that there is no time left for God's forgiveness." *The Death of Tragedy* (1961) 4-6; 331-32.

[32] Or, as Nietzsche put it, "Man is a rope, tied between beast and overman—a rope over an abyss." *Thus Spoke Zarathustra* preface 4 in *The Portable Nietzsche* ed. W. Kaufmann (1959) 126.

[33] For famous odes on the overwhelming potency of *eros* see Euripides' *Hippolytus* 525-62 and 1268-82, Sophocles' *Antigone* 781-90, and *Maidens of Trachis* 497-530.

[34] Pindar, *Pythian Ode* 8. 95-97, written in 446 BCE; similarly Sophocles' *Ajax* (c. 445 BCE) 124-26.

[35] "[Judaism's] ideal for man is charity in action rather than clarity of thought… Hellenism gave the world the 'heroic' outlook with its motto 'ever to excel and to surpass others.' Its counterpart in Judaism is the vision of divine holiness and the consciousness not of that wherein human nature excels but of where it requires correction." L. Roth *Judaism: A Portrait* (1960) 35-36.

[36] There were exceptions to this, such as afterlife for certain special heroes in the Elysian Fields (*Odyssey* 4. 561-69) or on the Isles of the Blest (Hesiod *Works and Days* 167-73); Orphism and the Eleusinian Mysteries (*Homeric Hymn to Demeter* 480-82) also promised afterlife to their initiates.

[37] On the "new music" see E. Csapo and W. Slater *The Context of Ancient Drama* (1995) 332-34; on the ant-like sound of Euripides' music see Aristophanes *Women of the Thesmophoria* 100.

[38] Attica (some 1,000 square miles, about the size of Rhode Island) was divided into 139 *demes* (villages), each of which belonged to one of ten tribes. In 431 BCE Attica had a population of some 310,000, including 110,000 slaves and 28,500 metics (resident foreigners); so Csapo / Slater *op. cit.* (1995) 286.

[39] In an attempt to link between the birth of tragedy directly to the birth of democracy, W. R. Connor has argued that "state-sponsored" tragedy at the City Dionysia did not begin, as has been traditionally thought, with Thespis' first production c. 534

BCE but rather began in 501/0 as a "freedom festival" to celebrate the overthrow of the Pisistratid tyranny and the establishment of Cleisthenes' democratic (tribal) reforms in 508/7. But the idea that tragedy was born so suddenly, like Athena out of Zeus' head, contradicts Aristotle, who says that tragedy developed little by little (*kata mikron*) and underwent many changes before it reached its natural end (*Poetics* ch. 4. 1449a 13-15). Furthermore if Connor's theory were correct, one would expect some primary source record of such a momentous event; but our main sources for Cleisthenes' reforms (Herodotus 5. 67-73; [Aristotle] *Constitution of Athens* 20-22) are silent about the postulated event. See Connor "City Dionysia and Athenian Democracy" *Classica et Mediaevalia* 40 (1989) 7-32; for a different sort of rebuttal, see K. Raaflaub "Zeus Eleutherios, Dionysos the Liberator, and the Athenian Tyrannicides. Anachronistic Uses of Fifth-Century Political Concepts" in *Polis and Politics: Studies in Ancient Greek History* eds. P. Flensted-Jensen, T. Nielsen, L. Rubinstein (2000) esp. 255-60. In this context M. L. West has cogently cast doubt on the certainty of several sixth-century dates for various tragedians: see "The Early Chronology of Attic Tragedy" *Classical Quarterly* 39 (1989) 251-54.

[40] Aristotle *Poetics* ch. 4, 1449a 13-15.

[41] Athenian democracy "officially" began with the overthrow of the Pisistratid tyranny in 510 BCE and the tribal reforms of Attica by Cleisthenes in 508/7. But the word "demo-cracy" ("people-power") was not coined until c. 450.

[42] Aeschylus' predecessor Phrynichus won his first victory c. 511-508 BCE.

[43] *Poetics* ch. 4, 1449a 15-19; Thespis, the winner of the first competition c. 534, apparently introduced the first actor; Sophocles introduced the third (and last) actor.

[44] See Aristophanes *Frogs* 1004-5 (405 BCE).

[45] J. Herington *Aeschylus* (1985) 41.

[46] J. Herington *Poetry Into Drama: Early Tragedy and the Greek Poetic Tradition* (1985) 144.

[47] See E. Robertson *The First Democracies: Early Popular Government Outside Athens* (1997).

[48] In Athens, the size of these three groups was 10, 500, and 6,000 respectively. On the tripartitite constitutional structure of Greek city-states see M. I. Finley *Politics in the Ancient World* (1983) 57-58.

[49] L .J. Samons (ed.) *Athenian Democracy and Imperialism* (1998) 6.

[50] My discussion draws heavily on L. J. Samons "Democracy, Empire, and the Search for the Athenian Character" *Arion* (Winter 2001) 128-57, especially 140.

[51] The word *parrhesia* does not appear in extant Aeschylus or Sophocles; it occurs in five plays of Euripides: *Hippolytus* 422 and *Ion* 672-75 refer to free-spokenness in Athens; *Orestes* 905, *Electra* 1049-56 and *Bacchae* 668 refer to it in Argos and Thebes; two other interesting passages refer to it in Athens, namely Aristophanes *Women of the Thesmophoria* 541 and Plato *Republic* 8. 557b. See A. Momigliano "Freedom of Speech in Antiquity" in *Dictionary of the History of Ideas* ed. P. Wiener vol. 2 (1973) 252-63.

[52] On the Athenian Assembly see M. I. Finley *Politics in the Ancient World* (1983) 70-96; on the Spartan Assembly see Thuc. 1. 67, 79, and 87-88; also P. J. Rhodes *Greek City-States: A Source Book* (1986) 76-80.

[53] On the (often rambunctious) informal vocal participation in the Assembly, see Judith Tacon "Ecclesiastic *Thorubos*: Interventions, Interruptions, and Popular Involvement in the Athenian Assembly" *Greece and Rome* 48 (2001) 173-92.

[54] Comedy, unlike tragedy, dealt with the particular problems of a particular city (Athens) at a particular time; see J. Henderson *Three Plays by Aristophanes: Stag-*

ing Women (1996) 3-30.

[55] See S. Goldhill "Greek drama and political theory" in *The Cambridge History of Greek and Roman Thought* eds. C. Rowe and M. Scholfield (2000) 60-87.

[56] Aristophanes, *Frogs* 1009-10, where Euripides is speaking to Aeschylus in their debate about why a poet should be admired; cf. 686-7, 1054-55. Other relevant Aristophanic passages on the dramatist as teacher: *Acharnians* 497-500, 634-5, 650-62, *Wasps* 650-1.

[57] On the cognitive value of the emotions, see M. Nussbaum in *The Encyclopedia of Ethics* eds. L. and C. Becker (1992) under "Tragedy" in vol. 2, 1254-57.

[58] This teaching of tragedy will later be opposed by the philosophical thesis of Socrates and his student Plato who will assert something like the following: That the structure of the world (*kosmos*), both empirically (i.e. the facts of life) and morally (e.g. the idea of the Good), is stable and rational; hence it can be understood by reason (*logos*, rational discourse) which is the sole and sufficient means of approaching the truth. Therefore human error, both intellectual and ethical, arises from a failure in the reasoning process (i.e. from ignorance). In other words, (from an ethical perspective), excellence or virtue (*arete*), being a kind of knowledge, can be taught; and because this is the case, i.e. that "virtue is knowledge" and its opposite (bad conduct) results from ignorance, it follows that man is largely self-sufficient; hence no change (*metabole*) or reversal (*peripeteia*) of fortune (such as tragedy enacts) can alter a person's happiness (*eudaimonia*) substantially. See further E. R. Dodds *op. cit.* ("Euripides the Irrationalist", 1973) 78-79.

[59] Thucydides 1. 70; cf. L. J. Samons "Democracy, Empire, and the Search for the Athenian Character" *Arion* (Winter 2001) 128-57.

[60] The fifth-century trireme (120 by 20 feet), carried 200 men. Its job was to sink the enemy. Under the power of its two sails, the trireme averaged 4-5 knots and covered 35-45 miles per day; in battle it could reach 7-8 knots. Cf. J. Morrison, J. Coates and N. Rankov *The Athenian Trireme* (second edn., 2000) 4-5, 102-6, 132-3. Athens' active fleet of 200 triremes would have required some 34,000 sailors and 4,000-5,000 hoplites. The cost of such an immense navy over a typical four-month sailing season would have been between 400 and 800 talents. See L. J. Samons *Empire of the Owl: Athenian Imperial Finance* (2000) 93, 207, 306.

[61] See John Wilson *Athens and Corcyra* (1987) 61-64.

[62] At Sybota, Corinth and her allies had 150 triremes, of which 30 were sunk; Corcyra had 110 triremes, of which 70 were sunk; Athens lost none of her 30 triremes; see Thuc. i. 45-54; N. Hammond *Studies in Greek History* (1973) 447-70; Morrison, Coates, Rankov op. cit. 62-69; Wilson op. cit. 33-64.

[63] The expedition against Potidaea eventually cost Athens 2,000 talents. An (Attic) talent was a large unit of currency (weighing 57 pounds) worth 60 minas or 6,000 drachmas; one drachma was the daily wage of a skilled laborer or a sailor. In 431 Athens had some 6,000 talents in reserve to fight the war (Thuc. 2.13). To get a sense of how much money this is, consider that the Parthenon, Athena's marble temple on the Acropolis, which took fifteen years to build (447-432 BCE), cost 470 talents. In 431, the year of Euripides' *Medea*, Athens collected some 400 talents in tribute money from her "allies"; it was this amount that was paraded by 400 porters, presumably each carrying a talent's worth of coins in a bag, through the orchestra at the opening of the festival—a lengthy reminder to the audience of 15,000 of the empire's power. R. Meiggs *Athenian Empire* (1972) 434; L. J. Samons *Empire of the Owl* (2001) 197-99.

[64] Athens is called a tyrant-like city by Pericles at Thuc. 2.63 and, even more explicitly, by Cleon at 3. 37.

[65] Athens' massive war-chest: 9,700 talents at its height in 448 BCE; so Thuc. 2.13.

[66] See S. Goldhill "The Great Dionysia and Civic Ideology" in *Nothing to Do with Dionysos: Athenian Drama in it Social Context* (1990) 101-4.

[67] Samons op. cit. (2001) chapters 3 and 4; cf. R. Meiggs *The Athenian Empire* (1972) 201-2.

[68] See A. Elliott *Euripides: Medea* (1969) 112.

[69] R. Rehm *Marriage to Death: The Conflation of Wedding and Funeral Rituals in Greek Tragedy* (1994) 118 and 202 n. 55.

[70] On the play's structure, see T. Buttrey "Accident and Design in Euripides' Medea" *American Journal of Philology* 69 (1958) 1-17.

[71] Battle of the sexes: 235-51, 569-75, 1291-92, 1366-68; Medea's "divided self":792-96, 1021-80, 1242-50.

[72] L. Cohn-Haft "Divorce in Classical Athens" *Journal of Hellenic Studies* 25 (1995) 1.

[73] [Aristotle], *Athenian Constitution* 26.4. Cf. Rehm op.cit. (1994) 97; 197 n.5.

[74] See E. Hall *Inventing the Barbarian: Greek Self-Definition Through Tragedy* (1989) 80, 175-6; cf. H. Bacon *Barbarians in Greek Tragedy* (1961) 151-2.

[75] M.L. Earle *The Medea of Euripides* (1904) 106.

[76] Sophocles *Tereus*, pre-415 BCE, fragment 583, 1-12 (Radt).

[77] Sophocles *Maidens of Trachis* 536-41, 547-9.

[78] On this topic see M. Blundell *Helping Friends, Harming Enemies: A Study in Sophocles and Greek Ethics* (1989) 26-59.

[79] Cf. H. Foley "Tragic Wives: Medea's Divided Self" in *Female Acts in Greek Tragedy* (2001) 243-71.

[80] Scholars debate vigorously the meaning of Medea's famous line 1079. Does she mean "My seething spirit (*thumos*) is stronger than my deliberations (*bouleumata*)" or "My seething spirit dictates my (murder) plans"? The second interpretation is to be preferred. Why? Because of one overwhelming fact: *bouleumata*, in all nine occurrences in Medea (270, 372, 449, 769, 772, 886, 1044, 1048, 1079) refers to concrete "plans"; 3x (270, 449, 886) to Creon's / Jason's "plan" about the new bride and Medea's exile and 6x to Medea's revenge plans. Most importantly, twice previously in this speech (1044, 1048, as also at 769, 772) Medea uses the word to refer to her murder plans against her boys. In sum, words of the *bouleu-* word cluster (i.e. *bouleumata* = 9x; *bouleuein* = 6x; *boule* = 2x) occur 17 times; all 17 refer either to the "exile" plans of Jason/Creon or to Medea's "revenge" plans. So the play offers compelling evidence to translate *bouleumata* specifically as "murder plans" rather than generally as "considerations." [The evidence of *kreisson* is a bit ambiguous since it can mean "stronger than" (as at 965) or "is master of" (as probably at 443-45: "Another, a queen, is master of your bed."). The decisive evidence about *bouleumata* tips the scales in favor of "is master of."] Hence the best reading is: "My seething spirit controls / is master of (*kreisson*) my plans (*bouleumata*) to kill my children." For a useful overview of various interpretations of lines 1078-80 see D. Mastronarde *Euripides: Medea* (2002) 393-7.

[81] On the Scylla see *Odyssey* 12.256-59; cf. Aeschylus *Agamemnon* 1232.

[82] N. Collinge "Medea Ex Machina" *Classical Philology* 57 (1962) 171; P. Arnott *Greek Scenic Conventions* (1978) 86.

[83] C. Sourvinou-Inwood suggests that Medea, in the finale, changed costume (a rarity in tragedy) and dressed in oriental garb, a dramatic move that would represent the child-killer "at her most other, most negative, and most symbolically distanced."

"Medea at a Shifting Distance: Images and Euripidean Tragedy" in *Medea: Essays in Myth, Literature, Philosophy and Art* eds. J. Clauss and S. Johnston (1997) 291-92. D. Mastronarde *Euripides' Medea* (2002) 41-42 argues that the lack of textual evidence makes this suggestion unlikely.

[84] Thuc. 3.81-82; translation by R. Crawley (1874).

[85] Arrowsmith "A Greek Theater of Ideas" *Arion* 2.3 (1963) 30-31, repr. in *Euripides: A Collection of Critical Essays* ed. Erich Segal (1968) 26-27.

[86] On this progression see C. Segal "The Menace of Dionysus: Sex Roles and Reversals in Euripides' *Bacchae*" in *Women in the Ancient World* eds. J. Peradotto and J. Sullivan (1984) 195-212.

[87] For a fine up-to-date "biography" of the god see A. Henrichs "Dionysus" in *The Oxford Classical Dictionary* [3] eds. S. Hornblower and A. Spawforth (1996) 479-82.

[88] The plot of the *Bacchae* can be outlined as follows:
   a) 1-433: Preparation for confrontation: situation in Thebes
      1. Dionysus' homecoming and introduction of his rites (Prologue: 1-63)
      2. conversion of Tiresias and Cadmus (Act 1: 170-369)
   b) 434-976: Confrontation: resistance to the god (Pentheus vs. the Stranger)
      1. confrontation #1: apparent defeat of the Stranger (Act 2: 434-518)
      2. confrontation #2: psychic capture of Pentheus (Act 3: 576-861)
      3. confrontation #3: decisive victory of the Stranger (Act 4: 912-976)
   c) 977-1392: Result of confrontation: fates of Pentheus, Agave, and Cadmus
      1. killing of Pentheus by Agave (Act 5: 1024-1152)
      2. Agave's madness / recovery; Dionysus' verdict (Epilogue: 1165-1392

[89] The actors appear in the following symmetrical ring pattern:
   a. Dionysus: god, disguised as man, describes his mission (Prologue)
   b. Tiresias / Cadmus: innocuous consequences of maenadism (Act 1)
   c. Pentheus: hunter of maenads (Act 1)
   d. Stranger: defeated by Pentheus [appearance] (Act 2)
   e. Pentheus: man as woman: cross-dressing (Act 3)
   d. Stranger: defeats Pentheus [reality] (Act 4)
   c. Pentheus: hunted by maenads, via report of messenger (Act 5)
   b. Agave / Cadmus: lethal consequences of maenadism (Epilogue)
   a. Dionysus: god, undisguised, on mission accomplished (Epilogue)
   I have borrowed the basic scheme from T. B. L. Webster *Greek Art and Literature, 500-430 B.C.* (1939) 159.

[90] See F. Zeitlin *Playing the Other: Gender and Society in Classical Greek Literature* (1996) 360-61.

[91] W. Arrowsmith speaks similarly about Euripides' *Orestes* produced in 408 BCE, just two years before the *Bacchae*: "I am tempted to see in the play Euripides' prophetic image of the final destruction of Athens and Hellas, or that Hellas to which a civilized man could still give his full commitment." *Euripides IV* eds. D. Grene and R. Lattimore (1958) 111.

[92] See R. Friedrich "City and Mountain: Dramatic Spaces in Euripides' Bacchae" *Proceedings of the XIIth Congress of the International Comparative Literature Association vol. 2 Space and Boundaries in Literature* (1988) 538-45.

[93] See C. Segal "Chorus and Community in Euripides' *Bacchae*" in *Poet, Public, and Performance in Ancient Greece* eds. L. Edmunds and R. Wallace (1997) 65-86.

[94] Cicero *On the Laws* 2.15; the comedy in question seems to be Aristophanes' lost *Seasons*, probably produced between 423 and 408.

[95] See F. Nietzsche *The Birth of Tragedy* (1872), esp. sections 1-5.

[96] See R. Seaford *Euripides' Bacchae* (1996) 50; although I disagree with Seaford's general interpretation, it will be clear from my notes how much I have learned from his commentary, especially with regard to the play's allusions to the Dionysiac mysteries.

[97] See W. Arrowsmith *op. cit.* ("A Greek Theater of Ideas", 1963).

[98] Cp. Segal *op. cit.* ("The Menace of Dionysus") 197 on the consequences of Pentheus' male-dominated perspective: "This society's extreme sexual differentiation, even with its preferential treatment of the masculine, is as inimical to male as to female psychic integration. The women become mad and leave the inner space which defines them and gives them their secure, if limited, identity; yet the men too suffer dismemberment."

[99] See B. Knox "Euripides: The Poet as Prophet" in *Directions in Euripidean Criticism* ed. Peter Burian (1985) 1-12.

[100] Thucydides: *The Peloponnesian War* 6.24 trans. R. Crawley (1876; Modern Library reprint 1951). For the theme compare Thucydides (3.84) on the civil war at Corcyra in 427 BCE, where the breakdown of law was so severe that fathers were killing their own sons. The historian speaks "of the savage and pitiless excesses into which men who had begun the struggle not in a class but in a party spirit, were hurried by their ungovernable passions (*orge*). In the confusion into which life was now thrown in the cities, human nature, always rebelling against the law and now its master, gladly showed itself ungoverned in passion (*orge*)..."

[101] Euripides revisited this theme of *eros* for war often but nowhere more bitterly than in 407/6 BCE (he died in the winter of that year); cf. *Iphigeneia at Aulis*, 808 and 1263.

[102] Translated by R. Crawley op. cit. (1876).

[103] See B. Knox "Divine Intervention in Euripidean Thought" in *Studi di Filologia Classica in Onore di Giusto Monaco* vol. 1 (1991) 223-30.

[104] "... too late for Athens." In 405-404 B.C. after their final defeat by Sparta at Aegospotami in the Hellespont (northeastern Aegean Sea), the Athenians saw their empire destroyed. After 395 BCE the city would regain some of her power but in 405-404 Athens was financially exhausted and starved into submission; portions of the city's walls had been razed; three thousand Athenians had been executed at Aegospotami and one hundred Athenian warships had been captured or destroyed in that battle (Sparta allowed her to keep twelve ships); democracy was then abolished; and the council of thirty oligarchs began their reign of terror. On all this see Plutarch *Life of Lysander* ch.11-15 and Xenophon *Hellenica* 2.1-3. Tragedy, like democracy, would continue in the fourth century but it was a pale shadow of its predecessor; see P. Easterling "The end of an era? Tragedy in the early fourth century" in *Tragedy, Comedy, and the Polis* eds. J. Henderson et al. (1993) 559-69.

[105] Oliver Taplin *Greek Tragedy in Action* (1978) 14.

MEDEA

Translation and notes by A.J. Podlecki

CHARACTERS

MEDEA, Jason's ex-wife; daughter of Aietes, king of Colchis
on the southeastern coast of the Black Sea
JASON, Medea's ex-husband; son of Aeson from Iolkos on
the east coast of Thessaly in central Greece
CREON, King of Corinth, whose daughter Jason marries
AIGEUS, King of Athens
CHORUS, Corinthian Women (married)
CHILDREN, two young sons of Medea and Jason
NURSE, an old and long-time slave of Medea's family (49)
TUTOR, an old slave of Jason's family (53), in charge of
Medea's and Jason's sons
MESSENGER

The scene° is a street in Corinth. Medea's house is in the background. Her elderly
"Nurse" steps out of the front door and addresses the audience.

Nurse°
 I wish that the ship Argo had never flown°
 through the dark Clashing Rocks° to the land of Colchis,°

The scene is before a house in Corinth, that in which Jason and Medea had lived with their two boys before Jason moved into Creon's palace to live with his new bride, Creon's daughter.

1 *Nurse*: As often in Euripides, a character appears and gives some background information. Here the "Nurse" explains that the present troubles of her mistress, Medea, can be traced back to the time when Jason set out from Thessaly (on the east coast of central Greece) with the Argonauts ("sailors of the Argo") to the land of Colchis (on the southeastern shore of the Black Sea) where he met the princess Medea who helped him secure the Golden Fleece.

1 *Argo*: this ship, whose name means "The Swift One," was built by the Argonauts (under Athena's inspiration) to fetch the Golden Fleece from Colchis, home of Aietes (Medea's father). This first great sailing expedition of the Greeks took place in the generation before Odysseus and Achilles (cf. *Odyssey* 12. 70, where the ship is called "world-famous").

2 *Clashing Rocks*: Homer identifies these as the "Wandering Rocks" near Scylla and Charybdis (*Odyssey* 12.59-72). These reefs, at the western end of the Black Sea near the mouth of the Bosporus (north of Istanbul), were believed to shift their position inexplicably, and so were particularly treacherous to sailors.

35

that in the forest glens of Mt. Pelion°
the pine had never been cut for her, never made into oars
for the hands of excellent sailors who hunted   5
the Golden Fleece for Pelias.° My lady, Medea,
would never have sailed to Iolkos' towers,°
her spirit struck senseless with passion for Jason.°
She wouldn't have persuaded Pelias' daughters°
to kill their father; wouldn't have settled here in Corinth,   10
with her husband and children. She tried to please
the people to whose land she had come, an exile,
and for her part to fit in with Jason in everything.
This, to my mind, is a woman's greatest safety:
not to take the opposite side from her husband.   15
    But now she *hates* everything and all that she once
loved most is diseased. Jason has betrayed his own children
and my lady for marriage and the bed of a royal bride;
he's married the daughter of Creon, who rules over this land.
And Medea – poor woman! – treated with dishonor,°   20
shouts "Where are the oaths? Your right hand given
in the greatest trust?" She calls upon the gods to witness

---

3   *Pelion*: a mountain (5,300 feet) on the coast of southeast Thessaly, from where the
    Argonauts set sail. In their war against the Olympian gods the giants attempted
    to pile the neighboring Mt. Ossa on Pelion to scale the heights of Olympus.
6   *Golden Fleece for Pelias*: Jason's uncle Pelias had treacherously deprived his half-
    brother, and Jason's father, Aeson, of the kingdom of Iolkos (7). When Jason turned
    up to claim the throne, Pelias attempted to get him out of the way by insisting
    that he perform an apparently impossible "labor," fetching the fabulous fleece of
    a golden ram from faraway Colchis. Pelias later reneged on his promise to turn
    the kingdom over to Jason.
7   *Iolkos*: modern Volo, on Thessaly's southern coast, seat of Pelias' kingdom.
8   *her spirit struck senseless*: it seems difficult to believe that the Medea of this play,
    coolly calculating the best means of avenging those who have wronged her, could
    ever have been "swept away" by her love for Jason. But that is what the story
    requires and is one of the myth's features as told by other writers.
9   *Pelias' daughters*: when Pelias refused to give up his rule to his nephew, who had
    successfully carried out the assigned task (see note on 6), Medea devised a ter-
    rible scheme to remove him. Having first demonstrated her magic abilities by
    rejuvenating a ram, she persuaded Pelias' daughters to cut up their father and boil
    him, promising them that this would have the effect of renewing his youth. It did
    not (cf. 485-6, 504-5). Euripides told this story in his very first play, *The Daughters
    of Pelias*, written in 455, just 3 years after Aeschylus' *Oresteia*; Clytemnestra, the
    protagonist of that famous trilogy, probably influenced Euripides' portrayal of
    Medea.)
20   *treated with dishonor*: this especially rankles Medea; besides the thought of all she
    has given up for what now turns out to have been a bad bargain (23), and her
    very human feeling of helplessness and inferiority at having her male support
    removed—not to mention sheer jealousy—her honor also is a stake (cf. 33).

what kind of return she has received from Jason.
She doesn't eat, surrenders to her sorrows;°
her life has melted into a river of tears   25
since realizing the wrong her husband does her;
she keeps her gaze fixed on the ground,
never looking up. She listens to friends' advice
no more than some rock or wave of the sea.
Oh, sometimes she'll turn her white cheek away   30
to herself, and let out a wail for her dear father,
her country, her home,° which she betrayed to come
with her husband, who has now so dishonored her.
She understands, poor woman, from what has happened,
how important it is not to leave one's homeland.   35
    She hates her children, does not enjoy seeing them.°
I'm afraid she may be planning something rash.
Her mind is dangerous. She will not endure mistreatment;
I know this lady and am terrified that she might
thrust a sharpened sword through her heart   40
or even kill the royal family and the bridegroom
and then take upon herself some greater disaster.
She's a frightening woman: not easily will someone
engage with her in hatred and sing a victory-song.   45

Medea's two young sons rush in, accompanied by their tutor.°

But here come the boys who have just finished
their running. They're not thinking about their mother's
troubles. For young minds aren't used to suffering.

TUTOR

You, my mistress' long-time household slave,
why are you standing here all by yourself   50
outside, crying out loudly about your troubles?
How is it that Medea is willing to be without you?

---

24 *she doesn't eat*: similarly Phaedra in *Hippolytus* (135-40); it is a dangerous sign when
    Euripidean women behave this way.

32 *her home*: the terrible crime of violating a close blood-bond is compounded by the
    thought that, at the pragmatic level, there is "no way back" for her. (She often
    returns to the topic; e.g. 166, 596 ff.).

36 *she hates her children*: a first hint (but as yet no more than that) that her grief and
    rage may be turned against her boys.

45-46 *Medea's two young sons*: they are accompanied by a "tutor," a slave whose function
    was to accompany male children during their day's activities. The scene which
    follows presents a lively, realistic dialogue between the two household slaves;
    the information that the Tutor brings regarding the King's edict of banishment
    could have been presented in fewer lines but the overall effect is of a relatively
    tranquil domestic scene (with only a few forebodings) before the storm breaks
    with Medea's entrance.

NURSE
Old man, attendant and tutor of Jason's children,
when masters' affairs take an unlucky turn,
good slaves feel it, too, and have sorrowful hearts.   55
I have come to such a pitch of suffering
that a longing filled me to come outside and tell
the earth and sky about my lady's sorrows.

TUTOR
Has she not yet, poor woman, stopped her wailing?

NURSE
I envy you! Trouble's starting, not at the half!   60

TUTOR
Foolish—if one may use this word of masters;
how unaware she is of the latest evils!

NURSE
What is it, old man? Don't grudge me your news.

TUTOR
Nothing. I've changed my mind about what I said.

NURSE
I beg you not to hide it from your fellow-slave.   65
If necessary, I can be quiet about it.

TUTOR
Without appearing to listen, I heard it said,
as I came to the place called "Dice" where the very old
sit and play, near the sacred spring of Peirene,°
that the king of this country, Creon, was going to issue   70
an edict exiling these children from the land of Corinth
along with their mother. Whether this report was correct,
I don't know. But I wish it were not so.

NURSE
And will Jason tolerate such treatment of his children,
even though at odds with their mother?   75

TUTOR
Old marriage-bonds are left behind by new ones,

Pointing to Medea's house.

and he has no friendly feelings for this house.

NURSE
We're ruined, then, if we must add a new evil
to the old one we've hardly saved ourselves from.

---

69 *Peirene*: Corinth's sacred spring which began on the height of Acrocorinth and
ran down to the lower city.

TUTOR (*somewhat threateningly*)
    But you must keep still and be quiet about the report,   80
    since this isn't the time for the mistress to learn it.

NURSE (*drawing the boys to her*)
    Children, do you hear what a father you've got?
    Damn—I won't say him; for he is still my master,
    but he's been caught being evil to his dear ones.

TUTOR
    And what human being *hasn't* been? Did you just find out   85
    that each man loves himself more than his neighbor?°
    Since, in fact, their father doesn't love these children
    because of his new marriage-bed.

The Nurse attempts to shield the children.

NURSE
    Go into the house, children; all will be well.

To the Tutor.

    And you keep them apart as far as possible;   90
    don't bring them near their angry mother.
    For I just now saw her glaring like a bull at them,
    as if to do something. She won't cut short her wrath,
    I'm sure, until it strikes someone like a thunderbolt.
    May she do something to enemies rather than friends.   95

From 96 to 213 the Nurse and Chorus outside and Medea within engage in an antiphonal exchange, half-sung, half-chanted. Medea's savage grief reverberates against the old servant's mounting terror.

MEDEA (*inside*)
    Oh!
    I'm miserable and wretched with suffering,
    Oh! Oh! I wish I could die.

NURSE
    There, I told you, dear children,
    your mother stirs her heart, stirs her wrath.
    Hasten quickly into the house   100
    and don't come into her sight;°

85-86 *Did you just find out that...?*:A surprising bit of cynicism from the Tutor. To some
    extent it exonerates Jason: he is just doing what most men do: put themselves
    first. It reminds us how exceptional Medea is: she gave herself over to her passion
    wholly and to some extent against her interest (and her reversed feelings will be
    just as all-consuming and self-destructive).

101 *don't come into her sight*: Medea's look had been described as bull-like (92) and there
    is a suggestion that the boys, by allowing themselves to be seen by their mother,
    will somehow trigger a savage burst of destructive energy, as if her generalized
    anger will focus on them if she sees them. (Medea will later be very much affected,
    almost disarmed, by her children's gaze, 1040-3.)

don't come near her, but watch out
for the savage bent,° the hateful nature
of her self-willed mind.°
Go now, go quickly inside!   105

They start towards the door, puzzled, but do not enter.

Clearly her groans are just the beginning:
the cloud of her grief starts, is rising,
will kindle to flames when her spirit fans it
to greater fury. What will it do,
that deeply brooding, inexorable soul,
stung by wrongs it has suffered?   110

The children have now entered the house with the Tutor.

MEDEA
Ah!
I suffered—miserable—suffered things
deserving loud laments.
Accursed children of a hateful mother!°
Perish with your father!
The whole house be damned!

NURSE
Ah! I am the one who is miserable.   115
What share do your *children* have in the wrongdoing°
of their father. Why do you hate *them*?
Oh, children, how I grieve for what you may suffer.
Terrible is the temperament of royalty°

---

103 *savage bent*: we are being prepared for a Medea whose actions will be less than
    human ("no more than some rock or wave of the sea," 29).
104 *self-willed*: a key word (*authadia* means literally "self-pleasing") in understanding
    Medea's motivation. She won't follow in the normal path that most women take;
    she showed imaginative individuality in a destructive way before (at Colchis and
    Iolkos), and it would be surprising if her atypicality did not manifest itself again
    in some farfetched, hardly imaginable way.
113 *Accursed children*: Surprisingly strong language; as offspring of a passionate love-
    gone-sour the boys stir their mother to equally passionate anger, but we suspect
    also that Euripides is preparing the audience for the outcome (cf. 36).
116-17 *What share do your children have...?*: Of course, this is "Everyperson's" viewpoint.
    Medea's reasoning is peculiar, stranger, for she is not (although she sometimes
    talks like) "Everywoman."
119-21 *the temperament of royalty*: it is not clear what prompts this philosophical dis-
    quisition by the Nurse (unless it is that Medea, as "royalty" displaced, has the
    sort of imperious temperament that the Nurse here warns against). This kind
    of homespun sententiousness is very common, not only in Euripides, but in the
    other dramatists. Here it emphasizes the gap between the great mythic figures of
    the stage and the ordinary members of the audience. [The phenomenon of tragic
    "catharsis," i.e. purification of emotions (Aristotle's *Poetics* 1449b28) requires

who, perhaps because they are rarely overruled   120
and always imperious, shift their moods violently.
In any event to become accustomed to living
on the basis of equality is better. I, at any rate,
hope to grow old securely in surroundings of simplicity,
not greatness, since, first of all, the *name* "moderation"   125
wins the prize for its fine sound and, secondly,
her *usage* is far better than "greatness" for humans.
Excess brings no advantage to mortals
and it pays back greater ruin
when a god is angry at a house.   130

The fifteen chorus members, who represent the women of Corinth, enter along one or both entrance ways [if one, probably the western, stage-left, one] and eventually take up their position in the orchestra, or dancing-place.

CHORAL ENTRANCE SONG *(from the orchestra)*°
I heard the voice, I heard the shout
of the unfortunate Colchian woman.°
Is she not yet calm? Tell me old woman.
For I was still inside, at the double-doors of the hall,
when I heard the wailing. And I find no joy,   135
woman, in the household's sufferings,
since friendship for it has a fixed place in my heart.

NURSE *(from the stage)*
The household has crumbled. It is no more.
He is held fast in the royal bed   140
while she, my mistress, secluded in her chamber,
pines her life away; her heart will not be warmed
by any word from friends.

MEDEA *(still from within her house)*
Ah!
I wish my head could be struck by a bolt of lightning°
from above! What good for me to live longer?   145
Oh, Oh. I wish my hateful life
would dissolve in death.

---

that the gap be a large one—the hero suffers on a gigantic scale—but not entirely
unbridgeable, for the audience must feel "what it must be like" to be an Oedipus
or a Medea].
131 *Choral Entrance Song.* The chorus, fifteen ordinary married Corinthian women, enter
singing in lyric meters; Medea (who is still secluded in her house) and the Nurse
interject remarks in anapests, which were probably chanted rather than spoken.
The whole effect is one of stylized and contrapuntal formality.
133 *unfortunate Colchian woman*: the Chorus sides with Medea, which helps to explain
why they so readily agree to her request for silence later.
144 *I wish my head*: the vehemence of Medea's language is noteworthy; the chorus thus
have the answer to their question at 132-3.

CHORUS (*from the orchestra*)

STROPHE 1

Do you hear, Zeus and earth and light?
Do you hear the song the bride
is wailing so miserably?°   150
Foolish woman, why long
for that terrible resting place?
Why hasten the end of death?
Do not pray for this. If your husband
now shows reverence for a new bridal bed,   155
do not rage at him for it. Zeus will see
that you get due justice. Save your tears.
Do not lament for your former partner too much.

MEDEA (*still from within her house*)
O great goddess, Justice,° and lady Artemis,   160
do you see what I suffer,
even though I bound my accursed husband
with mighty oaths? I wish I could see him
and his bride crushed, house and all, for the wrong that—unprovoked—
they dare to inflict on me.   165
Father! City!° How shameful it was
to kill my brother° and leave you!

NURSE
Do you hear how she cries out
her prayer to Justice and Zeus,°
whom men consider the steward of oaths?   170
There is no possible way my mistress'
rancor will just trickle away.

CHORUS

ANTISTROPHE 1

If only she would come out

149-50 *the song the bride is wailing*: a favorite type of paradox in Greek poetry; and of
course Medea is no longer a "bride."

160 *great goddess, Justice and lady Artemis*: the Greek word here for Justice is Themis,
an old personification embodying a natural and quasi-religious (as opposed to
legal and somewhat arbitrary) justice. Artemis was typically a woman's patron
divinity, who supervised childbirth and other female activities.

166 *Father! City!*: recollection of the terrible wrong done to her family once again sears
her soul (cf. 32).

167 *to kill my brother*: Apsyrtos (unnamed in the play), whose severed limbs Medea had
scattered from the Argo to delay her father's pursuit (cf. 1334).

169 *her prayer to Justice and Zeus*: The chorus had called upon Zeus (148, 158), but Medea,
so far, has not. A minor inconsistency, the reason for which is unclear (unless
Medea's reference to Jason's violation of their "mighty oaths" at 163 is considered
an *implicit* appeal to Zeus, who is the steward of such oaths).

where I could see her,
talk to her, try to relieve   175
the heavy weight of wrath
on her heart.
My eager concern
must never fail my friends.

To the Nurse.

Go, bring her here out of the house.   180
Tell her we are her friends.
Quick! Before she does some harm°
to those inside. For her sorrow is surging greatly.

NURSE

All right—but I fear I may
not persuade my mistress.   185
A nuisance, but I shall do you this favor.
Yet she glares at her servants like a mother lioness,°
when anyone comes near her to speak.
You wouldn't be mistaken if you called
those men of the past stupid, not sophisticated,   190
who discovered songs for festivities,
banquets and dinner parties—
sweet sounds for our lives.°
But no mortal has discovered how to stop
hateful human sufferings with music   195
and the intricate chords of the lyre's songs.
It is these sufferings which cause the violent deaths
and terrible disasters that overthrow houses.
Yet to cure *these* by singing would be profit indeed
for mortals. Why sing loud and long   200
when abundant banquets succeed on their own?
That's pointless. The party itself
brings joy in full measure for mortals.

CHORUS

EPODE

I heard the shriek,   205
the sorrowful wailing;
she cries out shrilly, painfully,
that her husband wrongs and betrays her.

---

182 *before she does some harm*: a further suggestion of imminent danger.
187 *like a mother lioness*: once again an indication that there is something inhuman, even
    bestial, about Medea; cf. 29, 92, 103.
193 *sweet sounds for our lives*: an interesting bit of introspection by a poet, perhaps an
    assessment of the limitations of his art.

She calls on Zeus' daughter, Justice,°
protectress of oaths,   210
who brought her over to Greece,
over the dark sea to the briny Bosporus,
gateway of the vast Black Sea.

Enter Medea.°

MEDEA
Women of Corinth, I have come out of the house
to avoid your reproaches. I know that many men   215
are really haughty, some where none can see them,
others openly. Some get a bad reputation
simply from living a life of ease and comfort.
People do not behave justly in hating
another on sight, with no injury done,   220
without learning fully the man's character.°
An alien, too, must especially blend with the city;°
but I don't approve, either, of the citizen who,
self-willed and boorish, gives offence to others.
This thing has fallen on me like a bolt from nowhere,°   225

209-10 *Justice, protectress of oaths*: Medea denounced Jason as a "breaker of oaths" (21-2, 162-3); here, she bitterly reproaches those divinities whose job it is to guarantee such oaths, and who in her case appear not to have done so. She will take matters into her own hands.

214 *Enter Medea* This speech is very different from what we might have expected, given the descriptions of Medea's pent-up fury and her own raptures of grief. Obviously, one intended effect is surprise. But why does she sound so ordinary, uttering what are almost platitudes and sounding more like Everywoman—and Greek Everywoman, at that—than a Black Sea witch? Many have thought her reasonable tone and careful, even tedious, argùmentation nothing more than a façade; she is not at all like this, as we and the characters in the drama will soon discover. In my opinion, it is likelier that we are being asked to believe in her as a woman scorned and, as a foreign woman would be in most Greek cities of the time, totally vulnerable. If we sympathize, I believe we are meant to. Medea has been dealt with callously, treacherously, even, and has nowhere to turn. She must, then, reach deep into a wholly different and utterly dark side of her nature to devise an escape.

215-21 The inconsequentiality of this section in particular has struck many critics. A partial explanation can be found in the fact that by this time (431 BCE) Athenians were evolving elaborate schemes for constructing a persuasive speech, and that an extended proem or "warm-up" was a required feature of this highly formalized style of speechwriting. Otherwise, we can say that she is really just trying to make the Corinthian women think that she is completely normal and even a bit chatty, to take them off the scent of her real intentions.

222 *An alien, too*: now we come to a point that is relevant to her own situation (although in 223-4 she veers again to inconsequentiality).

225 *like a bolt from nowhere*: the Greek is not quite so specific, but it seems legitimate to interpret it in light of 94.

destroying my soul. I'm ruined. The joy of living
is gone for me. I want to die, my friends.
The one who was everything to me (I know it)
has turned out the worst of men, my husband.
    Of all creatures that live and have understanding°   230
we women are the wretchedest breed alive;
first, we must use excessive amounts of cash°
to buy our husbands, and what we get are masters
of our bodies. This is the worst pain of all.
In fact, this is the greatest struggle,° whether he'll be   235
a good or bad one, for divorce brings no repute
to wives, and yet they can't deny their husbands.°
So coming into new rules and customs,
she must be a prophet, since she hasn't learnt at home°
how to deal in the best way with her bed-mate.   240
And if we manage to find a solution to this,
so husbands live with and don't feel chained to us,
our lives are a joy; but if not, it is necessary to die.
A man, however, when he becomes annoyed
with the company of those inside,   245
can go outside and stop his heart's distress.
We must look to only one other person.
They say that we spend all our time at home,
and live safe lives, while they go out to battle.
What fools they are! I'd rather stand three times   250
behind a shield than bear a child once!°

230-51 It is hard to imagine a stronger or more crystalline statement of the position put forward in the following 20 lines; they have rightly been considered a "classic" presentation of women's social vulnerability, and their applicability has extended beyond the Greece of Euripides' day.

232 *excessive amounts of cash*: the reference is to the dowry, which was often a considerable amount.

235 *the greatest struggle*: for of course, in an arranged marriage, the wife had little say in the choice of husband.

236-7 *divorce brings no repute to wives*: For a Greek man, divorce was relatively simple: he went before a magistrate and made known his intention. For a woman it was much more difficult to initiate, and involved a complicated legal process.

239 *she hasn't learnt at home*: another complaint of more general applicability. A girl marrying generally in her mid- or late teens must have been ignorant in some essential matters. (It could, however, also be argued that the male, too, was sexually immature. Though considerably older than his wife, his experience would have been limited by the fact that most of his social life was among members of his own sex.)

244-6 *a man...can go outside*: even more true in Euripides' day than perhaps at later periods. The opportunities for a woman in the fifth century to initiate any kind of social contact on her own were virtually non-existent.

250-1 *I'd rather stand three times*: it is difficult to imagine a more lapidary statement of the sentiment expressed in these famous epigrammatic lines.

But your reasoning is no doubt different from mine:
this is your city; you have fathers' homes;
you enjoy life and the company of friends.
I am alone and without a city;° my husband insults me.°   255
I was brought from a foreign land, a piece of plunder;
I have no mother or brother or kinsman°
to go to for shelter from my present adversity.
I only ask to obtain so much from you:°
if some method or scheme can be found for me   260
to pay my husband back for these sufferings.
Keep silent. A woman is generally full of fear, a coward
when it comes to self-defense or the sight of a sword;
but when she's been wronged in anything touching sex,   265
no mind is more homicidal than hers.°

CHORUS
I'll do as you ask. Justly, Medea, you'll pay
your husband back. No wonder you grieve for what's happened.
But I see Creon, ruler of this country,
coming here to announce some new decision.°   270

Enter Creon abruptly, with attendants.°

CREON
You! The scowling hater of your husband,
Medea, I order you to go from this land
an exile, and take your two children with you.

253-5 *this is your city...I am alone and without a city*: Medea turns to a new point. As a
    foreigner, even if she were Greek, she would, in the absence of a male citizen to
    represent her interests, have no civic status.
255 *my husband insults me*: The Greek word here (*hybris*) is very strong; in other contexts
    it might even imply "rapes me."
257 *no mother or brother or kinsman*: in the case of legal divorce, this much protection was
    afforded the female: she could return to her nearest male kinsman for protection
    (taking her dowry with her). Medea has of course forfeited this (see 167).
259 *I only ask to obtain*: in the view of some critics, Medea's long arguments thus far
    have been only posturing; she has been systematically ingratiating herself, pull-
    ing at the women's heart-strings, to elicit this promise that they do nothing to
    interfere with her revenge-plot, not even reveal it. There may be some truth to
    this view, but I think that it is easy to overstate the extent of her insincerity so far
    (cf. 214 note).
263-6 Medea closes this fine speech with a blood-curdling epigram.
270 *some new decision*: they may have heard the same rumor as the Tutor (67 ff.), or
    this is simply an anticipation.
270-1 *(Enter Creon)*: There is some evidence that there was a conventional distinction
    between the two entrance-ways to mark the direction from which the entering
    person was coming (or to which he or she was going). If so, Creon will enter from
    the western (stage-left) entrance, which marked arrivals from and departures to
    the city or harbor (east denoted the countryside).

And no delay! For I'm the one who gives
the orders here, and I won't go home again°   275
until I've cast you outside the country's borders.

MEDEA
Oh! How wretched and utterly ruined I am!°
For my enemies are letting out all their sail,
and no ready harbor from ruin awaits me.°
Though you've treated me foully, I shall still ask: 280
for what reason are you driving me out, Creon?

CREON
I fear you°—no need to dress up the language—
fear you'll work some incurable harm to my daughter.
And many things contribute to this fear:
you're clever and much versed in doing harm,   285
and you're grieving the loss of your husband's bed.
I hear you've threatened—that's the report that came—
to do something to me who gave her and to the bride
and to the bridegroom —*that's* what I must guard against.
It's better for me to feel your hatred *now*, woman,   290
than lament loudly later for showing softness.

MEDEA
Oh! Oh!
This isn't the first time, Creon;° it's happened often
that my reputation has injured me and done much harm.
A man who's naturally sensible should never

274-5 *I'm the one who gives the orders here*: I think that the poet gives such heavy emphasis
    not to portray Creon as a spluttering state-autocrat, but to show how massively
    opposed to Medea are the political forces of Corinth. It will take all her ingenuity
    (or another demonstration of her fabled magic) to overcome such opposition. The
    fact that Creon does "go home again" without having expelled her, but against
    his better judgement, shows how skillful Medea is at manipulating her male
    adversaries. Jason will later step into a similar trap.
277 *How wretched and utterly ruined I am!*: a conventional but effective feminine
    appeal.
278-9 *my enemies are letting out all their sail*: imagery from seafaring is pervasive in
    Greek poetry (cf. 523-4, 769-70), not surprisingly given the country's geography.
282 *I fear you*: Creon's instincts are correct. He senses Medea's capacity for working
    "incurable harm." That she succeeds in spite of this shows how skilled she is at
    getting her own way (even in human terms). It also adds another undertone of
    foreboding, a covert warning that springs of malign power lie just beneath her
    smooth surface.
292-301 *This isn't the first time*: again, Medea begins in a very roundabout and "rhetori-
    cal" way. Perhaps this is meant to characterize her as being able to feign pompous
    longwindedness to put her opponent off the scent. (My hesitations to describe it
    in this way stem from the fact that such rhetoricizing is common in Euripides,
    even when there seems to be no effort to characterize his speaker, as, for example,
    Hippolytus.)

bring up his children to be excessively wise.   295
Apart from the charge of idleness they get,
they earn hatred and jealousy from the citizens.
If you bring some new wisdom to stupid men
you'll seem to them useless and not wise;
if you're considered by the citizens better than those   300
who are reputed to be sophisticated,
you'll appear offensive.
This is the very thing that's happened to me;
since I'm a wise woman,° some are jealous,
others annoyed, yet I'm not over-wise.   305
You fear me—fear something unpleasant?
Don't be afraid of me, Creon, I haven't the means
to do harm to men who are the rulers.
What wrong did you do to me? You gave your daughter
to whom your spirit urged you. My husband's the one   310
I hate. You acted sensibly, I think, and now I don't begrudge
your affairs prospering. Go on with the marriage!
Be happy! But allow me to live in this country.
For although we've been treated unjustly, we'll say nothing;
we've been conquered by those more powerful.   315

CREON

Soothing words you've spoken, but in my mind
there lurks a fear° that you're planning something bad.
I trust you, then, by that much less than before.
A woman, just like a man, who is quick to wrath
is more easily guarded than one wise and silent.   320
Leave, go away at once; no further talk.
Since this is settled, you cannot devise a way°
to remain here, since you are an enemy of mine.

MEDEA

Don't, I implore you most humbly by your newly-married
daughter!

Medea falls before Creon's feet in a suppliant posture.

CREON

You're wasting words; you'll never be able to sway me.   325

---

304 *since I'm a wise woman*: Medea picks up Creon's charge at 285. By harping on this
  topic of "wisdom / cleverness" (the Greek noun *sophia* carries both meanings),
  Medea hopes to deflect fears that her skills, for which she was evidently renowned,
  may harm the royal family.
316-7 *in my mind there lurks a fear*: once again (cf. 282) Creon's instincts are to be wary.
  His generalization at 319-20 is correct: now that Medea has got control of herself,
  she is much more potentially dangerous than when she was "carried away" by
  her grief and anger.
322 *you cannot devise a way*: how wrong he is!

MEDEA
You'll drive me out? You'll not respect my prayers?

CREON
I cannot love you more than my own family.

MEDEA
O country of mine, how I remember you now!°

CREON
By far the dearest thing to me, after children.°

MEDEA
Ah! What an evil thing men's passionate desires are!   330

CREON
It all depends, I suppose, on how things turn out.

MEDEA
Zeus, don't fail to take account of the author of these miseries.°

CREON
Go, you foolish woman; end my suffering!

MEDEA
And what of *my* suffering? Who will relieve me of *it*?

CREON (*motions to attendants*)
An attendant here will take you away by force.   335

MEDEA (*grasping his hands and knees in supplication*)
Do not, I beg you, Creon, resort to this.

CREON
You're making trouble for nothing, it seems, woman.

MEDEA
I'll go into exile. I'm not pleading for pardon.

CREON
Well then, why are you applying force, refusing to release my hand?

MEDEA
A single day allow me to remain°   340
to think through where I shall go in exile
and find some means of life for my children.
Their father sets no stock on devising something for them.°

---

328 *O country of mine*: now that Medea must leave Corinth immediately, the thought
   that she has no place to go has its maximum impact on her (see 32-3, with note;
   166-7).
329 *after children*: an allusion to the importance of children, not only to Creon here, but
   later: to Aigeus, to Jason, to Medea herself.
332 *Zeus*: now at last, she does call upon the father of gods (see note on 169).
340 *A single day*: Medea's trump card; who could resist such an apparently trifling
   request?
343 *sets no stock on devising something*: but Jason will show some fatherly feelings (460-
   1).

Have pity on them! You are a father of children, too.°
It's natural for you to show them kindness.   345
My concern isn't for me if we go into exile;
my tears are rather for them and their misfortunes.

CREON
My nature is not tyrannical in the least;°
I've already lost much through showing respect.
I see the mistake I'm making now, woman,   350
yet you shall have this—but I'm warning you,
if the rays of the coming dawn shall look upon you
and the children within the boundaries of this land,
you'll die; this sentence is passed unerringly.
So remain, if you must, but only for one day.   355
You'll not do any of the terrible things I fear.

Exit Creon; Medea rises to her feet.

CHORUS LEADER
Poor woman,
oh, where ever will you go
overcome by your sufferings?
To what hospitable house   360
or land to save you from harm?
How a god has placed you, Medea,
in the way of a wave of harm, with no way out!°

MEDEA
Everything's totally ruined — who'll deny it?°
O, but don't suppose only for me.   365
Struggles still await the newlyweds
and sufferings for their kinsmen, not small ones.
Do you suppose I'd ever have flattered that man
unless devising something for my profit?
I'd never have talked to or touched him with my hands.   370
But he arrived at such a pitch of folly

344 *You are a father of children, too*: Medea picks up Creon's point at 329; we will be
    reminded again, in a gruesome way, of his affectionate nature at 1204 ff.
348 ff. Euripides goes to an extreme in presenting his secondary character in a favor-
    able, even sympathetic, light. When Creon says, "I see the mistake I'm making,"
    he uses a conventional phrase that is sometimes uttered by other, genuinely
    tragic, figures.
363 *with no way out*: but Medea, with demonic and self-destructive inventiveness, will
    discover one.
364-409 In this great speech Medea flings off the mask of fawning servility and feminine
    helplessness which she had duped Creon. We begin to hear the colossal pride
    which has sustained so severe a wound, and the rage which wells up from deep
    within her. Her enemies will soon discover the strength of her willpower and of
    her determination not to let such affronts go unavenged.

that, even though he might have spoiled my plans
by exiling me, he allowed me to remain this day,
in which I'll make three people corpses:°
father, daughter, and my husband.   375
  I have so many ways of killing them,°
I don't know which I'll try out first, my friends.
Perhaps I'll set fire to the bridal chambers,
silently stealing into the room where the bed is spread.   380
But one pitfall, there, for me: if I'm caught
creeping into the house and plotting something,
my death will give my enemies a laugh.°
Best to take the direct route, where my natural
skills can shine: murder them with poisons.   385
  Well, then; let's say they've died.
What city will accept me?
What foreign host will offer me asylum
in guaranteed safety, and defend my person?
There is none. I'll wait a little while longer,
and if some tower of refuge appears for me°   390
I'll proceed to the crime with silence and deceit.
But if an unmanageable disaster drives me away,
I'll take the sword myself, even if I am going to die,
and murder them, and move with force and daring.
No, by the mistress whom I most revere   395
of all, and chose to help me in my work,
Hecate, who lives in the recesses of my hearth,°
they'll not make my heart hurt and get off free!
Bitter and painful I shall make their marriage,
bitter Creon's marriage-connection and his exiling of me   400
from this land. Well, spare none of the things you know,
Medea, none of your schemings and devices.°

---

374 *I'll make three people corpses*: later the plan will be changed; she does not kill Jason
  (in any literal sense, that is), and cannot have foreseen Creon's death; this fits in
  with the rumored threats about which we have already heard (287-9).
376 *I have so many ways of killing them*: so this is premeditated murder.
383 *My death will give my enemies a laugh*: this is the typical "heroic" stance, not to
  become a laughing-stock to one's enemies, and so humiliated as well as vulnerable; see 404, 797, 1049.
390 *if some tower of refuge appears*: this is just what will happen with the arrival of King
  Aigeus at 663.
397 *Hecate*: in some versions of the story, Medea was a priestess of this underworld
  goddess, who taught her the art of witchcraft. According to one late account Hecate
  had married Aietes and was the mother of Medea and Circe.
401-2 *Well...Medea*: for a hero or heroine to address himself or herself by name is rather
  unusual. Perhaps it is intended to remind the audience that hers is a significant
  name, "She-who-devises."

Advance to the terrible! Now it's a test of courage.°
You see what they're doing to you? You mustn't be
laughed at by this Sisyphian marriage of Jason,°   405
since your father was noble, and his father, the Sun.°
You know how.

Turning to the Chorus, conspiratorially.

And what is more, we're women,
quite unable to manage good, but none more skilled
when it comes to crafting every kind of evil.°

FIRST CHORAL ODE °

STROPHE 1

The streams of sacred rivers run backwards: 410
justice and everything go in reverse.
It is *men's* plans that are treacherous
and oaths sworn in the name of the gods
are no longer fixed and firm;
but the tables will turn.   415
I will have renown.
Honor will come at last°

403 *a test of courage*: another "heroic" sentiment.
405 *this Sisyphian marriage*: Sisyphus was noted for deviousness and trickery, for which
   he was punished by being made to roll up a steep hill a boulder which he was never
   able to bring to the top (cf. *Odyssey* 11. 593-600). So Medea means here that Jason
   acted in an underhanded way in contracting his new marriage. (Some accounts
   made Sisyphus the founder and first king of Corinth and father of Creon; or even
   husband of Medea! In later times travelers were shown his tomb near Corinth.)
406 *your father...and his father, the Sun*: generations of heroic and semi-divine ancestors are looking upon Medea to see how "nobly" she will respond to the present
   challenge.
408-9 Epigrammatic lines which gave some grounds to those who, like Aristophanes
   (*Frogs* 1043-56), affected to be shocked at Euripides' portrayal of women (cf. the
   epigram at 263-6).
410-45 *First Choral Ode*: The Chorus now dance to a song whose matching stanzas
   (*strophe* answered metrically by *antistrophe*) are a sign of correspondingly matching
   dance-steps. Music was provided by a flute-player. In the first half, the women
   of Corinth respond to Medea's stated intention to seek revenge by asserting that
   women, whose achievements have been given less than their due by male poets,
   will now "have renown" (414), and would have had even more if there had been
   women poets who could have reported men's misdeeds as men, through the ages,
   have women's. In the second half they recapitulate some points already made:
   Medea's heart was maddened by love of Jason (see 8); she passed from the Black
   Sea through the "twin rocks" (see 2, 210-12). She is a foreigner in Corinth (222)
   and is being exiled (255) in dishonor (20, 33), with no father's home to return to
   (32-3, 166, 506 ff.).
417-20 *Honor will come*: Medea's honor will be redressed, but at what cost! And the
   women will continue to be "victims of bad reports," even more than before because
   of Medea's actions.

to the female race; no longer
will women be victims of bad reports.   420

ANTISTROPHE 1

The music of bards born long ago
shall cease to sing
of my faithlessness.
To us no talent of raising the lyre's
heavenly voice was given   425
by Apollo, leader of songs.
Otherwise I would have sung
a contrary hymn against the male race;
for the long ages have as much to tell
about men's lot as of women's.   430

STROPHE 2

Medea, you sailed from
your father's home
with maddened heart,°
and passed the twin rocks
of the sea. A foreign land   435
you live in. Your husband's bed
you've lost, poor woman.
The land now drives you away,
a dishonored exile.

ANTISTROPHE 2

The grace of oaths is gone.°
Shame no longer resides°   440
in great Greece,
but has flown skyward.
And for you no father's home
will give shelter from sorrows.
And another, a queen,
rules your bed
and has taken charge of your home.   445

Enter Jason from the western, stage-left, entrance way.

JASON
    This is not the first time I've seen°

---

433 *maddened heart*: driven mad, that is by love; see note on 8.

439 *The grace of oaths is gone*: because Jason has broken his oaths to Medea (21-2, 162-3, 209-10).

440 *Shame*: personified, as often; here it means a sense of decency and honor.

446 *not the first time*: from his first words Jason is shown to be pompous and undiplomatic; he will also reveal himself as incredibly insensitive and opportunistic.

what an irreparable evil a savage temper is.
You could have stayed in this country and this house
if you had borne more lightly the plans of your masters;°
but for your foolish words you'll be driven out.   450
It's no business of mine;° never stop
saying that Jason is the vilest of men.
But the things that you've been saying about the rulers—
consider it gain that you're punished only by exile.
I've always tried to smooth the ruffled temper   455
of the princes, and I wanted you to stay!
But you don't give up your folly, continually
carping at the rulers, so you'll be expelled.
        In spite of this I haven't rejected my loved ones,
but have come out of forethought for you, woman,°   460
so you won't go into exile with the children,
penniless, destitute. Exile brings with it°
a flock of sorrows. For even though you hate me,
I could never harbor malicious thoughts against you.

MEDEA
Vilest of creatures!° This is the worst thing   465
I can say about your so-called manliness!
You've come to us, you, the worst enemy
of the gods and me and the whole human race?
This isn't being bold or even brash,
to wrong loved ones and look them in the eye,   470
but the worst of all diseases of humankind,
a lack of shame.° But you were right to come,
for when I have spilled out my abuse of you,
my heart will be lightened and your ears will burn.
        I'll begin right back at the beginning.   475
I rescued you, as the Greeks know who were
your shipmates long ago aboard the Argo,
when you were sent to master the monstrous bulls

---

449 *if you had borne more lightly the plans of your masters*: like waving a red flag before
    Medea's fierce individualism.
451 *it's no business of mine*: but it is, or should be, even as a former husband, and one
    who has derived so much benefit from her.
460 *woman*: the word Jason uses (*gyne*) can also signify "wife"; perhaps an irony
    intended by the poet.
462 *Exile brings with it*: Jason's sententiousness strikes us as unfeeling, but may not have
    struck a Greek audience so. His offers of help seem well-intentioned enough; he may
    be thinking, but does not say, "What would people say if I didn't help you?"
465 *Vilest of creatures*: a not surprising vehemence on Medea's part.
472 *a lack of shame*: as the chorus had sung in the preceding ode, "Shame no longer
    resides in great Greece" (439-40).

with yokes and sow the furrow with seeds of death.°
The serpent who never slept, his twisted coils   480
protecting the golden fleece, I was the one
who killed it and held out to you a beacon of safety.
I betrayed both my father and my house°
and went with you to Pelias' land, Iolkos,
showing in that more eagerness than sense.°   485
I murdered Pelias by the most painful of deaths,
at the hands of his own daughters, and I destroyed
his whole house. And in return for this, you foulest of men,
you betrayed us and took a new wife,
even though you have children. Were you childless,°   490
one might forgive your passion for this marriage bed.
But now the trust of oaths is gone.° I do not know
whether you think those old gods no longer rule,°
and men's present laws are newly passed,
since you're conscious of having broken your oaths to me.   495
    Ah! You often clasped my right hand.
How fruitlessly I appealed to you,
you evil man! My hopes all misfired.
    Well, then, I shall deal with you as a friend:
what good am I supposed to get from you?   500
Still, if I ask, you'll be shown up as more shameful.
Now where should I go? To my father's house?
To my country which I betrayed to come with you?
To Pelias' wretched daughters? Of course, they would
welcome the slayer of their father into their home!   505
This is how things are: to my nearest and dearest
I stand an enemy, and those I shouldn't have wronged

---

479 *sow the furrow with seeds of death*: Medea's father (Aietes) put various obstacles in Jason's path to prevent him from getting the Golden Fleece: the fire-breathing bulls (478) and these "Sown Men" which sprang from the soil into which Jason had sown the dragon's teeth. Using her magic Medea helped him overcome these obstacles.

483 *I betrayed both my father and my house*: once again she returns to the point (31-2, 166) as if it were resting heavily on her conscience; it also reminds Jason of the magnitude of her sacrifice for him—and his debt to her.

485 *more eagerness than sense*: because, for all her reputation for wisdom (285, 303), Medea was foolish to trust Jason.

490 *Were you childless*: in ancient Greece concubinage was permitted, especially for purposes of producing a male heir to inherit a man's property and carry on the family name.

492 *the trust of oaths is gone*: for the importance of the theme see 162-3, 209-10, 418, 439, 495.

493 *those old gods no longer rule*: Medea emphasizes that in reneging on his oath never to forsake her Jason has transgressed an age-old rule of behavior, one of the most sacrosanct in the human ethical code.

are now my enemies because I did you a favor.
And in return for my services you've made me
envied among many Greek women: for I have *you*,   510
a splendid, trusted husband, for all my sorrow,
even if I must leave this country in exile,
deprived of friends, my children alone
and I alone with them; a fine blot on the new
bridegroom's record, that both the children and I
who saved you should wander over the earth as beggars.   515
    O Zeus, why did you give to men clear signs°
to distinguish counterfeit gold from true, but as for
humans, no stamp is impressed on their bodies
by which the bogus ones can be discerned?

Chorus Leader
    A terrible thing is temper and knows no cure   520
    when dear ones wrangle and fall to fighting each other.

Jason
    I must, it seems, not fall short of perfection
    in speaking, but just like an expert helmsman,
    haul up my sail and run before the storm
    of harsh words your tongue spews, woman.   525
    But since you so proudly prate about your favors,
    I believe the only one of gods or mortals
    who saved me during my voyage was—Aphrodite!°
    A subtle mind you have, but are very slow
    to grasp the story of how Eros forced you   530
    with his unerring arrows to save my person.
    Still, I don't insist on a strict accounting;
    the benefits you offered have worked out well.
    But what you got in return for saving me
    was far more than you gave, as I shall prove.   535
    First, instead of a barbarian land,°

516-19 *Zeus, why did you give...?*: the same idea is expressed in *Hippolytus* (925-31),
    written three years after *Medea*.

527-8 *the only one of gods...was Aphrodite!*: a similar argument is used by Helen in the
    Trojan Women (929 ff and cf. 982-9, where Hecuba retorts "Aphrodite is just a name
    given by humans to their lack of self-control!"), but here the sterile and ungallant
    remark characterizes Jason as especially unfeeling.

536-41 *First, instead of a barbarian land*: it seems incredible that Jason does not see how
    misapplied all his points are. These are hardly "benefits" (533), given that Medea
    has, by summary decree, been stripped of her status and must leave Corinth with
    (as yet) no sure destination, her reputation for murderous craft preceding her.
    Many commentators have felt that Euripides is scoring points against his smug
    contemporaries. If this is the way that superior Greeks treat those less privileged,
    let us have "barbarian" mores every time!

Greece is your country now; you have a taste of justice
and the use of laws not subject to force.
All the Greeks can see that you are wise,
so you have renown, but if you lived at the ends   540
of the earth, no one would take account of you.°
For me, I wouldn't care to have gold in the house
or a singing voice sweeter than Orpheus'°
unless I reached some pinnacle of fame.
    So much for my own efforts—and remember,   545
you were the one who called for a debate.
Now for the blame you cast at my royal match:°
in this I shall prove, first, that I am wise;
second, self-controlled; finally, a great friend
to you and to my children—wait and hear me out.°   550
When I moved my residence to here from Iolkos
bringing along a pack of problems with no solution,°
what luckier scheme could I have found than this,
to marry the King's daughter, I, a fugitive?
Not—what's chafing you—that I hated your bed   555
and was struck by desire for a new bride,
nor eager for a contest in child-producing;
I have enough and find no fault with them.
Uppermost in my mind was for us to live well-off,°
not destitute, for I know that an impoverished man   560
is shunned by all his friends. I wanted to raise

540-1 *if you lived at the ends of the earth*: as Medea has said, bitterly and often, she wishes
    she had never left Colchis.

543 *singing voice sweeter than Orpheus'*: Orpheus' power over beasts and the natural
    world through his music was proverbial. The platitude makes Jason's argument
    sound particularly hollow. Furthermore, Jason fails to see the irony that Orpheus,
    one of the Argonauts, because he loved his wife so passionately, descended into
    Hades to retrieve her, using his beautiful voice to bewitch the shades (cf. Eurip-
    ides' *Alcestis* 357-62).

547 *Now for the blame*: Jason apparently does not see that, so far from exonerating him,
    his new marriage arrangement comes across as coldly calculating and thus dimin-
    ishes our estimation of him still further. His "defense" reads like a case-study in
    opportunistic manipulativeness.

550 *wait and hear me out*: obviously Medea makes some kind of movement or gesture,
    perhaps turning away as if to leave.

552 *a pack of problems with no solution*: it is not clear what Jason is referring to beyond
    the fact that Medea's presence was an encumbrance to his new dynastic plans.

559 *for us to live well-off*: on the surface this sounds plausible enough. But considering
    how much Medea has sacrificed because of her single-minded passion for Jason,
    we see how far apart these two are (and must always have been, unless he expe-
    rienced a drastic sea-change), how little such mundane considerations could ever
    have mattered to her.

the children in a manner befitting my family,°
producing brothers for those I had with you,
to bind the family together so I might prosper.
What need have *you* of children?°   565
But it profits me to benefit those living
 by means of those to come. Was this a bad plan?
You'd agree, if the marriage didn't chafe you.
You women have come to such a point that you think,°
if things go right in bed, you have everything;   570
but if your sex-life is suffering, then you become
vicious enemies of all your best and dearest.
There ought to have been some other way°
for mortals to procreate—the female race could vanish!
Then, men wouldn't have had this misery.   575

CHORUS LEADER
Jason, you've packaged these arguments attractively;
still—though you may not want to hear it—I think
you're acting against justice in betraying your wife.°

MEDEA
How different I am from the rest of the human race!
For me, the man who is a villain, but clever   580
in speech, would have to pay the highest fine;
confident of cloaking his villainy in fine words,
he dares *anything*; still, he's not over-wise.
So stop putting a false face before me
with slippery words; one line'll lay you flat:°   585
if you hadn't been evil you would have persuaded me first,
then got married, not kept it quiet from dear ones.

JASON
And you, I suppose, would then have furthered that plan
had I mentioned the marriage, when, even now,

---

562 *in a manner befitting my family*: a note of self-importance, even snobbishness on
    Jason's part, only latent so far, is thus explicitly struck. Note also the egoistic tone
    "my family" and, in 564-5, "I might prosper."
565 *What need have you of children?*: can Jason have said anything more callous (and
    double-edged, in light of the way the plot will turn)?
569 *You women have come to such a point*: implying that women are narrowly focused
    on sex and have a romantic view of it, whereas men have a broader outlook; this
    is an uglier version of the kind of distinction Medea had made at 238-47.
573 *There ought to have been some other way*: Hippolytus makes a similar suggestion: men
    should have been able to "deposit a weight of gold, or iron, or bronze in one of
    Zeus' temples and then go around to collect 'a seed of children' of equivalent value"
    (*Hippolytus* 616-24; he doesn't say by what method the seed would grow).
578 *you're acting against justice*: this puts the charge against Jason in most explicit terms
    (cf. 209-10).
585 *lay you flat*: a wrestling metaphor (cf. 1214).

you dare not eject the great rancor from your heart.   590

MEDEA

That wasn't the reason; it would've looked bad
for you to be growing old with a barbarian wife.

JASON

No, I assure you, it was not for a woman's sake
that I undertook my present royal marriage,
but, as I've already told you, because I wanted   595
to rescue you and produce princely brothers
to help my children, a prop to support the house.

MEDEA

I want no share in a "happy" life that grieves me,
or "prosperity" that chafes against my heart.

JASON

Do you know how to change your prayer and thus appear   600
wiser? Pray that good never appear to you grievous,
nor think that you're unlucky when you're lucky.

MEDEA

Go on, insult me! You have somewhere to turn;
I shall leave this country in exile, alone.°

JASON

You chose it yourself! Don't blame anyone else!   605

MEDEA

By marrying someone else?° Forsaking you?

JASON

By casting impious curses against the rulers.

MEDEA

Yes, and I am in fact a curse to your house too!°

JASON

I don't intend to debate with you any further.
But if you wish me to give you or the children   610
extra money for your trip into exile, tell me;
I'm ready to give it with a lavish hand,
and write to foreign friends who will help you out.
You'd be foolish not to take up this offer, woman;°
you'll profit more by getting rid of your anger.   615

---

604 *I shall leave...in exile, alone*: Medea returns to an earlier theme (cf. 255).

606 *By marrying someone else?*: Medea's biting sarcasm is an effective thrust at Jason.

608 *I am a curse*: a covert warning that Medea will not take Jason's insult (603) lying
    down.

610-14 *if you wish...*: Jason is careful to preserve the proprieties, but this is a mere
    token: let it not be said that he is the kind of man who does not pay alimony and
    child-support.

MEDEA

I wouldn't have any dealings with *your* friends
nor take what *you* gave, so don't bother offering.
The gifts of an evil man bring no gain.°

JASON

I call upon the gods to witness°
that I was willing to do anything for you   620
and the children; but you reject favors and stubbornly
cast away your dear ones; you'll suffer the more for it.

MEDEA

Go away! Desire for your newly-wedded bride overwhelms you.
You've been away from her house too long! Go on,
play the bridegroom! Perhaps, if the gods support my words,   625
you've made a match you'll one day have cause to lament.

Exit Jason to Creon's palace.

SECOND CHORAL ODE°

STROPHE 1

When passionate desires°
descend in full force they never enhance
men's fame or virtue,
but if Aphrodite approaches   630
with reserve, there is

---

618 *The gifts of an evil man*: A proverb: cf. Sophocles' *Ajax* 665: "An enemy's gifts are
     no gifts and garner no gain."
619 *I call upon the gods to witness*: Jason is being legalistically (and moralistically) cor-
     rect; ritually and juridically, at least, his "hands are clean."
624-5 *Go on, play the bridegroom*: An ironic echo of 313 where Medea, addressing Creon,
     used a similar phrase.
627-62 *Second Choral Ode*: In the first half, the Chorus sing of the dangers of love when
     it goes to extremes (cf. Sophocles' *Antigone* 781-800); in the second half they return
     to the topic of exile and end with more general commiseration for Medea. The
     theme of "moderation in love" seems at first sight rather straightforward, but as
     applied to Medea's and Jason's situation it is not. So far from being immoderate,
     Jason seems incapable of loving at all; we have just heard him say that his new
     marriage is not due to infatuation, but a coolly calculated match of convenience
     (555 ff.) As for Medea, her uncontrolled passion for Jason is a thing of the past
     (8, 228, 526 ff.). And "never drive me to fight with my husband" (638-9) comes
     in rather oddly, considering that we have just witnessed a fight between Medea
     and Jason, but not one resulting from the fact that either one (unless Jason is dis-
     sembling) has "fallen in love" with someone else.
627 *passionate desires*: Aphrodite's agents, the Erotes; the violence of their activity contrasts
     with the peaceful picture at 835-45. Two other themes here are of more general
     relevance; "men's fame" (629; cf. 416) and "Lady Restraint" (*Sophrosune*, personi-
     fied, 635). Both have an indirect and negative application to Medea: her revenge,
     motivated as it is by perverted passion, will fly in the face of the Chorus' praises of
     "Restraint," and will bring her a kind of fame, but hardly one to be envied.

no goddess so gracious in her favors.
Mistress, never use me as a target,
shooting golden arrows
tipped with desire, unerring in aim.   635

ANTISTROPHE 1

Cherish me, Lady Restraint,
noblest gift of the gods.
And may fearsome Aphrodite never hurl
contentious passions and insatiable strife
against me, shattering my spirit
with longing for the beds of other men.   640
And may she shrewdly judge our bed-partners,
honoring those women's bridal-beds
that stay free from war.

STROPHE 2

My city, my home!
I pray never to go into exile,   645
never to lead that kind
of life of endless,
unmanageable suffering,
most pitiable of sorrows.
Die! To die would be better,   650
and bring my life's day to an end forever.
No pain is worse
than to lose one's country.

ANTISTROPHE 2

We saw, we don't have to take
another's word, Medea: 655
no city, no friend
will pity your pain,
the worst of sufferings.
May that man perish
without any favor
who refuses to honor his friends   660
by unlocking the door to a pure heart.
No friend of *mine* will he ever be!

Enter Aigeus, King of Athens.°

___

663 (*Enter Aigeus*). an unexpected arrival by the renowned Athenian king who enters
along the eastern (stage-right) ramp, just in the nick of time for, as Medea had said
(289-91), she needs some "tower of refuge" in order to proceed with her revenge-
plot. (Some critics, e.g. Aristotle *Poetics* 1461b21, have objected that his appearance is
unmotivated, and a bit too convenient for the plot. But it has also been pointed out
that the "children theme," especially as it ironically applies to Medea—she is willing
to help Aigeus attain his desire for children, while at the same time contemplating
the murder of her own—provides some continuity with the rest of the play.)

AIGEUS
Medea, greetings! No one knows a better prelude
than this when addressing friends.

MEDEA
Greetings to you, too, Aigeus, wise son of Pandion.°   665
From where are you coming to this land?

AIGEUS
I've come from Delphi, Apollo's ancient oracle.°

MEDEA
What took you to the earth's center of prophecy?

AIGEUS
To find out how I might become a father.

MEDEA
By the gods! You're childless at your time of life?   670

AIGEUS
Childless, indeed, by some cruel stroke of fate.

MEDEA
You're married?° You've had experience with women?

AIGEUS
Indeed, it's not for lack of a wife or marriage.

MEDEA
What did Apollo tell you about children?

AIGEUS
Words too wise for a man to understand.   675

MEDEA
Is it right for me to know the god's response?

AIGEUS
Certainly, for a clever mind indeed is needed.°

MEDEA
What did he say, then? Speak, if it is allowed.

---

665 *Greetings to you, too, Aigeus*: it is most unusual for a newcomer to appear without
being announced and without identifying him- or herself. How does Medea know
who it is? Of course, the playwright can presume his audience's familiarity with
the mythical tradition that included the subsequent cohabitation of Medea and
Aigeus in Athens. But Medea's instantaneous recognition of the new arrival
remains to be explained.

667 *I've come from Delphi*: a return journey from Delphi to Athens would not pass near
Corinth; Aigeus has detoured for a special reason (682 ff.).

672 *You're married?*: Medea is methodical, almost clinical, in her approach to Aigeus'
problem; an ancient note informs us that Aigeus had in fact had two wives.

677 *a clever mind...is needed*: Jason had mentioned Medea's international reputation (539).

Aigeus
Not to release the wine-skin's hanging neck°—

Medea
Until you do what, come to what place?   680

Aigeus
Until I come to my father's hearth once more.

Medea
But why, then, have you put your ship in *here*?

Aigeus
There is a man named Pittheus, ruler of Trozen°—

Medea
Most pious son of Pelops, as they say.

Aigeus
I want to share the prophecy with him.   685

Medea
Yes, for he is wise and has much experience.

Aigeus
And the dearest of my military comrades.

Medea
I wish you well; good luck in what you desire.

Aigeus (*looking at her closely*)
But why are your eyes, your skin melted with tears?°

Medea
Aigeus, my husband is the worst man in the world!   690

Aigeus
What's wrong? Be clearer about what's troubling you.

Medea
Jason is wronging me; I've done nothing to *him*.

Aigeus
Wronging you how? Tell it to me more clearly.

Medea
He has another woman in my place as mistress of his home.

Aigeus
You mean he's dared to do such a vile deed?   695

---

679 *Not to release the wine-skin's hanging neck*: this oracle was interpreted in antiquity
   to mean "have sexual intercourse"; no doubt rightly.
683 *Pittheus...Trozen*: Trozen was southeast of Corinth, in the area known as the Argolid.
   It is Pittheus' daughter, Aithra, whom Aigeus will impregnate, thus becoming
   the father of Theseus.
689 *melted with tears*: since the actors (all of whom were male) wore masks, no tears
   would have been visible. Medea probably puts her hands to her face, or attempts
   to cover it with her cloak, thus prompting Aigeus' question.

MEDEA
He has. His former "dear ones" are now dishonored.

AIGEUS
Did he fall in love or just come to hate your bed?

MEDEA
Deeply in love, the faithless traitor to his family.°

AIGEUS
Forget it then, if he's as bad as you say.

MEDEA
His passion was to get a marriage-alliance with kings.   700

Aigeus
Which king offers him this? Finish the story.

MEDEA
Creon, the man who rules this land of Corinth.

AIGEUS
You're right, then, to feel aggrieved, Medea.

MEDEA
I'm lost! What's more, I'm driven into exile.

AIGEUS
By whom? You mention now a new injury!   705

MEDEA
Creon it is who's driving me out of Corinth.

AIGEUS
And Jason allows it? I don't approve of that!

MEDEA
He says he doesn't, but must "put up" with it.

Medea falls before Aigeus as a suppliant.

I implore you solemnly, appealing by your beard
and knees, and make myself your suppliant:°   710
have pity, have pity on me in my misfortune;
don't allow them to drive me out, solitary, but take me
into your country and your home as a suppliant
at your hearth. May the gods fulfill your passionate
desire for children, and may you achieve a happy death.   715
You don't know what a lucky find this is!
For I can end your childlessness and enable you
to father children: for this I have magic drugs.°

---

698 *Deeply in love*: we know that Medea is being sarcastic in light of Jason's explanation
at 555 ff. and 593-4; she explains her meaning to Aigeus at 700.

709-10 *appealing by your beard and knees*: a most solemn form of supplication; Medea
had said something similar to Creon (324), equally effectively.

718 *I have magic drugs*: it is unusual and bold for Medea to advertise her magic powers
in this way (but cf. 384-5; 789); this is the "witch" in her speaking.

AIGEUS
  For many reasons, woman, I am eager
  to grant you this favor: first, for the gods' sake;°   720
  then, for the sake of the children that you've promised—
  for in this regard I have utterly failed.
  So be it, then. If you come to my country
  I shall try to protect you, as is just and as I agreed.
  But I tell you one thing in advance, woman—   725
  I'm not willing to escort you from this land.°
  If, however, you come to my home on your own, you'll stay
  there unharmed; I shall not surrender you to anyone.
  But secure your removal from this land on your own;
  for I wish to incur no blame, even from strangers.   730

MEDEA
  I accept the terms. Your faithfulness to your promise°
  is all the benefit I need of you.

AIGEUS
  Surely you trust me, don't you? What's troubling you?

MEDEA
  I do trust you. But Pelias' house and Creon
  are my enemies. If they try to drag me away,   735
  the yoke of your oath will keep you from giving me up.
  If you just promise and don't swear by the gods,
  you might become their friend; a summons from them
  might make you yield, for my claims are weak,
  whereas *they* have both wealth and royal power.   740

AIGEUS
  You have shown much foresight in your words.
  If you wish, I do not refuse to take an oath:
  it will mean greater safety for me, to have
  something to show your enemies as a plea,
  and it makes your case more secure. Name your gods.°   745

720 *first, for the gods' sake*: Aigeus has recognized the validity of Medea's complaints (703 ff.) and she has become his suppliant (709-10), so he feels a moral duty to her. At the human level, too, as he admits (711-12), he has a powerful motive for enlisting her help.

726 *I'm not willing to escort you from this land*: Aigeus probably feels that such escort might involve him in animosity with Corinth's rulers. More likely, however, the point is introduced to provide an excuse for Medea to show her self-reliance and arrange a spectacular exit on her own.

731 *faithfulness to your promise*: Medea, once burnt (by Jason), is twice shy. The plot takes an interesting detour to prolong the scene and also to demonstrate Medea's hard-nosed practicality.

745 *Name your gods*: a standard procedure in oath-taking. The solemnity of the undertaking is enhanced and Medea gets a chance to refer to her illustrious divine ancestry (746-7).

MEDEA
Swear by the soil of Earth and by the Sun, the father
of my father, and add all the rest of the race of gods.

AIGEUS
To do or not do what? Speak further.

MEDEA
Never to drive me out of your land yourself,°
or, if an enemy wants to take me off,   750
not to allow it willingly while you live.

AIGEUS
I swear by Earth, the holy light of the Sun,
and all the gods, to abide by what you say.

MEDEA
Enough. And to suffer what if you do not abide by this oath?

AIGEUS
The sort of things that happen to impious men.   755

MEDEA
Farewell, go on your way. All is well.
I shall come to your city by the quickest means
when I've done what I intend and got what I wish.°

CHORUS LEADER (*to Aigeus*)
May Lord Hermes the Escorter, Maia's son,°
bring you home, and may you accomplish   760
what you eagerly hope to obtain;
for you are a noble man, Aigeus,
as far as I can judge.

Exit Aigeus.

MEDEA °
O Zeus and Justice of Zeus and light of the Sun!°

To the Chorus.

Now, my friends, sweet victory over enemies   765
will be mine! I've set out along the road!

---

749 *Never to drive me out of your land yourself*: Medea's life at Athens was to be anything
but smooth; in fact, since Aigeus later expelled her from Athens for trying to poison
Theseus, he, like Jason, became an oath-breaker.
758 *when I've done what I intend*: an ominous hint of what is to follow.
759 *Hermes the Escorter*: one of the standard epithets of the gods' messenger (especially
as escorter of dead souls to the underworld).
764-810 With Aigeus' solemn promise to give her asylum, if she can get to Athens
herself, the missing link in Medea's intended chain of vengeance has been forged.
Success is now within her grasp and she allows herself to gloat as she works out
details of her murderous plan and begins to savor the evil fruits of success.

Now there's hope of paying out my enemies!
The one thing missing this man has provided:
a safe harbor after our plans are achieved.
I'll make fast my mooring line to him   770
when I come to Athena's town and citadel.
      Now I shall tell you exactly what I'm planning;
you'll hear, but not rejoice at what I say.
I'll send one from among my servants to Jason
and ask that he come to see me face-to-face,   775
and when he comes, I'll speak soft words to him—
I agree to what he wants and think it fine
for him to give me up and marry a princess,
a suitable plan and well devised by him.
I'll beg him for my children to remain   780
not because I want to leave my sons
in a hostile land for enemies to insult,
but merely to snare and kill the king's daughter.
The children I'll send off to the bride with gifts
in their hands, asking not to go into exile—   785
a fine-textured robe and a golden garland.
And if she takes the adornment and puts it on,
she and all who touch the girl will die.
Such is the poison with which I'll anoint the gifts.°
      There, I'm finished with that part of the plot.   790
But I groan at the kind of task that I must proceed
to accomplish.° For I shall put the children to death°—

---

764 *O Zeus and Justice of Zeus and light of the Sun*: solemn prayers of this kind usually
    involved naming three divinities: Zeus is summoned as supreme Olympian (cf.
    169, 332). Justice, sometimes personified as Zeus' daughter, means for Medea
    simply vengeance on those who have wronged her; she had called on justice under
    the name of Themis earlier, 160 (cf. 209-10, 578, and 1389, when it will be Jason's
    turn). The Sun is the purest, most powerful of natural elements, as well as her
    grandfather. The prayer sounds, and is meant to sound, almost sacrilegious.
789 *Such is the poison*: Medea's magic powers are hinted at in the matter of Pelias' daugh-
    ters (386-7, 504-5) and alluded to by her openly when she promised to help Aigeus
    overcome his sterility (718). Here the full range of her magic is revealed: she has
    preparations which render garments incendiary when they come in contact with
    the skin, and to which anyone who touches them will adhere (see 1212 ff.).
791-2 *the kind of task that I must proceed to accomplish*: Medea uses "heroic" language;
    to overcome her natural sympathies as a mother and kill her children will require
    a perverted kind of bravery.
792 *I shall put the children to death*: this is the first time Medea speaks of killing her
    boys. Critics differ about when exactly she makes this decision. My view is that,
    although the idea may have been circling around in her subconscious for some
    time (cf. the Nurse at 36, "she hates her children" and Medea at 112-3), it is only
    now that she finally determines to kill them. She might, after all, have arranged
    to kill Jason—threats against her husband were common knowledge (288)—and

my children. No one will save them from me.
When I have utterly ruined Jason's whole house,
I shall leave the country, accused of my dear children's   795
murder, and having dared the unholiest of deeds.
For to be laughed at by enemies is intolerable, friends.°
So what profit is there for me in living?
I have no country, no home, no shelter from misfortune.°
I made a mistake *then* in leaving the house of my father   800
and putting faith in the words of a *Greek* man.°
I'll punish him with a god's help.
The children he had by me he'll never see alive,
and those he hopes for by his newly-yoked bride
he'll not be able to beget, for she is evil   805
and evilly she *must* die by my poisons.
Let no one think of me as "poor" or "weak"
or "retiring," but quite the contrary, a millstone
around my enemies' necks, a boon to my friends.
The lives of people like that are most renowned.°   810

CHORUS LEADER
You shared your innermost thoughts with us, and so,
wishing as much to support society's laws
as to aid you, I tell you to give up your plan.

MEDEA
It cannot be otherwise. I understand why you speak
thus; you were not mistreated, as I was.   815

CHORUS LEADER
But how will you dare to kill your seed, woman?

---

perhaps also the bride and her father, but she now hits upon a truly fiendish form
of revenge: Jason's dynastic plans, at least as regards his children by her, will be
thwarted, and she will wound him most painfully by using the considerable love
which she knows he feels for their sons (see 1303ff.). But at what cost to herself!
It is not a casual decision, and she will several times come close to abandoning
her resolve (see 1040 ff.).

797 *to be laughed at by enemies*: the Greeks avoided, at all costs, public loss-of-face,
especially by ridicule (cf. 383, 404, 1049, 1355, 1362).

799-801 *I have no country... I made a mistake...I'll punish him*: Medea returns to these
well-worn themes of what she has "sacrificed," perhaps to confirm her resolve to
seek such terrible retribution from the one whom she holds responsible.

801 *the words of a Greek man*: this is Medea's retort to Jason's absurd claim that he benefited her in bringing her to Greece (536-7).

808-9 *a millstone...a boon*: the code of "helping friends, harming foes" governed the
entire Greek heroic ethos (cf. 765-7).

810 *The lives of people like that are most renowned*: Medea once again projects herself into
a vanished heroic past; what she forgets is that these heroes' actions in sacrificing
everything to their self-esteem (cf. Achilles) often brought misery to those around
them and sometimes death to themselves (cf. Ajax).

MEDEA
Because it is this that will sting my man most.

CHORUS LEADER
You'll only end up being the most miserable of women.°

MEDEA
So be it. From now on your speech is superfluous.
Go, you (*to the Nurse*), and bring Jason to me—   820
for I entrust to you all important tasks—
tell him nothing of what I've decided to do,
if you wish your mistress well, and are a woman.°

Exit Nurse to Creon's palace.

THIRD CHORAL ODE°

STROPHE 1
The Athenians, sons of Erechtheus,°
have long been prosperous;   825
the blessed gods' own children they are,
and sprung from a sacred land
that no invader has ever despoiled.°
They feed on wisdom most glorious,
treading always delicately   830
through crystalline air°
where once, it is said,

818 *the most miserable of women*: this puts "Everyperson's" case most clearly. No normal
       woman would act thus, for the prospect of such great remorse would forestall
       her. Medea is extraordinary—beyond comprehension—even in this, her ability
       to suppress "normal" humans instincts of motherhood.
823 *and are a woman*: Medea had similarly appealed to the female instincts of the Chorus
       at 407-8.
824-865 *Third Choral Ode*: The first part of the song is a hymn of praise to Athens, the
       gentle beauty of its landscape and its humane virtues; in short, its civilization (a
       not inappropriate theme to present to an audience which was to face war with
       Sparta within months). It is a shocking contradiction for so glorious a city to
       provide shelter to one who could contemplate such a heinous crime. In the last
       stanza they express their horror and disbelief at Medea's plan.
824 *Erechtheus' sons*: Erechtheus was an early king of Athens. The Athenians were often
       referred to as his descendants (see next note).
827-8 *sacred land that no invader has ever despoiled*: it was a constant boast by the Athenians,
       made even by Thucydides, that their country had never been subject to immigra-
       tion or invasion from abroad. According to their nationalistic mythology, they
       were descended from Erichthonios (often confused or identified with Erechtheus),
       who was the son of Hephaestus and Gaia, mother Earth. So they were literally
       indigenous, native sons!
831 *through crystalline air*: the bright violet-hued atmosphere of Athens was renowned,
       and often served as a theme for poetry.

the Holy Nine, Pieria's Muses,°
created golden-haired Harmony.

ANTISTROPHE 1

They celebrate in song how Aphrodite,°   835
drawing water at fair-flowing Cephisus' streams,°
sent moderate breezes
sweetly blowing over the land;
how she always puts on her hair
a fragrant garland of roses   840
and sends passionate desires
to be Wisdom's partners,°
to share all her manifold tasks
and, with her, to bring forth
every kind of virtue.   845

STROPHE 2

How, then, will this city
of sacred rivers or this land
that gives safe escort to friends,
accept you—the slayer of children,
the unholy one—with other refugees?   850
Consider the stroke at your young,
consider the killing you plan!
We all beseech you most humbly,
beg you in every way,
do not slay your children!   855

ANTISTROPHE 2

Where will you get the nerve,
either from the anger of your mind or the thought
of your children, to bring such terrible daring
to your hands and to your heart?
When your eyes gaze on the children,   860
how will you hold back tears°
for their slaying? You won't be able,
when the children beg
at your knees, to dip your hand

---

833 *Pieria's Muses*: Mt. Pieria in southern Macedonia (north of Mt. Olympus) was the
    site of an important cult of the Muses and according to some accounts they were
    born there.
835-41 *how Aphrodite... sends passionate desires to be Wisdom's partners*: a less threatening
    picture of Eros than in the preceding ode (629-35).
836 *Cephisus' streams*: one of Athens' two major rivers; the other was the Ilissus.
842 *Wisdom's partners*: Wisdom (*Sophia*) is personified as a goddess.
861 *hold back tears*: a very touching picture, full of poignant emotion. To this kind of
    appeal Medea seems impervious.

boldly in their blood. 865

Enter Jason.

JASON
I've come as bidden. For all your ill-will
I couldn't refuse you this at least, but let me hear
what new request you have to make of me, woman.

MEDEA
Jason, I'm asking you to forgive the things
I said before; it's natural that you should put up 870
with my moods, for the many intimacies we shared.
I started to go over it all in my mind
and rebuked myself: "Wretched woman, why
do I rage and rail at those who plan things well for me?
I shall only incur the wrath of the land's rulers 875
and my husband, who is doing his very best for us
by making a royal marriage and fathering kin
for my children. Should I not put aside my anger?
What's the matter? The gods are good.
Don't I have children? Don't I know that we 880
were outcasts from Thessaly and had no friends?"°
I thought this over and saw how very stupid I'd been,
how foolish the anger that filled me. But now I praise you
and think you showed sound sense° in taking on this
marriage for us; it was I who was foolish, lost control 885
when I ought rather to have joined in those plans°
and helped bring it off, to have stood by the bed,
and taken pleasure in welcoming your new bride.
But we are what we are—I won't say that we're bad—

873-81 *"Wretched woman...had no friends?"*: this remarkable monologue, in a long tradition of such lively addresses to oneself, serves a double purpose: it takes Jason
off his guard (as intended), but also ironically shows us the kind of "normal"
woman Medea might have been. For the position she voices here is one which any
ordinary Greek woman would probably have adopted under the circumstances,
realistically assessing her resources, and making the best of what she had. Medea's
matter-of-fact tone reminds us how extraordinary a person she is.

884 *showed sound sense*: Medea echoes the adjective *so-phron* (= sensible, prudent, self-
controlled) which Jason had primly used of himself at 549 and she cleverly uses
its antonym, *a-phron* (= foolish, lacking self-control) to describe herself in 885 (cf.
913). [Both these words have the same root as *so-phro-sune* (= restraint, prudence,
self-control) which the chorus had described as the "noblest gift of the gods" at 636.]
Ironically, in manipulating her husband, Medea has total control of her amorous
self, in contrast with the early days when Jason had "swept her away."

886 *I ought rather to have joined in the those plans*: she is, to our way of thinking, laying
it on a bit thickly, perhaps to show up Jason's obtuseness.

we women;° so you mustn't be bad just to get even   890
with us, nor oppose us with folly for folly.
I ask your forgiveness. I admit I was stupid then,
but now I've changed my plans for the better.
    O children, children, come here, come out,
come out of the house, embrace your father.   895

The boys enter with the Tutor.

Talk to him with me; lay aside with your mother
our previous hostility. Let us be friends.

The boys embrace Jason.

A truce has been called. Our anger is all gone.
Take my right hand in yours. The harm!
I'm thinking about the harm that still lies hidden!   900

They gather round and embrace Medea.

My dears, will you reach out your arms like this
when you have lived a long life?° Oh God!
I'm on the verge of tears and full of terror.
The long-standing quarrel with your father is over;
now I have filled your tender cheeks with my tears.   905

CHORUS LEADER
From my eyes, too, fresh tears spring.
I hope the harm proceeds no further than now.

JASON
Woman, I find no fault with your actions now,
or then: for it's natural that women get angry
when their husbands smuggle new brides into their houses.   910
But your heart has now taken a turn for the better.
You've recognized, at long last, the winning plan—
the thing a woman of self-control would do.

He addresses the children.

For you, boys, your father has thoughtfully arranged
a plan that will bring safety, with the gods' help.   915
I think you'll hold first place in Corinth
with your brothers, the ones who are still to come.
Just grow up strong—the rest your father will manage,
and whichever of the gods is on our side.°

889-90 *We are what we are...we women*: once again Medea plays on the dependent position
    of women; cf. 823. Her aside, "I won't say that we're bad," seems on the surface
    at least to conflict with her earlier statement at 408-9.

902 *when you have lived a long life*: Medea's words strike a particularly pathetic note in
    view of her murder plan; or her resolution may be slightly faltering.

915-19 *with the gods' help...whichever of the gods*: is this just conventional piety on Jason's
    part, or is it meant to show some lingering fear, as he deals with a woman such
    as he knows Medea to be? In any case, as it turns out, her powerful malevolence
    will overcome any help the traditional gods might have offered him.

I want to see you grow up big and strong,   920
and gain the upper hand over my enemies.°

Medea breaks down and weeps; Jason turns to her.

And you, why do you turn your fair cheek away?
Why shed such abundant tears?
Were you not pleased to hear what I just said?

MEDEA
It's nothing. I was thinking about these children.   925

JASON
Cheer up, then, for I'll take good care of them.

MEDEA
Very well. I don't distrust your words.
But a woman is naturally womanish and prone to tears.

JASON
Why, then, are you weeping so much for these children?

MEDEA
I bore them! When you were praying that they live,   930
pity came over me whether this would happen.

She pulls herself together.

Still, the reasons why I wanted you to come,
some I've already mentioned, here are the rest.
The rulers have decided to send me from the country.
(And it's best for me, too, I know it well,   935
not to be in your way or those in authority here;
I am thought of as the family enemy.)
All right, then, I'll go from this land into exile,
but in order that you bring up the children yourself,°
ask Creon that they not go into exile.   940

JASON
I don't know if I can persuade him but I must try.

MEDEA
Instruct the woman you married, then, to beg
her father not to drive them into exile.

JASON
Yes, and I expect I *will* persuade her,
especially if she's a woman like the rest.   945

920-1 *I want to see you*: a standard piece of "tragic" irony, in light of the sequel; among
  Jason's "enemies" (921), of course, first and foremost stands Medea.
939 *that you bring up the children yourself*: a master-stroke by Medea, appealing to
  Jason's fatherly instincts. This also serves as a prelude and excuse to use the boys
  as intermediaries in taking the gifts to the princess.

MEDEA

I, too, will join with you in this task:°
I'll send her gifts by far the most beautiful
now in existence, of this I'm quite certain;
the children will take them.

She turns to the servants.

Go, tell an attendant   950
to bring the adornment here as quickly as possible.

Exit attendant into Medea's house.

She'll think herself lucky, not once but a thousand times,
for having won *you*, the noblest of men, as her bedmate
and getting besides, adornments which the Sun-god,
my father's father, once gave to his descendants.   955

The attendant returns with a chest of gifts.

Come, children, take in your hands these wedding gifts;
give them to the lucky royal bride,
her dowry—gifts in no way to be despised.

JASON

But why, foolish woman, empty your hands of *these* gifts?
Do you think the royal house lacks robes, do you think   960
it lacks gold? Keep them, don't give these things away.
For if the woman thinks me worth anything°
she will place me above wealth, I am certain.

MEDEA

No! No! The proverb says that gifts persuade even the gods
and gold is stronger than a thousand words for mortals.   965
The spirit of luck is with her, the gods make
her fortune grow. She is young, and a princess.
To spare my children exile, I'd give life, not only gold.°
    Go children, to her father's wealthy home
and supplicate the young wife, *my* mistress.°   970
Beg her not to exile you from the land.
Give her this finery, and be especially careful
that she take the gifts in her hands herself.
    Go, quickly. Bring the news to your mother
that you have succeeded in what she longs to obtain.°   975

---

946 *join...in this task*: Medea uses another "heroic" turn-of-phrase; cf. 791-2.
962 *For if the woman thinks me worth anything*: in Jason's own mind, of course, there is
    no doubt, for he is sure that he is "beyond price" in his new bride's eyes.
968 *I'd give life*: whose life? Medea's ambiguity is perhaps calculated.
970 *my mistress*: a new, and false, note of submissiveness on Medea's part. Earlier (17)
    the Nurse had used the same expression to describe her relation to Medea.
975 *in what she longs to obtain*: ominous, as often with closing lines in this type of
    scene.

Exit Jason, the Tutor and the children.

FOURTH CHORAL ODE°

STROPHE 1

No hope remains, no hope at all,
that the children can live;
they have gone to be murdered.
The bride will accept, yes accept
a crown of gold, a crown of death
— poor girl— and around her golden hair
she will place with her own hands   980
the deadly jewels of Hades.

ANTISTROPHE 1

The graceful favor of the gifts
and their immortal gleam will persuade her
to put on the robe and golden crown.
But already she will adorn herself   985
as a bride among the dead.
Into such a trap she will fall,
into such a deadly fate—poor girl—
for in no way will she escape her doom!

STROPHE 2

And you, poor man! Cursed bridegroom,   990
son-in-law of princes! You don't realize
you're bringing destruction to the lives
of your sons, hateful death to your wife.
Miserable wretch! How wrong you've been,
how blind to your fate!   995

ANTISTROPHE 2

And next I lament *your* grief,
unhappy mother of these boys,
children whom you'll murder
because of your bridal bed which he deserted,
against the law! And now your husband   1000
lives with another woman as his wife!

The Tutor leads in the children.

976-1001 *Fourth Choral Ode*: Now that Medea's evil plan seems to be going forward, the chorus heighten the emotions of horror and revulsion at the impending crime. They picture, first, Creon's daughter as she is about to put on the beautiful but deadly gifts; next, they lament the disaster which, in entering this marriage, Jason has brought on Corinth's royal family, as well as on his own sons. Finally, they sympathize with the pain and sorrow which they imagine await Medea if she proceeds with the infanticide.

TUTOR°

Madam, your sons do not have to go into exile;
the royal bride gladly took the gifts in her hands;°
there's peace, now, with her and the children.

He looks at her directly.

Why are you so disturbed when you've succeeded?   1005

Medea screams.

TUTOR

A cry like that does not conform to my news.

Medea screams again.

TUTOR

                    Does my news mean
something I'm not aware of, something bad?   1010

MEDEA

You've brought the news you've brought. I don't blame you.

TUTOR

Why, then, is your gaze downcast and weeping?

MEDEA

I *must* weep, old man. The gods and I,
in my malevolence, have contrived these things.

TUTOR

Take heart! You, too, will journey back with the children's help.   1015

MEDEA

Ah! Others I'll send on a journey first.°

TUTOR

You're not the only woman to be unyoked from her children.
A human must try to bear misfortune lightly.

MEDEA

I'll do as you say. But go inside the house,

1002-1080 From a moral point of view this fifth "episode" is the play's central scene.
There is still a chance that, even after killing the princess, Medea will not murder
her sons. Euripides shows great skill not only in maintaining suspense until the
last possible moment, but in plumbing the depths of a mother's agonized soul as
she makes and unmakes her resolve to commit this unthinkable crime.

1003 *took the gifts in her hands*: just as Medea had instructed the children at 972-3.

1013-4 *The gods and I*: why does Medea invoke the gods to explain her action? Is it just
a manner of speaking, or does she perhaps believe that there is a destiny that the
Corinthian royal house, Jason, her children, and she herself are fulfilling?

1015-16 *journey...journey*: the translation misses a clever ambiguity in the Greek; both
verbs have the prefix *kata-*, which denotes "return from" as well as "down to."
The Tutor takes Medea (in 1016) to mean "the *return* journey *from* exile in Athens"
whereas Medea means "the journey *down to* Hades."

see that my boys get whatever they need for the day.   1020
The Tutor exits into Medea's house alone.

    Ah, children, children, you'll have a city and a home
in which you'll always live, deprived of me,°
your mother, whom you'll leave behind in her misery.
But I shall go to another land as an exile
before benefiting from you and seeing you prosper,   1025
before preparing your pre-nuptial baths and your brides,
before adorning your marriage-beds and holding high°
the wedding torches. O, how miserable my inflexible will has made me!°
For nothing, then, my children, I tended you,
for nothing I labored and wore myself down with toil,   1030
enduring harsh labor-pains at your births.
Oh, the hopes I had once for you were many
—that you would keep me in old age°
and, when I died, deck me out properly,
a sight for men to envy. Now, it's gone,   1035
that sweet concern. Deprived of you two
I shall drag out a grievous and painful life.
And you will never again see with your dear eyes
your mother, after leaving for another form of life.
    O god! Why do you turn your eyes to me,   1040
children? Why smile this final smile?
Ahh! What should I do? I have no heart,
women, when I see the bright eyes of the children.°

1019 *I'll do as you say*: once again (as in 1015-16) Medea's words are ambiguous. Does
    she mean simply to dismiss the Tutor's sententiousness; i.e. "I know; I'll try (to
    bear my fate lightly)"? Or is the accent rather on *lightly* (because Medea has, as
    she thinks, devised a diabolical means of escape from her misfortune)?

1022 *a home in which you'll always live*: the phrase has a sinister implication, i.e. "a
    dwelling-place in Hades."

1025-27 *benefiting...seeing...preparing...adorning...holding high*: this loss of maternal joys
    was a commonplace of mothers who were about to die; Alcestis on her deathbed
    speaks thus to her children (*Alcestis* 317-9). Medea's clichés would naturally be
    taken to mean "the children will be without their mother" (see 1022, "deprived
    of me"), but they take on a horrible hidden meaning when we realize that what
    will bring about this sad state of affairs is not Medea's being removed from her
    children, but her removal of them, by killing them.

1028 *my inflexible will*: the Nurse had earlier referred to Medea's "self-willed mind"
    (104; cf. 223), and Jason had accused her of acting "stubbornly" (621). This inflex-
    ibility (*authadia*) is one of Medea's distinguishing features.

1033 *keep me in old age*: it was a primary duty of Greek children to support their aged
    parents.

1040-43 *your eyes... bright eyes*: the Greeks thought that there was something special and
    uncanny about vision, and in poetry the eyes are often spoken of as a person's
    quintessential identifying mark.

I can not. Good-bye to those plans made before.
I shall take my children from the land.   1045
Why should I harm them, to hurt their father,
when I would harm myself twice as much?
No, I will not. Farewell to my plans.
    And yet, what's wrong? Do I want to be laughed at°
for letting my enemies off scot-free?   1050
The deed *must* be done! Ugh! The weakness
of even letting soft thoughts into my mind.°
Go into the house, children.

*An attendant leads the boys towards the door; Medea turns away from the door
towards the audience.*

The one for whom it is not right to attend my sacrifice,°
beware! My hand shall not be turned from its purpose!   1055
Ah! Ah!
Do not, my spirit, do *not* do this deed!° Let them live—
O wretched thing! Spare the children! If they are *alive*
there in Athens with us, they will gladden you.
No, by those Avenging Demons in Hades°
it is impossible that this should happen,   1060
to leave my children for my enemies to insult.
In any case, the deed has been done
and there will be no escape.
    Already the crown is on her head
and wrapped in the robe, the princess-bride dies.   1065
I know it for certain. But now I am setting out
on a most painful road, and sending them on one
more painful still. I wish to talk to the children.

An attendant leads the boys back to Medea.

1049 *Do I want to be laughed at…?*: Medea dreads the prospect of her enemies gloating
    over her reverses; similarly 383, 404, 767.
1052 *soft thoughts*: such signs of weakness are repugnant to Medea, although she was
    prepared to make a pretense of "soft words" (776) when it was expedient to do
    so.
1054 *attend my sacrifice*: Medea uses the formal language of one preparing a solemn
    sacrifice, with a warning to outsiders or non-adherents to the cult to depart. Here,
    "my sacrifice" is the slaying of her children.
1056-80 *Do not, my spirit*: in the best poetic tradition going back at least to Archilochus
    in the seventh century, Medea addresses her *thumos*, "spirit," "inner self"— in
    some contexts, even, "self-consciousness"— as if it were an independent force
    driving an individual to act in a certain way. And in Medea's case this explana-
    tion is perhaps near the truth.
1059 *Avenging Demons*: supernatural agents called up by victims of aggression to
    seek vengeance on their aggressors; sometimes identified with the curses of the
    injured party.

Give, children, give your right hands°
to your mother to kiss.   1070
O dearest hands, lips dearest to me
and form and face of my children so well born!
May you both be blessed—but *there*. For matters here
your father has destroyed. O sweet embrace,
O soft skin, most pleasant breath of my children.   1075
Go in, go in! I can look upon you no longer because
I am conquered by evils. On the one hand I understand
what sort of evils I am going to dare and endure,
but my seething spirit dictates my plans,
the same spirit which causes the greatest evils for mortals.°   1080

An attendant leads the boys into Medea's house, for the last time.

CHORAL INTERLUDE°
I have often gone
through subtle debates, searched
the fine points of argument
more than befits a woman.°
But we, too, have a Muse   1085
who shares her wisdom with us—
not with all, but a small
segment of women might perhaps be found
who are not strangers to the Muse.
My conclusion is that people   1090
who've never borne children
are much happier
than parents.
The childless have no experience
whether children bring happiness   1095
or sorrow—they don't have them!
They've missed many sufferings.

1069-75 *Give, children, give your right hands*: a very moving account of the display of
affection between parent and child, with its delineation of every detail of the
boys' youthful charm. The poet is exploiting the poignancy of this last farewell
and showing us how strong are the maternal instincts which Medea has had to
suppress.

1078-80 *I understand*: verses frequently quoted by ancient moralists and famous as an
expression of the ethical problem of *akrasia*, weakness of will ("I know the right
course of action, but don't do it").

1081-1115 *Choral Interlude*: the chorus-leader chants a series of anapests on the theme,
"Children are a lot of trouble and worry, and what good is it anyway, if as often
happens, they die young?"

1084 *more than befits a woman*: because Greek women were supposed to be seen—sometimes—but almost never heard; i. e. they were expected to be submissive and
dependent on the males about them.

But those who have at home
a delightful brood, I see them
worn out by constant concerns: 1100
first, how to feed and raise them,
and leave them enough to live on.
Then, whether they're laboring
for good children or bad is unclear.
I'll mention one last evil,   1105
the worst of all for humans.
Let's say they've successfully raised them:
their children are now grown up,
and they're good. Then, if a divinity
so decrees, Death snatches   1110
the children away to Hades.
What profit, then, for mortals
if the gods add to our other woes
this most painful grief,
only for the sake of children?   1115

MEDEA
My friends, I've waited and watched a long time,
to learn how things turned out over there.

A Messenger, extremely agitated, enters from stage-left.

Now finally I see this man coming,
one of Jason's attendants. His troubled breathing
shows that he has some bad news to report.   1120

MESSENGER
You've done a terrible deed, against the law!
Medea, flee, flee! Take any conveyance you can,
some kind of ship or earth-treading chariot!

MEDEA
What happened, then, to warrant such hasty flight?

MESSENGER
Died, they've just now died. The princess   1125
and Creon her father, died because of your poisons.

MEDEA
The best possible word you could speak!°
You'll be for ever after among my benefactors and friends!

MESSENGER
What are you saying? Are you sane, not mad, woman,

1127 *The best possible word*: Medea is referring to the first word of the Messenger's
previous statement, "died." Her almost ghoulish glee in savoring every grisly
detail of her victims' death-agonies horrifies the Messenger, who cannot believe
that she is not insane (1129).

who committed outrage against the royal hearth   1130
and show delight, not fear, in hearing the news?

MEDEA
I, too, am able to give an account to match yours.°
But take your time, my friend; tell me, then,
how did they die? For twice the pleasure
you'll give, if they died a horrible death.   1135

MESSENGER°
When the two children whom you bore went
with their father and came into the bridal quarters,
we servants who were suffering with your troubles
were gladdened to hear the rumor going around that you
and your husband had settled your previous quarrel.   1140
One of us kissed a child's hand, another
a golden head. But I, because of my joy,
followed the children into the women's quarters.
The mistress whom we now honor in your place,
before she saw your two children come in,   1145
kept her gaze eagerly fixed on Jason.°
But then she held her veil before her eyes
and turned her white cheek in the other direction,
out of loathing at the children's entry. Your husband
tried to dispel the girl's livid anger   1150
by saying to her: "Please don't be angry at dear ones;
put aside your wrath and turn your head;
please consider my loved ones yours as well.
Take the gifts and, as a favor to me,
ask your father to save these children from exile."°   1155
    The girl, when she saw the finery, couldn't resist,
but agreed to all her husband's requests. Before he
and your sons had proceeded far from the palace
she took up the embroidered dress and began to put it on;
then she placed the golden tiara upon her locks   1160
arranging her hair in a brightly reflecting mirror,
smiling at her body's lifeless image.°
Then she got up from her chair and walked around

1132 *an account to match yours*: Presumably Medea means she could justify her actions
    by repeating the tale of her mistreatment by Jason and his new in-laws.
1136-1230 The Messenger follows Medea's instructions to "take his time" for his account
    fills almost 100 lines. For grim realism and horrible detail, it is matched only by
    the Messenger's account of the killing of Pentheus (*Bacchae* 1043-52).
1146 *kept her gaze eagerly fixed on Jason*: it appears, then, that if for Jason the marriage
    was a calculated act of self-interest, for his bride it was a love-match.
1155 *ask your father*: Jason is thus following Medea's instructions (942-3).
1162 *her body's lifeless image*: ironical, in view of what will soon befall.

the house, skipping lightly with delicate feet,
thoroughly pleased with the gifts, again and again   1165
looking behind to make sure the hem was straight.
What happened from here on was a terrible sight:
Her complexion turned pale; she stumbled
sideways; her body shook. She hardly managed
to reach her chair without falling flat on the floor.   1170
One of her old serving women, supposing
that a fit of Pan or some other god was upon her,°
cried out for joy, but then she saw around her mouth
the white foam oozing, the eyes in their sockets
rolling wildly, the blood all gone from her skin.   1175
Then, in place of her earlier cry of joy, she let out
a great wail of grief. At once a maid rushed
to her father's quarters, another to tell the new
husband of his bride's misfortune; the whole house
resounded with pounding of running peoples' feet.   1180
     Before a swift sprinter could have run his two hundred
yard course and come back to the starting-point,
the girl came out of her faint, opened her eyes
and let out a terrible moan in her misery.
For a double agony was now assaulting her: 1185
first the gold diadem which lay upon her head
sent out a remarkable stream of devouring flame,
and also her fine-wrought robe, your children's gift,
was eating the white skin of the unfortunate girl.
She got up from her chair and ran, all on fire,   1190
shaking her hair and her head this way, that way,
trying to cast off the crown. But fixed fast
the gold binding held, and the fire, as she shook
her hair, simply flared up twice as strong.
She fell to the floor, overmastered by her misfortune,   1195
unrecognizable to anyone but a parent;°
the usual look of her eyes could not be seen,
nor her lovely face, but down from the top of her head
was dripping blood all mixed together with fire.
And from her bones the flesh oozed off, like tears of resin   1200
from a pine, ripped by the hidden jaws of the poison;
it was a dreadful sight. All of us were afraid
to touch the corpse; what happened to her was a lesson.

1172 *a fit of Pan*: such occurrences, especially sudden and violent reactions in an indi-
    vidual or group, were attributed to Pan (hence the word "panic").
1196 *unrecognizable to anyone but a parent*: a pathetic touch, which also prepares the way
    for her father's entry and emotional reaction.

Her father, poor wretch, unaware of the disaster,°
burst into the house and fell upon the corpse. 1205
At once he groaned and threw his arms around her,
kissed her and spoke as follows: "My unlucky child,
which divinity destroyed you so shamefully?
Which one has left me, old tomb of a man, bereft of you?
Alas, I wish I could die with you, child!" 1210
When he had brought his sobs and laments to an end
and wanted to make his aged body rise
he stuck fast to her delicate robes like ivy
to branches of bay; it was a fearful wrestling match.
He wanted to get up on his knees and rise, 1215
but she held fast. If he used force and pulled,
he tore the aged flesh from his bones.°
Finally the ill-starred man gave up the ghost
and expired; the suffering was too much for him.
They lie now, corpses, child and aged father 1220
together, a calamity that calls for tears.
    No account need be taken of your situation,
for you will devise an escape from punishment.
I have often considered the human condition a shadow,°
and I would not hesitate to say that those 1225
who seem to be wise and concern themselves with learning,
these risk being called the biggest fools.
For no mortal man is truly blessed;
when wealth flows one may have more luck
than another, but is not for that reason blessed. 1230

Exit Messenger.

CHORUS LEADER
It seems that a divinity has inflicted on Jason today
a mass of sufferings, but with justification.
Poor girl, Creon's daughter, how you stir our pity,
you who have gone to Hades' halls in death
on account of your marriage-bond with Jason. 1235

1204-21 *Her father, poor wretch*: the scene has been building to this encounter between
    loving father and doomed daughter; one aspect of the "children theme" thus
    reaches its grim conclusion.
1217 *he tore the aged flesh*: Creon's "wrestling match" with his daughter is described
    as a *sparagmos*, "a tearing to pieces." The same word is used of Agave's "tearing
    to pieces" of her son Pentheus (*Bacchae* 1127, 1135, 1220). *Sparagmos* properly
    describes the rending of an *animal* victim in the frenzied rites of Dionysus, thus
    making these *human* deaths all the more tragic.
1224 *the human condition a shadow*: a frequent image in Greek poetry (e. g. Sophocles
    Ajax 125-6) to describe the transitoriness of human happiness and its susceptibil-
    ity to reversals.

MEDEA

My friends, I have resolved upon the deed, to kill the boys
as quickly as possible and flee from this country.
I shall not, by delaying, give my children over
to another, more unfriendly, hand to murder.
In any case, their death is inevitable, and since   1240
they must die, I who gave them birth shall kill them.
Up then! Arm yourself, my heart!
Why wait to do the dreadful evil that must be done?
Come, my wretched hand, take up the sword,
take it and go to life's goal of grief!   1245
Do not be cowardly, do not remember the children,
how very dear they are, how you bore them.
For this short day, at least, forget all about your children,
then grieve. Even if you kill them, still you bore them,
you loved them. Alas, what an unlucky woman I am!°   1250

Exit Medea into her house.

FIFTH CHORAL ODE°

STROPHE 1

Earth and dazzling ray of Sun,°
look down, look down on this murderous woman,
keep her from laying her bloody,
kin-murdering hands on her own sons.
From your golden race   1255
they sprang; we are afraid
that a god's blood may flow
because of men's misdeeds. Stop her, prevent it,

1250 *Alas, what an unlucky woman I am!*: we are left with an impression of Medea the
   mother, whose instincts of nurture and protection of her young, though sup-
   pressed and perhaps perverted, nevertheless still run deep. The messenger at 1229
   had made the point of what an ephemeral thing "good luck" is; for Medea it has
   entirely passed and what awaits her is a life of misery (1245).
1251-92 *Fifth Choral Ode.* As Medea exits for the first time in the play, the Chorus sing
   a song to "cover" the decisive action occurring offstage. The first strophe and
   antistrophe, pitched at a high emotional level, contain phrases whose meaning is
   ambiguous, but the over-all sense is clear: since the Sun's divine blood flows in
   Medea's veins (see, e.g., 406), murdering her children is sacrilegious. What is the
   point of having borne children, if you later kill them? Such a great crime calls for
   divine vengeance. Strophe 2 is, strikingly, interrupted by dialogue from the boys
   within, *as they are being murdered.* In antistrophe 2 the Chorus scour the traditional
   tales for an analogue to such a horrendous crime, and can only come up with one,
   the case of Ino (on whom see note to 1284).
1251-2 *Earth and dazzling ray of Sun*: two powerful primal elements (personified),
   to whom characters often appeal in tense situations, even in preference to the
   Olympian gods. An appeal to the Sun is additionally appropriate, since Medea
   is his grand-daughter.

O light born from Zeus! Drive from the house
the wretched, murderous Fury of Vengeance!°   1260

Empty is your labor of childbirth,°
empty now, and gone; lost the lovely offspring
you bore when you left the straits most unwelcoming,
the dark Clashing Rocks.° Wretched woman,
why does wrath fall so heavy on your mind   1265
and violent murder answer violent murder?
For grievous to mankind are the stains
of kinsmen's blood and sorrows,pursue
those who kill their own, echoing their misdeeds,
sorrows sent by the gods to fall upon their homes.   1270

Boys (*within*)
  Ah!

Chorus Leader
  Do you hear, do you hear, the children's cry?   1273
  O miserable unfortunate woman!   1274

First Boy (*from within*)
  O, what should I do? Where run from mother's attack?   1271

Second Boy (*from within*)
  I don't know, dearest brother. We're slain!   1272

Chorus Leader
  Should I go into the house? I think I should try   1275
  to save the children from death.

First Boy (*from within*)
  Yes, by the gods, save us. We are in need.

Second Boy (*from within*)
  For now the snares of the sword are ready to strike!°

1260 *Fury of Vengeance*: Medea seems to be identified with the Erinys (Fury), an earth
  goddess who, with her sisters, avenged crimes against family members or others
  of dependent status.
1261 *Empty is your labor*: the chorus echo a sentiment expressed earlier by Medea
  herself (see 1029 ff.).
1262-4 *the straits...and dark Clashing Rocks*: see 2 above, with note.
1278 *ready to strike*: Note the convention that killing was not actually depicted on the
  Greek stage here comes close to being broken, since the boys' vivid account and
  blood-curdling shrieks make us feel we are actually present at the murder.

CHORUS LEADER
Wretched woman, you must have been rock°
or iron to kill the children seedlings   1280
you bore with a fate inflicted by your own hand.

ANTISTROPHE 2
Of one woman, one only I have heard
that she cast her hand at her own dear children:
Ino,° driven mad by the gods, when Zeus' wife
expelled her from home to wander.°   1285
She impiously killed her children
and leapt, poor wretch, into the sea,
stepping over an ocean cliff,
dying with the two children she slew.
What, I ask, could be more terrible?   1290
O, the many sufferings that women's love-life brings—
the harm you have already done among humans!°

Jason rushes in.°

JASON
Women, who stand in attendance near this house,
is the one who did these terrible things, Medea,
still at home, or has she made good her escape?   1295
She must now either hide beneath the earth
or take wing and fly up to heaven's height°
to avoid reprisals from the household of the King.
Is she sure she can kill the princes of the land,
and then escape from this house, free and unpunished?   1300

1279. *you must have been rock*: the point is made yet again that Medea is something
inhuman, an elemental force of nature (cf. 29).

1284 *Ino*: a daughter of Cadmus of Thebes and the typical "evil stepmother" to the
children (by his first marriage) of her husband Athamas. To punish her the goddess Hera drove Ino mad and, after killing one of her sons by Athamas, she leapt
with the other into the sea. (There were other examples of mythical mothers who
slew their children, e.g. Procne and Agave, but these are conveniently ignored so
the Chorus can make the point that there was "one woman, one only" who had
acted as terribly as Medea.)

1284-5 *Zeus' wife expelled her*: Hera, who had befriended Athamas' children; the implication is that, as noted above, she drove Ino insane.

1291-2 The Chorus ends by drawing a general conclusion, not only from Ino's case but
also Medea's (cf. Jason's oversimplification, 569 ff.).

1293ff. (*Jason rushes in.*) It is noteworthy that in this final scene Jason is portrayed as far
more believably human, even sympathetic, than he has been up until now. Suffering seems to have ennobled him, or at least to have made him less pompous.

1297 *take wing and fly*: Jason has no idea how close he is to describing the way in which
Medea actually will escape.

Still, I care less for her than for the children;°
she will fall victim in turn to those she wronged.
I have come, however, to save my children's lives,
to keep the king's family from making them pay
for the foul murder committed by their mother.°   1305

CHORUS LEADER
Poor Jason! You do not know what evil you're in,
or else you wouldn't have spoken like that.

JASON
What is it? I suppose she wants to kill me, too.

CHORUS LEADER
Your children are dead, their mother's hand killed them.

JASON
Ah! What are you saying? You've destroyed me, woman!°   1310

CHORUS LEADER
Realize finally that your children are no more.

JASON
Where did she kill them? Inside or outside the house?

CHORUS LEADER
If you open the doors you will see your boys' bloody bodies.

JASON (*shouting, and pounding on the house door*)
Attendants, unlock the bolts as fast as you can,
release the latches! Let me see the double evil,   1315
the victims, their killer whom I'll punish.

*Medea appears on or above the roof, with the corpses of her sons, in a chariot drawn
by winged dragons.*°

MEDEA
Why are you trying to move and unbar the gates,
seeking the corpses and me who made them so?
Stop your exertions. If you need something from me,
tell me what you want; your hand shall *never* touch me.   1320

1301 *I care less for her than for the children*: Jason does not come in saying "What she did
to my bride!" We are about to discover how much he really cares for his sons.
1304-5 *making them pay for the foul murder*: such possible reprisals had been envisaged
by Medea (1238-9).
1310 *You've destroyed me, woman!*: he addresses Medea, although he cannot see her.
1317 Medea's appearance "above," on the roof of the stage-building or suspended
from the so-called "machine," comes as a shock to the audience as well as to Jason.
Although from her remarks to Aigeus earlier that she would "come to his city by
the quickest means" (757) we might have supposed that she was thinking about a
way of escaping from Corinth, nothing has suggested this particular supernatural
conveyance. It takes the place of the device with which many of Euripides' other
plays end, the "god or goddess (speaking) from the machine" (*deus ex machina*).

This chariot here my father's father, the Sun-god,°
has given to me, to ward off my enemies' might.

JASON
You hateful creature! Woman by far most loathsome
to the gods, to me, and to the entire human race!
A mother, you dared to thrust a sword   1325
into your children, thus making me a childless ruin.
And doing this, you look upon the Sun and earth,°
though daring the foulest of crimes? Go to damnation!
My sense has returned, though then I lacked it
when I took you from your home and a foreign land   1330
and brought you to a Greek home, a great evil,
betrayer of your father and the land that gave you birth.°
The gods have inflicted your Avenger against me.°
After killing the brother who shared your hearth,°
you went aboard the Argo, the ship of beautiful prow.   1335
    That was the way you began. Then you married
this husband here and bore me children,
but because of the bed and sex you murdered them.
No Greek woman would ever have dared this.
Yet I ranked you over them, and married you,   1340
a wife who hated and ruined me,
a lioness not a woman,° who have a nature
more fierce even than that of Etruscan Scylla.°
But not by casting ten thousand insulting remarks
could I sting you, so savage is your inborn nature.   1345
Be damned, shamefully defiled with your children's blood!
It is left for me now to lament my fate.

1321 *my father's father, the Sun-god*: for Medea's descent from the Sun see 406, 476-7,
    954-5.
1327 *you look upon the Sun and earth*: Medea, as it were, desecrates the purity of these
    elemental forces, the same ones the Chorus had invoked at 1251-2.
1332 *betrayer of your father*: he repeats the accusation which she had so often made
    against herself (31-2, 166-7, 502-3, 799 ff.; and cf. 441 ff., 643 ff.).
1333 *your Avenger*: for this "avenging Spirit" see note on 1059. Jason seems to mean that
    he is now being punished for his complicity in Medea's previous crimes.
1334 *who shared your hearth*: another interpretation of this phrase is "(killed) at the
    hearth," which would make Medea's crime even worse, since the hearth was the
    sacred center of family gatherings.
1342 *a lioness not a woman*: the Nurse had earlier said that Medea's glare was like that
    of a "mother lioness" (188). The theme of Medea's bestial nature is thus rounded
    off (cf. 29, 92, 103, 1279-80).
1343 *Etruscan Scylla*: the monster described by Homer (*Odyssey* 12.89 ff.; cf. Vergil, *Aeneid*
    3.420 ff.) as having six heads with three rows of teeth, and twelve feet, which snatched
    six of Odyseus' best sailors as they sailed through the straits of Messene between Sicily
    and Italy in that part of the Mediterranean called by the Greeks the Etruscan Sea.

Now I shall never enjoy my new bride's bed,
nor be able to speak to the children I bred and raised,
yet alive in this world, for I have lost them.   1350

MEDEA
I would have stretched out a long speech refuting
your arguments, if father Zeus didn't know
what you got from me and what you did in return.
You were not about to treat my bed with dishonor
and spend a pleasant life laughing at me.°   1355
Nor were the princess and the father who gave her
to you going to exile me and get off scot-free.
So then, call me a lioness, if you like,
or a Scylla who dwells in the land of Etruria,
for I've fittingly driven my sting into your heart.   1360

JASON
Yet you grieve, too, and share in the disaster.

MEDEA
True, but grief is gain, if it stops you from laughing at me.

JASON
O children, what an evil mother you encountered!

MEDEA
O children, how your father's illness killed you!°

JASON
At least it wasn't my right hand that killed them.   1365

MEDEA
No, your insults and your newly-formed marriage.

JASON
Did you *really* think it proper to kill them because of the marriage bed?

MEDEA
Do you think that this is small suffering for a woman?°

JASON
For a self-controlled woman, but for you a world of evil.°

MEDEA
These children no longer live; *that* will sting you.   1370

1355 *laughing at me*: for the theme of the intolerability of having enemies gloat over
   one's setbacks see 383, 404, 797 and 1049.
1364 *your father's illness*: a slightly unusual description of Jason's behavior in abandoning Medea for the princess.
1368 *small suffering for a woman?*: Medea seems to confirm the charge made by Jason
   at 569 ff., and which the Chorus echoed at 1291-2.
1369 *For a self-controlled woman*: self-control / good sense (*so-phron*) was the virtue by
   which Jason had set so much stock (cf. 549, 635, 884, 913).

JASON

Alas, they do live, as Avenging Spirits°
who will bring down pollution on *your* head.

MEDEA

The gods know who was the first to inflict suffering.

JASON

And they know, truly, how loathsome your heart is.

MEDEA

Loathe on, then. I detest your shrill barking.

JASON

And I yours. We are easily done with each other.   1375

MEDEA

How? What should I do? I very much want to.

JASON

Allow me to bury the corpses and weep for them.

MEDEA

No, indeed, my hand will bury them,
after bringing them to Hera's shrine on the cliff,°
so none of my enemies will insult them by pulling   1380
down their tombs. In this country of Sisyphus,°
we shall assign a sacred feast and rituals°
as a memorial of this impious murder forever after.
I myself am going to Erechtheus' country,°
Athens, to live with Aigeus, son of Pandion.   1385
Since you are base, your death will be fittingly mean:
you'll be struck on the head by a piece of your ship, Argo,°

1371 *Avenging Spirits*: Jason means that the children's deaths will "cry to heaven for
vengeance" and that (he hopes) Medea will be punished for her crime by some
divine agency.

1379 *Hera's shrine on the cliff*: an important sanctuary of Hera, who had "on the cliff" as
one of her cult-titles at Corinth and elsewhere; the ancient sources are not very clear
about its location (perhaps in the direction of Sicyon on the Gulf of Lechaion).

1381 *country of Sisyphus*: Corinth; on Sisyphus see note on 405.

1382 *we shall assign a sacred feast and rituals*: several of Euripides' plays end with a similar
charter for the performance of some such generally quite minor local festival, and
many of these are known from the sources to have been celebrated until much
later than the poet's own time (for this one, see Pausanias 2.3.6). It is not clear
what the poet's purpose was in thus connecting an occurrence in his play with
an actual contemporary event. (Note that a memorial celebrated by the people of
Corinth in honor of Medea's sons makes more sense with the version of the story
that had the children murdered by the people, who later tried to expiate their
deed by setting up a festival.)

1384 *Erechtheus' country*: Athens; see note on 824.

1387 *struck on the head by a piece of your ship, Argo*: There were other variants: Jason had
dedicated the mast of the Argo in Hera's temple, but as he was going out it fell on

a bitter termination to your marriage with me.

JASON°
May the children's Fury and Justice,°
avenger of murder, destroy you!°   1390

MEDEA
What god, what spirit, listens to you,
breaker of oaths, deceiver of friends?°

JASON
You polluted slayer of your children!

MEDEA
Go home and bury your bride!

JASON
I am going, deprived of my two children.   1395

MEDEA
There's more lamenting to come—wait for old age.°

JASON
O dearest children!

MEDEA
                    Dearest to their mother, not to you.

JASON
And yet you killed?

MEDEA
                    To cause you pain.°

JASON
O, I am miserable. I wish I could
kiss the dear lips of my children.   1400

MEDEA
Now you talk to them, now you greet them.
Before you drove them away!

---

him and killed him (ancient note on *Medea* 1286); or Medea predicted that Jason
would commit suicide (Neophron's play).

1389-end This closing section between Medea and Jason is in anapaests, a rhythm
which denotes a rise in the level of excitement.

1389-90 *the children's Fury and Justice, avenger of murder*: Furies were often said to work
as agents or emissaries of the personified goddess Justice, whom Medea herself
had invoked at 764. (On the Furies see 1260, 1371.)

1392 *breaker of oaths*: Medea returns, one last time, to her charge of faithlessness against
Jason (cf. 162-3, 209-10, 439, 492, 495).

1396 *wait for old age*: Medea means that if he somehow survives the falling ship-timber
(1387) and lives to old age, he will have no offspring to perform the expected
attendance on elderly parents (cf. 1033).

1398 *To cause you pain*: Medea puts her motive with razor-like simplicity.

JASON

    In the name of the gods allow me
    to touch the soft skin of the children.°

MEDEA

    It cannot be. Your words have been uttered in vain.

JASON

    Zeus, do you hear how I am rejected?   1405
    Do you see what she is doing to me,
    this polluted child-murdering lioness?°
    But with the breath and force that are in me
    I will raise a dirge, and summon the gods,
    calling on them to witness°   1410
    how you killed my children and now keep me
    from touching them with my hands and burying their bodies.
    Would that I had never begotten them,
    to see them murdered by you!

Medea, in the chariot of the Sun, flies off with the corpses towards Athens; Jason exits down a side ramp.

CHORUS

    Zeus is steward of many things on Mt. Olympus°   1415
    and many things, too, beyond expectation
    the gods accomplish. The expected does not turn out;
    for the unexpected the gods find a way.
    Such is the end of this business.

Exit Chorus from the orchestra.

1403 *allow me to touch*: Jason's moving appeal does not move Medea. We sympathize
    with the anguished father in a way that would have seemed impossible because
    of the highly unfavorable impression he made in the earlier scenes.

1407 *this polluted child-murdering lioness*: he repeats some of the language of 1393 and
    the animal image of 1342.

1409-10 *summon the gods, calling on them to witness*: this reminds us of an earlier legalism
    by Jason (619), but he has far more justification here.

1415-19 Some critics excise these final anapestic lines by the Chorus on the grounds that
    they are bland and are found in almost the same form at the end of *Andromache*,
    Helen, *Bacchae* and *Alcestis*. But they seem inoffensive enough and by their very
    conventionality would have served notice to the audience that the play really
    was over.

HIPPOLYTUS

Translation and notes by Michael R. Halleran

CHARACTERS

APHRODITE, goddess of fertility, sexuality and beauty
HIPPOLYTUS, (bastard) son of Theseus and the queen of the Amazons
ATTENDANTS, Hippolytus' fellow hunters
SERVANT, slave of Theseus' palace
CHORUS, (married) women of Trozen
NURSE, aged and trusted servant of Phaedra
PHAEDRA, wife of Theseus, stepmother of Hippolytus
THESEUS, husband of Phaedra, father of Hippolytus
MESSENGER, companion of Hippolytus and slave of Theseus' house
ARTEMIS, goddess of childbirth, hunting, and chastity

Aphrodite enters from one of the two eisodoi, *long side entrance ramps.*°

APHRODITE

I am powerful° and not without a name among mortals
and within the heavens. I am called the goddess Cypris.°
Of those who dwell within Pontus
and the boundaries of Atlas° and see the light of the sun,

Setting: The play is set in Trozen, with the *skene* building representing the palace. Statues of Aphrodite and Artemis stand on opposite sides of the acting area.

Aphrodite enters: Euripides always opened his plays with an expository speech laying out the drama's background. When a divine character delivers the prologue, as is the case here, the references to the future create an irony in which the audience knows what awaits the play's mortals characters but the latter do not. Aphrodite may have appeared on the roof of the *skene* building or at ground level. In either case, like the other divine characters who deliver the prologues in Euripides' plays, she makes no direct contact with the mortal characters and departs before Hippolytus arrives.

1 *powerful*: Aphrodite's power is announced at the very outset, the first word in the Greek text.

2 *Cypris*: A common name, especially in poetry, for Aphrodite, reflecting her association with the island of Cyprus.

3-4 *Pontus . . . boundaries of Atlas*: the Black Sea and Straits of Gibraltar respectively, that is, from the ancient Greeks' perspective the eastern and western limits of the known world.

I treat well those who revere my power,   5
but I trip up those who are proud towards me.
For this principle holds among the race of the gods also:
they enjoy being honored by mortals.
I shall now show you the truth of these words:
Theseus' son, Hippolytus, the Amazon's offspring,°   10
reared by pure Pittheus°—
he alone of the citizens of this land of Trozen
says that I am by nature the most vile of divinities.
He spurns the bed and doesn't touch marriage,°
but honors Apollo's sister, Artemis, the daughter of Zeus,   15
considering her the greatest of divinities.
Always consorting° with the virgin through the green wood,
he rids the land of beasts with swift dogs,
having come upon a more than mortal companionship.
I don't begrudge them these things; why should I?   20
But I will punish Hippolytus this day
for the wrongs he has done me. I won't need much toil,
since long before this I prepared most of what has to be done.
      When he once came from Pittheus' house
to the land of Pandion° for viewing the rites
at the holy Mysteries,° his father's noble wife   25
Phaedra looked at him and her heart was seized
with a terrible passion, according to my plans.
And before coming to this land of Trozen
she set up there a temple to Cypris°
beside Pallas' very rock,°   30
overlooking this land, since she was in love with one

---

10 *Amazon's offspring*: nowhere in the play is Hippolytus' mother named. What is
     emphasized consistently is that he is a bastard, the illegitimate offspring of Theseus
     and the (non-Greek) Amazon.
11 *Pittheus*: Hippolytus' paternal great-grandfather; his daughter Aethra was Theseus'
     mother.
14 Remarkably what Aphrodite demands from Hippolytus is not simply ritual
     observance, but his participation in her realm, the world of sex and marriage.
17 *consorting*: The word, often used in a sexual sense, suggests the unnaturalness
     (from Aphrodite's viewpoint) of this association.
24 *land of Pandion*: Athens, as Pandion was one of the city's legendary kings.
25 *Mysteries*: These were the rites celebrated at Eleusis, outside of Athens, in honor
     of the goddess Demeter. This detail suggests Hippolytus' religious piety while
     offering a plausible motive for his visit to Athens.
29-33 An ancient inscription links the temple of Aphrodite with the shrine of Hip-
     polytus.
30 *Pallas' very rock*: the Athenian acropolis; Pallas is another name for Athena.

who was distant. In the future people will name the goddess
as established there because of Hippolytus.
After that, to escape the pollution of the Pallantids' blood,°
Theseus left the land of Cecrops°   35
and, resigned to a year in exile,
sailed with his wife to this land.
And now the poor woman, moaning and overwhelmed
by the goads of passion, is dying
in silence°—none of the household knows her disease.   40
   But not like this is this love destined to turn out;
I will reveal the matter to Theseus and it will be brought
to light.° As for the young man who wars against me,
his father will kill him with the curses the lord of the sea,
Poseidon, gave to Theseus as a gift,   45
that he could pray to the god three times not in vain.
Phaedra will keep her good reputation,°
but still she will die. For I do not value her suffering more
than my enemy's paying me
such a penalty that I am satisfied.   50
   But I see Theseus' son coming here,
Hippolytus, who has just abandoned the toil of the hunt;
I will depart from this place.
A band of many lively attendants follows him
and shouts with him, honoring the goddess Artemis   55
in hymns. He does not know that the gates of Hades
lie open and that this is the last light he sees.

Aphrodite exits by the same eisodos *she entered from.*
Hippolytus and his attendants enter from the opposite eisodos.

---

34 *Pallantids' blood*: The Pallantids ("sons of Pallas") were Theseus' cousins (sons of
    Aegeus' half-brother Pallas, not to be confused with the alternate name for Athena).
    In a dispute over his right to rule after his father's death, Theseus killed his cousins
    and went into exile for a year as atonement for shedding kindred blood.
35 *land of Cecrops*: Cecrops was a legendary king of Athens. Greek poetry used many
    such periphrases for common names like Athens.
40 *in silence*: Enjambed to appear at the end of its clause and the first word in this line,
    silence is highlighted at this early stage of the drama. Speech and silence form an
    intricate leitmotif in this play.
42 Not quite. The order of events—revelation, Hippolytus' death, and Phaedra's
    death—is the opposite of what transpires. While Theseus *eventually* learns the
    truth, this line creates a false expectation of how events will unfold.
48 *good reputation*: This is the overriding motivation for her actions—her good
    name.

HIPPOLYTUS

Follow me, follow, hymning
the child of Zeus, heavenly Artemis, who cares for us.   60

HIPPOLYTUS AND ATTENDANTS

Lady, lady, most revered,°
offspring of Zeus,
hail, I say, hail, daughter
of Leto and Zeus, Artemis,   65
most beautiful by far of maidens,
you who in the expanse of heaven
dwell in the hall of your great father,
in the gold-rich house of Zeus.
Hail, I say, most beautiful,   70
most beautiful of those on Olympus.

HIPPOLYTUS

For you, mistress, I bring this plaited wreath.°
I fashioned it from an untouched meadow,
where neither the shepherd thinks it right to feed   75
his flocks nor the scythe has yet come, but a bee
goes through the untouched meadow in springtime.
And Reverence° cultivates it with river water
for those to whom nothing is taught, but in whose nature°
moderation° has been allotted in everything always—   80
for these to cull; but for the wicked it is not right.
So, dear mistress, receive from a reverent hand
a band for your golden hair.
For I alone of mortals have this privilege:
I am your companion and converse with you,   85

61-71 This brief song employs the language commonly found in hymns: frequent
address, repetitions, and references to the god's attributes, parentage, dwellings
and sites of worship.

73-87 Hippolytus addresses the statue of Artemis on stage and offers it the garland
he has fashioned from his special meadow. The language is particularly charged,
juxtaposing images of religious observance and purity with suggestions of sexual
violation, since a meadow was a proverbial site for sexual activity.

78   *Reverence*: The Greek word *aidos* is difficult to translate. It refers to a complex set
of emotions, most particularly those that inhibit one from improper behavior.

79-80 Hippolytus wants to restrict his meadow not only to the pure but those who
are so *by nature*. The late fifth century was engaged in a lively debate over nature
and nurture. Throughout the play, Hippolytus emphasizes his *natural* qualities
and virtues.

80   *moderation*: No concept is more fundamental to this play than *sophrosyne*; which
relates especially to Hippolytus and Phaedra, both of whom use the word in a
range of senses.

hearing your voice, though without seeing your face.°
May I reach the end of my life's course just as I began it!

A servant enters from the palace.

SERVANT
Lord—for we must call the gods masters—°
would you take some good advice from me?

HIPPOLYTUS
Yes, indeed. Otherwise I wouldn't seem wise.   90

SERVANT
Now, do you know the law that is established among mortals?

HIPPOLYTUS
I don't know. *What* are you asking me about?

SERVANT
To hate what's proud° and not friendly to all.

HIPPOLYTUS
Rightly—for what mortal who is proud is not irksome?

SERVANT
And there is some charm in being affable?   95

HIPPOLYTUS
Very much so, and profit with little effort.

SERVANT
Do you suppose that this same thing holds among the gods too?

HIPPOLYTUS
Yes, if we mortals follow the same laws as the gods.

SERVANT
Why then don't you address a proud goddess?

HIPPOLYTUS
Whom? Be careful that your tongue doesn't slip in some way.   100

SERVANT
This one, who stands near your gates.

---

86 *without seeing your face*: Hippolytus' close relationship to Artemis has limits—he
never sees her; see below, 1391-2.

88-120 The servant serves a large function in a small scene—a foil for both Hippolytus' rash actions as well as Aphrodite's. The dialogue, highlighted by the rapid
exchange of single lines (*stichomythia*) is finely nuanced, as the servant tries to
steer Hippolytus to a safer course.

93 *proud*: The word *semnos*, appearing 4x in this dialogue, covers both negative ("arrogant," "proud") and positive ("august," "revered") senses. Its multivalence allows
the servant to suggest subtly that Hippolytus' "proud" behavior might offend a
"proud" goddess.

HIPPOLYTUS
Since I am pure, I greet this one from afar.

SERVANT
And yet she is proud and renowned among mortals.   103

HIPPOLYTUS
I like none of the gods who are worshipped at night.   106

SERVANT
One must, child, engage in the honors due the gods.   107

HIPPOLYTUS
Among both gods and mortals one cares for one, another for another. 104

SERVANT
May you be fortunate, having all the sense you need.   105

HIPPOLYTUS
Go, attendants, enter the house
and take care of the meal; after hunting a full table
is a pleasurable thing. And we must curry   110
the horses, so that, after I have sated myself with food,
I may yoke them to the chariot and give them their proper
exercise. But to that Cypris of yours I say good riddance.°

Hippolytus and his attendants exit into the palace.

SERVANT
The young when they think that way°
should not be imitated. But I, as is fitting for slaves to speak,   115
will pray to your statue,
mistress Cypris; and you should be forgiving.
If someone because of his youth has an intense spirit
and speaks rashly about you, pretend not to hear him;
for gods ought to be wiser than mortals.°   120

The servant exits into the palace.
The chorus, fifteen women of Trozen, enter from one of the eisodoi, *likely the same one used by Hippolytus and his attendants.°*

---

113 *of yours . . . I say good riddance*: Both phrases suggest Hippolytus' contempt. The latter is weaker than "go to hell" but probably stronger than the now somewhat quaint "good riddance."

114 Like Pentheus in the *Bacchae*, Hippolytus is characterized by his youth. See, e.g., Aphrodite's description at 43.

120 The gods, suggests the servant, should be wiser than mortals. This pithy axiom lingers in counterpoint to the play's actions.

121ff. Women of Trozen constitute the chorus. By virtue of their sex, they will be sympathetic to Phaedra. In their opening song, commonly called the *parodos*, they express their concern for and ignorance about Phaedra's condition. After the religious discourse of the prologue, their opening domestic scene stands in sharp

CHORUS

STROPHE A

There is a rock which, they say, drips water from Oceanus,°
and it pours forth from its cliffs
a flowing stream, where pitchers are dipped.
There a friend of mine   125
was soaking purple
robes in the stream's water
and laying them down on the back of a hot,
sun-struck rock; it was from there
that word of my mistress first came to me: 130

ANTISTROPHE A

that she wastes away in bed with a sickness,° and keeps herself within
the house, and delicate robes
shadow her blonde head.
And I hear that today is the third   135
day that she has kept
her body pure of Demeter's grain°
by starvation,
wishing to run ashore on the wretched boundary
of death because of a secret trouble.   140

STROPHE B

Are you frenzied, girl,°
possessed by Pan or Hecate,
or the holy Corybantes
or the mountain mother?
Or are you wasting away   145
because of offenses against Dictynna° of many animals,
because you neglected to make ritual offerings?

---

contrast—something both mundane and particularly female. Formally the song has
two strophic pairs (strophe and antistrophe) and a concluding stanza (epode).

121 *Oceanus*: The fresh-water river that the Greeks believed circled the (flat) earth.

131 *sickness*: Throughout the play, Phaedra's passion for Hippolytus and her response
to it are described as a sickness.

137 *Demeter's grain*: Demeter was the Greeks' goddess of grain.

141-4 The chorus speculate that Phaedra's illness might be caused by divine possession, either of *Pan*, god of the woods, or *Hecate*, chthonic goddess, associated with
childbirth, or the *Corybantes*, male attendants of Cybele, who was one manifestation
of the *mountain mother*, imported from Anatolia.

146 *Dictynna*: a Cretan goddess identified with Artemis, at least in her role of "mistress
of wild things."

For she roams also through the Mere°
and over the sandbar
in the wet whirlpools of the brine.   150

ANTISTROPHE B

Or does someone in the house
tend to your husband,
the noble-born leader of the Erechtheids,°
with a union hidden from your marriage bed?°
Or has a seafarer sailed   155
from Crete° into the harbor
that is most welcoming to sailors,
with a message for the queen,
and she is bound to her bed
in grief over her troubles?   160

EPODE

A bad, wretched helplessness
from labor pangs and mindlessness
is wont to dwell
with women's difficult temperament.
Once this breeze rushed through
my womb; I called to the heavenly   165
helper of labor, ruler of arrows,
Artemis,° and, with the gods' blessing,
she always comes, making me envied.

The Nurse enters from the palace with Phaedra on a couch or bed carried by attendants.

CHORUS LEADER
  Look, the old nurse brings her here,°   170

---

148 *Mere*: most likely the precinct of Artemis Saronia (the Saronic Gulf was the body
   of water closest to Trozen) where the goddess had a shrine.
153 *Erechtheids*: Athenians, descended from their legendary ruler Erechtheus.
154 *union hidden from your marriage bed*: Theseus had a deserved reputation as a phi-
   landerer.
157 *from Crete*: Phaedra was a native of Crete, the site of many unhappy passions. See
   below on 337.
168 *Artemis*: Patron of wild things, the hunt, and chastity, Artemis was also a goddess
   of childbirth.
170ff Phaedra arrives on stage from the palace on a couch carried by attendants, along
   with her Nurse. The object of the chorus' concern is now before their (and the
   audience's) eyes, but the revelation they seek proceeds on a circuitous course. This
   long scene (170-524) is broken up by changes in meter and structure (sustained
   speeches and rapid dialogue). The Nurse offers a conventional pragmatism,
   expressed with many platitudes, to contrast with Phaedra's high moral posture.
   Here she mixes complaints about her plight (caring for her mistress) with general

outside the house before the doors.
A hateful cloud grows upon her brows.
My soul desires to learn what in the world it is—
why the queen's complexion
has changed color.   175

NURSE

O the ills and hateful diseases of mortals!
What am I to do for you, what not to do?
Here is your daylight, here's your bright air.
Now the bed where you lie sick
is outside the house.   180
Your every word was to come here,
but soon you'll rush back into the house.
You're quickly frustrated and delight in nothing;
what's at hand doesn't please you, but whatever's absent
you think dearer.   185
It's better to be sick than to care for the sick:
the one is simple, but the other brings
both mental anguish and toil for the hands.
All life is painful for mortals
and there is no cease from toils.   190
　　But whatever else is dearer than life,
darkness surrounds and hides it with clouds.
Indeed we clearly are madly in love
with this, whatever this is that shines on earth—
because of inexperience of another life   195
and the lack of revelation of the things beneath the earth;
we are carried along vainly by tales.

PHAEDRA

Lift up my body, hold my head upright!°
My limbs are weak.
Seize my beautiful arms, attendants!   200
This headdress on my head is heavy.
Take it off,° spread out my locks on my shoulders!

---

reflections on the woes of humankind.
198ff Phaedra's excited lyrical expressions are confusing to the Nurse's literal-minded-
　　ness. The contrast between the two is achieved in part through different rhythms.
　　The Nurse speaks in "regular" anapests, as she has in the first part of this scene, while
　　Phaedra's three central outbursts (208-11, 215-22, and 228-32) are anapests, but of a
　　more lyrical variety. Very likely they differed in delivery from the Nurse's lines.
202 *Take it off*: Removal of a woman's headdress symbolically suggested the loss of
　　her chastity. Similarly, in letting down her hair, Phaedra might be seen as trans-
　　gressive.

NURSE

Take heart, child, and don't move
your body so impatiently.
You will bear the disease more readily   205
with calm and a noble spirit.
It is necessary for mortals to toil.

PHAEDRA

Ah!
How I wish I could draw a drink
of pure water from a fresh spring,
and lie down beneath poplars   210
in a grassy meadow and take my rest!

NURSE

Child, what are you crying aloud?
Don't say these things before a crowd,
hurling words mounted on madness.

PHAEDRA

Take me to the mountains! I will go to the woods°   215
and to the pine trees, where the beast-slaying
dogs run on the heels of dappled deer.
Please, by the gods! I desire to shout to dogs,
hold a pointed weapon in my hand
and hurl a Thessalian spear   220
past my yellow hair.

NURSE

Why in the world, child, are you so distressed at heart?
Why do *you* care about hunting?
Why do you desire flowing spring water?   225
There's a hillside with water here, near
the city walls, where you could have a drink.

PHAEDRA

Artemis, mistress of the sea's Mere
and the hippodrome which resounds with hoof beats,
I wish that I could be on your plain   230
breaking in Enetic foals!°

NURSE

What now is this word you have hurled, out of your mind?
In your desire for the hunt, you set out just now

215ff All the activities which Phaedra describes are associated with Hippolytus.
231 *Enetic*: The Enetoi, inhabitants of the area north of the Adriatic Sea, were famed
    for their horses.

to go to the mountains, but now you desire
foals on the waveless sands.   235
These things need much divination
to tell what god is pulling on your reins
and knocking you out of your wits, child.

PHAEDRA
Wretched me, what in the world have I done?
Where have I wandered from good thinking?   240
I was mad, I fell because of ruin from a divinity.°
Ah, ah, miserable one!
Dear Nurse, cover my head again;
I am ashamed° of what I have said.
Cover me. Tears come from my eyes,   245
and my look is turned to shame.°
To have one's thinking made straight is painful,
but madness is an evil. To die
without awareness is best.

NURSE
I'm covering you; but when will death   250
conceal *my* body?
A long life has taught me many things:
mortals should engage with one another
in moderate friendships
and not to the inmost marrow of the soul,   255
and the mind's affections should be able to be easily loosed—
easy to push aside and to draw tight.
But for one person to labor over two,
as *I* feel pain for this one,
is a difficult burden.   260
They say that exacting conduct in life
brings about more falls than delight
and is at war more with health.
So I praise excessiveness less than

---

241 *I was mad... ruin from a divinity*. Inexplicable behavior was commonly described
    as madness and ascribed to the gods. Passion was also frequently described as
    madness. The ruin (*ate*) that comes from the god does not excuse the human's
    responsibility for her/his actions.
243-4 *Cover my head...I am ashamed*: Aware that she has uttered a lyrical and cryptic
    expression of her desire for Hippolytus, Phaedra seeks to be covered up—a return
    to a "chaste" state. Note also that Phaedra expresses her shame even at what she
    has said. This scene may well echo one from an earlier play, in which it seems that
    Hippolytus veiled his head in response to Phaedra's sexual overtures.
246 Probably a reference to blushing.

"nothing in excess;"°   265
and the wise will agree with me.

Chorus Leader
Old woman, trusted nurse of the queen,°
We see here Phaedra's wretched fortunes,
but it is unclear to us what her sickness is.
We would like to learn and hear about it from you.   270

Nurse
I don't know, despite my questions; she doesn't wish to tell.

Chorus Leader
Nor what the source of these pains is?

Nurse
You've come to the same point; she's silent about all these things.

Chorus Leader
How weak she is and how her body is wasted away!

Nurse
Of course, when it's been three days since she has eaten.   275

Chorus Leader
Because of some madness or trying to die?

Nurse
To die, you ask? This fasting *will* end her life.

Chorus Leader
What you say is remarkable, if her husband accepts this.

Nurse
She hides her pain and denies that she is sick.

Chorus Leader
But can't he tell by looking at her face?   280

Nurse
No, he's actually abroad, away from this land.°

Chorus Leader
But aren't *you* using force in trying
to learn about her sickness and the wandering of her wits?

Nurse
I've gone to all lengths and still have accomplished nothing.

---

265 *"nothing in excess"*: This maxim, associated with Apollo's oracle at Delphi, was a
commonplace of Greek life.

267 The scene now returns to the standard spoken meter of tragedy, iambic trimeter.

281 Theseus is conveniently out of the country. In other versions of the story he
is in Hades. In this play a simple visit to the oracle at Delphi accounts for his
absence.

Even so I will not now give up my zeal,   285
so that *you* may be present and bear witness to
how I am by nature to a mistress in misfortune.
        Come now, dear child, let's both forget
our earlier words. You become more pleasant
in loosening your gloomy brow and path of thought,   290
and where I didn't follow you well before,
I'll give that up and move on to better words.
And if you have a sickness that can't be spoken of,
women are here to help treat the disease.
But if your misfortune can be divulged to men,   295
speak, so that it can be mentioned to doctors.
        So, why are you silent? You shouldn't be silent, child,
but either refute me, if I say something wrong,
or agree with my good advice.
Say something. Look over here. Poor me!   300
Women, we labor at these toils in vain,
and we're no closer than before. For then she was not
softened by words and she is not persuaded now.
But know *this*—and then be more stubborn
than the sea°—if you die, you will betray your°   305
children, who won't have a share of their father's house.
No, by the Amazon, mistress of horses,
who gave birth to a master for your children,
a bastard who thinks he's legitimate, you know him well,
Hippolytus . . .

PHAEDRA
                Oh no!°

NURSE
                        Does this touch you?   310

PHAEDRA
    You've destroyed me, dear nurse, and by the gods
    I beg you to be silent from now on about this man.

NURSE
    You see? You have your wits, but even though you do,

304-5 The sea's stubbornness was proverbial.
305-6 The Nurse wisely appeals to Phaedra through her children. Their ability to suc-
        ceed in life is prime motivation for Phaedra's actions; see 421-5.
310 *Oh no*: Silent for more than sixty lines, Phaedra finally breaks her silence at the
        mention of Hippolytus. Two changes of speakers in a single line of iambic verse
        were extremely rare, thus underscoring the effect of this moment of recognition
        and revelation.

you don't wish to help your children and save your life.

PHAEDRA
I love my children; I am storm-tossed by another fortune.   315

NURSE
Are your hands pure of blood, child?

PHAEDRA
My hands are pure, but my mind is polluted.°

NURSE
This isn't some harm conjured by an enemy, is it?

PHAEDRA
No, a dear one unwillingly destroys me unwilling.°

NURSE
Theseus—has he wronged you?   320

PHAEDRA
May *I* not be seen doing him harm.°

NURSE
So what is this terrible thing that incites you to die?

PHAEDRA
Let me err; for I'm not erring against you.

NURSE
I will *not*, not willingly, but my failure will lie with you.

PHAEDRA
What are you doing? Are you using force, hanging upon my hand?°   325

NURSE
Yes, and your knees, and I will never let go.

PHAEDRA
Bad, bad these things will be for you, wretched one, if you learn them.

NURSE
Why, what could be worse for me than not to succeed with you?

---

317 This statement is remarkable in its attention to inward purity. Purity was typically
a matter of outward states, while mental purity was a concept slow to develop in
ancient Greece.

319 *unwillingly*: At this point Phaedra does not fault Hippolytus. This will change after
she hears his denunciation of women and attack on her later in the play.

321 For this focus on appearances (*not be seen*) in ethical statements, see on 403-4.

325 At this juncture, the Nurse takes Phaedra's hand and knees in a gesture of ritual
supplication. This act brought a socio-religious compulsion on the supplicated to
comply with the request. As is evident in this scene, maintaining physical contact
with the supplicated was essential. The Nurse's desperation is seen in her taking
this extreme act.

PHAEDRA
You will die. The deed, however, brings me honor.

NURSE
And then you hide it, although I'm supplicating for your good?   330

PHAEDRA
Yes; I'm trying to devise good from what's disgraceful.

NURSE
Won't you then appear more honorable if you speak?

PHAEDRA
Go away, please by the gods, and let go of my right hand!

NURSE
No, since you're not giving me the gift you ought.

PHAEDRA
I will give it, for I respect your supplication.   335

NURSE
I'll be silent now. From here the word is yours.

PHAEDRA
O wretched mother,° what a passion you had!

NURSE
The one she had for the bull, child? Or what is this you're saying?

PHAEDRA
And you, my poor sister, wife of Dionysus!

NURSE
Child, what's wrong? Are you reviling your kin?   340

PHAEDRA
And I the third unfortunate one, how I'm dying!

NURSE
I'm alarmed. Where will this story end up?

PHAEDRA
From there, not recently, comes my misfortune.

NURSE
I'm no closer to knowing what I want to hear.

PHAEDRA
Ah! If only you could say for me what I must say!   345

---

337 *Wretched mother*: Phaedra refers to her mother, Pasiphaë, who was struck with passion for a bull. At 339 she refers to her sister Ariadne, whose love affair with Dionysus ended (in some accounts) unhappily. Phaedra puts herself in the context of her family of unhappy Cretan women. In this play, unlike in an earlier version, Phaedra is determined *not* to fulfill her family's pattern of disastrous passion.

NURSE

I am not a prophet who can know what's unclear surely.

PHAEDRA

What is this thing which they call people being in love?

NURSE

Something most pleasant, child, and painful at the same time.

PHAEDRA

My experience would be the second one.

NURSE

What are you saying? You're in love, child? With what man?   350

PHAEDRA

Whoever this one is, the Amazon's . . .

NURSE

You mean Hippolytus?

PHAEDRA

                                        You hear this from yourself, not me.°

NURSE

Oh no! What are you saying, child? How you've destroyed me!
Women, this is unendurable, I will not endure
living. I look upon a hateful day, a hateful light.   355
I will hurl my body, throw it down, I will die
and be free of life. Farewell, I am no more.
For those who are virtuous desire what's bad,
against their will but still they do. Cypris then is no god°
but whatever else is greater than god,   360
who has destroyed Phaedra here, and me and the house.

CHORUS LEADER

Did you note—ah!—did you hear—ah!—
the wretched sufferings,°
not to be heard, which the queen cried aloud?
May *I* die, dear one, before I arrive
at your state of mind! Oh no! Ah, ah!   365
Oh woman wretched because of these griefs!
Oh the pains that hold mortals!
You're ruined, you've brought to light what's evil.
What awaits you this whole day?
Something bad for the house will be accomplished.   370

---

352 Phaedra never brings herself to say his name in this scene.
359-60 Here, and elsewhere in this play (see, e.g., 447ff. and 1268ff.), Aphrodite is
   described as a force of nature as much as a god.
362-72 This brief lyric section (matched metrically at 669-79) divides this long scene
   into smaller units.

It is no longer unclear where the fortune sent from Cypris
ends, o wretched child from Crete.

PHAEDRA

Women of Trozen, you who dwell°
in this farthest forecourt° of Pelops' land,
already at other times during night's long expanse   375
I have thought in general about the ruin of mortals' lives.
And they seem to me to do worse
not because of their natural judgment; for many are capable
of sensible thinking. No, we must look at it like this:°
we know what's good and recognize it,   380
but we don't toil to accomplish it, some through laziness,
others because they prefer some pleasure
other than the good. There are many pleasures in life,
long conversations and leisure—a delightful evil—
and respect;° and there are two kinds,° one not bad,   385
the other a burden on the house. If what is appropriate
were clear, there would not be two with the same letters.°
Since then this is in fact what I think,°
there is no drug by which I was going to weaken
and fall into the opposite thinking.   390

373-430 In this long speech (her longest in the play), Phaedra explains the course of
   her actions and the principles by which she has decided to take her life. While
   many scholars have viewed this as Phaedra's articulation of her moral failing,
   more recent interpretations see in this speech Phaedra's expression of her high
   moral standards—and, implicitly, her stark contrast with her counterpart in the
   earlier play.
374 *forecourt*: From her (normally) Athenian perspective, Phaedra imagines Trozen as
   the "forecourt" of the Peloponnese, across the Saronic Gulf.
379-81 Socrates, a contemporary of Euripides, asserted that no one willingly errs (the
   so-called Socratic paradox). Phaedra argues that in fact we often do know what
   is right, but fail to accomplish it for one reason or another. It is uncertain to what
   degree Euripides is responding directly to Socrates' argument, but at the very
   least the play is engaging with contemporary intellectual debates.
385 *respect*: *Aidos* may seem to sit oddly at the end of this list of pleasures, but from
   Phaedra's perspective it is what helps her to protect her good name.
385-6 *two kinds*: This phrase constitutes a major interpretative crux: are pleasure or
   respect of two kinds? The Greek does not allow for a definitive answer, but it is
   likely that the phrase refers to pleasures. At the same time, it is important to note
   that by its emphatic placement and thematic importance, respect stands out among
   these pleasures that can be both good and bad.
387 Either there would be one more word or one less thing. The statement reflects
   contemporary interest in the correctness of names.
388-90 These lines make clear that Phaedra's general thinking (see 376) applies to her
   own situation.

I will tell you my path of thought also.
When passion wounded me, I started to consider how
I might best bear it. So I began with this,
to keep quiet about this disease and conceal it;
for nothing can be trusted to the tongue, which knows how   395
to admonish the thoughts of others,
but itself comes to possess the most evils by its own doing.°
Secondly, I took care to bear the folly well,
trying to subdue it with moderation.
And third, when I couldn't manage   400
to master Cypris in these ways, it seemed to me good to die,
the best plan (no one will deny it). °
For may I neither be unnoticed when I do good things,
nor have many witnesses when I do disgraceful ones.°
I knew that the deed and the sickness brought a bad name,   405
and in addition to this I knew well that I was a woman,
an object of hatred to all. May she perish most wretchedly
whoever first began to disgrace her bed
with other men! It was from noble households
that this evil began among women.   410
For whenever what's disgraceful seems fine to the noble,
it will seem very much so to the base.
I also hate women who are chaste in reputation
but secretly have engaged in bad, reckless acts.
How in the world, Cypris, mistress from the sea,   415
can they look their spouses in the eye
and not shudder because the darkness, their accomplice,
and the timbers of the house might at some time speak.
This is the very thing that is killing me, dear ladies,
that I never be convicted of disgracing my husband   420
nor the children I gave birth to. No, may they flourish°

395-7 This sentiment is shown to be painfully true in the following scene.
401-2 That dying was better than living poorly was a commonly expressed Greek
    sentiment.
403-4 Ancient Greece was what is frequently called a "shame culture," one in which
    excellence and its opposite were measured by external standards and one's worth
    was not easily distinguished from one's reputation. Phaedra is *not* suggesting here
    (or at 420-1) that she would tolerate her own improper behavior provided that
    she was not apprehended. (Note her strong condemnation of hypocrisy at 413-4.)
    Rather she uses these phrases to express her repugnance at such behavior.
421-5 Phaedra is deeply concerned with her children's reputation as well. See 717 and
    above on 305-6.

and dwell in the famous city of Athens as free men
with free speech,° with a good reputation in regard to their mother.
For this enslaves a man, even one who is boldhearted,
whenever he is aware of his mother's or father's wrong doings.   425
This alone, they say, contends with life—
having a just and good mind.
But time reveals the base among mortals, whenever it happens to,°
placing a mirror before them, as before a young maiden;
may I never be seen in company with these.   430

CHORUS LEADER

Ah! Ah! Everywhere moderation is a fine thing
and harvests a good reputation among mortals!

NURSE

Lady, your situation just now scared me terribly for a moment.°
But now I realize that I was foolish; and among mortals   435
second thoughts are somehow wiser.
For what you've experienced is nothing extraordinary
or unaccountable: the goddess's anger struck against you.
You're in love along with many mortals (what's remarkable
    about that?);
will you then destroy your life on account of passion?   440
Surely there is no advantage to those who desire others,
and those who are going to do so, if they must die. For Cypris,
when she flows greatly, is something that cannot be borne;
she goes gently after the one who yields, but whomever
she finds thinking extravagant and proud thoughts,   445
she takes him and you can't imagine how badly
she treats him. Cypris goes through the air
and is in the swell of the sea, everything is born from her;
she is the one who sows and gives desire,
from which all of us who live upon the earth are born.   450
    Now those who know the writings of the ancients
and themselves are constantly engaged in poetry

---

422 *free speech*: one of the most cherished of Athenian rights.
428-30 The speech's concluding image is provocative, evoking themes of both sexuality (the maiden's concern with her physical appearance) and revelation, which lie at the heart of this speech.
433-81 The Nurse has recovered and offers a rebuttal of Phaedra's view. She emphasizes what she views as common sense and yielding to the forces of nature. Conveniently for her argument, she focuses on passion in general and not the particulars of Phaedra's situation—union with her stepson.

know how Zeus once desired a union°
with Semele, and they know how beautiful-shining Eos
once snatched Cephalus up into the company of the gods   455
because of desire; but still they dwell in heaven
and do not flee out of the way of the gods, but they put up,
I think, with being conquered by misfortune. And *you*
will not bear it? Your father then ought to have begotten you
on special conditions or under the rule of other gods,   460
if you will not put up with these laws.

    How many indeed of those who are very sensible do you think,
when they see their marriage bed is sick, pretend not to?
And how many fathers help their errant sons to bear°
their passion? For this is held as one of the wise principles   465
of mortals: what isn't good goes unnoticed.
Surely, mortals should not try too hard to perfect their lives;
and you wouldn't make too precise the roof which covers
a house. Since you've fallen into as much misfortune
as you have, how do you think you could swim out of it?   470
But if, being human, you have °
more good than bad, you'd be very well off.

    Come on, dear child, stop your poor thinking and stop acting
outrageously—for this is nothing other than outrage
wishing to be mightier than the gods—   475
and endure your passion; a god has willed this.
And even though you are sick, bring an end to your sickness in some
    good way.
There are incantations and bewitching words;°
some drug for this sickness will appear.
Certainly men would be late in discovering contrivances,   480
if we women are not going to discover them.

453ff In support of her position, the Nurse uses two examples from well-known myths
    to make an *a fortiori* argument: the gods suffer from passion and endure, so too
    should mortals. In the first case, Zeus' union with Semele led to the latter's incendi-
    ary destruction when Semele asked her unidentified lover to appear to her in his
    full glory, the thunderbolt, as it turned out. In the example of Eos' mortal lover
    Cephalus, the latter's abandonment and decrepit aging (he received immortality
    but not eternal youth) are fundamental to the tale. The Nurse omits any reference
    to these unpleasant aspects of the stories.

464-5 The example of fathers helping their sons with their illicit romances stands in
    ironic and tragic counterpoint to the events of the play.

471-2 This maxim, with its pessimistic view of human happiness, was commonly
    expressed in Greek literature.

478-9 The words are ambiguous—incantations and drugs either to drive away her
    passion or induce passion in the virgin Hippolytus.

CHORUS LEADER
Phaedra, she speaks more helpfully
for the present circumstances, but it's you I praise.
This praise, however, is harder to handle than
her words and more painful for you to hear.   485

PHAEDRA
This is what destroys well-governed cities°
and the homes of mortals—overly fine words;°
for one shouldn't speak what's pleasant to the ear
but what will give good repute.

NURSE
Why this lofty speech? It's not refined words   490
you need but the man. As quickly as possible we must
    understand things clearly,
speaking out about you frankly.
For if your life were not in such circumstances
and you were in fact a chaste woman, I would never
for the sake of your sexual pleasure be leading you on   495
to this point; but, as it is, the contest is a great one—
to save your life, and this shouldn't be begrudged.

PHAEDRA
You've spoken terrible things; won't you shut your mouth
and not utter such disgraceful words again?

NURSE
Disgraceful, but these are better for you than fine ones;   500
and the deed is better, if it will save you,
than the name, in which you will exult and die.

PHAEDRA
Ah! Don't, by the gods—for you speak well but disgracefully—
go beyond this, since my soul is well tilled by passion,
and if you speak finely about what's disgraceful   505
I will be consumed by what I'm now fleeing.

486-524 In the concluding section of this long scene, the Nurse persuades Phaedra to
    let her act on her mistress' behalf. The contrast presented in the two positions
    defined in their two speeches is now seen in the thrust and parry of dialogue. The
    Nurse persuades Phaedra through highly ambiguous speech. Throughout this
    exchange there is a deliberate lack of clarity as to what the Nurse is planning to
    do. Phaedra expressly forbids the Nurse to talk to Hippolytus (520) but is weary
    and weakened enough (note 504-6) to allow the Nurse to act in some way on
    her behalf. The playwright is thus able to suggest that Phaedra is no party to the
    Nurse's scheming while creating suspense as to what will happen next.
486-7 This condemnation of rhetoric is found frequently in contemporary literature, a
    response to the increasingly important role it played in Athenian life.

NURSE

Fine, if this seems best to you . . . you ought not to be erring,
but if in fact you are, obey me; the favor is second best.
I have in the house love-charms that are enchantments
for passion, and it just occurred to me   510
that they will stop you from this disease
without disgrace and without harming your mind, if you don't
 become cowardly.
But we need to get some token of that one who's desired,
either a lock of hair or something from his garments,
and join together one delight from two.   515

PHAEDRA

Is this remedy something applied or drunk?

NURSE

I don't know. Wish to profit, child, not to learn.

PHAEDRA

I'm afraid that you'll appear too clever for me.

NURSE

Know that you'd fear everything. What *do* you fear?

PHAEDRA

Please don't mention any of this to Theseus' offspring.   520

NURSE

Let it be, child. I'll arrange these things well.
Only may you, mistress from the sea, Cypris,°
be my accomplice. The other things I have in mind
it will suffice to tell friends within.

The Nurse exits into the palace.

CHORUS

STROPHE A

Eros, Eros, you who drip desire°   525

522-4 Most likely Phaedra (the character, not the actor playing her) did not hear the
 Nurse's closing words. One of the conventions of the fifth-century stage allowed
 one character to break off contact with another without the second character hearing the first's following words. Here the Nurse has stopped speaking to Phaedra
 and addresses Aphrodite's statue.
525-64 The first *stasimon*. As the Nurse is inside propositioning (as it turns out) Hippolytus and before we learn of these actions, the chorus sing of Eros' power, while
 Phaedra is by the palace door. This song has a common structure: two stanzas
 on a general theme (the destructive power of Eros) followed by two with specific
 examples of this principle (Zeus and Semele and Heracles and Iole). The Trozenian women focus on the destructive power of passion, or, more particularly,
 illicit passion.

down into the eyes° as you lead sweet delight
into the souls of those you war against,
never may you appear to me with harm
or come out of measure.
For the shaft neither of fire nor of the stars is superior   530
to Aphrodite's, which Eros, the son of Zeus,
sends forth from his hands.

ANTISTROPHE A

In vain, in vain along the Alpheus°   535
and in the Pythian home of Phoebus°
the <land> of Hellas slaughters more and more oxen,
but Eros, the tyrant of men,
the holder of the keys to Aphrodite's
dearest inner chambers, we do not venerate,   540
although he destroys mortals and sends them through every
misfortune whenever he comes.

STROPHE B

The filly in Oechalia,°   545
unyoked in marriage,
with no man and no wedding before, Cypris
yoked her away from Eurytus' house,
like a running Naiad or a Bacchant,
with blood, with smoke,   550
in a bloody wedding,
and gave her away in marriage to Alcmene's son. Oh
wretched in your wedding!

525-34 The opening of this song echoes the form of cult hymns; for the language, see
    above on 61-71. *Eros*: The son of Aphrodite and (depending on the myth) various
    fathers, Eros is here depicted as a warrior. His arrow was a common attribute; the
    military images are more fully developed here. Frequently, there is little functional
    difference between Eros and Aphrodite, as here the first half of the song sings
    about the power of Eros, while the second half refers to Aphrodite.
526 *down into the eyes*: the eyes were imagined as both the site of erotic desire and the
    source of infatuation.
535 *Alpheus*: major river that flowed through Olympia, the site of the Olympic games
    and one of Zeus' main shrines.
536 *Phoebus*: the god Apollo, who had a prominent shrine in Delphi (in central Greece),
    which could be referred to with the adjective Pythian.
545-54 Heracles was infatuated with Iole, daughter of Eurytus, king of Oechalia. When
    Eurytus refused to give his daughter in marriage to Heracles after he had won an
    archery contest with her as prize, Heracles destroyed his city.

ANTISTROPHE B

Holy wall°   555
of Thebes and mouth of Dirce,°
you could confirm how Cypris is when she comes.
Giving the mother of twice-born Bacchus
in marriage
to a flaming thunderbolt,   560
she brought her to sleep in a bloody doom.
For she is terrible, and blows on all there is, and like
a bee she flits.

Phaedra is standing near the palace door.

PHAEDRA
Silence, women! We are destroyed.°   565
CHORUS LEADER
What in the house terrifies you, Phaedra?
PHAEDRA
Hold on. Let me learn fully what those within are saying.
CHORUS LEADER
I'm silent. But this is an inauspicious prelude.
PHAEDRA
Woe is me!
Ah! Wretched because of my sufferings.   570
CHORUS LEADER
What speech are you crying aloud,
what words are you shouting?
Tell me what report rushes over your mind
and scares you, lady.
PHAEDRA
We're ruined. Stand by these gates   575
and hear the clamor that falls within the house.
CHORUS LEADER
You're by the door, it's your job to convey
the talk within the house.
Tell me, tell me, *what* is the trouble that has come?   580
PHAEDRA
The child of the horse-loving Amazon, Hippolytus,

555-64 For the story of Semele, native of Thebes, and Zeus, see above on 453ff.
556 *Dirce*: a famous Theban spring.
565-600 In this exchange, Phaedra speaks almost exclusively in "calm" iambic rhythms,
    while the chorus express their anxiety and excitement in lyrics.

cries aloud, reviling my attendant terribly.

CHORUS LEADER

I hear a voice, but I have nothing clear.   585
Shout out what sort of cry has come,
come through the gates to you.

PHAEDRA

Look, now he clearly declares her "matchmaker of evils,"
"betrayer of your master's bed."   590

CHORUS LEADER

Woe is me for these ills!
You are betrayed, my dear.
What can I devise for you?
For what was hidden has been revealed. You're ruined—
ah!, woe, woe!—betrayed by friends.   595

PHAEDRA

By speaking of my misfortunes she destroyed me,
trying to cure this disease, as a friend but improperly.

CHORUS LEADER

What now? What will you do, you who have suffered
what can't be remedied?

PHAEDRA

I don't know, except one thing—to die as quickly as possible;
this is the only cure for my present miseries.   600

Phaedra withdraws from the palace door, but does not exit.
Hippolytus enters from the palace, followed by the Nurse.

HIPPOLYTUS

O mother earth, and the sun-filled sky,
what unspeakable words I heard uttered!

NURSE

Be quiet, child, before someone hears your cry!

HIPPOLYTUS

It's not possible to be silent, when I've heard terrible things.

599-600 It should be noted that at this point Phaedra's plan is still to die (as quickly as possible); vengeance on Hippolytus becomes an issue only after the following scene.

600 *Phaedra . . . does not exit.* The staging of this scene is controversial. Some critics, in order to account for Phaedra's apparent misunderstanding of Hippolytus' intentions, assume that she departs and then returns at the end of the scene. But this would be very much opposed to what we know of fifth-century practice. Most likely, Phaedra remains on stage and effectively serves as the silent, indirect and obvious object of Hippolytus' attack. In the only scene in which these two characters appear on stage together, they do not acknowledge each other's presence.

NURSE
    Yes, I beg you by this fair right arm of yours.°   605
HIPPOLYTUS
    Don't bring your hand near me, don't touch my robes!
NURSE
    Oh, I beg you by your knees, *don't* destroy me!
HIPPOLYTUS
    Why do you say that if, as you say, you've spoken nothing bad?
NURSE
    That conversation, child, was *not* for all.
HIPPOLYTUS
    Surely what's good is better when spoken among many.   610
NURSE
    Child, *don't* dishonor your oath!
HIPPOLYTUS
    My tongue is sworn, my mind unsworn.°
NURSE
    Child, what will you do? Will you destroy your friends?
HIPPOLYTUS
    I spit this out! No one who's unjust is a friend of mine.
NURSE
    Forgive; it is natural for humans to err, child.   615
HIPPOLYTUS
    Zeus, why did you establish women in the sun's light
    as counterfeit, an evil for human beings?
    If you wanted to propagate the human race,°
    you should not have provided this from women,
    but mortals ought to place bronze or iron   620
    or a weight of gold in your temples
    and buy offspring in exchange for a set value,
    each one for its price,

---

605 The Nurse attempts (unsuccessfully) to supplicate Hippolytus, as she had (successfully) supplicated Phaedra; see above on 325.

612 A line parodied several times by the comic playwright and Euripidean contemporary Aristophanes. It is also not Hippolytus' considered opinion, as he makes clear later in this scene (656ff.), but it expresses his disgust and outrage at the Nurse's proposal.

618-24 This bizarre wish reflects both contemporary misogyny and is paralleled elsewhere in Euripides. For all its extremity, this wish is in keeping with Hippolytus' extraordinary rejection of sex and marriage, and, it should be remembered, is the young man's initial response to what he believes to be his stepmother's sexual overture.

and then dwell in their homes free, with no females.
[But, as it is, first of all, when we are about to lead an evil   625
into the house, we pay out the wealth of the house.]
And this is how it's clear that a woman is a great evil: a father
who has begotten and reared her, gives a dowry in addition,
and sends her out of the house so he can be rid of the evil.
    And the man who in turn takes this ruinous creature   630
into his house rejoices when he adds a pretty ornament
to the worst statue, and he toils, wretched one,
to deck her out with robes, while draining the prosperity
of the house. [This has to happen: he marries well and
enjoying his in-laws keeps for himself a bitter marriage bed,   635
or getting a good marriage and harmful in-laws
he suppresses the misfortune with the good.]
It's easiest for the man who has a "nothing;" but a woman
set up foolishly in the house is harmful.
And I hate a clever woman; not in my house may there be   640
one with more thoughts than a woman should have.
For Cypris engenders wickedness more often
in the clever ones; the clueless woman
is deprived of foolish wantonness by her slight intelligence.
A servant should not go indoors to a woman,°   645
but one should set up voiceless savage beasts to dwell
with them, so that they can neither address anyone
nor in turn hear any word from them.
But, as things are, they devise evil plans
within, and servants carry them outside.   650
    So you too, evil one, you came to traffic with me
about my father's undefiled marriage bed.
I will wash these things away with flowing river water,
splashing it against my ears. *How* could I be base,
who feel impure just hearing such things?   655
But know well, woman, my piety saves you:
if I hadn't been caught off guard by taking oaths to the gods,
I would never have kept from declaring this to my father.
But, as things are, I will go away from the house so long as Theseus°
is out of the country, and I will keep my mouth silent.   660
But I'll return when my father does and I will watch
how you look at him, you and that mistress of yours.

645ff. A thinly veiled attack on the Nurse's action.
659-62 The dynamics of the plot require Hippolytus' absence from the next part of the
    drama, just as they were helped by Theseus' absence in the first half.

[I will know that I have tasted your daring.]
May you both perish! I will never have my fill of hating
women, not even if someone says that I'm always saying this.   665
For truly they too are always somehow evil.
Either then let someone teach them to be chaste,
or let *me* always trample on them.

Hippolytus exits down the eisodos *by which he first entered.*

PHAEDRA

Oh wretched, ill-fated°
destinies of women! What device or word do we have,   670
now that we've been tripped up, to loose the knot of words?
We've met with retribution.° Oh earth and light!
Wherever will I escape this fortune?
How, friends, will I hide my pain?
What god could appear as a helper, what mortal   675
as an ally or accomplice in unjust deeds?
For my trouble
goes across the boundary of life—a difficult crossing.
I am the most ill-fated of women.

CHORUS LEADER

Ah, ah, it's all over, and your servant's schemes,   680
lady, have failed; things go badly.

PHAEDRA

O most evil one and destroyer of friends,
what you've done to me! May my ancestor Zeus °
strike you with fire and destroy you by the roots.
Didn't I tell you—didn't I anticipate your mind?—   685
to be silent about the things about which I'm now disgraced?
But you didn't control yourself; so no longer will I die
with a good reputation. Ah, I need new words:°
for this man, his mind whetted by anger,
will denounce me to his father for your errors,   690
will tell aged Pittheus the situation,
and will fill the entire land with the most disgraceful words.

669-79: Phaedra's brief lament matches metrically the chorus leader's lyrics at 362ff.
   At 680, the characters return to regular spoken iambics.
672: *we've met with retribution*: The phrase need not mean that Phaedra imagines she
   is being justly punished, only that she recognizes that she has met with retaliation.
683: *ancestor Zeus*: Phaedra's father, Minos, was son of Zeus and Europa.
688: *new words*: The first hint of her planned response to Hippolytus' denunciation.

May you perish, you and whoever is eager
to give improper help to unwilling friends!

NURSE

Mistress, you can fault what I did wrong,					695
for this biting pain conquers your judgment.
But I too can speak to this, if you'll accept it.
I reared you and am devoted to you; while seeking remedies
for your disease I found not what I wished.
But if I had fared well, indeed I'd be held among the wise.		700
For we get a reputation for intelligence in proportion to our fortune.

PHAEDRA

What?! Is this just and satisfactory for me,
that you wound me and then give way in words?

NURSE

We're talking too much. I wasn't moderate.
But it's possible, child, to be saved even from this.			705

PHAEDRA

Stop talking. You didn't give me good advice
before and what you attempted was evil.
But go, out of the way, and take thought
for yourself; I will arrange my own things well.°

The Nurse exits into the palace.

But you, noble-born children of Trozen,					710
grant me this request at least:
conceal in silence what you have heard here.°

CHORUS LEADER

I swear by proud Artemis, daughter of Zeus,
that I will never reveal any of your ills to light.

PHAEDRA

Well spoken—thank you. I will tell you one thing further:		715
I have a remedy for this misfortune
so that I can hand over a life of fair repute to my children°
and myself profit considering how things have fallen out.
For I will never disgrace my Cretan home,
nor will I come before Theseus' face					720
with disgraceful deeds done, for the sake of one life.

---

709 A strong echo of the Nurse's words at 521 with the addition of *my own*.
712 Because of their constant presence, the chorus' complicity is necessary for plotting on stage.
717-21 Phaedra states her prime motivation—ensuring her children's good name and avoiding disgrace.

CHORUS LEADER

What incurable ill are you about to *do*?

PHAEDRA

To die; but how—this I will plan.

CHORUS LEADER

Speak no words of bad omen.

PHAEDRA

                              And you, give me no bad advice.
In being rid of my life this day, I will delight   725
Cypris, the very one who destroys me.
I will be worsted by a bitter passion.
But in death I will be a bane for the other,°
so that he may learn not to be haughty
at my ills; and by sharing this disease   730
in common with me he will learn to be moderate.°

Phaedra exits into the palace.

CHORUS

STROPHE A

May I be within the hidden recesses of the steep mountain;°
there may a god make me
a winged bird among the flying flocks!
And may I fly high
over the sea waves of the Adrian coast°   735
and the water of the Eridanus,°
where the unhappy girls drip amber-gleaming tears°
into the dark-colored swell   740
in lamentation over Phaethon!

728-31 Immediately before she exits to kill herself, Phaedra enunciates a further motivat-
    ing force—vengeance against Hippolytus for his haughtiness over her. The Greeks
    upheld a code of "help friends/harm enemies," one facet of which was that an
    enemy's gloating over one's misfortunes was intolerable. Just as Hippolytus has
    implicitly rejected Phaedra as a "friend" (see 613-4), so too will Phaedra treat him
    as an enemy, and by this code will seek vengeance against him.

731 An echo of Hippolytus' words at 666.

732-75 Often called an "escape ode," the second *stasimon* expresses the chorus' anxiety
    in response to Phaedra's ominous departure. Structurally its four stanzas fall into
    two halves, the first fanciful and mythological, the second historical and, then,
    immediate.

735 *Adrian coast*: Gulf of Venice

737 *Eridanus*: fabulous river in the far west, later identified with the Po.

738-41 *Phaethon*: The son of Helius, the sun god, he doubted his paternity and asked
    to steer the god's chariot as proof. This trip ended in catastrophe and Phaethon's
    sisters were turned into poplar trees, shedding amber as their tears.

ANTISTROPHE A

May I reach the apple-sown shore
of the Hesperides,° the singers,
where the lord of the sea's dark-colored Mere
no longer provides a path for sailors,   745
but ordains a holy boundary
of heaven, which Atlas holds,°
and the ambrosial springs flow past where Zeus lay,°
where very holy earth, the giver of prosperity,   750
increases blessedness for the gods!

STROPHE B

O white-winged Cretan
ship, you who conveyed my mistress
from her prosperous home
through the roaring sea waves of the deep,   755
a delight that proved most ruinous for the marriage.
For indeed there were evil omens at both ends of her journey—
both when she flew from the land of Crete to glorious Athens
and when they tied the woven rope-ends to the shores of Munichus° 760
and stepped onto the mainland.

ANTISTROPHE B

Because of this her wits were crushed
by a terrible disease   765
of impious passion from Aphrodite.
And foundering under this hard misfortune she will attach°
a suspended noose from the bridal chamber's beams,
fitting it around her white neck,   770
since she feels shame at her hateful fortune,°
and chooses instead a repute of good fame and rids

---

742 *Hesperides*: These were commonly depicted as singers and served as the guardians
    of the garden where the golden apples given to Hera as a wedding gift from her
    grandmother Ge (Earth) were planted.
747 *Atlas* traditionally held up the earth and was connected with the golden apples
    in various stories.
749 *where Zeus lay* (749) seems to refer to his original lovemaking with Hera.
757 The Greeks were very sensitive to omens, especially connected to an important
    event, such as the departure and arrival of Theseus' ship.
760 *Munichus*: the eponymous hero of the older port of Attica, the Munichia.
767ff. Most unusually, the chorus express an almost clairvoyant picture of what the
    audience will soon witness. In general, in Greek myth and literature, women kill
    themselves by hanging and not by the sword.
771-5 These lines provide a concise and powerful summary of Phaedra's major concerns
    presented in the first half of the play.

her mind of its painful passion.   775

NURSE WITHIN

Oh! Oh!°

Everybody around the palace, come and help!

Our mistress, the wife of Theseus, is hanging.

CHORUS LEADER

Ah, ah! It's all over. The queen is no more,

hanging in a suspended noose.

NURSE WITHIN

Won't you hurry? Won't someone bring a two-edged   780

blade so we can loose this knot around her neck?

CHORUS LEADER

Friends, what should we do? Do you think we should enter

the house and free the queen from the tightly drawn noose?

ANOTHER CHORUS MEMBER

What?! Aren't young servants at hand?

Meddling doesn't bring safety in life.   785

NURSE WITHIN

Stretch out the wretched corpse and make it straight;

this was a bitter tending of the home for my master.

CHORUS LEADER

The unhappy woman is dead, from what I hear:

they're already stretching her out as a corpse.

Theseus enters from one of the eisodoi.

THESEUS

Women, do you know what in the world is the servants' shouting

~ ringing deeply~ in the house that has reached me?   790

For the house doesn't see fit to open its doors and give me

a friendly greeting upon my return from the oracle.

It can't be that something bad has happened to old Pittheus,

can it? His life is already advanced, but even so   795

his departure from this house would be painful to me.

CHORUS LEADER

Your misfortune doesn't concern the old,

Theseus; the death of the young pains you.

THESEUS

Oh no! It's not my children's life that is plundered, is it?

776-89 A voice from within (presumably the Nurse's) is heard, proclaiming Phaedra's
    death, while the chorus hesitate to take action. The fact of the queen's death is thus
    established (immediately) before Theseus' return to the palace.

CHORUS LEADER
    They're alive, but their mother is dead, the most painful
        thing possible for you.   800

THESEUS
    What are you saying? My wife is dead? By what fortune?

CHORUS LEADER
    She fixed a suspended noose to hang herself.

THESEUS
    Chilled by grief or from what misfortune?

CHORUS LEADER
    We know only so much; for I too just arrived at the house,°
    Theseus, to mourn your troubles.   805

THESEUS
    Ah! Why am I wreathed with these plaited leaves°
    on my head, since my visit to the oracle brought me misfortune?
    Open the doors of the gate, servants,
    unloose their fastenings, so I may see the bitter sight
    of my wife, who in dying has destroyed me.°   810

As the chorus sing, the ekkyklema *(stage trolley) is wheeled out with Phaedra's corpse.*

CHORUS
    Oh, oh wretched one because of your miserable ills!°
    You suffered, you did
    so much that you've confounded the house.
    Ah for your reckless daring—
    you died violently and by an unholy misfortune
    in a wrestling match with your own miserable hand!   815
    Who, wretched one, consigns your life to darkness?

THESEUS
    Woe for my pains! I, wretched me, have suffered

804-5 Their vow of complicit silence requires this lie to Theseus.
806-7 Theseus wears a garland of leaves in connection with his visit to the oracle. His tearing it up contrasts with Hippolytus offering a garland to Artemis in the play's opening.
810 In response to Theseus' command, the doors are opened and Phaedra's body revealed. This is accomplished by means of the *ekkyklema*, a wheeled platform that allowed for interior scenes to be made visible to the audience and on-stage characters. Once on stage, Phaedra's corpse serves as the physical object of Theseus' grief and, with the soon-to-be-discovered note, the damning proof (in his father's eyes) of Hippolytus' guilt. It also serves as a potent visual backdrop to the debate between father and son later in this scene.
811-55 Theseus' lamentation and the choral comments are all in lyric meters.

the greatest of my ills. O fortune,
how heavily you've come upon me and the house,
an unperceived stain from some malignant spirit—°
no, you're the destruction that makes my life unlivable!   820
O wretch, I see a sea of ills so great
that I will never swim back out of it
or pass through the wave of this misfortune.
With what word, wife, with which one shall I, wretched me,
correctly address your heavy-fated fortune?
For like a bird you are vanished from my hands,
you rushed from me with a swift leap to Hades.
Ah, ah, miserable, miserable are these sufferings!   830
From somewhere long ago I am recovering
a fortune sent by the divinities because of the faults
of some ancestor.

CHORUS LEADER

Not to you alone have these ills come, lord, but along°
with many others you have lost your cherished wife.   835

THESEUS

Beneath the earth, beneath the earth, I want to die,
move to the gloom there and dwell in darkness,
oh wretched me, since I am bereft of your dearest
companionship. For you destroyed more than you perished.
From where, wretched wife,   840
did this deadly fortune come to your heart?
Could someone say what happened, or is it in vain that
the royal house holds a throng of my servants?
Woe is me, <wretched> because of you,
<woe,> what a pain I have seen for the house,   845
unendurable, unspeakable! Oh, I'm destroyed.
The house is empty, and the children are orphaned.
<Ah, ah!> You left, you left us, o dear
and best of women, of however many
the light of the sun and night's starry-faced   850

---

819 Like many characters in Greek tragedy, Theseus suggests that his misfortune
    comes from an avenging spirit, stirred most likely (see also 831ff. and 1379ff.)
    by an ancestral crime. "The sins of the fathers are visited on the sons." Whereas
    in some dramas, the motif of an avenging spirit is fully developed, in this play
    it appears more as a commonplace to express the incomprehensible and is not
    woven into the play's fabric.
834-5 Statements such as these were the stock phrases of consolation, no more effective
    in Euripides' time than in our own.

brightness look upon.

CHORUS

O wretched Theseus, how much ill this house holds;
my eyes are wet with floods of tears at your fortune.
But I've been shuddering for some time at the calamity to come.   855

THESEUS

Ah, ah!
What is this tablet° hanging°
from her dear hand? Does it wish to declare something new?
What—did the unhappy one write me a letter about our marriage bed
and children, asking for something?
Take heart, wretched one: there is no woman   860
who will come into Theseus' bed and house.
Look, the impression of the dead woman's°
gold-wrought seal here seeks my attention.
Come, let me unwind the strings of the seal
and see what this tablet wishes to say to me.   865

CHORUS LEADER

Ah, ah, a god brings in this further,
new ill in succession. ~In light of what has happened,
what terrible thing could there be to meet with?~
For ruined, no longer living, I say—
ah, ah!—is my masters' house.   870
[O spirit, if it's somehow possible, don't overturn the house,
but listen to my prayer;
for from somewhere I see, like a prophet, a bird of bad omen.]

THESEUS

Oh woe! What an ill upon ill this is, another one,
unendurable, unspeakable! Oh wretched me!   875

856ff. The meter returns to spoken (iambic) rhythm as Theseus discovers the tablet
attached to Phaedra's wrist. When he discovers what the tablet reveals, he breaks
out again in lyric rhythms (874ff.) until the point at which he formally declares
Hippolytus' crime and punishment. The chorus leader also delivers his words in
lyric meters, returning to spoken meter after Theseus does.

856 *tablet*: The note left on the tablet is a convenient plot device, allowing Phaedra to
communicate (falsely) with her husband. Intensity is added to the scene by the
personification of the tablet (see 857, 863 and 877-80) and the irony of what Theseus
imagines it will reveal and what it in fact does.

862-5 Phaedra's tablet was two pieces of wood, coated with wax for inscription and
connected by a hinge. It was wound with string and sealed with wax and the
"signature" of an embossed ring.

CHORUS LEADER
What is it? Tell me, if I may be told at all.

THESEUS
The tablet cries out, cries out insufferable things.
Where can I escape the weight of ills? For I'm gone,
ruined, since I've seen, wretched me, such, such a song
taking voice in writing.   880

CHORUS LEADER
Ah! You are revealing a word that is the leader of ills.

THESEUS
I will no longer keep this destructive,
hard-to-express evil within the gates of my mouth.
O city!
Hippolytus dared to touch my marriage bed   885
by force, showing no honor for the revered eye of Zeus.
Father Poseidon, you once promised me
three curses; with one of these
make an end of my son, and may he not escape this
day, if the curses you gave me are sure.   890

CHORUS LEADER
Lord, by the gods, take this back and undo this prayer;
for you will recognize later that you erred. Listen to me.

THESEUS
Impossible. And in addition I will drive him from this land,
and he will be stricken by one of two fates:
either Poseidon will revere my curses   895
and send him dead into the house of Hades,
or exiled from this country he will wander
over a foreign land and drag out a painful life.

CHORUS LEADER
Look, here your son Hippolytus himself is at hand,
at just the right moment. Relax your evil anger, lord   900
Theseus, and plan what's best for your house.

Hippolytus enters with some attendants by the same eisodos *by which he
departed.*

---

886 Zeus was concerned with upholding justice in general and, among many other
     things, marriage in particular (despite his own infidelities).
887-90 Three curses (or wishes) are a folktale motif, adopted by this myth. Not having
     used one of them before, Theseus is uncertain of their efficacy. So, he immediately
     follows this curse with his own proclamation of exile.

HIPPOLYTUS

   I heard your shout, father, and came°
   quickly. And I still don't know what
   you're groaning over; but I'd like to hear it from you.
   Ah! What's this? Your wife, father, I see that she is   905
   dead. This is most remarkable:
   I just left her; she saw this light not long ago.
   What has happened to her? How did she perish?
   Father, I wish to learn from you.   910
   You're silent. But there is no place for silence in troubles.
   [For the heart desiring to hear everything
   even in troubles is convicted of being greedy.]
   It is not just, father, for you to conceal your misfortunes
   from your *friends* and those even more than friends.   915

THESEUS

   O mankind, so often wrong and useless,
   why do you teach countless skills
   and devise and discover everything,
   but one thing you do not know nor have you yet tracked down—
   to teach good sense to those who have none?°   920

HIPPOLYTUS

   You're talking about a clever man who can compel
   those who don't have good sense to have it.
   But you're being subtle at an inappropriate moment, father,
   and I fear that your speech goes too far because of your troubles.

THESEUS

   Ah, mortals ought to have established a sure sign   925
   of friends and a means of distinguishing their minds,
   to tell who is a true friend and who isn't.
   And all men ought to have two voices,°
   one just, the other how it happened to be,
   so that the one thinking unjust things could be refuted   930
   by the just one; and we would not be deceived.

HIPPOLYTUS

   What?! Has some friend slandered me to you,

902ff. With Hippolytus' arrival, the scene is set for a debate between him and his father. Almost all of Euripides' plays contained such a formalized debate (commonly called an *agon*), reflecting the increasing contemporary interest in rhetoric and the practice of the law courts. The "prosecutor" (Theseus) goes first, the "defendant" (Hippolytus) second, their long speeches punctuated by a bland choral comment and followed by rapid dialogue between them.

920 On learned versus innate qualities, see above n. on 79-80.

and am I afflicted with this sickness, when I am not at all
   responsible?
I'm alarmed: your words go astray,
beyond sense, and alarm me.   935

THESEUS
Ah, mortal mind!—where will it end up?
What limit will there be to its daring and over-boldness?
For if generation after generation
it will expand, and the next one will surpass in wickedness
the one that went before, the gods will have to attach   940
another land to earth to contain
those who are by nature unjust and evil.
Look at this man, who, though born from me,
disgraced my marriage bed and is convicted
clearly by this dead woman of being most evil.   945
   But, since I've already come into pollution, show
your face here, before your father.
You consort with the gods as a superior man?
You are virtuous and pure of evils?
I couldn't be persuaded by your boasts   950
so that I think poorly and attribute ignorance to the gods.
Now pride yourself and through your vegetarian diet°
be a huckster with your food, and with Orpheus as lord
play the bacchant and honor many vaporous writings—
for you're caught. I proclaim to everyone   955
to flee from such men as these; for they hunt you down
with their solemn words, while they devise disgraceful deeds.
   This woman is dead; do you think that this will save you?
In this most of all you're convicted, o you most evil one:
for what sort of oaths, what arguments could be stronger   960
than this woman here, so that you escape the charge?
Will you say that she hated you, and, of course, that °
the bastard is naturally at war with the legitimate offspring?
You're saying that she's a bad merchant of her life,
if she destroyed what's dearest because of her enmity towards you. 965

928ff. Another fanciful wish (see 618ff.), inspired perhaps by ventriloquism.
952ff. It is clear from the opening scene (109-11) that Hippolytus is no vegetarian. This
   and the facile references to Orpheus (legendary character around whom a cult
   arose) and Dionysiac religion ("play the bacchant," a bacchant being a female
   devotee of the god of wine and the sap of life, Dionysus) suggest that Theseus is
   relying merely on the caricature of a "holy man" to attack his son.
962-3 On the theme of illegitimacy in this play, see above n. on 10.

Or will you say that sexual folly is not inherent in men,
but in women? I know that young men
are no less likely to fall than women,
whenever Cypris stirs up a young mind;
and the fact that they're male helps them.   970
      Now then—why do I contend like this with your arguments
when the corpse before us is the surest witness?
Get out of this land as an exile as quickly as possible,
and don't go to god-built Athens
nor the boundaries of the land my spear holds sway over.   975
For if after suffering these things I am to be worsted by you,
Isthmian Sinis° will never bear witness
that I killed him but say that I boast in vain,
and the Scironian rocks° that border on the sea
will deny that I am harsh to the wicked.   980

CHORUS LEADER
I don't know how I could say that any mortal is
fortunate; for what was highest is turned upside down.

HIPPOLYTUS
Father, the fierceness and intensity of your mind are°
terrible; but if someone should unfold this matter,
though it has fine words, it is not fine.   985
I am unaccomplished at giving speeches before a crowd,°
but more skilled before a few of my peers; and this too
is natural: for those who are inadequate in the presence
of the wise are more eloquent at speaking before a crowd.
But nevertheless, since this disaster has come,   990
I must speak. And I will first begin my speech
where you first tried to catch me,
seeking to demolish me without a chance to reply.
You see this light and earth; in these there is no man—

---

977 *Isthmian Sinis*. Sinis, an inhabitant of the Corinthian Isthmus, was one of many
    thugs dispatched by Theseus on his original journey from Trozen to Athens.
979 *Scironian rocks*: The brigand Sciron gave his name to these cliffs (on the Saronic coast
    of the Isthmus) after being killed by Theseus by being hurled from them.
983-1035 Hippolytus, with no physical evidence and unwilling to break his oath, has
    little with which to mount his defense. So he relies on assertions of his virtue and
    arguments from probability—how it was unlikely that he could have done this
    deed. Such arguments do not disprove the "facts" of the case, of course, but were
    popular in contemporary oratory.
986-7 A commonplace of Greek rhetoric, but also a reflection of Hippolytus' narrow
    range of experience. Fifth-century Athens was very much a public community in
    which citizens were expected to play an active part in the life of the city.

even if you should deny it—more virtuous by nature than me.   995
For I know first of all how to revere the gods
and to associate with friends who do not attempt wrong
but who would be ashamed either to give evil commands
to their friends or to repay disgraceful deeds in kind;
I am not someone who laughs at his companions, father,   1000
but the same to friends when they're away as when nearby.
And by one thing I am untouched, the thing by which you
    now think you have me:
to this very moment my body is pure of sex.
I don't know this deed except by hearing of it in stories
and seeing it in pictures; for I am not eager   1005
even to look at these things, since I have a virgin soul.
    Suppose my chastity does not persuade you; let it go.
You *must* show in what way I was corrupted.
Was it that her body was more beautiful
than that of all women? Or did I expect, if I took°   1010
an heiress as wife, that I would dwell as lord in your house?
I was a fool then, no, completely out of my mind.
Or will you say that rule is sweet? For those who are sensible
~not at all, unless~ it has destroyed the mind
of those mortals who like monarchy.   1015
But I would like to be first at victories
in the Hellenic games, but in the city second,
prospering always with the best as friends.
For this has political power, and the absence of danger
gives a delight greater than rule.   1020
    One of my arguments hasn't been spoken, you have the rest:
if I had a witness to my true character and I were being tried
while this woman saw the light, you would have seen
who was base by examining them with the facts. But,
as things stand, by Zeus of oaths and by the plain of earth,   1025
I swear to you that I never touched your marriage,°
never would have wished to, never would have conceived
the idea. Indeed may I then perish with no glory, no name,°
[cityless, homeless, an exile wandering over the land,]

1010-1 Legally (from the perspective of fifth-century law), Hippolytus would have
    no claim on Theseus' rule by virtue of marriage to Phaedra. But in myth (see the
    stories of Jocasta, Penelope, and Clytemnestra), being the husband of a widow
    seems to have offered some claim to the dead king's household.
1026 Hippolytus cannot break his oath to the Nurse, but he can swear his innocence
    to his father.
1028 On the theme of reputation in this play, see above n. on 48.

and may neither sea nor earth receive   1030
my flesh when I'm dead, if I am by nature an evil man.
What it was she feared that she destroyed her life,
I don't know, for it's not right for me to say more.
She who was unable to be virtuous acted virtuously,°
but I who was able to be so did not make good use of it.   1035

CHORUS LEADER

You've spoken an adequate rebuttal of the charge
in offering oaths to the gods, no small pledge.

THESEUS

Isn't this man by nature an enchanter and sorcerer,
who is confident that he will master my spirit
with his easy disposition, after he's dishonored the one
    who begot him?   1040

HIPPOLYTUS

I marvel very much at the same in you too, father;
for if you were my son and I your father,
I would surely have killed you and would not be punishing
    you with exile,
if you had dared to touch my wife.

THESEUS

How like you is what you've said! You will not die   1045
in this way, according to this law you've set up for yourself;
for a quick death is easiest for an unfortunate man.
No, an exile from your fatherland, you will wander°
over a foreign land and drag out a painful life.
[For these are the wages for an impious man.]   1050

HIPPOLYTUS

Oh no! What are you doing? You won't even wait for time
to inform against me, but will drive me from the land?

THESEUS

Yes, beyond Pontus and the territories of Atlas,
if I somehow could, so much do I hate you.

1034-5 These enigmatic lines, illustrating the shifting semantics of the word *sophrosyne*
(*virtue*, more broadly "moderation," on which see above n. on 80), offer a concise
summary of the play's fundamental dichotomy (from Hippolytus' perspective):
Phaedra was not (in general) virtuous, but performed one act that was chaste (her
suicide by which her passions were defeated), while Hippolytus, who generally
was virtuous, could not use this quality to help himself.

1048-9 Throughout this confrontation with his son, Theseus makes no reference to the
curse, only to the exile (see also 973-5). He has no control over the curse—only
the exile.

HIPPOLYTUS

Without examining oath or pledge or the words of prophets,   1055
will you throw me out of the land without a trial?

THESEUS

This tablet, without receiving any mantic lot,
accuses you persuasively; and I say good riddance
to the birds flying overhead.

HIPPOLYTUS

O gods, why then do I not loose my mouth,°   1060
since I am destroyed by you, whom I revere? No, I will not;
I would not in any way persuade those whom I must,
and I would violate in vain the oaths which I swore.

THESEUS

Ah, how your piety will be the death of me!
Get out of your fatherland as quickly as possible.   1065

HIPPOLYTUS

Where then will I turn, wretched me? What guest-friend's
house will I go to, when I've been exiled on such a charge?

THESEUS

Whoever enjoys bringing in as their guests
those who corrupt their wives and who do wrong
while they help to guard their houses.

HIPPOLYTUS

Ah! To the heart; this is near tears,   1070
if I appear evil and seem so to you.°

THESEUS

Then you should have wailed and learned at that time,
when you dared to act outrageously against your father's wife.

HIPPOLYTUS

O house, I wish you could utter a voice for me
and bear witness whether I am by nature an evil man!   1075

THESEUS

Cleverly you flee to voiceless witnesses;

1060-3 Hippolytus entertains briefly the possibility of speaking the truth about Phaedra
and the Nurse but concludes that it would be unsuccessful and violate his oath
as well. Some critics have emphasized that only the presumed ineffectiveness of
violating his oath leads Hippolytus to keep it, but it should also be noted that
when confronted with the reality of exile he does not in fact violate the sanctity
of his oath to the gods.

1071 Appearing evil to his father is painful, but whatever his father may believe, Hippolytus does not doubt his own virtue (see 1100-1).

but the deed, without speaking, reveals that you are evil.

HIPPOLYTUS

Ah!

I wish that I could stand opposite and look at myself,
so that I could cry over how badly I suffer.

THESEUS

Much more have you practiced revering yourself°   1080
than showing piety towards your parent, as a just man should.

HIPPOLYTUS

O wretched mother! O bitter birth!
May none of my friends ever be a bastard!

THESEUS

Take him away, slaves. Haven't you heard me
for some time declaring his exile?   1085

HIPPOLYTUS

Any one of them who touches me will regret it.
But you yourself, if that's your desire, thrust me from the land.

THESEUS

I'll do this, if you don't obey my words;
for no pity for your exile comes upon me.

HIPPOLYTUS

It is fixed, so it seems. Oh wretched me,   1090
since I know these things, but I don't know how to reveal them!
O daughter of Leto, dearest to me of the divinities,°
partner, fellow hunter, I will be exiled
from glorious Athens. So farewell to the city
and land of Erectheus! O plain of Trozen,   1095
you have so much happiness to be young in,
farewell! Looking at you for the last time I address you.
Come, my young companions of this land,
speak to me and escort me from this country,
since you will never see another man   1100
more virtuous, even if this doesn't seem so to my father.

Hippolytus exits down the eisodos *opposite the one by which he entered.*
Theseus exits into the palace, and then the ekkyklema *is wheeled in.*

1080-1 Athenians considered reverence towards one's parents the highest obligation
        in the mortal realm.
1092ff. Hippolytus addresses Artemis' statue, as he had when he first arrived on stage.

CHORUS

STROPHE A

Greatly does the gods' concern, when it comes to mind,°
relieve my distress; and although one conceals his
    understanding in hope, he falls short of it°   1105
when looking among the fortunes and deeds of mortals.
For things come and go from here and there,°
and the life of men changes, always wandering.   1110

ANTISTROPHE A

Would that destiny from the gods grant me this in answer to my
    prayers—
fortune with prosperity and a heart untouched by pains;
and may my views be neither exacting nor counterfeit,   1115
but may I share in a life of good fortune, changing
my adaptable ways for the next day always.°

STROPHE B

For no longer do I have a clear mind, and what I see is contrary
    to my hope,   1120
since we saw, we saw the brightest star
of the Greek land rushing to another land
because of his father's anger.   1125
O sands of the city's shore,
o mountain thicket where
he used to kill beasts with swift-footed dogs
in the company of holy Dictynna!   1130

ANTISTROPHE B

No longer will you mount the yoked team of Enetic foals,
holding the course around the Mere as you exercise
your horses; your sleepless music beneath the strings' frame   1135
will cease throughout your father's house.
The resting places of Leto's daughter°
will be ungarlanded in the deep verdure;
and by your exile maidens have lost   1140

1102-50 In this song (third *stasimon*) the chorus express their despair about divine justice
    in the wake of Hippolytus' exile and their grief and anger over it.

1105-7 Somewhat opaque in their expression, these lines seem to suggest the contrast
    between an attitude of optimism and the reality of what has transpired.

1108-10 Life's inconstancy was commonly expressed by the Greeks.

1117-9 This wish for an adaptable nature echoes the Nurse's attitude at 253ff. and
    contrasts with Hippolytus' at 87.

1138 *Leto's daughter:* Artemis.

the bridal contest for your bed.°

EPODE

But in tears at your misfortune
I will endure
a luckless lot. O wretched mother,
you gave birth in vain! Ah,   1145
I am furious at the gods.°
Oh, oh!
Yoked Graces,° why do you send this wretched man,
not at all responsible for his ruin,
out of his fatherland, away from this house?   1150

A companion of Hippolytus enters, by the same eisodos *by which Hippolytus and his attendants departed.*

CHORUS LEADER
Look, I see here a companion of Hippolytus°
with a gloomy look, hastening quickly to the house.

MESSENGER
Where could I go, women, to find the ruler of this land,
Theseus? If you know, tell me; is he inside this house?   1155

Theseus enters from the palace.

CHORUS LEADER
Here he is, coming outside the house.

MESSENGER
Theseus, I carry a report worthy of your and the citizens' concern,
both those who dwell in the city of Athens
and those within the boundaries of the Trozenian land.

THESEUS
What is it? It can't be that some upsetting misfortune   1160

1141 A reference to Hippolytus' marriage might seem odd, but such a thought was conventional and prepares subtly for the cult that will be established for Hippolytus at the play's end.

1146 *furious at the gods*: an extremely strong statement.

1148 In art the three *Graces* (Charites), associated with Aphrodite, were routinely depicted joined together. The word *yoked* might also suggest their role in marriage and procreation.

1151 So-called "messenger scenes" were customary in Greek tragedy. They allowed for the description of off-stage actions (the miraculous bull from the sea was beyond the technical abilities and the aesthetic taste of the Greek theater) and expanded the scope of the drama. This "messenger" (in fact, he conveys news, not a message) is not a neutral party but a companion of Hippolytus. This explains his ability to report in vivid details what happened and gives another opportunity for someone to declare Hippolytus' innocence.

has befallen the two neighboring cities,° can it?

MESSENGER

Hippolytus is no more, or nearly so; though precariously
balanced in the scales, he still sees the light.

THESEUS

At whose hands? It can't be that someone whose wife he disgraced
    forcibly,
as he did his father's, got angry at him, can it?   1165

MESSENGER

His own team of horses destroyed him,
and the curses from your mouth, which you prayed
to your father, the lord of the sea, against your son.

THESEUS

O gods and Poseidon, how you truly are my father after all,°
since you've listened to my curses! *How* did he perish?   1170
Tell me, in what way did the club of Justice
strike him after he disgraced me?

MESSENGER

We were near the wave-beaten shore,
in tears as we groomed the horses' coats
with currycombs; for a messenger had come telling us   1175
that Hippolytus could no longer dwell in this land,
since he had been banished by you to a wretched exile.
And he came to us at the shore in the same strain of tears,
and a countless assembly of friends
<and> age-mates was walking along behind him.   1180
Finally he ceased from his groans and said:
"Why do I carry on this way in my grief? My father's words
must be obeyed. Harness the yoke-bearing horses
to the chariot, servants, for this is no longer my city."

    And then from that point every man hurried,   1185
and faster than one could say it, we had readied
the horses and set them right by our master.
He seized the reins from the rail with his hands,
fitting his feet right into the footstalls. And first

1161 *two neighboring cities*: Athens and Trozen, linked more politically than geographi-
    cally.
1169 Like all mortal children of gods, Theseus could not be sure of his paternity.
    Now, the curses prove to him that Poseidon is his father. The confirmation of this
    paternity stands out after the brutal confrontation between father and son in the
    previous scene.

he opened his palms upwards and said to the gods,° 1190
"Zeus, may I be no more, if I am by nature an evil man;
but may my father perceive how he dishonors me,
either when I am dead or while I still see the light."
At that moment, taking the goad into his hands he began to lay it
upon the horses all at the same time; and we attendants 1195
were following our master below the chariot near the bridle,
along the road that goes straight to Argos and Epidaurus.°
     And when we were coming into the desolate territory,°
there is a headland beyond this land,
lying towards what is by then the Saronic Gulf. 1200
From there an echo from the earth, like Zeus' thunder,
let forth a deep roar, hair-raising to hear;
the horses stood their heads and ears straight
towards the heavens, and we were very afraid
about where in the world the voice came from. And looking 1205
towards the sea-loud coast we saw a supernatural wave
fixed towards the heavens, so that my eye
was robbed of the sight of the coast of Sciron,
and it was covering the Isthmus and the rock of Asclepius.°
And then swollen and foaming with 1210
froth all around it, with a blast from the sea it advanced
toward the shore where the four-horse chariot was.
And along with its very swell and triple crest
the wave spewed forth a bull,° a savage monster.
The whole land was filled with its voice 1215
and was giving a hair-raising roar in reply, and the sight of it
appeared greater than we who were looking on could absorb.
     And at once a terrible panic fell upon the horses;°
my master, who was very familiar
with the ways of horses, snatched the reins in his hands 1220
and he pulled them, the way a sailor does an oar,
leaning his body backwards on the reins. But biting

1190 This was the habitual gesture for praying to the gods of the upper air.
1197 *Argos and Epidaurus*: Cities to the west and northwest respectively of Trozen.
1198 *desolate territory*: In Greek myth, miraculous phenomena typically occur in isolated areas.
1209 *Isthmus*: of Corinth, near which the *rock of Asclepius* (of unknown precise location) presumably stood.
1214 *bull*: The bull was associated with Poseidon and could represent untamed masculinity. Bulls also played a role in Phaedra's and Theseus' family histories.
1218ff. The master horseman, Hippolytus is ruined by his horses, just as, e.g., the hunter Actaeon was killed by his hunting dogs.

on the fire-forged bits with their jaws, they carried him
against his will, heeding neither the helmsman's hand   1225
nor the harness nor the well-made chariot. And whenever,
holding the tiller, he steered their course toward the soft ground,
the bull would appear in front to turn them back,
and drive the four-horse team mad with fear; and whenever
with their maddened minds they rushed towards the rocks   1230
it would follow nearby in silence alongside the rail
until it finally tripped up and overturned
the chariot, smashing the wheel's rim against the rock.
Everything was mixed together: the wheels' hubs
and the axles' pins were leaping up,   1235
and the wretch himself, bound up in the reins'
inextricable bond, was being dragged, smashing
his own head against the rocks and shattering his flesh,
and shouting out in a way that was terrible to hear:
"Stop, you who were reared in my stables,   1240
don't wipe me out! Oh my father's wretched curse!°
Who wishes to come and save the best of men?"
And many of us who wished to do so were left behind
with our slower pace. And, freed from the bonds,
the cut leather reins—I don't know how—   1245
he fell still breathing a *little* life;
and the horses and the disastrous monstrous bull
disappeared—I don't know where in the rugged land.
    I'm only a slave in your house, lord,
but I will never be able to do this,   1250
to believe that your son is evil,
not even if the entire race of women should be hanged,
and someone should fill the pine forest on Ida°
with writing; for I know that he is good.

CHORUS LEADER

Ah, a misfortune of new ills is accomplished,   1255
and there is no escape from destiny and necessity.

THESEUS

Because of my hatred of the man who has suffered this,

1241 It is not clear how Hippolytus learned of his father's curse, but it is not implau-
    sible that he might have heard of it. In any case, such matters did not commonly
    trouble ancient playwrights.
1253 *Ida*: A reference to one of two wooded mountains, most likely the one near Troy,
    famous from Homer.

I took delight in these words; but now feeling a sense of shame
before the gods and him, because he is my son, I neither
take delight in these ills nor am I distressed at them.   1260

MESSENGER

What now? Bring him here, or what should
we do with the wretched one to satisfy your will?
Think about it; but if you take my counsel,
you will not be savage towards your son in his misfortune.

THESEUS

Bring him here, so that I can see him before my eyes   1265
and refute with arguments and the misfortunes from the gods
the one who denied that he defiled my bed.

Hippolytus' companion exits down the eisodos *by which he entered.*

CHORUS

You lead the unbending mind of gods and of mortals captive,°
Cypris, and along with you is
the one with many-colored wings°, encompassing them   1270
with his very swift wing;
Eros flies over the earth
and over the sweet-echoing briny sea,
and he bewitches anyone whose maddened heart
he rushes against, winged and gold-shining—   1275
the young of the mountains and those of the sea,
whatever the earth nourishes
and the blazing sun looks upon,
and men; over all of these, Cypris,   1280
you alone hold sway in royal power.

Artemis enters on high.°

1268-81 The chorus' final song (fourth *stasimon*) is very short, a hymn to the power of
   Cypris and Eros, in the wake of what has transpired. This song will be followed
   immediately by Artemis' arrival. Just as in the play's beginning Aphrodite's exit
   was followed by a song to Artemis, here near the play's conclusion a song to
   Aphrodite immediately precedes Artemis' appearance.

1270 *the one with many-colored wings*: Eros.

1281 *Artemis enters on high.* Divine epiphanies were part of Greek literature and especially favored by Euripides at the end of his plays. Here the goddess informs the
   characters of information they could not have known otherwise, helps to effect
   the reconciliation of father and son, predicts the future, and establishes a cult for
   Hippolytus. Artemis would have appeared on the roof of the *skene*, brought there
   by the *mechane*, a crane-like device developed for this purpose. Her position, literal
   and metaphoric, contrasts sharply with the mortals who suffer at ground level.
   Initially she speaks in anapests (a meter suggesting greater formality); at 1296 she
   converts to standard iambic meter.

ARTEMIS

> You, the noble-born son of Aegeus,
> I command you to listen:
> I, the daughter of Leto, Artemis, address you.   1285
> Why, wretched Theseus, do you take delight in this,
> killing your son impiously,
> when you were persuaded of unclear things by your wife's
> lying words? But it was a clear ruin you got.
> Why then do you not in your disgrace hide in Tartarus,°   1290
> or change to a winged life above
> and lift your foot out of this pain? For you have no share
> of life among good men.   1295
> Listen, Theseus, to the state of your ills.
> And yet I'll accomplish nothing, except to pain you.°
> But I came for this: to reveal your son's mind
> as just, so that he may die with a good reputation,
> and your wife's frenzied lust or, in a way,°   1300
> nobility. For stung by the goads of the goddess
> most hateful to us who take delight in virginity,
> she fell in love with your son; and trying to overcome
> Cypris with her reason she was destroyed,
> against her will, by the contrivances of her Nurse,   1305
> who, after she obtained his oath, revealed the sickness
> to your son. And he, as was in fact just, did not go along
> with these words, nor in turn, since he is pious by birth,
> did he retract the pledge of his oath when he was abused
> by you. And she, in fear that she would be found out,   1310
> wrote lying letters and destroyed
> your son by her tricks, but still she persuaded you.

THESEUS

> Ah!

ARTEMIS

> Does this story sting you, Theseus? Be still,
> so that you may hear what happened next and groan more.
> Do you know that you had three sure curses from your father?   1315
> You took one of these, o you most evil one, to use against your son,

---

1290 *Tartarus*: Serves as another name for Hades, the underworld.

1297ff. Like Phaedra, Artemis is concerned both with preserving a good reputation (Hippolytus') and vengeance.

1300-1 *frenzied lust or . . . nobility*: This alternative explanation juxtaposes two aspects of Phaedra's situation—the divinely caused passion for her stepson and her nobility in combating it.

when you could have used it against an enemy.
Now your father from the sea, being well disposed towards you,
gave only what he had to, since he had agreed.
But you appear evil in both his eyes and mine,   1320
since you waited for neither proof nor the voice
of prophets, didn't bring things to the test, didn't allow
long time to inquire; but sooner than you should have,
you hurled curses against your son and killed him.

THESEUS
Mistress, may I perish!

ARTEMIS
                            You did terrible things, but even so   1325
it is still possible for you to obtain forgiveness even of them;°
for Cypris wanted these things to happen,
sating her desire. This is the custom of the gods:°
no one is willing to oppose the desire
of whoever wants something, but we always stand aloof.   1330
For—know this well—if I hadn't feared Zeus
I would never have come to this degree of disgrace,
to allow the dearest to me of all mortals
to die. But first of all your not knowing°
frees your error from wickedness;   1335
and then your wife in dying did away with
the refutation of her words, so that she persuaded your mind.
These evils then have burst upon you especially,
but it is painful for me too; for the gods do not enjoy it°
when the pious die, but we destroy   1340
the base along with their children and houses.

Hippolytus enters supported by attendants, by the same eisodos *by which he left.*°

1326 Artemis does not say that she will forgive Theseus, only that he might obtain
    forgiveness. Forgiveness is not a common attribute of Greek gods.
1328-30 Artemis states as principle what is implicit in much of Greek literature—the
    gods' non-intervention, even to help their favorites.
1334-5 Theseus' ignorance makes him less culpable, but no less responsible.
1339-40. By echoing the traditional imprecation against oath-breakers, this phrase
    invites an implicit comparison with Hippolytus, who did not break his oath.
1341 In his arrival, weak and near death and accompanied by attendants, Hippolytus
    echoes Phaedra's first appearance. Hippolytus' self-lamentation, cries of innocence
    and prayer for death are all in lyric meters, the excited rhythms matching the
    intensity of his words and situation.

CHORUS LEADER

 Look, here the wretched one approaches,
 his youthful flesh and blond head
 mangled. Oh pain for the house,
 what a double grief has been brought to pass for the house, 1345
 seizing it by the gods' will!

HIPPOLYTUS

 Ah, ah!
 I am wretched! I've been mangled
 by unjust divine pronouncements from an unjust father.
 I am ruined, wretched me, woe is me! 1350
 Pains shoot through my head,
 and a spasm throbs in my brain.
 Stop, let me rest my worn-out body.
 Ah, ah!
 O hateful team of horses,
 nourished at my hand, 1355
 you've destroyed me,
 you've killed me.
 Ah, ah! By the gods, gently
 hold on to my wounded flesh with your hands, servants.
 Who stands by my side on the right? 1360
 Lift me properly, move me carefully,
 ill-starred and accursed
 because of my father's errors. Zeus, Zeus, do you see this?
 Here I am, the reverent and god-revering,
 here I am, the one who surpassed everyone in virtue, 1365
 I'm walking into a death clear before my eyes,
 having utterly lost my life
 and toiled in vain
 performing labors of piety for men.
 Ah, ah! 1370
 Even now pain, pain comes over me—
 let go of wretched me!—
 and now may death the healer come to me!
 Add death to my pain, death for me the unfortunate.
 I desire a two-edged weapon, 1375
 to rend me asunder and put
 my life to sleep.
 Oh my father's wretched curse!

A blood-tainted inherited evil°
of long-ago ancestors   1380
breaks its bounds,
and does not stay in place,
and has come upon me—why in the world me,
who am completely blameless of evils?
Woe is me, woe!
What can I say? How can I rid   1385
my life
of this suffering and make it painless?
Would that the black-as-night
compulsion of Hades might lay me,
the ill-starred, to sleep!

CHORUS LEADER
O wretched one, what a misfortune you've been yoked to;
your nobility of mind destroyed you.   1390

HIPPOLYTUS
Ah!
Oh divine fragrance. Even in my troubles
I recognized you and my body was lightened.
The goddess Artemis is in this place.

ARTEMIS
O wretched one, she is, the dearest to you of the gods.

HIPPOLYTUS
Do you see me, mistress, how wretched I am?   1395

ARTEMIS
I see you; but it is not right for me to shed a tear from my eyes.°

HIPPOLYTUS
You don't have your huntsman or your attendant.

ARTEMIS
No; but you who are dear to me are dying.

HIPPOLYTUS
Or your horseman or the guardian of your statues.

ARTEMIS
No, for Cypris, the wicked one, planned it this way.   1400

HIPPOLYTUS
Ah! I understand what divinity has destroyed me.

1379-83 See above on 819.
1396 The gods keep their distance from mortals' suffering; see also 1437-8.

ARTEMIS

She found fault with your homage, and she was vexed at your virtue.°

HIPPOLYTUS

Single-handedly she destroyed the three of us, I realize.

ARTEMIS

Yes, your father, and you, and his wife, third.

HIPPOLYTUS

I groan then also for my father's bad fortunes.°   1405

ARTEMIS

He was completely deceived by the divinity's plans.

HIPPOLYTUS

O father, most wretched because of your misfortune!

THESEUS

I am ruined, child, and I have no pleasure in life.

HIPPOLYTUS

I groan for you more than me at this error.

THESEUS

If only I could become a corpse instead of you, child!   1410

HIPPOLYTUS

Oh the bitter gifts of your father Poseidon!

THESEUS

Would that they had never come to my lips!

HIPPOLYTUS

What?! You surely would have killed me, so angry were you then.

THESEUS

Yes, we were tripped up in our judgment by the gods.

HIPPOLYTUS

Ah! Would that the race of mortals could be a curse on the gods.°   1415

ARTEMIS

Let it be. For not even under the darkness of earth°
will the anger of the goddess Cypris that stems from her

1402 Artemis' view of Aphrodite's motivation is, predictably, somewhat different from the latter's stated reasons in her prologue speech.

1405ff. From here on, Hippolytus, despite his ruin at his father's hands, expresses concern and sympathy for him.

1415 Remarkably, this curse is made against the gods. Cf. the chorus' words at 1146.

1416ff. Just as Aphrodite took vengeance on Hippolytus, Artemis will take vengeance on one of Aphrodite's favorites, not named here but almost certainly Adonis, who died gored by a boar while hunting. *Unavenged . . . take vengeance*: from the same verbal root and part of the same matrix of honor/payment; cf. Aphrodite's words at 8 and 21.

desire rush down against your body unavenged,
thanks to your piety and noble mind.
For I will take vengeance by my hand   1420
with these inescapable arrows on another, one of hers,
whatever mortal is her very dearest.
    But to you, o miserable one, in return for these ills,
I will give the greatest honors in the city°
of Trozen: unyoked maidens before marriage   1425
will cut off locks of their hair for you, who over a long time
will enjoy the fruits of their tears' deepest mourning.
Always the maidens will be inspired to sing songs
about you, and Phaedra's love for you will not
fall away nameless and be kept silent.   1430
But you, o child of aged Aegeus, take
your son in your arms and embrace him.
For in ignorance you killed him, and it is likely
that mortals err greatly when the gods bring it about.
And I urge you not to hate your father, Hippolytus;   1435
for you have your fate with which you were destroyed.
And so farewell; it is not right for me to see the dead
nor to defile my sight with final breaths.
And I see that you are now near this evil.

Artemis exits.

HIPPOLYTUS
Farewell to you too as you go, blessed maiden;   1440
easily you leave a long companionship.°
I dissolve the strife with my father, since you wish it;
for also before I obeyed your words.
Ah, darkness now comes down upon my eyes.
Hold on to me, father, and straighten my body.   1445

THESEUS
Ah! Child, what are you doing to me, the ill-starred?

HIPPOLYTUS
I'm dead, and already I see the gates of the dead.

1424ff. Artemis promises a cult for Hippolytus, in which he will be honored in death
    by Trozenian maidens, who will offer him locks of their hair before their marriage.
    Hippolytus, who rejected sex and marriage during his life, will be venerated by
    young women before their marriage.
1441 This line has been interpreted as reflecting various attitudes—from resentment to
    pious resignation. At the very least it underscores the profound separation between
    gods and mortals. The play concludes with the mortal players only.

THESEUS
Leaving my hand impure?

HIPPOLYTUS
No, since I free you from this bloodshed.

THESEUS
What are you saying? You're acquitting me of blood?   1450

HIPPOLYTUS
I call to witness Artemis who subdues with arrows.

THESEUS
O dearest one, how noble you are revealed to your father.

HIPPOLYTUS
O farewell to you, too, father, I bid you a long farewell.

THESEUS
Ah, for your pious and noble mind!

HIPPOLYTUS
Pray that you have legitimate sons such as me.   1455

THESEUS
Don't now leave me, child, but endure!

HIPPOLYTUS
My enduring's over; I'm dead, father.
Cover my face with my robes as quickly as possible.

THESEUS
Famous Athens and the boundaries of Pallas,
what a man you will lack! Oh wretched me,   1460
how much, Cypris,will I remember your evils!

Theseus exits into the palace and attendants carry in Hippolytus' corpse.

CHORUS
This grief to be shared by all the citizens°
came unexpectedly.
There will be a splashing of many tears;
for sorrowful tales about the great   1465
hold greater sway.

The chorus exit down the eisodos *by which they arrived.*

1462-6 All of Euripides' plays end with a choral coda, providing formal closure to the
drama, not that different from the "THE END" that appears at the conclusion of
many films.

HERACLES

Translation and notes by Michael R. Halleran

CHARACTERS

AMPHITRYON, Heracles' mortal father
MEGARA, Heracles' wife
CHORUS of Theban elders
LYCUS, usurper of power in Thebes
HERACLES
IRIS, messenger of the gods
LYSSA, Madness personified
MESSENGER
THESEUS, king of Athens
HERACLES' AND MEGARA'S THREE SONS
LYCUS' ATTENDANTS

Setting: Outside the palace of Heracles in Thebes, Amphitryon, Megara, and her three sons by Heracles sit as suppliants on the steps of the altar of Zeus Soter (Zeus the Rescuer), seeking to escape death at the hands of Lycus, the recent usurper in Thebes. In typical Euripidean fashion, the play begins with a speech which conveys the basic background information to the audience and helps to establish the play's mood.

AMPHITRYON

What mortal does not know of the man who shared his marriage
    bed with Zeus,
Amphitryon of Argos,° whom Alcaeus, Perseus' son,
once begot, me, the father of Heracles?
I took Thebes here as my home, where the earth-born
crop of Spartoi° grew up, whose race Ares°   5

---

2 Argos was an important city in the eastern Peloponnese (see map).
5 Cadmus, the legendary founder of Thebes, killed a serpent and, following the goddess Athena's advice, sowed half of its teeth. From these teeth sprouted up the Spartoi (the "sown men"), who fought one another (incited, according to some accounts, by Cadmus throwing a rock among them) until only five remained. The prominent families of Thebes claimed to be descended from these. They should not be confused with the Spartans, inhabitants of Sparta.
5 Ares, the Greek god of war, is perhaps used here metaphorically for battle, but he was the father of the serpent whose teeth were sown.

saved in small number, and these populated the city of Cadmus
with their children's children. From these came
Menoeceus' son Creon, a ruler of this land.
Creon was the father of Megara here,
whom all the Cadmeans° once celebrated   10
with flute and song, when the famous Heracles
led her as wife to my house.
But my child, leaving behind Thebes, where I had resettled,
Megara here and his in-laws,
was eager to dwell in the Argive fortifications,   15
the Cyclopean city,° from which I'm in exile since I killed
Electryon.° And trying to ease my misfortunes
and wishing to dwell in his fatherland,
he pays to Eurystheus° a great price for the return—
taming the earth—whether subdued by Hera   20
and her goads or by necessity.
And he's finished toiling with the other labors,
but for the last one he's gone through the mouth of Taenarum°
to Hades, so he might bring back to the light
the three-bodied dog;° and from there he has not returned.   25
There is an old story among the Cadmeans
that there used to be a certain Lycus, Dirce's husband,
who ruled this seven-gated city°
before the white-horse ones, Amphion and Zethus,°
offspring of Zeus, became the rulers of the land.   30

---

10 The Cadmeans, taking their name from Cadmus, were the early inhabitants of
    Thebes; in this play and elsewhere the name is used virtually as a synonym for
    "Thebans."
16 "The Cyclopean city" refers to Mycenae (see map) with its famous fortifications,
    the city in the Peloponnese which gave its name to the Bronze Age culture of
    the Greeks. Here and elsewhere in Greek tragedy, Mycenae and Argos are used
    interchangeably to refer to the same place, in part because of their geographical
    proximity.
17 Amphitryon unintentionally killed Electryon, Alcmene's father. Blood-guilt com-
    monly provides a motive for exile in Greek myths.
19 Eurystheus was Heracles' mortal persecutor. The two were cousins: Electryon,
    Alcmene's father, was half-brother of Eurystheus' father, Sthenelus.
23 Taenarum was a cape in the southernmost Peloponnese, thought to be an entrance
    to the underworld, Hades.
25 The three-bodied dog was Cerberus, the watchdog of the underworld. Capturing
    him was Heracles' final labor.
28 Thebes was often referred to by its most salient feature, its seven gates.
29 Amphion and Zethus, sons of Zeus and the mortal Antiope, were in many accounts
    the founders of Thebes. The precise significance of the epithet "white-horse ones"
    is uncertain.

His child, named after his father with the same name,
not a native Cadmean, but coming from Euboea,°
killed Creon and having killed him rules the land,
after falling upon this city sick with faction.
And for us the marriage bond to Creon   35
turns out to be, it seems, the greatest ill.
With my son in the chambers of the earth
this new ruler of this land, Lycus,
wishes to do away with Heracles' children,
killing them and his wife, so he can quench bloodshed with
    bloodshed   40
and me (if one may reckon even me, a worthless old man,
among men), lest these children someday reach manhood
and exact payment for the blood of their mother's kin.
But I (for my child, when he departed for the dark gloom
of earth, left me behind in this house   45
as a housekeeping nurse for the children)—
to prevent Heracles' children's death, I, along with their mother,
sit at this altar of Zeus Soter,°
which my noble offspring set up as a dedication
for his victory in war after his defeat of the Minyans.°   50
And we keep these positions, lacking everything—
food, drink, clothing—lying on
the ground without bedding. For locked out
of the house, we sit here in need of rescue.
Some of our friends I realize are not reliable friends,   55
while others who truly are cannot help.
Such is misfortune for mortals:
May no one who is even moderately friendly to me
ever meet with it! It is the surest test of friends.

MEGARA

Old man, who once destroyed the city of the Taphians°   60
when you gloriously commanded the army of Cadmeans,
how nothing of the divine is clear for mortals!

---

32   Euboea is a large island off the eastern coast of the northern portion of Greece (see map).
48   Taking shelter at an altar was supposed to offer protection to the suppliants. Soter ("Rescuer") was one of Zeus' many cult titles.
50   Heracles led the Thebans in a victorious batle against the Minyans, inhabitants of northern Boeotia, whose principle city was Orchomenus.
60   The Taphians were a people located in the Taphian islands and Cephallenia near the Acarnanian coast in northwestern Greece. Amphitryon led one of the groups which joined forces in defeating them.

I, for instance, on my father's side was not excluded from good fortune:
He once was celebrated as great because of his prosperity,
since he held power, for the love of which   65
long spears leap against successful men,
and he had children. And me he gave to your son,
joining me to Heracles in a splendid union.
But now all these things have died and flown away.
And you and I are about to die, old man,   70
along with Heracles' children, whom I protect
like a bird with her chicks crouched beneath her wings.
And one after another of them falls to questioning:
"Mother," they say, "Where in the world has he gone to?
What is he doing? When will he return?" Fooled by their youth   75
they seek their father, but I put them off,
telling them tales. And they are all alarmed
whenever the door creaks, and leap up
as if to fall at their father's knee in greeting.
So now, old man, what hope or means of rescue   80
do you have at hand? I look to you.
We could not escape from the land's boundaries in secret
(for the guards at the borders are stronger than we are)
nor in our friends do we any longer have hope
of rescue. Whatever plan you have,   85
speak out. Otherwise death is certain.

AMPHITRYON

Daughter, it is not very easy to give advice on matters such as these
lightly, with earnestness but without effort.
In our weakness let us prolong the time.

MEGARA

Do you want some further pain? Or do you so love the light?   90

AMPHITRYON

Yes, I rejoice in it and love its hopes.

MEGARA

So do I, but you ought not to think the impossible, old man.

AMPHITRYON

In delays there are cures for ills.

MEGARA

But the time between is painful and stings me.

AMPHITRYON

Be that as it may, daughter, a fair sailing might come   95
from your present ills and mine,

and still my child, your husband, might return.
But be calm and check the flood of the
children's tears and soothe them with words,
concealing your deceptions, miserable though they are, with tales   100
for even mortals' misfortunes grow weary,
and blasts of winds are not always strong,
and the fortunate are not fortunate to the end.
For all things stand apart separating from one another.
That man is the best, the one who always   105
trusts in hopes.° It is a bad man who is at a loss.

The chorus, composed of fifteen old men of Thebes, now enters the orchestra
down one of the eisodoi *(entrance ramps) singing and dancing.*°

CHORUS
                    STROPHE
To the high-vaulted halls and the old man's
bed we set forth, pivoting for support
around our staffs,
aged singers of lamentations,   110
like the white bird,°
mere words, the nocturnal semblance
of night-time dreams,
feeble, but eager still,
O, children, fatherless children,   115
old man, and you, wretched mother,
who lament your husband
in the halls of Hades.

                    ANTISTROPHE
Let's not grow weary of foot and heavy
in our limbs, like a yoked foal   120
bearing the weight of

---

106 Hope was by no means viewed by the Greeks primarily as a good; more often
     than not it was seen as negative, a sign of weakness or delusion. Here Amphitryon
     seems to be making a virtue of necessity.
106 The arrival of the chorus is preceded by no particular preparation or announce-
     ment, but the audience was accustomed to the choral entrance early in the play.
     While being very sympathetic to the family, the chorus emphasizes here in the
     opening song and later (e.g., 268ff.) their weakness and inability to help them,
     making the need of another rescuer the more keenly felt. This opening song (*paro-*
     dos) is short, having only three stanzas of modest length.
111 The swan was proverbial for its whiteness, renowned for its singing (especially
     for its dying song) and associated with Apollo and poets.

wheel-drawn baggage
up a steep, rocky cliff.
Grab the hands and garments of anyone
whose footstep falters and is weak.   125
Old man, escort old man,
who before now, when young,
at one time held a youthful spear, allied
in the toils of his comrades,
and was no disgrace to the most glorious fatherland.   130

EPODE

Look how these eyes' Gorgon-gleaming°
flashes are like
those of their father.
Misfortune is not wanting in the children,
nor is charm.
Greece, such ones,   135
such allies you will lack
in losing these.

But look—I see this one coming near the house,
Lycus, the ruler of this land.

Lycus has entered with attendants from one of the eisodoi.

LYCUS°
I will question Heracles' father and his wife,   140
if I may. And I may, since in fact I've become
your master, ask what I wish.
For how long do you seek to prolong your life?
What hope, what defense do you perceive against death?
Do you believe that their father, who lies dead in Hades,   145
will come back? Since you must die,
you are bringing on yourselves more grief than you deserve,
you, in putting forth empty boasts throughout Greece

---

132 The Gorgons were female monsters, decorated with snakes, who would turn to
     stone anyone who looked at them. Here, and elsewhere in the play, "Gorgon-
     gleaming" means something like "fierce-eyed."
140 Lycus has arrived with attendants (as is clear from 240ff.), played by actors with
     non-speaking roles, so-called "mute" characters. He delivers at once a speech
     (*rhesis*) which will function as a foil for Amphitryon's long defense of Heracles. The
     first half of this scene with the pair of "set" speeches on a topic is called an *agon*,
     contest. Such contests are particularly characteristic of Euripides, unsurprisingly
     in light of his interest in the sophists and the importance they placed on rhetoric
     and debate.

that Zeus shared with you your wife and was partner in your child,
and you that you were called wife of the most excellent man.   150
So what is the august deed your husband has accomplished,
if he killed and destroyed a marsh snake°
or the Nemean beast, which he claims, after he subdued it with snares,
to have killed by the strangling of his arms?°
Relying on these achievements do you try to contend? On account of
        these   155
ought Heracles' children not to die?
He got his reputation, although he had no courage,
in fighting beasts, and was not brave in other matters,
he who never held a shield in his left hand
nor came near a spearpoint, but carrying his bow and arrows,   160
the most cowardly weapon, was ready for flight.°
The test of a man, of his courage, is not bow and arrows
but staying steadfast in the ranks and looking, even face-to-face,
at the swiftly advancing swathe of troops.
My behavior involves not shamelessness, old man   165
but prudence, since I know that I killed
Creon, this woman's father, and hold his throne.
Therefore I don't wish, when these children grow up, to have left behind
avengers against me and pay the penalty for what I did.

AMPHITRYON
Let Zeus defend Zeus' part of his   170
child. As for me, Heracles, it's my concern
to reveal in words this man's stupidity
about you, for I will not let someone speak ill of you.
First, then, the unspeakable° charges (I consider the accusation
of cowardice against you, Heracles, among unspeakable ones),   175

---

152 With the phrase "marsh snake" Lycus refers to one of Heracles' labors, the killing
     of the Lernean hydra (see below n. on 421), but does so in language which belittles
     the accomplishment.
154 Lycus implies that a similarity between the words "snares" (*brochois*) and "arm"
     (*brachionos*) allows Heracles to claim more than is true about his subduing of the
     Nemean lion (see below n. on 359).
161 The attack on Heracles' bravery is meant to dismiss any favor which might be owed
     to the children of a brave benefactor. The debate between Lycus and Amphitryon
     on this matter may reflect contemporary tactical arguments, but more importantly
     it offers an opportunity for Amphitryon to sing the praises of Heracles and to
     show him as more than a man of brawn. It should also be observed, as is clear
     from this play and many places in Greek literature and art, that Heracles did not
     exclusively or even primarily use the bow as his weapon.
174 Certain accusations (e. g. parricide) were not to be spoken in Athens; to do so could
     lead to prosecution for slander, unless the accusations could be proven true.

with the gods as witnesses these I must dismiss from you.
I ask Zeus' thunderbolt and his four-horse chariot,
where you stood and pierced the creatures of earth,°
the Giants, in their sides with your winged shafts,
and then celebrated the victory song with the gods.   180
Those wanton four-legged creatures, the race of Centaurs,°
go to Pholoe and ask them, most evil of kings,
what man they would judge most excellent,
if not my son, who you claim only seems so.
And should you ask Abantid Diphrys,° which reared you,   185
it could not praise you, since nowhere
have you done a noble deed to which your fatherland could
     bear witness.
And you criticize that very clever invention, the archer's equipment;
Listen now to my side and become wise.
The heavily armored soldier is a slave to his armor: 190
having only one defense, when he's broken his spearpoint
he is unable to save himself from death.
And if those arrayed in battle with him are cowardly,
he himself is dead because of the cowardice of those near him.
But for anyone who can aim well with the bow   195
this is the single best thing: after shooting thousands of arrows
with others he can save himself from death,
and standing afar he wards off the enemy,
striking them with unseen arrows as they watch,
not offering himself to his opponents,   200
but being well on guard. In battle this
is especially wise—to hurt your enemies
while saving yourself, without being anchored to chance.

---

178 Here and later (1190-92) reference is made to Heracles' service to the gods during the so-called Gigantomachy, the Battle of the Giants (against the gods). The Giants were monsters born to Uranus (the original sky god) and Earth, after he was castrated by his son Cronus and his blood impregnated Earth. They waged war against Zeus and the other Olympians and were defeated. The subject was popular in literature and art.

181 The Centaurs were hybrid creatures, having the torso of a man and the trunk of a horse, and were generally considered uncivilized. Heracles, when entertained with wine by the Centaur Pholus at Pholoe in Arcadia (see map), fought off other Centaurs who were attracted by the wine's scent.

185 The Abantes were a tribe in Euboea (see above n. on 32), where the mountain Diphrys was also located. Lycus came to Thebes from Euboea, and thus Amphitryon by metonymy says that Abantid Diphrys reared Lycus. Heracles has glorious and far-flung witnesses to his achievements, while Lycus doesn't have the support of his "hometown."

These arguments hold the opposite opinion
from yours concerning these matters.   205
But these children, why do you wish to kill them?
What did they do to you? In one respect I think you're wise,
if, base yourself, you fear the offspring
of the best. But this is still grievous for us
if we must die because of your cowardice,   210
a fate which you ought to be suffering at our hands, we who are your
    betters,
If Zeus had just thoughts towards us.
But if all you wish is to hold the sceptre of this land unharassed,
allow us to leave the land as exiles;
and you will do no harm by violence nor suffer violence   215
whenever the wind of god changes for you.
Ah!
Land of Cadmus (I will come against you now
in flinging my words of reproach),
is such the protection you give Heracles and his children,
who by himself did battle with all the Minyans°   220
and made Thebes able to see with a free man's sight?
Nor do I praise Greece (and I will never endure being
silent), finding it most cowardly towards my child,
when it should have come bearing fire, spears, arms
to these young birds, in return for the toils of his hand   225
in cleansing the sea and the earth.
But, children, neither the city of the Thebans
nor Greece is strong enough for you. And you look to me,
a friend with no strength, nothing except the sound of my voice.
The might we had before is wanting,   230
my limbs tremble with age and my strength is faint.
But if I were young and still master of my body
I would take up a spear and bloody those
blond locks of his, so that when he saw my spear
he'd flee in cowardice beyond the bounds of Atlas.°   235

Chorus Leader

Don't the good among mortals have the resources
for arguments, even if they're sluggish at speaking?

---

220 See above, n. on 50.
235 Atlas held up the heavens somewhere in the farthest west; the bounds of Atlas
    are the limits of the civilized world.

LYCUS

You, speak ill of me with the words you've exalted yourself with,
but I, in return for these words, will do you ill.
Go now, some to Helicon, others to the glens of Parnassus,°   240
and order woodsmen to cut down
trees; and when they are brought into the city,
pile up the wood, fitting it around the altar,
and kindle and burn them up,
all of them, so that they may learn that not the dead man   245
rules this land, but I do now.
As for you, old men, since you're opposed to
my views, you will lament not only
the children of Heracles, but also your own house's
fortunes, when it suffers something, and you'll remember   250
that you are slaves of my rule.

CHORUS LEADER

Children of earth, whom Ares once sowed
after leaving the serpent's grasping jaw desolate,°
will you not lift up your staffs, the supports
of your right hand, and bloody this man's   255
impious skull, who, not a Cadmean,
but a most base outsider, rules over my people?
But you will never rule over me with impunity
nor will you have the many things I toiled and labored for
with my hands. Go back where you came here from   260
and show your insolence. As long as I'm alive you will never kill
Heracles' children. Not by that much earth
is he hidden below, after leaving behind his children.
Since you have destroyed this land,
he who helped it does not obtain what he ought.   265
Am I a busybody then in helping my friend°
when he's dead and most needs his friends?
Right hand, how you desire to pick up a spear,

---

240 Helicon and Parnassus are mountains, the former not far from Thebes, the latter
      a considerable distance away in Phocis (see map).
253 See n. on 5 above; the chorus leader is addressing the chorus.
266 The word translated here as "friend," *philos*, is important in this play (see already
      Amphitryon at 55ff.) and in Greek culture generally. Although "friend" is its best
      English equivalent, *philos* had a wider range of meaning in Greek: it included those
      related by blood or marriage as well as non-family members, referring to anyone
      who was near and dear. Central to Greek ethics was the principle of helping your
      friends (*philoi*) and hurting your enemies (*echthroi*), a principle which motivates
      much of the action of this play.

but you lost the desire by your weakness,
since otherwise I would have stopped you, Lycus, from calling me a
    slave   270
and we would have lived honorably here in Thebes,
in which you delight. A city does not have good sense
when it's sick with faction and bad counsels;
otherwise it would never have gotten you as ruler.

MEGARA

Old men, thank you. On account of friends   275
friends ought to show just anger.
But in your anger at the ruler on our account
may you suffer no ill. Hear, Amphitryon,
my opinion, if I seem to you to be saying anything.
I love my children. How could I not love   280
those I bore and for whom I toiled? And death
I consider terrible, but I think whatever mortal
strives against necessity is stupid.
But we, since we must die, ought to die
not wasted by fire, giving laughter   285
to our enemies, which to my mind is a greater ill than death.°
We owe many fine things to our house:
You got an illustrious reputation for combat
so that it's intolerable for you to die through cowardice,
while my husband needs no witnesses for his glory,   290
and he would be unwilling to save these children
at the price of their getting a bad reputation. For the noble
are distressed at their children's disgraces;
and I must not thrust away the example of my husband.
Look at how I consider your hope.   295
Do you think that your child will come back from beneath the earth?
And who of the dead has come back from Hades?
But maybe we might soften this man with words?
Impossible. One should flee the stupid enemy
and yield to those who are wise and well bred,   300
since more easily, submitting to their sense of shame, you would come to
    friendly agreement.
Already it's occurred to me that we might obtain

---

286 Greek culture, which has often been called, with some exaggeration, a "shame
    culture," placed great importance on the external, public manifestations of excel-
    lence and its opposite. Hence the point made here about being the object of laughter
    for one's enemies and the importance attached below (289ff.) to reputation. See
    above, n. on 266.

exile for these children. But this would be miserable,
investing them with rescue at the cost of wretched poverty,
since for friends in exile, they say,   305
hosts have a kindly look for only one day.
Endure death with us, which awaits you in any case.
We call upon your nobility, old man.
Whoever struggles against the fortunes of the gods
is eager, but his eagerness is senseless.   310
For no one will ever make what must happen not happen.

CHORUS LEADER

If someone had treated you insolently
when my arms had strength, I would have stopped him easily.
But now I'm nothing. From this point it's up to you to see
how you will break through these bad blows of fortune.   315

AMPHITRYON

Neither cowardice nor a craving for life
keeps me from death, but I wish to save
my child's children. But I seem to desire the impossible in vain.

He leaves the altar.

Look, this neck is ready for your sword:
Stab me, kill me, throw me from a cliff.   320
But give us two one favor, lord, we ask:
Kill me and this wretched woman before you kill the children,
so that we don't look upon a dreadful sight,
the children breathing their last and calling, "Mother,
Grandfather." But the rest, if you're eager,   325
accomplish it; for we don't have the might to prevent death.

MEGARA

I, too, beg you to add a favor to this favor,
so you alone may serve the two of us two-fold:
Open the house (we are locked out)
and let me clothe the children in the garments of the dead   330
so that this at any rate they can receive from their father's house.

LYCUS

This will be done. I command attendants to open the doors.
Go inside and get dressed; I don't begrudge the robes.
But when you've put on your garments
I will come to you to give you to the earth below   335

Exit Lycus with his attendants down the eisodos *from which they entered.*

MEGARA

Children, accompany your wretched mother's step

into your father's house, where others
rule over the property, though the name is still ours.

Exit Megara with the children into the palace.

AMPHITRYON
Zeus, in vain I got you as a sharer of my wife,
in vain I called you partner in my child.   340
You were after all less of a friend than you seemed.
I, a mortal, defeat you, a great god, in excellence,
for I did not betray Heracles' children.
But you knew how to go secretly into beds,
taking others' wives when no one offered,   345
but you do not know how to save your friends.
You are some ignorant° god or by nature unjust.

Exit Amphitryon into the palace.°

CHORUS°

STROPHE A

Phoebus° cries woe,
after a song of good fortune,
as he strikes the beautiful-voiced lyre   350
with a golden pick;

---

347 The word translated as "ignorant" (*amathes*) also suggests "unfeeling, insensitive."

347 The stage in Greek tragedy was in general not very busy, with relatively few entrances and exits, and these rarely occurred in quick succession. Therefore it is striking to find the successive exits of Lycus, Megara with the children, and Amphitryon within twelve lines of each other. (In only one other place in all of Euripides is there anything comparable [*Ion* 442ff.].) As a result, emphasis falls on Amphitryon's final, brief and biting word against Zeus. Elsewhere in Euripides we find such "challenging prayers" to gods, but this one has a special point because of its position in the drama.

347 The chorus, already in the orchestra, now dances and sings its second song, commonly called the first *stasimon*, "standing song." The song, intended as a *threnos*, a lamentation of the presumed-dead Heracles, is more of an *encomium*, a eulogy in praise of his accomplishments, particularly his "labors". Heracles' labors were many, and which of them constituted the canonical twelve varies according to author, time and place. In this song, as frequently, the focus is on Heracles as a benefactor to mankind. The ode has an interesting structure: the repeated metrical pattern of the strophes and antistrophes is the norm, but the repeated short stanzas (called mesode after the strophe and epode after the antistrophe) after each of the stanzas is remarkable. The central ten stanzas of the song each describe one labor, except for Antistrophe B and Mesode C, which describe two each.

348 Phoebus is another name for the god Apollo, appropriately invoked as a god of song, especially of those played on the lyre.

And I wish to celebrate in eulogy
as a crown for his labors
the son who went into the gloom of earth
and of the dead—
whether I am to call him the offspring of Zeus
or of Amphitryon.   355
Excellent deeds achieved with noble toil
are glory for the dead.

MESODE A

First° he rid Zeus' grove
of the lion,   360
and putting the skin on his back
he covered his blond head
with the dread beast's tawny gaping jaws.

ANTISTROPHE A

And he once laid low with his murderous arrows
the mountain-dwelling race   365
of savage Centaurs,
killing them with his winged shafts.°
The beautiful-swirling Peneius
and its vast, barren fields
bear witness to this,
as do the dwellings on Mount Pelion   370
and the neighboring settlements of Mount Homole,
where filling their hands with pine trees°
the Centaurs would subdue the land of Thessalians
by their ridings.

EPODE A

And killing the golden-horned,   375
dappled-back hind,
the scourge of farmers,
he honors the beast-slaying
goddess of Oenoe.°

---

359 Subduing the Nemean lion was the canonical first labor. After strangling it to death
   (its skin was invulnerable), Heracles put on its skin and jaws, and this became his
   characteristic garb in literature and art. Nemea is in the northern Peloponnesos .
367 On the Centaurs in general, see above, n. on 181. A different group of Centaurs
   is referred to here, as the geography of this passage (the river Peneius, Mount
   Homole, etc.) places them in Thessaly and environs.
372 To use as weapons.
379 The goddess of Oenoe, located at the border of the Argolid and Arcadia (see

Strophe B

And he mounted the four-horse chariot   380
and with curbs subdued
Diomedes' mares, who in their murderous stalls
would despatch with unbridled zeal
bloody meals with their jaws,
harsh eaters, delighting   385
in human flesh. And he went
beyond the silver-rich banks
of the Hebrus,
as he toiled for the lord of Mycenae.°

Mesode B

And on the Pelian headland
along the streams of Anaurus   390
he killed with his arrows
Cycnus,° murderer of strangers, Amphanae's
unsociable inhabitant.

Antistrophe B

And he went to the maidens of song°
and their dwelling in the west   395
to pluck by hand the golden fruit
from the apple-bearing leaves,
after killing the tawny-backed serpent,
who guarded them coiling around
with its coils, unapproachable.
And he travelled into the recesses of the salty   400
sea, making calm waters
for mortal oarsmen.°

---

map), is Artemis, the goddess of the hunt, to whom the offering of the so-called
Cerynitian hind is appropriate.

388 The mares of Diomedes were located up north in Thrace (see map), where the
Hebrus flowed; Heracles had to subdue these man-eating horses for Eurystheus,
the lord of Mycenae.

392 According to some traditions, Cycnus, a son of the war-god Ares, beheaded strangers on their way to Apollo's shrine at Delphi, and Apollo urged upon Heracles
the task of killing him. The geographical references in this passage, however, seem
to place the event near Mount Pelion and Amphanae, in Magnesia.

394 The maidens of song were the Hesperides, dwellers of the far west, whose golden
apples were protected by a fierce snake.

402 The seventh labor in this song is rather unspecifically expressed: Heracles calmed
the waters for mortals. Note that this stanza contains two labors.

EPODE B

And going to the home of Atlas°
he drove his hands
under the middle of heaven's vault   405
and held up the starry dwellings
of the gods by his manly strength.

STROPHE C

And he went through the hostile swell of sea°
to the horse-riding host of Amazons
around Moetis with its many rivers,   410
gathering all of his friends
together from Greece
to pluck the ruinous quarry
of the gold-decked warrior's belt
from the warlike maiden's robe.   415
And Greece seized the foreign maiden's
famous spoil, and
it is preserved in Mycenae.

MESODE C

And he burned up the thousand-headed,
much-destructive hound of Lerna,   420
the hydra,°
and smeared its venom on his shafts,
with which he killed the three-bodied
herdsman of Erytheia.°

ANTISTROPHE C

And he both went through other races   425
with glorious success and sailed into

---

403 For Atlas see above, n. on 235. Elsewhere Atlas plucked the golden apples while
    Heracles held up the world. The chorus gives Heracles credit for both deeds.
408 This refers to the Black Sea (the marsh, Moetis, was located north of it), where
    Heracles did battle with the Amazons, a group of legendary woman warriors,
    whose leader is alternately called Antiope and Hippolyte. In this battle Heracles
    was victorious and made off with the leader's belt, often translated as "girdle,"
    which he dedicated at Hera's shrine in Mycenae.
421 Usually the second labor, the subduing of the Lernean hydra, provided Heracles
    with the venom for his arrows; Lerna was located south of Argos.
424 The herdsman of Erytheia, located in southwest Spain, was Geryon, a three-bodied
    or three-headed creature, whose cattle Heracles had to bring to Eurystheus. Note
    that this Mesode, like Antistrophe B, contains two labors.

much-lamented Hades, his final labor,°
where, wretched one, he is finishing off
his life, nor did he come back.
His halls are bereft of friends,   430
and Charon's boat awaits
the children's life's journey,
which has no return, and is god-forsaken
and unjust. The house looks to your° arms
and you're not here.   435

EPODE C

But if I had the strength of my youth
and could wield the spear in battle,
and were joined by my comrades,
I would champion the children
with might. But as things stand, I lack   440
my blessed youth.

And now I see these people,° wearing
the garments of the dead,
the children of the formerly, once great
Heracles, and his loving wife,   445
pulling beside her their children,
who cling to her feet which guide them, and the old father of Heracles.
I am wretched!
I am no longer able to hold back
my old eyes' tears.   450

*Megara, with the children clinging to her feet, and Amphitryon have come forth from
the palace.*

MEGARA

Well then. Who is the priest, who is the sacrificer of the ill-starred?
[or the murderer of my wretched life]
These sacrificial victims are ready to be led off to Hades.
Children, we are being led off, a not pretty yoke of corpses,

---

427 Going down into Hades to fetch its watchdog, the multi-headed Cerberus, was
     Heracles' last labor, the one from which his family and the chorus despair of his
     returning. Charon (432) was the ferryman of Hades, on whose boat one crossed
     the river Styx and entered the underworld.
434 The chorus is addressing Heracles, even though he's absent; such addresses are
     not uncommon in choral songs.
442 The song has ended and the chorus now announces in anapests the entrance of the
     family in their funereal garb. Entrances immediately after choral songs are gener-
     ally not announced in Greek tragedy, but are commonly announced in situations
     such as this one, the slow and solemn entrance of a group, a "moving tableau."

the old man and the young and their mother all together.   455
Wretched fate, mine and the children's,
these, whom my eyes gaze on for the very last time.
I gave you birth, and I reared you for your enemies
to abuse, laugh at, and destroy.
Oh!
Much have I fallen from my hopeful expectation,   460
which I once had from your father's words.
To *you*° your now dead father used to assign Argos
and you were going to live and rule in Eurystheus' house,
wielding power over the fertile Pelasgian° land;
and he used to put around your head the lion's   465
skin, with which he used to arm himself.
And *you* were lord of chariot-loving Thebes,
taking possession of my land as inheritance,
since you would win over the one who begot you,
and he would place in your right hand his club   470
as protection, finely wrought, a make-believe gift.°
And to *you* he promised to give Oechalia,°
which he had once sacked with his well-aimed arrows.
Your father would exalt you three
with three kingdoms, proud in his manly strength.   475
And I would pick out brides
from the land of the Athenians, from Sparta, and
Thebes, contracting marriages, so that moored
by stern cables,° you would have a happy life.
But this is all gone: fortune changed   480
and gave you instead Keres° to have as brides
and wretched me tears to bear as the ritual bath water.°
Your father's father here gives the marriage feast,
deeming Hades your father-in-law, a bitter marriage tie.

---

462 Megara now addresses her three sons in turn.
464 The adjective Pelasgian here refers to Argos (for which see above, n. on 2).
471 The club was the symbol of Thebes and hence is appropriately given to the son who was to rule over Thebes; similarly the first son was given Heracles' lion skin since the lion was the symbol of Argos, the land he was to rule over.
472 There were several different cities called Oechalia; presumably Euripides means the one in Euboea (see map). Heracles had sacked this city because of his passion for the king's daughter, Iole.
479 Metaphors from sailing are common in Greek literature (and in this play), as one might expect from a seafaring people.
481 The Keres were dreadful spirits of death.
482 Ritual baths were customary for both bride and groom prior to the Athenian wedding ceremony.

Oh! which of you first, which one last   485
am I to place against my breast? Whose mouth to kiss?
Whom to hold? Would that I like a shrill-winged
bee could gather the laments from all,
gather them, and give forth a single flood of tears.
Dearest, if any voice of mortals is heard   490
in Hades, I say this to you, Heracles:
Your father and children are dying, and I am being destroyed,
who before now was called happy by mortals because of you.
Help! Come! Appear to me even as a shadow!
For coming even as a dream you would be enough,   495
for they are cowards who are killing your children.

AMPHITRYON
You, keep trying to conciliate those below, woman,°
while I throw my hands to heaven and call on you,
Zeus, if you are going to help these children at all,
to save them, since soon you won't be able.   500
And yet you've been called often; I labor in vain,
for death, it seems, is inevitable.
But, old men, the things of life are short;
see that you go through it as pleasurably as you can,
without pain from morning to night,   505
since time doesn't know how to preserve
hopes, but is gone in flight, eagerly tending its own affairs.
Look at me, I who was admired by mortals,
as I accomplished illustrious deeds—but fortune robbed me
in one day, like a wing to the sky.°   510
Great prosperity and reputation—I don't know for whom
these are secure. Farewell. Now, comrades,
for the last time you look upon this dear man.

MEGARA
Ah!
Old man, I see my dearest one—or what am I to say?

AMPHITRYON
I don't know, daughter; I can't speak.   515

MEGARA
This is the man we kept hearing was beneath the earth,
unless I'm seeing a dream in the daylight.

---

497 Amphitryon refers to Megara's concluding prayer for Heracles' return from the
    underworld.
510 The phrase seems proverbial for the precariousness of prosperity.

What am I saying? What sort of dream do I see, out of my mind?
This one is no other than your child, old man.
Come on, children, cling to your father's robes,   520
go, be quick, don't let go, since for you
he is not at all inferior to Zeus Soter.°

Heracles has entered from one of the eisodoi.

HERACLES

Greetings, roof and gate of my hearth,
how joyfully I behold you on my return to the light!
Ah! What is this? I see my children before the house   525
with their heads wreathed with the dead's ornaments,
and my wife among a throng of men,
and my father crying at what misfortunes?
Let me draw near and learn from them:
Wife, what strange thing has come to the house?   530

MEGARA

Dearest of men...

AMPHITRYON

You who come as a saving light to your father...

MEGARA

Have you arrived, were you saved, coming in the nick of time for your
    dear ones?

HERACLES

What are you saying? What disturbance do I arrive at, father?

MEGARA

We were on the verge of being killed. But you, old man, forgive me,
if I snatched before you what you ought to be telling this man.   535
For the female is somehow more pitiable than males,
and my children were on the verge of death, and I on the verge of
    destruction.

HERACLES

Apollo, with what an opening do you begin your speech!

MEGARA

They're dead—my brothers and aged father.

---

522 Megara's command, as the ensuing words make clear, is not followed at once. The
     conventions of the Athenian stage allowed the action on one part of the stage to
     become "fixed" or artificially slow while the action on the other side took place.
     Note that Heracles does not address his family until after giving a customary greet-
     ing to the house and after making a brief aside explaining that he will approach
     and speak to them.

HERACLES
What are you saying? What did he do or what sort of death did
    he meet?   540

MEGARA
Lycus, the new ruler of the land, killed him.

HERACLES
In combat or because the city was sick?

MEGARA
Because of faction. And he controls Cadmus' mighty seven-gated city.

HERACLES
But how could fear have reached you and the old man?

MEGARA
He was going to kill your father, me, and the children.   545

HERACLES
What are you saying? Why did he fear my orphaned children?

MEGARA
Lest they some day exact vengeance for Creon's death.

HERACLES
What is this adornment of the children, fitting for the dead?

MEGARA
We are dressed already in these clothes of death.

HERACLES
By force you were about to die? I am wretched!   550

MEGARA
Yes, bereft of friends, and we kept hearing that you were dead.

HERACLES
And how did this loss of heart come to you?

MEGARA
Eurystheus' heralds kept announcing it.

HERACLES
But why had you left my house and hearth?

MEGARA
By force. While your father was ousted from his covered bed.   555

HERACLES
Didn't reverence keep them from dishonoring the old man?

MEGARA
Reverence? That goddess dwells far from this land.

HERACLES
Was I so lacking in friends in my absence?

MEGARA

What friends does one have in misfortune?

HERACLES

Did they despise the battles I endured against the Minyans?   560

MEGARA

Friendless, I tell you again, is misfortune.

HERACLES

Throw off these hellish wreaths
and show rescue's gleam in your eyes,
a dear exchange for the shadow below.
And I—for now is the time for the work of my hand—   565
first will go and raze the house
of the new ruler, cut off his impious head
and hurl it for dogs to tear. And whoever of the Cadmeans
I discover to be bad after benefiting from me,
with this victorious club I will subdue them,   570
while others I will tear apart with winged arrows
and fill the entire Ismenus° with the carnage of corpses.
And the clear flowing of Dirce will be red with blood.
For whom should I defend more than my wife,
children and old father? Farewell labors!   575
In vain I worked on them rather than these tasks.
Indeed I ought to risk dying in defense of these children,
since they were doing so for their father. Or how can I call it good
that I did battle with the hydra and lion
on Eurystheus' missions, but will not toil over my children's   580
threatened death?° I shall not then
be called Heracles "the victorious" as before.

CHORUS LEADER

It is just for a father to help his children
and aged father and his partner in marriage.

AMPHITRYON

It is your nature, child, to be a friend to your friends   585
and hate your enemies. But don't be overly eager.

HERACLES

Which of these things is hastier than it should be, father?

---

572 Ismenus and Dirce were the two rivers of Thebes.
581 Heracles seems to say that he will toil to avert his children's death, threatened by
     Lycus, but the language also suggests (ironically, not in Heracles' unconscious)
     that he is laboring to complete their murder.

AMPHITRYON

    The ruler has many poor men as allies,
    who seem prosperous in their own estimation;
    they staged an uprising and destroyed the city   590
    to rob from their neighbors, since their own patrimony
    was spent and gone and had escaped through their laziness.
    And you were seen approaching the city, and since you were seen, be
        careful
    lest you have caused the enemy to gather and you fall unexpectedly.

HERACLES

    I don't care if the whole city saw me.   595
    But seeing a bird on an inauspicious perch°
    I recognized that some pain had fallen against the house,
    and so by forethought I entered the land secretly.

AMPHITRYON

    Good. Go inside now, address Hestia°
    and let your paternal house see your face.   600
    The ruler will come in person to drag off and kill
    your wife and children and slaughter me too.
    Waiting here you'll have everything
    and you'll profit in safety. Don't throw your city into disorder
    before you set this right, child.   605

HERACLES

    I'll do this, since you've given good advice, I'll go inside the house.
    Coming back after some time from the sunless chambers
    of Hades and Kore° below, I'll not disdain
    to address first the gods in the house.

AMPHITRYON

    Did you really go into Hades' house, child?   610

HERACLES

    Yes, I led the three-headed beast to the light.

AMPHITRYON

    Conquering it in battle or by the gifts of the goddess?°

---

596 Augury was practiced in the Greek world.
599 The goddess of the hearth.
608 Kore, also known as Persephone, was the daughter of the goddess Demeter and
    Zeus and the bride of Hades.
612 One version of the story related that Persephone helped Heracles in defeating
    Cerberus.

HERACLES

In battle, but I was successful after seeing the rituals of the mysteries.°

AMPHITRYON

And is the beast really in Eurystheus' house?

HERACLES

The grove of the Chthonian° and the city of Hermione have it.   615

AMPHITRYON

And Eurystheus doesn't know that you've come up from the earth?

HERACLES

He doesn't know, since I came to learn the situation here first.

AMPHITRYON

Why were you under the earth for so long?

HERACLES

I spent time bringing back Theseus from Hades, father.°

AMPHITRYON

And where is he? Has he gone to his fatherland?   620

HERACLES

He's gone to Athens, glad to have escaped from below.
But come on, children, accompany your father into the house.
So your entrances into it are fairer
than your exits from it, right? But be brave,
and shed no more tears.   625
And you, my wife, compose yourself,
stop trembling, and, all of you, let go of my robes.
I'm not winged and I don't intend to flee my dear ones.
Ah!
The children don't let go, but cling to my robes
so much more. Did you come so close to the razor's edge?   630
Taking them by the hand I will lead these little boats
and like a ship I will pull them in tow; for I do not refuse
the care of my children. All mortals are equal:
they love their children, both superior mortals
and those of no account. They differ in money: 635

---

613 The language of this line strongly calls to mind the Eleusinian mysteries, celebrated
in Eleusis, a city near Athens, rites which promised a type of "rebirth." Some
accounts had it that Heracles was initiated into these mysteries before his trip to
the underworld.

615 "The Chthonian" is Demeter, the fertility goddess in whose honor the Eleusinian
mysteries were held, who had a shrine at Hermione, near Troezen (see map).

619 Theseus, the ruler of Athens, had gotten stuck in Hades when he tried to help his
friend Pirithous abduct Persephone, and he was rescued by Heracles.

some have it, others don't; but everyone loves his children.

Heracles exits with the children into the palace; Amphitryon and Megara follow them in.

CHORUS°

STROPHE A

Youth is dear to me;
but old age, a constant burden
heavier than the crags of Aetna,°
lies on the head, covering over   640
and darkening the eyes' light.
May I have neither the wealth
of an Asian° empire
nor my house full of gold,   645
have them instead of youth,
which is fairest in wealth,
fairest in poverty.
Painful and murderous old age
I hate. May it perish into   650
the waves! Would that it had never
come to the homes and cities
of mortals, but always let it be borne off
through the sky on wings.

ANTISTROPHE A

If the gods had intelligence   655
and wisdom regarding men's affairs,
those who excel would win a double youth,°
a clear sign of their excellence,
and after their death   660
they would run a double course and
come back to the rays of the sun;
but the ignoble would have
a single life to live.
And by this it would be possible to recognize
both the good and the bad,   665

---

637 The previous song was a type of lament (*threnos*); this one is a type of epinician, a victory song for Heracles who has triumphantly returned from the underworld.

639 Aetna was a volcanic mountain on the island of Sicily; the monster Typhoeus was thought to dwell under it.

644 Asia was proverbial for its wealth.

657 This notion, perhaps strange-seeming to us, is found elsewhere in Euripides (*Supplices* 1080ff.).

just as among the clouds
sailors can count the stars.
But as things are now, there is no marker from the gods
that is clear for the noble and the base.   670
But a lifetime as it rolls along
only increases wealth.

STROPHE B

I will not cease mixing together
the Graces and the Muses,°
the sweetest yoking.   675
May I never live without music,°
but may I always be crowned.°
An old singer, I still
celebrate Mnemosyne,
I still sing   680
Heracles' victory song
beside the wine-giving Bromius,°
beside the song of the seven-toned lyre
and the Libyan° pipe.
In no way will I abandon   685
the Muses, who set me dancing.

ANTISTROPHE B

The Delian maidens° around the temples' doors
whirling in their beautiful dances
sing a paean° in praise
of Leto's noble child.   690
I will sing paeans in celebration
at your° house,

---

674 The Muses were the patrons of poets and the source of poetic inspiration. Their mother was Mnemosyne (see 1679 below), the personification of memory. The Graces were personifications of loveliness and grace.

676 The word translated, *amousias*, suggests both "without music" and "without the Muses."

677 The crowning is both a sign of devotion and a reference to the crown of the victor.

682 Bromius, "the roarer," is a cult name for Dionysus, the god of wine and ecstatic experience.

684 The wood of the Libyan lotus tree was said to be good for making the pipe (*aulos*).

687 Delos, a tiny island in the Aegean sea, was the birthplace of Apollo and an important site for his worship.

689 The paean was a song particularly associated with Apollo, "Leto's noble child."

692 "Your" refers to Heracles; see above, n. on 434.

an old singer, like a swan
from a white throat.° For what is good
provides themes for hymns.   695
He is the child of Zeus. Surpassing
in excellence more than in noble birth,
with toil he made life
calm for mortals
by destroying terrifying beasts.   700

Lycus arrives with attendants from the eisodos *he previously used just as or just after Amphitryon enters from the palace.°*

LYCUS

Just in time, Amphitryon, you come out of the house;
for a long time now you've been adorning yourselves
with garments and ornaments of the dead.
But come now and tell Heracles' children and wife
to appear outside this house;   705
on these conditions you promised to die voluntarily.

AMPHITRYON

Lord, you persecute me when I'm in a wretched state
and you maltreat me outrageously now that he's dead;
you ought, even if you hold sway, to strive for this moderately.
But since you are compelling us to die,   710
we must acquiesce; may what you wish be done.

LYCUS

Where then is Megara? Where are the children of Alcmene's child?

AMPHITRYON

I think that she, to judge from outside...

LYCUS

What's this? What opinion do you hold with certainty?

AMPHITRYON

She's sitting as a suppliant at the holy altar of Hestia°...   715

LYCUS

To no purpose she supplicates to save her life.

---

694 The swan was sacred to Apollo at Delos and was also associated with singers (see
    above n. on 111). The "white throat" refers to the chorus of old men as well as to
    the swan.
700 The following scene is very short, as the action culminating in Lycus' murder
    moves rapidly. It involves one of Euripides' favorite patterns, the deception of
    someone who is led into the *skene*, where another or others wait in ambush.
715 For Hestia see above, n. on 599.

AMPHITRYON

And she is calling on her dead husband in vain.

LYCUS

He's not here and will never come.

AMPHITRYON

No, unless one of the gods should raise him up.

LYCUS

Go to her and bring her out of the house.   720

AMPHITRYON

If I did that, I'd be a partner in the murder.

LYCUS

Well, since you have this scruple,
I, who lack these fears, will bring forth
the children along with their mother. Come, follow, attendants,
so that we can gladly see a respite from these toils.   725

Lycus and attendants exit into the palace.

AMPHITRYON

You, then, go, go where you should. The rest perhaps
another will take care of. Expect, if you act badly,
to fare badly.° Old men, opportunely
he goes and he will be trapped by sword-bearing
men and nets, thinking that he'll kill those near him,   730
the utterly evil man. And I'm off so I may see the corpse
fall. For an enemy's death as he pays the penalty
for his deeds affords pleasure.

Amphitryon exits into the palace.

CHORUS°

—A change from ills! The former lord gloriously   735
turns his life back from Hades.
Oh,
justice and the lot from the gods which flows back again!

---

728 After these words Amphitryon, whose language up to this point in this scene has
      been misleading, explicitly predicts the murder which awaits Lycus. Lycus and
      his attendants have probably already entered the *skene* at this point, but even if
      they have not, the conventions of the Greek theater permitted such "words at the
      back" which the audience would hear, while the departing character(s) would
      not.

734 At this point begins a brief "epirrhematic" scene, in which the chorus in song
      alternate with an actor in spoken rhythms (Lycus from within); the third *stasimon*
      proper commences at 763. The choral parts in this section (734-62) are probably
      sung by individual members of the chorus.

—Finally you went where you will pay in death the penalty   740
for treating your betters with outrage.

—Joy makes me shed tears.
He came back,
which never before in my thoughts would I have expected   745
to experience, the lord of the land.

—But, old men, let us examine also the events within
the house—to see if someone fares as I wish.

LYCUS *(within)*
Oh! Woe is me!

CHORUS
—This song begins in the house, dear   750
for me to hear. Death is not far off.
The ruler cries out,
groaning the prelude of murder.

LYCUS *(within)*
Entire land of Cadmus, I am being killed by stealth.

CHORUS
—Yes, for you were trying to kill; endure paying fully   755
the retribution, paying the penalty for your deeds.

—What mortal, staining the gods with lawlessness,
spread the mindless tale
about the blessed Olympians,° that the gods
do not hold power.

—Old men, the impious man is no more.   760
The house is quiet. Let us turn to dances.
[The friends whom I wish are successful.]

CHORUS°

STROPHE A

Dances, dances
and festivals are celebrated
throughout the holy city of Thebes.
Changes from tears,   765
changes of fortune

---

758 The Olympians are the gods who dwell on Mount Olympus, the generation of
Zeus; they are the chief Greek gods.
762 The third *stasimon*. The chorus is convinced of divine justice and of Zeus' paternity
of Heracles because he has returned successfully and killed the villain Lycus.

give birth to songs.
The new king is gone, and the former one
holds sway, leaving the harbor of Acheron.°   770
Hope came beyond expectations.

ANTISTROPHE A

The gods, the gods
take care to heed
the unjust and the holy.
Gold and good fortune,
bringing with them unjust power,   775
lead mortals from their senses.
For no one dares to look to the future
as he neglects the law and favors lawlessness.
He smashes the dark chariot of wealth.   780

STROPHE B

Ismenus,° be garlanded,
and polished streets of the seven-gated
city and beautiful-flowing Dirce,
start the dancing,
and, leaving your father's water,   785
nymphs, daughters of Asopus,° join me in singing
the victorious contest
of Heracles.
Wooded rock of the Pythian,°   790
and home of the Heliconian° Muses,
extol with joyous sound
my city, my walls,
where the race of Spartoi° appeared,
a band of bronze-shielded warriors, who handed down   795
the land to their children's children;
they are a holy light for Thebes.

ANTISTROPHE B

Two kindred marriage

---

770 Acheron was one of the rivers of the underworld.
781 For Ismenus and Dirce, see above, n. on 572.
786 The daughters of Asopus are the river divinities, nymphs, descended from the
      river god Asopus; the river ran near Thebes.
790 This refers to Mount Parnassus (see above n. on 240), the home of Pythian Apollo
      and the Muses.
791 Mount Helicon in Boeotia was another home of the Muses.
794 For the Spartoi, see above n. on 5.

beds, mortal and
of Zeus, who came to the bed   800
of Perseus' granddaughter.° How
believable to me was your long-ago union,
Zeus, revealed, when it seemed unlikely.
Time revealed brightly   805
the might of Heracles,
who came forth from the chambers of the earth,
leaving the nether home of Pluto.°
You° were a better ruler to me
than the ignoble lord,   810
who now, looking on the contest
of swords, makes clear
whether justice
still pleases the gods.°

The figures of Iris and Lyssa appear on high.°

—Ah! Ah!   815
Do we have the same fear,
old men, since I see such a phantom above the house?

—In flight, in flight
raise your sluggish limbs, get out of the way.

—Lord Paean°   820
may you avert pains from us.

IRIS

Don't be afraid, old men, in seeing this offspring of Night,

---

801 Perseus' granddaughter was Alcmene. Note that the vocative which begins this
   stanza is never picked up; such "hanging vocatives" are not uncommon in choral
   poetry.
808 Pluto is another name for Hades.
809 The chorus addresses Heracles; see above, n. on 434.
814 The song which confidently asserts belief in the justice of the gods, a theodicy,
   concludes with "proof" of this—Heracles' victory over Lycus. The concluding
   "Whether justice still pleases the gods" is rhetorical on the part of the chorus, but
   the following appearance of Iris and Lyssa "answers" this rhetorical proposition.
814 Iris, the messenger god, and Lyssa, whose name means "madness", which she
   personifies, appear on high, most probably in the *mechane*, which causes the fearful
   cries of the chorus. (The chariot referred to by the chorus at 880 is most likely not
   physically present, only metaphorically.) This appearance of the gods in mid-play
   is most surprising. And nowhere else is there a more violent rupture between a
   song and the following action.
820 Paean is a name for Apollo in his capacity as a healing god.

Lyssa, and me, the servant of the gods,
Iris; for we come with no harm to the city,
but against one man's house we wage war,   825
who they say is from Zeus and Alcmene.
Until he completed fully his bitter trials
necessity was keeping him safe, nor would his father Zeus
allow either me or Hera to harm him at any time.
But since he's gone through the toils of Eurystheus,   830
Hera wishes to attach to him kindred blood
by his killing of the children, and I wish the same.
But come then, pull together your implacable heart,
unmarried maiden of dark Night,
and against this man drive, stir up   835
fits of madness, disturbances of mind to kill his children,
and leapings of his feet; let out the murderous cable
so that conveying through Acheron's° strait
his crown of beautiful children, killed in familial murder,
he may recognize what sort is Hera's anger against him   840
and learn mine. Otherwise the gods are nowhere
and mortal things will be great, if he doesn't pay the penalty.°

LYSSA

I am sprung from a noble father and mother,
from Night and the blood of Uranus.°
I hold an office that the gods don't like to admire   845
and I don't delight in going against mortals dear to me.
But before seeing her stumble I wish
to advise Hera and you, in the hope that you heed my words.
This man, whose house you send me against,
is not undistinguished either on earth or among the gods.   850
Taming the desolate land and savage sea,
he alone restored the honors
of the gods which fell at the hands of impious men.
And so I do not advise you to plot great evils.

IRIS°

Don't you give advice about Hera's and my plans.   855

---

838 On Acheron, see above, n. on 770.
842 This line has often been interpreted to mean that Heracles is to be punished for "hybris", arrogant behavior towards the gods. Neither this line nor the play supports this view.
844 Uranus was the sky god two generations before Zeus.
854 At this point the meter shifts to trochaic tetrameters, a rhythm often used to express excitement.

LYSSA

I'm trying to lead your step to the better instead of evil.

IRIS

Zeus' wife didn't send you here to be sensible.

LYSSA

I call on Helius° to witness that I'm doing what I don't wish to do.
But if indeed it's necessary for me to serve Hera and you,
yes, I'll go. Neither is the sea so fierce as it moans with waves   860
nor an earthquake nor the raging thunderbolt breathing forth pangs
as the race I'll run against Heracles' chest;
and I'll smash his halls and hurl the house on him,
after I've killed the children first. And the killer° will not know   865
that he's slain the children he begot until he casts off my madness.
There, look. See, he's tossing his head from the starting line°
and in silence he twists and distorts his Gorgon-gleaming eyes
and cannot control his breathing, and like a bull set to charge,
he roars horribly. I call up the Keres of Tartarus°   870
swiftly to screech and accompany me like dogs a huntsman.
Soon I will set you° dancing all the more and play for you a pipe of fear.
Iris, raise your noble foot and go to Olympus,
while I enter the house of Heracles unseen.

Lyssa and Iris exit separately.°

CHORUS°

Otototoi, groan! The bloom of your city,   875
the child of Zeus is cut off,
wretched Greece, you who will lose,
will lose your benefactor, set to dancing
by a raging madness singing in his ears.

---

858 Helius, the sun god, was frequently called to witness because he could literally oversee everything.

865 Lyssa claims that both she and Heracles will be the murderers of the children. On such "double determination" see below, n. on 1135.

867 Heracles is imagined in the initial stages of madness, first as a runner in a race, then a bull.

870 Tartarus is the underworld; for the Keres, see above, n. on 481.

872 "You" is addressed to Heracles.

874 Lyssa dismounts from the *mechane* to the roof of the *skene* and probably descends via a ladder at the back of the stage building; Iris exits on the machine.

874 The following brief scene (875-921) has three sections: the chorus alone (875-85), the chorus with Amphitryon speaking from within (886-909), and the chorus with the "messenger"(910-21). The predominant rhythm is dochmiac, which typically indicates, as it does here, great excitement.

The most grievous one is gone in her chariot   880
and lays the goad
on the horses to cause ruin,
a Gorgon° of Night with the hissing of
a hundred snakes, Lyssa with the petrifying gaze.

In a moment a divinity overturns the fortunate,
quickly the children will breathe their last at their father's hands.   885

AMPHITRYON *(within)*
Oh, wretched me!

CHORUS
Oh Zeus, the Poinai,° crazed, eating raw flesh,
acting unjustly, will at once lay low your race
with ills and make it childless.

AMPHITRYON *(within)*
Oh roof!

CHORUS
The dances without drums begin,
not pleasing to the thyrsus of Bromius.°   890

AMPHITRYON *(within)*
Oh house!

CHORUS
The spirits go for blood, not for the streams
of a Dionysian libation of wine.

AMPHITRYON *(within)*
In flight, children, away!

CHORUS
                        This is a ruinous song,
ruinous, which is played upon the pipe.   895
He hunts down and pursues his children. Never will Lyssa revel
without accomplishment in the house.

AMPHITRYON *(within)*
Aiai, the ills!

CHORUS
Yes, *aiai!* How I grieve for the old   900
father, and the mother, whose

---

883 For Gorgon see above, n. on 131; here it is used figuratively.
887 The Poinai are personifications of vengeance.
890 The thyrsus was a staff entwined with ivy or grape vines and tipped with a pine
     cone. It was used in the worship of Dionysus, who was known also by the title
     Bromius, "the roaring one". Note here and elsewhere the Dionysiac and music
     images in connection with Heracles' madness.

children were born in vain.

Look, look, a storm shakes the house, the roof collapses.°   905

AMPHITRYON (*within*)

Look, look! What are you doing in the house, child of Zeus?

You send a hellish disturbance against the house, Pallas,

as once you did against Enceladus.°

Enter messenger from the palace.°

MESSENGER

You who are white with age...

CHORUS

                                    What shout do you   910

call me with?

MESSENGER

                          Insufferable things for the house.

CHORUS

                                                        I will send for

no second prophet.

MESSENGER

The children are dead.

CHORUS

                          Aiai!

MESSENGER

Lament what is truly lamentable.

CHORUS

                                    Ruinous murders,

ruinous hands of a parent.   915

MESSENGER

One could not say more than we have suffered.

---

905   The collapse of the palace probably was not indicated by any special effects but
      left to the audience to imagine. It is assumed within the play to have occurred.

908   Pallas Athena once subdued the Giant Enceladus. Her appearance here is beneficent
      as she prevents Heracles from parricide. Just as the audience is asked to imagine
      the collapse of the palace, so too they are asked to imagine the sudden appearance
      of the goddess Athena described by Amphitryon; she was not visible on stage.

908   The "messenger" emerges from the palace and provides to the chorus and audience
      news of what happened within. So far all the audience knows is Lyssa's plans,
      cries from within and the intervention of Athena. The following scene with its long
      narrative provides the details of Heracles' murder of his family. "Messenger" is
      a traditional, although somewhat misleading, name for the character who offers
      news, not messages; here he is a household servant. Since violent actions and
      other difficult-to-stage events were only rarely enacted on the tragic stage, this
      character was very useful for providing such information.

CHORUS
How did the father's lamentable madness, mad destruction,
which you reveal, come upon the children?
Explain in what way these ills from a god
rushed against the house,   920
and make clear the wretched fortunes of the children.

MESSENGER°
There were rituals before the hearth of Zeus,°
purifications for the house, since Heracles had killed
the land's ruler and thrown him out of this house.
And the beautiful band of children was standing around him,   925
and so were his father and Megara, and already the basket had circled
around the altar, and we were keeping a holy silence.
As he was about to take the burning torch with his right hand
to dip it into the water, Alcmene's child
stood in silence. And as their father delayed   930
the children looked at him; and he was no longer himself,
but diseased in the rolling of his eyes
and after sprouting bloodshot veins in his eyes
he was dripping down froth from his thick beard
and he spoke with deranged laughter,   935
"Father, why do I sacrifice with purifying fire
before killing Eurystheus, and have twice the trouble?
To set these things right is the work of a single blow of my hand.
And when I bring here Eurystheus' head
I'll purify my hands of the present murder.   940
Pour out the libations, throw the baskets from your hands.
Who'll give me my bow and arrows? Who my hand's weapon?
I'll go to Mycenae; I must seize
crowbars and axes to shatter totally with iron tools
the Cyclopean foundations,° fitted together   945
with lines marked in red and with chisels."
After this, walking he claimed that he had a chariot,
not having one, and he was mounting the chariot's rail,
and he was striking with his hand as if, I suppose, with a goad.
The servants felt both fear and laughter together,   950
and looking at one another they said,

---

921 The rhythm returns to iambic trimeter.
922 Heracles begins the rituals of purification (involving the basket, containing barley
    and a knife, and a torch) needed to cleanse himself of Lycus' blood. The need for
    purification does not imply moral guilt.
945 On the Cyclopean foundations, see above, n. on 16.

"Is our master teasing us or is he mad?"
But he was going back and forth throughout the house,
and rushing into the middle of the men's quarters,° he claimed
he had arrived at the city of Nisus° , and stepping within the house   955
and lying down on the ground, just as he was, he prepared himself
a meal. After delaying for a short time
he said he was going to the wooded plains of the Isthmus.
And then he stripped off his garments
and was competing against no one, and himself by himself   960
was being proclaimed victor over no one, after demanding
an audience.° Roaring terribly against Eurystheus
he was in Mycenae by his account. His father,
taking him by his mighty hand, addressed him:
"Child, what's wrong? What is the nature of this aberration?   965
Surely it's not that the bloodshed of those
you just killed has made you frenzied?"° But he, thinking it was
    Eurystheus'
father trembling as a suppliant to touch his hand,
pushed him away, and prepared his ready quiver
and arrows for his own children, thinking he was killing   970
those of Eurystheus. They, trembling with fear,
were darting, one here, one there, one to his poor mother's
robes, another beneath a pillar's shadow,
and another cowered like a bird under the altar.
Their mother cried out, "You begot them, what are you doing?
    are you killing   975
your children?"And the old man and the crowd of servants called out,
but he, twisting his child in a circle away from the pillar,
a terrible turning by the foot, stood opposite
and struck him in the liver. And on his back,
breathing out his life, he drenched the stone pillars.   980
But his father raised a shout and added this boast:
"This one dead nestling of Eursytheus
has fallen at my hands, paying fully for his father's hatred."
And he was aiming his bow at another, who had cowered
around the altar's foundation, thinking that he was hidden.   985

---

954 Men and women had separate quarters in a Greek house of Euripides' time.
955 The city of Nisus is Megara on the Isthmus of Corinth (see 958 below), so called
    after its king Nisus.
962 Corinth, where Heracles imagines he is, was the site of athletic games, the Isthmian
    games, every two years.
967 The Greeks believed that bloodshed could cause madness; that is not what causes
    Heracles' frenzy here.

and the wretch fell at his father's knees first,
and throwing his hand towards his father's chin and neck°
said, "Dearest father, don't kill me;
I am yours, your child, you won't be killing Eurystheus'."
But he, since the child stood within the ruinous bow's range,   990
rolling his wild-looking Gorgon's eyes,
raised his club above his head, like a smith forging iron,
struck it against the child's blond head,
and shattered the bones. After killing the second child,
he went to sacrifice a third victim in addition to these two.   995
But first the wretched mother carried him off
inside the house and locked the doors.
But he, as if at the Cyclopean walls themselves,
was digging and levering the door frames, and tearing out the posts
laid low wife and child in one shot.   1000
And then he galloped towards his father's murder.
But a phantom came, as it appeared to view
Pallas, brandishing a spear over her helmet's crest,
and she threw a rock against Heracles' chest,
which checked him from his raging murder and sent him   1005
into sleep; he fell to the ground, striking his back
against a pillar, which had broken in two
in the roof's collapse and was lying on the foundations.
But we, freed from our flight,
with the old man's help, attached bonds of twisted knots   1010
to the pillar, so that when he ceased from sleep
he would not do anything in addition to these deeds.
And the wretch sleeps an unblessed sleep,
after killing his children and wife. And for my part, I
don't know who of mortals is more miserable.   1015

The messenger exits either back into the palace or down one of the eisodoi.

CHORUS°

There was a murder which the rock of Argos° keeps,
then most infamous and unbelievable to Greece—
that of Danaus' children;°

---

987 The gestures described are the traditional ones of supplication.
1016 The chorus now sings a brief, astrophic song in which they try to compare Heracles'
   deeds to those of previous mythological characters familiar to the audience. Such
   use of *exempla* is common in Greek poetry. Here it allows the chorus/Euripides
   to underscore the horror of the deeds.
1016 The rock of Argos is the citadel of the city of Argos.
1018 With the exception of the eldest, Hypermnestra, all fifty daughters of Danaus,
   after being forced to marry their cousins, killed them on their wedding night.

but these deeds of the wretched son of Zeus
surpassed, outstripped those former ills.   1020

I am able to tell of Procne's° murder of one child,
sacrificed to the Muses; but you, begetting
three children, destroyer,
joined a raging mad lot in killing them.

Aiai! What lamentation   1025
or wailing or song of the dead or what
dance of Hades am I to sound?

Ah! Ah!
Look, the doors of the high-gated
house are parting.°   1030
Oh me!
Look at the miserable children
lying before their wretched father,
who sleeps a terrible sleep after the children's murder,
and around Heracles' body   1035
there are these bonds
and many strong knots, attached
to the stony pillar of the house.

And the old man, like a bird lamenting its pangs
over its unfledged children, following   1040
with bitter steps, is here.

Amphitryon enters from the palace, following the ekkyklema *with the corpses and
the sleeping Heracles.*°

AMPHITRYON
Old men of Cadmus, in silence, in silence

1021 Procne, in order to take vengeance on her husband Tereus for his rape and brutal
treatment of her sister Philomela, killed their son, Itys. It remains unclear why the
son is said to be sacrificed to the Muses.
1030 Although there is still some debate on the issue, it is very likely that here the
device known as the *ekkyklema* was used. It would allow the audience now to see
the interior scene described by the messenger: the corpses of the children and
Megara and the sleeping and bound Heracles. Amphitryon, who is not part of
this tableau, follows the *ekkyklema* on foot and is announced in iambic trimeters
by the chorus at 1039-41.
1042 The following scene (up to 1086) is a charged lyric scene between the chorus and
Amphitryon, of which the central theme is the fear of an awakened Heracles.
There is considerable movement in this scene, with Amphitryon trying to get the
chorus to be quiet and to move away from the sleeping Heracles and Amphitryon
himself moving away in fear (see 1070 and 1081ff.).

will you not let this man relaxed in sleep
forget his ills completely?

CHORUS
Old man, with tears I groan over you, and   1045
the children and the victorious man.

AMPHITRYON
Move farther off, don't
make a sound, don't shout, don't
rouse him from his bed
while he rests calmly   1050
in sleep.

CHORUS
Oimoi!
How much bloodshed this is...

AMPHITRYON
Ah, ah! You'll destroy me.

CHORUS
That has
been spilled and rises up.

AMPHITRYON
Won't you cry out a silent
lamentation, old men?
Or he'll wake up, loosen the bonds, and destroy the city,   1055
destroy his father and shatter the house.

CHORUS
It's impossible, impossible for me.

AMPHITRYON
Silence, let me listen to his breathing. Come, let me lend an ear.   1060

CHORUS
Is he sleeping?

AMPHITRYON
Yes, he sleeps an accursed sleep that is no sleep,
he who killed his wife, killed his children
with the twang of the bow.

CHORUS
Now groan...

AMPHITRYON
                    I groan.

CHORUS
The destruction of the children...

AMPHITRYON

Oimoi!   1065

CHORUS

And of your child...

AMPHITRYON:

Aiai!

CHORUS

Old man.

AMPHITRYON

Silence, silence!
He's awake, he's turning over. Come,
I'll conceal myself, hidden within the house.   1070

Amphitryon moves away from Heracles.

CHORUS

Courage. Night holds your son's eyelids.

AMPHITRYON

Look out, look out. Wretched,
in my woes I don't shrink from leaving
the light, but I'm afraid that if he slays me, his father,   1075
he'll contrive ills on top of ills
and have more kindred bloodshed
in addition to these Erinyes.°

CHORUS

You should have died then, when you came home
after punishing the murder of your wife's brother
by sacking the very famous city of the Taphians.   1080

AMPHITRYON

Flight, flight, old men, move away from
the house. Flee the mad
man who's waking.
Or soon, throwing a second murder on top of murder,   1085
he'll be frenzied again throughout the city of Cadmeans.

Amphitryon flees from the waking Heracles.

CHORUS

Zeus, why did you hate your child
so cruelly and lead him into this sea of ills?

1077 The Erinyes were spirits of punishment, especially of kindred bloodshed. Amphitryon means that Heracles, if he kills his father, will incur more spirits of vengeance,
in addition to those he has from the murder of his children.

HERACLES°

Ah!

I'm alive and I see what I ought to see,
the sky and the earth and these shafts of the sun.   1090
But how I've fallen into a billowy and terrible
disturbance of my wits and I'm drawing hot breaths,
shallow ones, not securely from the lungs.
Look, why with my vigorous trunk and arms
moored like a ship with bonds   1095
do I sit against stonework that is broken in two,
sitting next to corpses?
My winged shafts and bow are strewn on the ground,
which before now stood beside my arms
and protected my sides and were protected by me.   1100
Surely I haven't descended again back into Hades,
after completing the course from Hades for Eurystheus?
But I see neither the Sisyphean rock°
nor Pluto nor the scepters of Demeter's daughter.
I'm astounded. Where in the world am I that I'm at a loss?   1105
Hello! Who of my friends is near or far
to cure this ignorance of mine?
For I recognize nothing clearly of what I'm used to.

AMPHITRYON

Old men, shall I draw near my ills?

CHORUS

And I with you, I won't abandon these misfortunes.   1110

HERACLES

Father, why do you weep and cover your eyes,
standing far away from your dearest child?

AMPHITRYON

Child, yes, even though you're badly off you are mine.

HERACLES

What pain do I suffer, which you're crying over?

1089 Heracles gradually comes to and begins to recognize his surroundings. He
    remains confused, however, and more information will come from Amphitryon,
    who slowly reenters the scene, after fleeing his son at 1081ff.
1103 Sisyphus was a notorious trickster, punished in the underworld by being com-
    pelled to roll a rock up a hill, only to have it roll down again *ad infinitum*. Heracles,
    entertaining the possibility that he might have returned to Hades, remarks that
    he sees none of the familiar sights, Sisyphus' rock, Pluto (see above, n. on 808) or
    the scepters of Demeter's daughter (see above, n. on 608).

AMPHITRYON
Things that even a god, should he learn of them, would lament.   1115

HERACLES
The boast is great, but you haven't yet named the misfortune.

AMPHITRYON
No, for you yourself can see, if you're now sane.

HERACLES
Tell me if you're adding some strange new thing to my life.

AMPHITRYON
If you're no longer a hellish reveller, I'd explain.

HERACLES
Ah! Again you've spoken this curious riddle.   1120

AMPHITRYON
Yes, I'm examining whether you're now firmly sane.

HERACLES
I don't recall at all my mind being frenzied.

AMPHITRYON
Should I loosen my child's bonds, old men, or what am I to do?

HERACLES
And tell me who bound me; for I feel ashamed.

AMPHITRYON
Know this much of your ills; leave the rest alone.   1125

HERACLES
Is silence enough for what I wish to learn?

AMPHITRYON
Zeus, do you see these things from Hera's throne?°

HERACLES
But have we suffered something hostile from that quarter?

AMPHITRYON
Let the goddess be and take care of your own ills.

HERACLES
I'm ruined; you'll speak of some misfortune.   1130

AMPHITRYON
Look, behold these fallen corpses of children.

HERACLES
Oimoi! What is this sight I see in my wretchedness?

1127 Amphitryon's remark suggests Zeus' subservience to Hera's wishes in this matter.

AMPHITRYON

You strove, my son, after a war that was no war against the children.

HERACLES

What war did you mention? Who killed them?

AMPHITRYON

You and your bow and arrows and the god who is responsible.°   1135

HERACLES

What are you saying? What did I do? Father, you're announcing ills.

AMPHITRYON

You were mad. You're asking for painful explanations.

HERACLES

Am I the murderer of my wife too?

AMPHITRYON

All these deeds are of your hand alone.

HERACLES

Aiai! A cloud of lamentation surrounds me.   1140

AMPHITRYON

For these reasons I lament your fortunes.

HERACLES

Did I smash my house where I raged in madness?

AMPHITRYON

I know nothing except one thing: everything of yours is in misfortune.

HERACLES

Where did the sting of madness seize me? Where did it destroy me?

AMPHITRYON

When you were purifying your hands with fire around the altar.   1145

HERACLES

Oimoi! Why do I spare my life,
since I've become the murderer of my dearest children?
Shall I not go to leap from a smooth rock
or by striking a sword into my liver
become an avenger of my children's blood,   1150
or by kindling my vigorous flesh with fire
thrust away my life's infamy which remains?
But interrupting my thoughts of suicide
here comes Theseus, my kin° and friend.

1135 The role of the god does not remove Heracles' own responsibility for these deeds. The Greeks accepted a notion of "double" or "over" determination for actions: a divine agent as well as a mortal share the responsibility. Here are named mortal agent, god, and weapon.

1154 Theseus was Heracles' cousin on both his mother's and father's (Zeus') sides.

I'll be seen and the pollution° of child murder   1155
will come to the eyes of the dearest of my friends.°
Oimoi, what shall I do? Where am I to find solitude from
ills, taking wing or going beneath the earth?
Come, I'll throw a shadow around my head,
for I'm ashamed at the evils I've done,   1160
and I wish in no way to afflict the blameless
by striking this man with blood guilt.

Heracles covers his head.

Theseus has entered from one of the eisodoi.°

THESEUS
I arrive with others, who remain along the streams
of the Asopus,° armed soldiers of the land of the Athenians,
bearing, old man, an allied force to your child.   1165
For a report came to the city of the sons of Erechtheus°
that Lycus had snatched this land's scepter
and was waging war and battle against you.
And making a return for what Heracles began
in saving me from below, I have come, old man, if you have   1170
any need of my hand or of my allies'.
Ah! Why is the ground full of these corpses?
It can't be that I've been left behind and have arrived
too late for these unexpected ills. Who killed these children?
Whose was this wife I see?   1175
Children don't stand near the spear;
no, I discover, doubtless, some other new ill.

AMPHITRYON
Lord who holds the olive-bearing hill...°

1155 It was believed pollution could be spread by contact and even by sight or hearing.

1156 The word translated as friend, *xenos*, means stranger, guest, and host. Here it refers to the friendship which develops in the context of the host-guest relationship, an important one for the the Greeks, and one protected by no less a power than Zeus himself.

1162 Theseus' arrival is a mild surprise; we have heard of his return from Hades earlier in the play, but there was no reason to expect that he would arrive at this crucial juncture. He has "partial vision" upon entrance, seeing initially only part of the stage.

1164 For the Asopus, see above, n. on 786.

1166 Erechtheus was one of the legendary early kings of Athens.

1178 From 1178-1213 the exchange between Amphitryon and Theseus is in lyric, predominantly dochmiac, rhythms, again indicating excitement. "Olive-bearing hill" refers to Athens, famous for its olive industry.

THESEUS
Why do you address me with a pitiable° prelude?

AMPHITRYON
We have suffered miserable sufferings at the hands of the gods.   1180

THESEUS
These children over whom you cry, whose are they?

AMPHITRYON
My suffering offspring begot them
and their begetter, enduring bloodshed's pollution, slew them.

THESEUS
What are you saying? What did he do?

AMPHITRYON
Deranged by an impulse of madness   1185
with arrows dipped in the hundred-headed hydra's blood.°

THESEUS
You've spoken dreadful things.

AMPHITRYON
We're gone, gone, nothing.

THESEUS
Speak no ill-omened word.

AMPHITRYON
You command one wishing so.

THESEUS
This contest is Hera's. But who is this among the corpses, old man?

AMPHITRYON
This one is mine, my much-suffering child, who went   1190
to the plain of Phlegra° as a warrior with the gods
to the battle where the Giants were killed.

THESEUS
Oh! Oh! Who of men is so ill-starred by nature?   1195

AMPHITRYON
You couldn't know another mortal
who has suffered more and been forced to wander more.

1179 Pitiable, probably because of the music which accompanied the address, not because of the words themselves.

1186 See above, n. on 421.

1191 The plain of Phlegra, the site of the battle of the Giants (see above, n. on 178), was variously located. Euripides probably thought of it as up north on the tip of Chalcidice (see map).

THESEUS
Why does he cover his miserable head with his robes?

AMPHITRYON
Feeling shame before your eyes
and your kindred friendship   1200
and at the murder of his children.

THESEUS
But if I came to share the pain? Uncover him.

AMPHITRYON
Child, drop the robe
from your eyes, throw it off, show your face to the sun.
My weight joins my tears in wrestling against you.   1205
I supplicate you, falling about your chin
and knee and hand,° breaking forth into
an old man's tears. Oh, child,   1210
check your fierce lion's spirit, by which
you are being led to a murderous, impious course,
wishing to join ills to ills,° child.

THESEUS
Well now, I tell you, sitting in a sorry state,
to reveal your face to friends;   1215
for no darkness holds so dark a cloud
that it could hide your misfortune and ills.
Why do you shake your head and show your fear?
So that the defilement of your greeting may not strike me?
It doesn't matter at all to me if I fare badly along with you. 1220
I fared well with you once. It must be credited to
when you brought me safely into the light from the dead.
I hate friends' gratitude which grows weak with age
and anyone who wishes to benefit from the good things
but not to sail with friends in misfortune.   1225
Stand up, unveil your miserable head,
look at me. Whatever mortal is noble
bears what falls from the gods,° and does not refuse it.

HERACLES (*now unveiled and standing*)
Theseus, do you see this contest of my children?

THESEUS
I have heard and you show the ills to my sight.   1230

1209 On these gestures see above, n. on 987
1213 Suicide in addition to the murders.
1228 The metaphor, from dicing, is common in Greek literature.

HERACLES
Why then did you uncover my head to the sun?

THESEUS
Why? As a mortal you can't stain the things of the gods.

HERACLES
Flee, miserable one, my unholy pollution.

THESEUS
There is no avenging spirit° from friend to friend.

HERACLES
Thank you. I don't regret that I helped you.   1235

THESEUS
And I, faring well then, pity you now.

HERACLES
Am I pitiable after killing my children?

THESEUS
I weep for your sake at external misfortunes.

HERACLES
Have you found others in worse ills?

THESEUS
You touch heaven from below with your bad fortune.   1240

HERACLES
For that reason I'm prepared to die.
[There is probably a lacuna here, most likely of no more than two lines.]

THESEUS
Do you think that the gods care at all about your threats?

HERACLES
God is stubborn, and I toward the gods.

THESEUS
Hold your tongue, so you don't suffer something greater by your proud
     talk.

HERACLES
I'm filled with ills and there's no longer a place where they can be
     stowed.   1245

THESEUS
But what will you do? Where are you borne in anger?

HERACLES
Dying, I will go where I returned from, below the earth.

1234 The avenging spirit of the dead which causes pollution; see above, n. on 1077.

THESEUS
You've spoken the words of a common man.

HERACLES
Yes, but you're giving me advice when you're outside misfortune.

THESEUS
Is it the Heracles who endured many things who says this?   1250

HERACLES
Not so many. Toiling must have its limit.

THESEUS
The benefactor and great friend to mortals?

HERACLES
They're no help to me, but Hera holds sway.

THESEUS
Greece would not endure your dying through ignorance.

HERACLES
Listen now to how I'll contend with words against   1255
your advice. And I will reveal to you
that my life both is unlivable now and was so before.
First of all, I came from this man, the sort who, needing purification
after killing my mother's aged father,°
married Alcmene, who gave me birth.   1260
And whenever the foundation of a family is not laid down
correctly, it's inevitable that the offspring be unfortunate.
And Zeus, whoever this Zeus is, begot me as an enemy
to Hera (Don't you, old man, be angry:
I consider you, not Zeus, my father),   1265
and when I was still at the breast
the wife of Zeus sent Gorgon-gleaming snakes
into my cradle so that I might die.°
And when I attained the cloak of a vigorous
body, what need is there to mention the toils I endured?   1270
What sort of lions or three-bodied
typhons° or Giants or war against
four-legged Centaurs° did I not dispatch?
And after killing the dog with heads all around that kept growing back,

---

1259 See above, n. on 17.

1268 Even as an infant Heracles was impressively strong: he strangled the snakes.

1272 In Hesiod's *Theogony* Typhon has a hundred heads, all snakes, but such numbers were not always immutable. The plural for Typhons here and Giants and Centaurs below suggests the host of Heracles' many labors. For the Giants and Centaurs see above, n. on 178 and 181.

the hydra, I both went through herds   1275
of thousands of other labors and arrived among the dead
to convey Hades' three-headed watch-dog
into the light at Eurystheus' orders.
And this final labor I, the sufferer, endured,
killing my children, to cope the house with ills.   1280
And I have come to this point of necessity: It is not religiously permitted
for me to inhabit my dear Thebes. And even if I do remain,
into what sort of temple or gathering of friends
shall I go? For the ruin I have forbids my being addressed.°
But am I to go to Argos? How, when I'm fleeing my fatherland?   1285
But come now, am I to set off for another city?
And then to be looked at askance when recognized,
locked up by bitter and sharp tongues:
"Isn't this Zeus' son, who at one time killed his children
and wife? Let him get the hell out of this land."   1290
[For a man once called blessed
reversals are something bitter; but the one for whom things always
go badly, since he's innately unfortunate, feels no pain.]
To this point of misfortune I think I'll one day come:
the earth will cry out forbidding me   1295
to touch the land, and the sea and the rivers'
streams to travel across them, and I'll closely resemble
Ixion, driven round chained to a wheel.°
[And this is the best—for none of the Greeks,
among whom we were blessedly successful, to look at me.]   1300
Why then should I live? What gain shall I have
in possession of a worthless, unholy life?
Let the famous wife of Zeus dance,
striking Olympus'° sparkling floor with her shoes.
For she has achieved the purpose she wished,   1305
turning upside down the first man of Greece
from the foundations. Who would pray
to such a goddess? One who because of a woman,
in jealousy over Zeus' union, destroyed

1284 See above, n. on 1155.
1288 The image, as R. Renehan suggests, is of a tongue having a door and Heracles
    being locked up, figuratively of course, because in exile he would not able to
    respond to these taunts.
1298 Ixion, the first murderer in Greek mythology, was absolved of his crime by Zeus
    and repaid the favor by trying to rape Hera. As punishment for this he was chained
    to a spinning wheel.
1304 Mount Olympus, the home of the gods.

Greece's benefactor, who was not at all blameworthy.   1310

CHORUS
This contest is from none other of the gods
than Zeus' wife. You perceive this well.

THESEUS
<If you were going to be the only person defiled by misfortune>
I would advise you <to kill yourself> rather than suffer ills.
But no one of mortals is untouched by fortune,
nor of the gods, if, as I assume, the stories of poets aren't false.   1315
Have they not joined in illicit unions
with one another? Have they not defiled their fathers
with bonds for the sake of ruling? But nevertheless they dwell
on Olympus and endure their errors.°
And yet what will you say if, a mortal, you   1320
make these fortunes too much to heart, when the gods do not?
Well, abandon Thebes because of the law
and accompany me to the city of Pallas.°
There after I've purified your hands of the pollution°
I'll give you a house and a share of my possessions.   1325
And the gifts from the citizens that I have after saving
fourteen youths by killing the Cnossan bull,°
I'll give these to you. And everywhere sections of land
have been apportioned to me; these will be given your name,
and from now on will be so called by mortals   1330
while you're alive. And whenever you go to Hades,
the entire city of the Athenians will extol you in honor
with sacrifices and memorials of stone.
For it is a fine crown for the citizens to get a good reputation
in the eyes of the Greeks for helping a good man.   1335
And with this favor I will repay you for
saving me; for now you are in need of friends.
[Whenever the gods give honor, there's no need of friends
for the god helping when he wishes is sufficient.]

1319 The adulterous behavior of Zeus and of other gods was infamous. Binding one's
father for the sake of rule refers to Zeus' actions against his father Cronus and
Cronus' against his father Uranus. Euripides here and elsewhere (most notably at
Hippolytus 451ff.) has a character employ an argument based on divine behavior:
"If the gods do x and put up with it, shouldn't you also accept x?"
1323 Athens.
1324 The pollution caused by the murder of his family; see above, n. on 922.
1327 Theseus killed the Cnossan (Cretan) Minotaur, a half-man, half-bull creature,
and saved the fourteen youths who would otherwise have been offered up to
the monster.

HERACLES

    Oimoi! These things° are incidental to my ills;   1340
    for I don't believe that the gods put up with
    illicit unions and binding hands with chains—
    neither did I ever think this proper nor will I be persuaded—
    nor that one is by nature master of another.
    For a god, if he is truly a god, lacks   1345
    nothing; these are the wretched stories of poets.°
    But I take care, even in these ills,
    that I not, by leaving the light, incur a charge of cowardice.
    For anyone who cannot withstand the blows of fortune
    would not be able to withstand a man's weapon.   1350
    I will brave death; and I will go to your
    city and owe you a thousand thanks for your gifts.
    But indeed I tasted a thousand labors,
    none of which I refused, nor did I let fall
    streams from my eyes, nor would I ever have thought   1355
    that I would come to this —to shed tears from my eyes.
    But as things are now, as it seems, I must be a slave to fortune.
    Well now. Old man, you see my exile
    and you see that I'm the murderer of my children.
    Give these corpses burial and lay them out,   1360
    honoring them with tears (for me the law does not permit),
    leaning them against their mother's breast, and giving them to her
       embrace,
    the wretched partnership that I, the sufferer,
    killed, unwillingly. And when you've covered the corpses in the earth,
    dwell in this city miserably, but do it nevertheless.   1365
    [Force your spirit to bear my ills with me.]
    Children, I, the father who engendered and begot you,
    killed you, nor did you benefit from my fine things
    which I was preparing, achieving a good reputation
    in life for you, a fine advantage from your father.   1370
    And you, miserable one, I destroyed, an unequal return
    for steadfastly preserving my bed,
    enduring at home long care for the house.
    Oimoi for my wife and children, *oimoi* for myself!

1340 "These things" is somewhat vague, but refers to what Theseus has just said, the
      arguments that Heracles goes on to dispute.
1346 The attack on the gods would have been familiar to some, at least, of the Athenians,
      since the very same argument was made by the poet-philosopher Xenophanes,
      who lived in the second half of the sixth and into the fifth century.

How miserably I've fared and am unyoked   1375
from my children and wife. Mournful joys of
kisses, and mournful partnership with these weapons.
For I'm at a loss whether I should keep these or abandon them,
which falling against my sides will say this:
"With us you killed your children and wife; you carry us,   1380
the murderers of your children." Then shall I bear these
in my hands? Saying what? But stripped of the weapons
with which I achieved the finest things in Greece,
am I to die shamefully, subjecting myself to my enemies?
These must not be left behind, but miserably be saved, even though
    they pain me.   1385
In one thing, Theseus, work with me: come and
help me convey the savage dog to Argos,
lest in grief, bereft of my children, I suffer something.
Land of Cadmus and all Theban people,
cut your hair,° mourn with me, go to the grave   1390
of the children. And mourn for all of us together,
both the corpses and me. We are all completely ruined,
miserable, struck down by one blow of fortune from Hera.

THESEUS

Stand up, unfortunate one; enough of tears.°

HERACLES

I couldn't: my limbs are stiff.   1395

THESEUS

Yes, misfortunes overpower even the strong.

HERACLES

Oh!
May I be a rock right here, forgetful of ills.

THESEUS

Stop. Give a hand to a helping friend.

HERACLES

But may I not wipe blood off on your robes.

THESEUS

Wipe it off, spare nothing; I don't refuse.   1400

HERACLES

Bereaved of my children, I have you as my child.

1390 A sign of mourning.
1394 It seems that Heracles has sunk again to the ground. But it is possible that he has
    remained seated among the corpses throughout his conversation with Theseus.

THESEUS

Put your arm on my neck, and I will lead.

Heracles rises and leans on Theseus for support.

HERACLES

A dear yoking; the other was disastrous.
Old man, one ought to get such a man as a friend.

AMPHITRYON

The fatherland which begot this one is blessed in its children.   1405

HERACLES

Theseus, turn me around so I may see the children.

THESEUS

What for? With this remedy, will you feel better?

HERACLES

I desire it, and I wish to embrace my father.

AMPHITRYON

Look here, child, for you're striving after what's dear to me too.

They embrace.

THESEUS

Do you thus no longer remember your labors?   1410

HERACLES

All those ills I endured are less than these.

THESEUS

If someone sees you, he'll not approve your being womanly.

HERACLES

In your view, am I to go on living, though humbled? But I don't think I
did so before.

THESEUS

Very much so. In your sickness you are not the "famous Heracles."

HERACLES

What sort were *you* below, in your ills?   1415

THESEUS

In courage I was a man less than everyone.

HERACLES

How then do you reproach me that I'm cast down by ills?

THESEUS

Go forward.

HERACLES

Farewell, old man.

AMPHITRYON
You too, my child.

HERACLES
Bury the children, just as I said.

AMPHITRYON
And who *me*, child?

HERACLES
I will.

AMPHITRYON
Coming when?

HERACLES
Whenever you die, father.   1420

[**AMPHITRYON**
How?

HERACLES
I will send for you from Thebes to Athens.]
But bear the children in, pains that are hard to bear.
And I, having destroyed my house with shameful deeds,
all ruined, will follow Theseus, a little boat in tow.°
Whoever wishes to acquire wealth or strength   1425
more than good friends thinks badly.

Heracles exits with Theseus down the same eisodos *from which Theseus first arrived.*

CHORUS°
We go, pitiable and much lamenting,
after losing the greatest of friends.

The ekkyklema *with the corpses is rolled back into the palace and Amphitryon follows it in; the chorus leaves the orchestra via the* eisodos *from which they entered.*

1424 At line 631 Heracles was the tugboat for the "little boats" (i.e. his children). Now
   the tables have turned: *he* is the "little boat in tow" and Theseus the tugboat.
1426 The last two lines are in anapoetic dimeters, a marching rhythm for the chorus'
   exit.

BACCHAE

Translation and notes by Stephen Esposito

CHARACTERS

AGAVE, mother of Pentheus, leader of the Theban Bacchae

CADMUS, grandfather of Pentheus and Dionysus; father of Agave; founder and former king of Thebes

CHORUS, fifteen Bacchae (frenzied female worshippers of Dionysus) from Lydia (in Asia Minor); also called "maenads" (mad-women)

DIONYSUS, (= "The Stranger"): son of immortal Zeus and mortal Semele; first cousin of Pentheus; appears both as a god (1-63 and 1329-51) and as a human, i.e. as the disguised Lydian "Stranger" (434-518, 604-861, 912-976)

MESSENGER #1, herdsman from Thebes

MESSENGER #2, slave of Pentheus

PENTHEUS, son of Agave and Echion; first cousin of Dionysus; successor to his grandfather Cadmus as king of Thebes; probably 18-20 years old

SOLDIER, one of Pentheus' guards

TIRESIAS, blind old prophet of Thebes

Setting: The time is the heroic past before the Trojan War, in the third generation after the founding of Thebes. The scene is the palace of King Pentheus on the acropolis of seven-gated Thebes, one of the most powerful cities of Mycenean Greece. Thebes was also a center of Dionysiac cult and a chief city of Boeotia ("Cow-land"), a region of central Greece; the city was dominated to the south by Mt. Cithaeron, some ten miles away.

The wooden facade of Pentheus' palace forms the back-drop at center stage and shows several Doric columns supporting an entablature (591, 1214). To one side is a fenced-in, vine-covered sanctuary containing the tomb of Semele (Dionysus' mother) and the smouldering ruins of her house (7-12).

PROLOGUE

Enter Dionysus, stage left, disguised as an exotic young holy man from Asia; he carries a thyrsus,° wears a smiling mask, fawnskin cloak and ivy wreath.

DIONYSUS

I have come to this land of Thebes as the son of Zeus.   1

Dionysus is my name. Semele, the daughter of Cadmus,

---

1   *Thyrsus*: A long, light fennel-stalk crowned with a bundle of ivy.

gave me birth after being forced into labor by fiery lightning.
Exchanging my divinity for human form I have arrived
at Dirce's streams and the waters of Ismenus.°   5
I see the tomb of my thunder-struck mother here
near the palace and the fallen ruins of her house
smouldering with the still living flames of Zeus' blast,
a memorial of Hera's undying hybris° against my mother.
I praise Cadmus who keeps this ground untrodden,   10
a shrine for his daughter. But it was I who covered her sanctuary
all around with the grape-vine's clustering foliage.
    After leaving the gold-rich fields of the Lydians
and Phrygians, I moved on to Persia's sun-parched plateaux
and Bactra's walls and the bleak land   15
of the Medes° and opulent Arabia
and all of Asia Minor whose parts hug the salty sea
with beautifully-towered cities
full of Greeks and barbarians mixed together.
I first came to this Greek city   20
only after I had roused to dancing all those Asian lands
and established my rites there so that I might be seen by mortals as a
    god.
    It was this very Thebes, of all the Greek lands, that I first incited
to female shrieks of ecstasy, wrapping her in fawnskins,
putting into her hands the thyrsus, my ivy javelin.   25
I did this because my mother's sisters, of all people,°
denied that I, Dionysus, was begotten from Zeus. Semele, they say,
was seduced by some mortal but then, by Cadmus' clever contrivance,
she charged the error of her bed to Zeus. For this reason,
because Semele had lied about her union with the god,   30
her three sisters sneered that Zeus had killed her.
To punish that slander I myself stung those same sisters,°
hounding them from their homes with fits of frenzy so that now,
knocked out of their senses, they make their homes on Mt. Cithaeron.°

---

5 Dirce and Ismenus: The two small rivers of Thebes. Dionysus was washed in the
   waters of Dirce at the time of his birth (cp. 519-22).
9 Hera: Zeus' seventh and permanent wife. She was bitterly jealous of her husband's
   frequent affairs. For an example of Hera's jealousy, see *Heracles* 840 and 1308-10.
16 Medes: Inhabitants of Media (Asia), southwest of the Caspian Sea.
26 Semele's sisters (= Dionysus' aunts): Agave, Autonoe, and Ino.
32-37 *Dionysus' opening act of war*: This begins the play's action. All Thebes' women
   are driven into a frenzy and onto the mountain. *The play, then, takes place in a city
   without women* (except for the chorus of Asian maenads in the orchestra) until
   Agave's entry at 1168.
34 Cithaeron: A mountain sacred to Dionysus, ten miles south of Thebes.

I forced them to wear the vestments of my mysteries   35
and the entire female seed of Cadmeians, all who were women,
I drove from their homes in madness. Mingled together
with Cadmus' daughters, the women of Thebes sit beneath green firs
on roofless rocks. For this city must learn well,
even if it doesn't want to learn, that it is still uninitiated in my bacchic
    rites.   40
I must vindicate my mother Semele
by revealing myself to mortals as the god whom she bore to Zeus.
    Cadmus, then, has passed the power and privileges of his monarchy
to the son of his daughter Agave. But that one, Pentheus,
fights against the gods by fighting against me. He thrusts me away   45
from his libations and mentions me nowhere in his prayers.
For this reason I shall show him and all Thebans
that I am a god. After setting matters here in order
I will move on to another land, revealing myself there too.
But if the city of Thebans, with wrath and weapons,   50
seeks to drive the Bacchae down from the mountain
I will wage war on the city, marshalling my army of maenads.°
For this reason I have changed my appearance to a mortal one
and transformed my shape into the nature of a man.

Dionysus turns and addresses the entering chorus; they show no sign of hear-
ing him.

    Hail, my sisterhood of worshippers,° you who left Mt. Tmolus,°   55
bulwark of Lydia, women I wooed from foreign lands.
Comrades in rest, companions of the road,
raise up those drums native to Phrygia's cities,
the invention of mother Rhea° and myself.
Surround this royal house of Pentheus!   60
Strike your drums so that Cadmus' city may come to see!
Meanwhile I shall hasten to the folds of Mt. Cithaeron
to join the choral dances of my Theban Bacchae.

Exit Dionysus, stage left, towards Cithaeron; enter Chorus, orchestra left,

---

52   *Maenads* ("frenzied women") are the same as Bacchae ("female devotees of Bac-
     chus"), though the term *maenads* (occurring mainly in the play's second half)
     highlights their frenzy.
55   *"Sisterhood of worshippers"*: *Thiasos* is the religious term for cult groups devoted to
     Dionysus.
55   Tmolus: Mountain in Asia Minor, sacred (64) to Dionysus.
59   Rhea: A Greek goddess (a Titan, sister and wife of Kronos, and mother of Zeus)
     who is here identified with the Asiatic goddess Cybele, the great Mother Goddess
     of Phrygia in Asia Minor.

wearing dresses, fawnskins and (probably) turbans. Each bacchant carries a tambourine-like drum.

CHORAL ENTRANCE SONG°

PRELUDE

From the land of Asia I hasten, leaving behind Tmolus, sacred mountain,
swift in my sweet toiling for Bromios the Roaring God°   65
wearied but not wearied,
praising Bacchus, crying out "euoi."°
Who is in the street, in the street?°
Who is in the palace? Let him come outside to watch.
Let everyone keep their lips pure in holy silence.° I shall forever sing   70
in Dionysus' honor the hymns that custom has prescribed.

HYMN TO DIONYSUS

STROPHE 1

O blessed is he who, happy in his heart,°
knows the initiation rites of the gods,°
purifies his life and
joins his soul to the cult group,°   75
dancing on the mountains, with holy purifications
celebrating the Bacchic rituals.
O blessed the man who dutifully observes
the mysteries of the Great Mother, Cybele.°
Swinging high the thyrsus   80
and crowned in ivy°

FIRST CHORAL SONG (64-169): The chorus of fifteen Asiatic Bacchae now enters the orchestra. The young, vigorous women, in their maenadic costumes and masks, sing and dance excitedly to the music of a reed-piper.

65   *Bromios* ("the Roarer"): A cult name of Dionysus (22x in the *Bacchae*).

67   "Euoi": An exclamation of joy used in the cult of Dionysus to praise the god.

68   "Who is in the street, in the street?" is one of this song's three cultic formulas (cp. 83, 152; 116, 165).

70   Reverential silence customarily preceded ritual acts such as this "cultic" entrance by the chorus.

72-77 *Prerequisites for Dionysiac happiness:* a) knowledge of the mysteries; b) living a pure life; c) initiation into the *thiasos*; d) participation in the mountain rituals honoring Dionysus.

73   Knowledge of the Dionysiac mysteries was secret except to initiates.

75   *Joining one's soul (psyche) to the cult group (thiasos):* refers to the soul's union with god or to a loss of the self as a result of the merging of individual with group consciousness as physical exhaustion is translated into physical well-being.

79   Cybele: An Asiatic goddess worshipped in Asia Minor as the 'Great Mother' of all living things.

81   Ivy: Being "ever-green" ivy symbolized the vine god's vigor and vitality.

he serves Dionysus.
Onward you Bacchae, onward Bacchae, °
escort the roaring Bromios home,
a god and the son of a god! Escort him   85
down from the Phrygian mountains into Greece's wide-wayed streets,
streets wide for dancing, Bromios the Roaring God!

ANTISTROPHE 1

At that time when Dionysus' mother was pregnant°
Zeus' thunder flew down
forcing her into the pangs of labor.   90
She thrust the child from her womb prematurely
and was herself slain by the bolt of lightning.
Immediately Zeus, the son of Cronus,
received the baby in his own birth chambers
concealing it in his thigh.   95
Stitching his leg back together
with golden clasps
he hid the infant from Hera.
When the Fates ordained it°
Zeus gave birth to a bull-horned god   100
and crowned him with crowns of snakes.
This is why maenads fling round in their hair
beast-eating snakes, the spoil of their hunting.

STROPHE 2

O Thebes, nurse of Semele,   105
crown yourself with ivy!
Abound, abound
with rich berry-laden evergreen creepers!
Rave with bacchic frenzy
carrying your branches of oak or fir!   110
Crown your garments of dappled deerskin
with the fleece of white wool!
Make the violent fennel-wands holy all round!°

---

83   Another ritual cry, like "Who is in the street?" (68); it recurs at 152-53.
88-98 *Zeus' two male pregnancies:* Besides giving birth to Dionysus from his thigh, Zeus
     gave birth to Athena from his head.
99   The Fates: The three spinning sisters who regulated each individual's life.
113 *Potential violence of the thyrsus:* Of this paradoxical sentence Dodds (82) writes: "The
     startling conjunction of *holiness* and *violence* (*hybris*) expresses the dual aspect of
     Dionysiac ritual as an act of controlled violence in which dangerous natural forces
     are subdued to a religious purpose. The thyrsus is the vehicle of these forces; its
     touch can work beneficent miracles (704 ff.), but can also inflict injury (762)...."

Immediately the whole land will dance
whenever the roaring Bromios leads the bands of revellers   115
to the mountain, to the mountain °
where the female mob waits
driven away from their looms and shuttles
stung by the goad of Dionysus.

ANTISTROPHE 2

O secret chamber of the Kouretes°   120
and holy haunts of Crete,
haunts where Zeus was born,
where in their caves the triple-crested Korybantes
invented for me this cylinder
covered with tightly stretched hide.   125
During the intense bacchic dancing they mixed its sound
with the sweet-humming breath of Phrygian reed-pipes
putting the drum into Mother Rhea's hands
to beat out time for the joyous cries of the Bacchae.
From the divine Mother the frenzied Satyrs°   130
won the instrument for themselves
and joined it to the dances
of the biennial festivals
in which Dionysus delights.°

EPODE

Sweet is the pleasure the god brings us in the mountains°   135
when from the running revellers
he falls to the ground clad in his sacred fawnskin. Hunting
the blood of slaughtered goats for the joy of devouring raw flesh
he rushes through the mountains of Lydia, of Phrygia.
Hail to the Roaring God, Bromios our leader! Euoi!   140
The ground flows with milk,
flows with wine,

---

116 *Mountain as **the** place for the activity of the Maenads:* 'To the mountain, to the mountain'
     is another cultic formula (cp. 68, 83); it recurs at 165, 977, 987.
120 Kouretes: The male devotees of Rhea Cybele; similarly the Korybantes of line
     123.
130 Satyrs: Immortal fertility spirits of the wild who were hybrids of man and beast.
134 Every other year at Delphi, in the uplands of Mt. Parnassus, a night festival in
     mid-winter was held in which women danced under torch-light in honor of Dio-
     nysus
135-39 *The three key elements of Dionysiac ritual:* a) going to the mountain to dance (*orei-
     basia*), which took place only in the winter; b) tearing-to-pieces an animal's body
     (*sparagmos*); c) devouring the animal's raw flesh (*omo-phagia*).

flows with the nectar of bees.
The Bacchic One,° lifting high
the bright-burning flame of the pine-torch,   145
like the smoke of Syrian frankincense,
springs up and rushes along with his wand of fennel.
Running and dancing he incites any wanderers,
shakes them with shouts of joy
tossing his luxuriant locks to the wind.   150
Amidst the cries of "euoi" he roars out:
  "Onward you Bacchae,
  Onward Bacchae,
  glittering pride of gold-flowing Mt. Tmolus.°
  Sing and dance for Dionysus   155
  as the rumbling drums roar!
  Glorify him joyously!
  "Euoi, euoi!" Yes, sing out
  your Phrygian incantations.
  As the holy flute   160
  roars holy hymns,
  glorify him, maenads,
  as you climb
  to the mountain,
  to the mountain!"   165
Sweetly rejoicing, then,
like a filly grazing with her mother,
the bacchant leaps
swift and nimble on her feet.

ACT I°

Enter Tiresias slowly and without escort, stage right; he wears a white mask and is
dressed like a bacchant, carrying a thyrsus and sporting a fawnskin cloak.

---

144 *"The Bacchic One"* is Dionysus himself.
154 'Gold-flowing Mt. Tmolus' refers to the gold dust carried down Tmolus into the
        Pactolus, a tributary of the Hermus River in central Asia Minor.
ACT I (170-369): Thebes' two most prominent authorities, the old "believers" Tiresias
        and Cadmus (city seer and city founder), encounter the young sceptic Pentheus
        (king). Act I sets the stage for the main event, the fierce power struggle of Acts II,
        III, and IV (434-976). The two outer scenes (170-214 = 45 lines, 330-369 = 40 lines)
        frame the longer center episode (215-329 = 115 lines) which features the contest
        between the young prince and Apollo's blind old prophet.

TIRESIAS *(knocking at the palace door)*
> Who is at the gates? Call Cadmus from the palace,   170
> Agenor's son, who, after leaving the city of Sidon,°
> fenced this citadel of Thebes with ramparts.

The door opens and a servant appears.

> Let someone go and announce that Tiresias is looking for him.
> He knows why I have come and what arrangements I have made.   175
> Though I'm an old man and he still older, we will twine together thyrsi
> and wear fawnskin cloaks and crown our heads with shoots of ivy.

Enter Cadmus from the palace, also dressed like a bacchant.

CADMUS
> O dearest friend, how delighted I was to hear the wise voice
> of a wise man when I was in the palace.
> I have come prepared, wearing these trappings of the god.   180
> As vigorously as we can we must exalt Dionysus to greatness
> since he is my daughter's son [who has revealed himself as a god among
>   men.]
> Where must we go to dance?
> Where ply our feet?
> Where shake our grey heads?   185
> Old man to old man, instruct me, Tiresias. You're the expert.
> I won't tire, day or night,
> striking the ground with my thyrsus.
> Gladly we've forgotten that we're old men.

TIRESIAS
>   Then you experience the same excitement I do.°
> For I, too, feel young and will try to dance.   190

CADMUS
> Then shall we not take a chariot to the mountain?

TIRESIAS
> But if we don't go on foot, the god wouldn't be honored in the same way.

CADMUS
> Shall I lead you, one old man guiding another, like a tutor does a child?

---

171 Sidon: A major port city of Phoenicia (modern Syria) ruled by Agenor.
189-214 *Opening dialogue of Tiresias and Cadmus.* The point here is "to exhibit a Dionysiac
     miracle of rejuvenation: by the magic of the god they are filled for a time with
     'a mysterious strength and exaltation'.... If the old men are filled with power,
     it should be because they are filled with faith. But Cadmus at least is not filled
     with faith, only with a timid worldliness. His real creed is 'the solidarity of the
     family.'" (Dodds 90)

TIRESIAS
> The god will lead us there without toil.

CADMUS
> And will we be the only men in the city to dance in honor
>> of Bacchus?   195

TIRESIAS
> Yes, since only we reason well. The rest are fools!

CADMUS *(finally yielding)*
> We're tarrying too long. Come on, take hold of my hand.

TIRESIAS *(stretching out his hand)*
> Here, then. Let's join hands so we make a pair.

CADMUS
> Since I'm a mortal, I'll not despise the gods.

TIRESIAS *(taking Cadmus' hand)*
> We don't use clever subtleties on the gods.   200
> For there is no argument that throws down the ancestral traditions,
> those we received from our fathers, possessions as old as time itself.
> No, not even the cleverness schemed up by the sharpest minds!

CADMUS
> Will someone say that I show no respect for old age
> just because I intend to dance all decked out in ivy wreaths?   205

TIRESIAS
> No! For the god has not determined whether it is the young
> or the old who must dance. On the contrary,
> he wishes to receive honors in common from everyone
> counting nobody out in his desire to be exalted.

Enter Pentheus, stage left, in a hurry; he is dressed in his royal robes and attended by guards.°

CADMUS
> Since you can't see this light of day, Tiresias,   210
> my words will proclaim for you what is going on.
> Here comes Pentheus, Echion's son, running towards the house.
> It is to him that I have entrusted the power of this land.
> How flustered he is! What calamity, I wonder, will he report?

PENTHEUS° *(at first not noticing Cadmus and Tiresias)*
> While I happened to be out of the country   215

---

215 *Pentheus' age:* About 18-20 years; he is "a young man" at 274, 974.
215-62 *Pentheus' monologue as a second prologue,* "a counter-manifesto to the first (prologue) - having heard the god's programme of action, we now listen to man's."
(Dodds 97)

I heard about strange new evils throughout the city —
that our women have abandoned their homes
for the sham revelries of Bacchus
frisking about on the dark-shadowed mountains
honoring with their dances the latest god, Dionysus, whoever he is.   220
They've set up their mixing bowls brimming with wine
amidst their cult gatherings and each lady slinks off in a different
    direction
to some secluded wilderness to service the lusts of men.
They pretend to be maenads performing sacrifices
but in reality they rank Aphrodite's pleasures before Bacchus!   225
    I've shackled with chains all those I captured
and thrown them into the public jails where my soldiers keep guard.
And all those who remain at large, I'll hunt down from the mountains°
[Ino and Agave, who bore me to Echion,
and Actaeon's mother, I mean Autonoe.]   230
After fastening them tight in nets of iron
I'll put a stop quickly to their destructive bacchic revelry.
    They say, too, that some stranger has come here
a quack dealer in spells from the land of Lydia
his long locks and golden curls all sweet-smelling   235
his cheeks dark as wine, his eyes full of Aphrodite's charms.
Day and night he surrounds himself with young girls
alluring them with his mysteries of joy.
But if I capture him within this land
I'll put a stop to his beating the thyrsus and tossing his hair.   240
In fact I'll cut his head right off his body!
    This is the guy who claims that Dionysus is *a god*.
Indeed he claims that Dionysus was once sewn into Zeus' thigh.
The truth is that Dionysus was incinerated by fiery lightning
along with his mother Semele because she had lied about her union
with Zeus. Aren't these terrible slanders worthy of hanging?   245
What outrageous acts of hybris this stranger commits, whoever he is!

Pentheus, as he turns to enter the palace, finally notices Cadmus and Tiresias.

    But here's another wonder. I see the sign-reader,
Tiresias, outfitted in dappled fawnskins
and my own mother's father. How completely laughable,   250
revelling about with his thyrsus like a bacchant!
I am ashamed, sir, to see your old age so devoid of common sense.
Won't you shake off that ivy!

---

228 *Pentheus as a hunter:* The image is frequent (e.g. 839, 871, 960, 1022).

Won't you get your hands free of that thyrsus, grandfather?
Turning abruptly from Cadmus to Tiresias.

It's you, Tiresias, who have persuaded him to this folly.   255
By introducing yet another new divinity to mankind, you hope
for more augury from the birds and more money from reading the omens
in the sacrificial fires.° If hoary old age weren't protecting you
you'd be sitting in chains with the rest of the Bacchae
for importing these sinister rituals. For whenever the liquid joy°   260
of the grape comes into women's festivals, then, I assure you,
there's nothing wholesome in their rites.

CHORUS LEADER
What impiety! Don't you respect the gods, stranger?
Don't you respect Cadmus who sowed the earth-born crop?°
Are you, the son of Echion, going to shame his race?   265

TIRESIAS *(letting go of Cadmus' hand)*
Whenever a wise man sets out to argue an honest case
it's no great undertaking to argue well.
Your tongue runs smooth like a wheel, as if you were a man of reason,
but your words reveal no reason.
If he behaves recklessly, an able and articulate man   270
turns out to be a bad citizen because he lacks good sense.
    Now as for this new god whom your laughter mocks
I couldn't describe his greatness and how powerful he'll be
throughout Greece. For there are two things, young man,
that are the primary elements among humans. First there's the goddess
    Demeter.   275
She's the earth but you can call her by whatever name you wish.°
She nourishes mortals with dry foods. But he who came afterward,
Semele's offspring, invented the wet drink of the grape
as a counter-balance to Demeter's bread. He introduced it°
to mortals to stop their sorrow and pain.   280
Whenever men are filled with the stream of the grape-vine
they can sleep and forget the evils of the day.

---

257 That money motivated prophets is a common charge in tragedy.
260-61 Pentheus implies that the maenads intoxicate themselves with wine. This insinu-
    ation is not true (686-88); the maenads preferred water and milk (704-10).
264 *Cadmus and the myth of the Sown Men:* Cadmus slew the dragon guarding Thebes
    and sowed its teeth, from which, miraculously, sprang earth-born warriors ("the
    sown men") with whose help he founded the city.
276 Demeter as Earth Goddess: Tiresias is referring here to the fact that many Greeks
    derived the name "De-meter" from *ge meter* which means "earth mother."
279-80 *Dionysus as the inventor of wine:* Bread and wine, the two staples of the ancient
    Mediterranean diet, were the gifts of Demeter and Dionysus respectively.

No other medicine alleviates human suffering.
Dionysus, being a god, is poured out as a libation to the gods
so that it is through him that men receive blessings.   285
  Furthermore, why do you laugh at him and the story
that he was sewn into Zeus' thigh? I'll teach you how elegant this is.
When Zeus snatched the infant from the fiery thunderbolt and carried
  him
up to Mt. Olympus as a god, Hera wanted to throw the child out of
  heaven.
But Zeus contrived a counter-scheme such as only a god could devise.
Breaking off a part of the sky that encircles the earth he fashioned one
  piece   291
into a dummy Dionysus. Using this as an offering of peace
Zeus palmed off the dummy as the real thing to Hera, thus pacifying
her hostility.° Over time humans, changing the word sky,
have come to say that he was sown in Zeus' thigh.   295
This story was invented because people couldn't believe
that Dionysus, a god, had once been held hostage to Hera, a goddess.
  This god is a mantic prophet too. For Bacchic revelry
and mania produce much mantic power:°
whenever this god comes into the body in full force   300
he makes the frenzied foretell the future.
He also shares some of Ares' bellicose spirit;
for fear and mania spread panic through a marching militia
dispersing the battle formation before it ever even touches the spear:
this, too, comes from Dionysus.   305
One day you will even see him on the cliffs of Delphi
bounding with pine torches across the plateau between Parnassus' twin
  peaks
brandishing and shaking his Bacchic wand.
He shall be made mighty throughout Greece. So obey me, Pentheus.
Don't be so sure that force is what dominates human affairs   310
nor if you have an opinion but that opinion is sick, imagine that your
  opinion

---

294 Tiresias appears as a kind of 'theological sophist.' His string of puns here
  ("piece...peace, sky...thigh") is the most remarkable etymological argument in
  the 350 year span of archaic and classical Greek literature (Stanford 175). Despite
  Tiresias' claim (200) that he is not using cleverness (*sophia*) on the gods, he does
  present himself as the worst sort of sophist, combining a certain religious conser-
  vatism with a flare for relativism that was so popular in the late fifth century.
299 Tiresias again makes an etymological connection, this time between 'madness'
  (*mania*) and "mantic" (*mantis*, "seer"). The mantic "sees" because he is driven mad
  by some higher power.

makes you somehow wise. Accept the god into this land and pour liba-
tions to him!
Become a bacchant and crown your head with a wreath!
   It is not Dionysus who will force women to be self-controlled°
in Aphrodite's realm. No, their chastity resides in their nature.°   315
[Self-control in all things always depends on character.]
Just consider the facts. For even in the revelries of Bacchus
the self-controlled woman, at least, will not be corrupted.
   You see how you rejoice whenever the crowds gather
at the palace gates and the city glorifies the name of Pentheus.   320
Dionysus too, I am sure, takes delight in receiving honor.
So I, for one, and Cadmus, whom your laughter mocks,
both of us will crown ourselves with ivy and dance,
a grey-haired old pair. But still we must dance.
Nor will I fight against the gods because I've been pressured   325
by your words. For you are most painfully mad so that
neither with drugs nor without them could you cure your disease.

CHORUS LEADER

Old man, you do not shame Apollo by your words.
Indeed, by honoring the great god Bromios, you reveal your wisdom.

CADMUS

My son, Tiresias has advised you well.   330
Live with us rather than outside the law.
For now you flutter about and think without thinking well.
Even if this god does not exist, as you claim,
let him be considered a god in your eyes. Lie for a good cause,
say that he is Semele's child. In this way she might seem   335
to have given birth to a god and honor might accrue to our entire family.°
   You see the horrific death of Actaeon,°
how the dogs he bred ripped him to pieces
and ate his raw flesh after he boasted in the mountain meadows

---

314-18 *Dionysus as beyond good and evil?* Tiresias is responding to Pentheus' charge (at
   222-25) of the maenads' sexual immorality. As Dodds (111) observes, "Dionysus
   is not immoral; he is non-moral—morality is irrelevant to religion of the Dionysiac
   type...."
315 *What determines human ethics?* "It is *physis* [personal character], not *nomos* [social
   convention] that determines conduct.... Here once more Teiresias speaks the
   language of the fifth century and thinks in terms popularized by the Sophistic
   movement." (Dodds 111).
336 It is family pride, not truth, that motivates Cadmus, thus calling to mind Plato's
   observation: "There are many who carry the thyrsus but few who are devotees
   of Bacchus." (*Phaedo* 69c)

that he was better than Artemis at hunting with hounds.   340
Don't let that happen to *you*.

Holding an ivy wreath out for Pentheus.

    Come here. Let me crown you with ivy.
Join us in giving honor to the god.

PENTHEUS *(pulling back quickly)*
Get your hand away from me! Go play the revelling bacchant
but don't wipe that folly of yours off on me!
I'm going to punish this teacher of your mindlessness.   345

Turning to his attendants.

Guard, off quickly!
Go to the seat where this seer here reads his birds.
Tear it up with crowbars.
Turn the whole place upside down!
Toss his sacred woolen wreaths to the blowing winds.   350
Then he'll really feel my sting!

Exit a guard down one of the side-ramps.

    And you other guards, go up through the city
and track down this effeminate looking stranger
who brings a new disease to the women and dishonors their beds.
And if you capture him, lead him here in chains   355
so that he's brought to justice by being stoned to death°
and sees a bitter bacchic revelry in Thebes!

Exit other guards down the other side-ramp.

TIRESIAS
O wretched man, how ignorant you are of what you're saying!
Now you're completely mad whereas before you had only momentarily
    lost your mind.
    Let's go, Cadmus, and on behalf of this man,   360
even though he is savage, and on behalf of the city,
let us beseech the god to do nothing sinister.
Come with me and bring your ivy staff.
You try to support my body and I'll try to support yours.
It is a shameful thing for two old men to fall.   365

337-40 *Actaeon as a negative role model:* Actaeon is the paradigm of the hunter who
    becomes the hunted on account of his *hybris*. Actaeon boasted that he was a better
    hunter than Artemis, goddess of hunting. For this offense Artemis transformed
    the young man into a stag. He was then torn apart by his own hounds who did
    not recognize their master. Actaeon was Pentheus' first cousin.
356 First Pentheus threatened decapitation (240-41), then hanging (246), now stoning
    (356-57).

Still, let come what may, since we must be slaves to Bacchus, Zeus' son.
But beware, Cadmus, lest Pentheus bring the pain pent up in his name°
into your house. I don't say this by any prophetic skill but rather
on account of the facts. For Pentheus is a fool and says foolish things.

Exit Cadmus and Tiresias, stage left, propping one another, using their thyrsi
as canes, heading off to Mt. Cithaeron; Pentheus stays on stage.

CHORUS OF ASIAN BACCHAE°

STROPHE 1

O Holiness, queen of the gods!°   370
O Holiness, as you make your way
on golden wings across the earth,
do you hear these words of Pentheus?
Do you hear his hybris,
blaspheming Bromios, Semele's son,   375
he who is first among the blessed divinities
at the banquets decked with bright bouquets?
For Dionysus has the power
to join in the Bacchic dances of the cult group,
to laugh as the reed-pipe sings,   380
to put an end to anxieties
whenever the liquid joy of the clustered grapes
visits the feasts of the gods,
whenever the goblet casts sleep over men
during the ivy-wreathed festivities.   385

ANTISTROPHE 1

Misfortune is the result°
of unbridled mouths
and lawless folly.
The tranquil life and prudent thinking°   390
remain untossed by storms and hold the house together.
For although the dwellers of heaven

---

367 *Meaning of Pentheus' name: Pentheus* as bringer of *penthos,* "pain." This is Tiresias'
    third and most charged pun on Pentheus' name as "Man of Pain."
SECOND CHORAL SONG (370-433): One of Euripides' most famous escape prayers; it
    responds to the preceding action by denouncing Pentheus' impiety and appealing
    to the spirit of Reverence.
370 "Holiness" (*Hosia*), apparently a cult word, is invoked as the opposite of Pentheus'
    hybris.
386-91 The chorus is alluding to the present quarrel between Pentheus and his grand-
    father Cadmus.
390 *Tranquility and prudence:* The two key Dionysiac virtues for the chorus.

inhabit the upper sky far away,
still they look down on human affairs.
So cleverness is not wisdom°   395
nor is it wise to think thoughts unfit for mortals.°
Life is short. Given such brevity
who would pursue ambitious ends
and lose what lies at hand?
These, in my opinion at least,   400
are the ways of madmen and evil counsellors.

STROPHE 2

If only I could go to Cyprus
island of Aphrodite°
home of the Love gods
those erotic bewitchers of mortal minds   405
inhabitants of Paphos°
which the hundred mouths
of a foreign river°
fertilize without rain!
If only I could go to exquisite Pieria°   410
home of the Muses°
sacred slope of Olympus!°
Take me there, Bromios, roaring spirit
who leads the Bacchic throng amid shouts of joy.
There the Graces live, and there Desire.°
And there it is lawful for the Bacchae to celebrate your mysteries.   415

---

395 *The clever sophist's wisdom is folly:* From the chorus' point of view Pentheus' "clever-
     ness" (*to sophon*) is the opposite of their own Dionysiac "wisdom" (*sophia*), which
     consists of reasoning well.
396 *Nothing in excess:* Violators of this adage inevitably suffer.
403 Cyprus: birthplace of Aphrodite, goddess of sexuality, who was born from Cronus'
     severed penis.
406 Paphos: a town of Cyprus, famous for its temple of Aphrodite.
408-9 The "foreign river" that fertilizes Paphos is the Nile.
410 Pieria: The Muses' birthplace, a hilly area of Macedonia near Mt. Olympus.
411 Muses: The nine daughters of Zeus and Mnemosyne (Memory), goddesses of music
     and the arts. This connected them with Dionysus, god of music and theater. One
     tradition says they nursed baby Dionysus.
412 Olympus: a mountain range on the coast of Thessaly.
414 Graces (*Charites*): three daughters of Zeus who personified life's joys and all the
     pleasures of domain of Dionysus, with whom their cult was long associated.

ANTISTROPHE 2

The god who is the son of Zeus
delights in festivities
and loves Peace, the goddess
who bestows bliss and nourishes youths.°
In equal measure he has given   420
to the rich and the humble°
so that mankind now possesses wine,
bringer of joy, banisher of care.
He hates the man whose concern is not this —
by day and by friendly night°   425
to live to the end a life of blessedness.
It is wise to keep one's heart and mind
at a distance from men of excess.
Whatever beliefs the common folk
have come to adopt and still practice,   430
these I would accept.

ACT II°

Enter Soldier, stage left, with several guards leading the captured Stranger (Dionysus disguised); his hands are bound.

SOLDIER

Pentheus, we stand before you having captured this prey
after which you sent us; our mission has been accomplished.   435
We found this wild beast tame. He didn't try to escape
but gave his hands to us willingly.
He didn't even turn pale or change his wine-flushed complexion.
Rather, laughing, he bid us to bind and carry him off.
He even stood still so as to make my task easy.   440
Feeling ashamed I said to him: "Stranger, not willingly
do I arrest you but by the orders of Pentheus who sent me."
Now as for the Theban Bacchae whom you shut up
and seized and bound in chains at the public jail,°

---

419 Peace (*Eirene*) is associated with Dionysus because she, too, enriches human life.
421 *Dionysus as the democratic god* **par excellence:** He gives wine to all.
425 Night is "friendly" because Dionysus' mysteries are celebrated mostly in nocturnal darkness (485-86).
ACT II (434-518): *The apparent defeat of the Stranger* is presented in three phases (bound, un-bound, and re-bound): a] 434-450: he is brought on stage in chains b] 451-502: Pentheus temporarily releases his prisoner c] 503-518: Pentheus, in anger, chains the Stranger again, sending him off to prison.
444 The reference is to the Theban maenads whom Pentheus had jailed at 226-27.

those women are gone, let loose and skipping off,   445
off to the mountain meadows, calling out to Bromios as their god.
The chains, of their own accord, came loose from the women's feet
and the keys unlocked the jailhouse doors without a human hand.
This man has come here to Thebes full of many miracles;°
but what happens next must be your concern, not mine.   450

PENTHEUS *(To his guards)*
Release this man's hands. Now that he's in my net
he won't be swift enough to escape me.

The guards remove the chains.

    Well, stranger, your body is indeed quite shapely, at least
for enticing the women. And that's why you came to Thebes, isn't it?
Those long side-curls of yours show for sure you're no wrestler,   455
rippling down your cheeks, infected with desire.
And you keep your skin white by deliberate contrivance,
not exposed to the sun's rays but protected by the shade,
hunting Aphrodite's pleasures with your beauty.
First, then, tell me who you are and from what family.   460

THE STRANGER
I have no hesitation about this. It's easy to tell.
Surely you've heard of the flowering mountains of Tmolus.

PENTHEUS
I have. They circle round the city of Sardis.°

THE STRANGER
I am from there and Lydia is my fatherland.

PENTHEUS
And from what source do you bring these rites to Greece?   465

THE STRANGER
Dionysus himself, the son of Zeus, sent me.

PENTHEUS
And does some local Zeus exist there, one who begets new gods?

THE STRANGER
No, we have the same Zeus who yoked Semele here in Thebes.

---

449 *Bacchae as a miracle play:* Tiresias had attempted to prove Dionysus' existence
    by using rational arguments (272-318). Pentheus rejected them. Now he will be
    confronted with a series of miracles, first physical (449; cp. 667, 693, 716), then
    psychological, which present a different (i.e. non-rational) kind of proof of Diony-
    sus' existence. The effect of the miracles on Pentheus is summarized by Dionysus
    at 787.
463 Sardis: Capital of Lydia (in Asia Minor) and a famous seat of Cybele's worship.

PENTHEUS
> And was it in a dream or face to face in daylight that he forced you into
> > his service?

THE STRANGER
> It was face to face. He looked at me, I at him.° And he gave me his sacred
> > rites freely.   470

PENTHEUS
> And those rites—in your view, what form do they take?

THE STRANGER
> That is forbidden knowledge for any mortals who are not Bacchae.

PENTHEUS
> And what benefit does it hold for those who sacrifice?

THE STRANGER
> It is unlawful for you to hear but the benefit is worth knowing.

PENTHEUS
> You coined that answer cleverly so that I might wish to hear.   475

THE STRANGER
> On the contrary. For the rites of the god hate the man who practices
> > impiety.°

PENTHEUS
> Since you say that you saw the god clearly, what form did he take?

THE STRANGER
> Whatever form he wanted. It wasn't for *me* to dictate that!

PENTHEUS
> Very clever, these empty-worded evasions of yours.

THE STRANGER
> To the ignorant man any speaker of wisdom will seem foolish.   480

PENTHEUS
> Did you come here first to introduce your god?

THE STRANGER
> No, every one of the foreigners dances these rites.

PENTHEUS
> That's because they're much more foolish than the Greeks.

---

470 *The Stranger's initiation into Dionysus' rites:* In this face to face encounter the initiate
becomes a virtual mirror of the god, an incarnate visual double, which indeed, as
we know, the Stranger is.

476 Impiety is a charge made three times (490, 502) by the Stranger against Pentheus.
In 399 B.C. the same accusation was brought against Socrates and led to his death
(Plato *Apology* 35d).

THE STRANGER
In this case, at least, they're wise though their customs are different.

PENTHEUS
Do you celebrate these sacred rites at night or in the day?   485

THE STRANGER
At night mostly, since darkness induces devotion.

PENTHEUS
No, darkness is devious and corrupts women.

THE STRANGER
Even in the day someone could devise shameful deeds.

PENTHEUS
You'll pay a penalty for your evil sophistries.

THE STRANGER
And you for your ignorance and impiety toward the god.   490

PENTHEUS
How bold this bacchus!° What a gymnast with words!

THE STRANGER
Tell me what I must suffer. What terrible deed you will inflict on me?

PENTHEUS
First I'll cut off those luxurious curls of yours.

THE STRANGER
My hair is sacred. I'm grooming it for the god.

PENTHEUS
And furthermore, hand over that thyrsus you're holding.   495

THE STRANGER
If you want it, you take it. This wand I carry belongs to Dionysus.

PENTHEUS (*apparently backing off the challenge*)
And we'll lock you up in prison.

THE STRANGER
The god himself will set me free whenever I wish.

PENTHEUS
Yes, when you call him, that is, from your jail cell beside the
    other Bacchae!

THE STRANGER
Even now he is nearby and sees what I am suffering.   500

PENTHEUS
Well, where? To *my* eyes, at least, he's invisible.

---

491 *"How bold this bacchus!"* A fine (unconscious) irony since "this bacchus" before
    Pentheus is indeed Bacchus (cp. 622, 1020). But he has no clue.

THE STRANGER

Right where I am. But because you're so impious you can't see him.

PENTHEUS [to his soldiers]

Guards, seize this man. He insults me and Thebes.

THE STRANGER

From a wise man to fools, I order them not to bind me.

PENTHEUS

And I order them to bind you. I have more power than you!   505

THE STRANGER

You don't know what your life is—neither what you're doing nor
     who you are.°

PENTHEUS

I am Pentheus, son of Agave and of my father Echion.°

THE STRANGER

Indeed you are and that name spells your misfortune.

PENTHEUS (To his soldiers)

Get out of here! Lock him up near the horse stables
so that he sees only pitch darkness.   510

(To the Stranger)

Do your dancing there!

The choristers start beating on their drums as the guards handcuff the Stranger.

                                And as for these women you've brought
as collaborators in your evil deeds, either we'll sell them
or I'll keep them as family possessions, slaves at my looms, after, that is,
I've stopped their hands from banging out that rat-a-tat-tat on their
     drums.

THE STRANGER

I'm ready to go. For whatever is not fated, I'm not fated to suffer.   515
But know well that as a punishment for these insults
Dionysus will pursue you — the very god you claim doesn't exist.
Since when you wrong us, it is him you throw into chains.

The Stranger is lead off by the soldiers into the palace, followed by Pentheus.

---

506 *Limits of knowledge:* Dionysus' riddle-like accusation recalls the all-too-accurate jab
     of the seer Tiresias at another proud Theban king: "Though you have eyes, you
     see neither where you are in evil nor where you live nor with whom you share
     your house!" (*Oedipus the King* 412)

507 *Pentheus' blindness:* The literalness of his response (i.e. giving his own name and
     his parents') underscores the king's striking ignorance of what he is doing (by
     binding the Stranger) and of who he is as a man (by thinking he has power over
     the Stranger).

CHORUS OF ASIAN BACCHAE°

STROPHE 1

Hail, daughter of Achelous,°
venerable Dirce,° happy maiden,   520
since you once washed Zeus' infant son
in your streams
when Zeus, his sire, snatched him
from the undying flame and hid the child
in his own thigh, shouting out   525
   "Go, Dithyrambus,°
   enter this male womb of mine.
   I hereby reveal you to Thebes, Bacchic child,
   where you shall be called Dithyrambus from the manner of your
     birth."
But you, O blessed Dirce, reject me   530
though you have my ivy-crowned
bands of revellers on your banks.
Why do you spurn me? Why do you flee?
Yet one day soon — I swear by the grape-clustering
delights of Dionysus' vine —   535
one day soon you will take heed of Bromios.

ANTISTROPHE 1

Pentheus reveals
his earth-born descent,
sprung from the serpent,
Pentheus whom earth-born Echion,   540
the Snake-Man, begot
as a fierce-faced monster
not a mortal man
but like a murderous Giant who wrestles the gods.°

THIRD CHORAL SONG (519-75): Reacts to the preceding action and registers the
   growing wrath of the Bacchae at Pentheus and his threat to imprison them (which
   could not be carried out since stage conventions virtually dictated that the chorus
   remain in the orchestra). Dionysus' wilder aspects, which had been largely ignored
   in the first two odes, begin to emerge here.
519 Achelous: A large river in west central Greece.
520 Dirce: The small river in the western quarter of Thebes.
526 *"Dithyrambus":* A sacred name for Dionysus. The dithyramb was Dionysus' special song, performed by choruses at revelries of wine, music, and wild abandon-
   ment.
544 The chorus compare Pentheus' earth-born descent to the chthonic descent of the
   giants who fought against the Olympian gods. Like the monstrous Giants, Pentheus
   is a symbol of *hybris.*

Soon he will bind me,   545
Bromios' servant, in a noose.
Already he detains my fellow-reveller
inside the palace
hidden in a dark prison.
Son of Zeus, Dionysus,   550
do you see this, how your proclaimers
struggle against oppression?
Come down from Mt. Olympus, lord,
brandishing your golden thyrsus!
Restrain the hybris of this murderous man!   555

EPODE

Where, then, on beast-nourishing Mt. Nysa,°
are you, Dionysus, leading with your thyrsus
the revelling bands?
Or where on the Corcycian peaks of Mt. Parnassus?°
Or perhaps in the thickly-wooded lairs   560
of Mt. Olympus where once°
Orpheus playing the lyre
gathered together the trees with his music,
gathered together the wild animals?
O blessed Pieria,   565
Euios° worships you and will come
to dance together with bacchic revelries.
He will lead his whirling maenads
after crossing the swift-flowing Axios   570
and the river Lydias, father of happiness
and bestower of prosperity to mortals.°
It is Lydias' sparkling waters,
so I've heard, which fertilize
that land and make it famed for horses.°   575

---

556 Nysa: A mystical mountain that traveled wherever the god's cult did.
559 Parnassus: A mountain near the Gulf of Corinth, towering over Delphi.
561-64 Orpheus' magical music. This famous Thracian singer enchanted both the animate and inanimate worlds. Like Dionysus, he brought joy and unity.
566 *Euios* is a ritual name for Dionysus; see 67n.
572 Axios and Lydias: two Macedonian rivers running into the Thermaic Gulf in the northwest Aegean Sea.
575 Macedonia was famous for breeding fine horses.

ACT III°

The stage is completely empty and silent. Suddenly from offstage:

THE VOICE *(of Dionysus)*
> Io!
> Hear my voice, hear it!°
> Io Bacchae, io Bacchae!

CHORUS LEADER *(in the orchestra)*
> Who is here, who is it?
> From where does the voice of Euios summon me?

THE VOICE
> Io! Again I speak,   580
> the son of Semele, the son of Zeus!

CHORUS LEADER
> Io! Master, master!
> Come into our revelling band,
> O Bromios, Bromios!

THE VOICE
> Shake the very foundation of this world, august Goddess
>   of Earthquakes!   585

CHORUS LEADER
> Ah, ah!
> Look how quickly Pentheus' palace
> will be shaken to its fall!
> Dionysus is in the palace.
> Worship him!   590

PART OF THE CHORUS *(in response)*
> We worship him.
> Didn't you see the stone lintels reeling, breaking apart

---

*ACT III (576-861): Structural and thematic center of the **Bacchae**.* Three main parts: a) 'palace miracles' (576-641); b) first messenger scene (660-786); c) tempting of Pentheus (787-861). The famous first episode contains a series of *supernatural* events which constitute the 'palace miracles'; a) the earthquake which shakes the palace (583-93, 623); b) Pentheus' hallucinations about the bull, the burning palace, and the light (615-31); c) the blazing of Zeus' lightning at Semele's tomb (594-99, 623-24); d) the (off-stage) collapse of the stable in which Dionysus had been jailed (633-34).

576 *Voice of god:* "Nowhere else in Greek tragedy is a god heard calling from off-stage, let alone accompanied by thunder and lightning." (Taplin 120)

576-603 *Lyric Dialogue #1:* The *Bacchae* features three *sung* dialogues (cp. 1024-42, 1168-99). All three immediately follow a choral ode and are intensely emotional sequences which alternate between an actor *singing* from the stage and the chorus (or chorus-leader) *singing* from the orchestra. Here the theme is Dionysus' liberation of his band of maenadic worshippers from Pentheus.

there on the columns?° Bromios, the roaring lord of thunder, is here,
raising his ritual shout of triumph in the palace.

THE VOICE (*calling on the Earthquake goddess*)
Fire up the blazing torch of lightning!
Burn it, burn the palace of Pentheus!   595

ANOTHER PART OF THE CHORUS
Ah, ah! Don't you see the fire, don't you see it
around Semele's sacred tomb,
the thunder-hurled flame
that long ago Zeus' bolt left behind?
Throw your trembling bodies to the ground!   600
Maenads, throw your bodies down!
For the king, Zeus' son, will come rushing
upon this house, turning it upside down.

The terrified chorus throw themselves onto the orchestra floor; perhaps a crash is heard.
Enter the Stranger from the palace.

THE STRANGER
Women of Asia, are you so paralyzed with fear
that you've fallen to the ground? It seems you felt   605
the Bacchic god shaking apart Pentheus' house.
Come on, lift up your bodies! Take courage! Cast off your trembling!

CHORUS LEADER
O greatest light of our bacchic revelry! Euoi!
How delighted I am to see you! Before I felt such a deep loneliness.°

THE STRANGER
Had you reached despair when I was summoned,   610
thinking I would fall in Pentheus' dark dungeons?

CHORUS-LEADER
Indeed we had. Who would have protected us if you had met misfor-
    tune?
Tell me, how were you freed after meeting that impious man?

THE STRANGER
I saved myself easily and without any toil.

592-93 *Was the earthquake represented on stage?* Given the simplicity of fifth century stage
    mechanisms, this scene was probably meant to be conjured in the mind's eye.
609 *Choral reaction to the liberation of the Stranger.* The Bacchae move from fear (604),
    trembling (607), loneliness (609) and despair (610) — all the result of the earth-
    quake and fire at Semele's tomb — to joy (609) at seeing the great *light* (608) which
    they identify with the god. Their experience of the initiation-like ritual into the
    Dionysiac mysteries stands in stark contrast to Pentheus' experience at 616ff.

CHORUS LEADER

But didn't he bind your hands in tight nooses?   615

THE STRANGER

In just this I mocked him. He thought he had bound me°
when in fact he never even laid a hand on us but fed on his hopes.
Finding a bull° in the stables where he had led me as a prisoner
he threw nooses around its knees and hooves,
breathing out fury, sweating profusely from his body,   620
gnashing his teeth into his lips. But I, sitting calmly nearby,
just watched. In the meantime Bacchus came
and shook the palace, kindling a flame on his mother's tomb.
When Pentheus saw this, thinking the palace was burning,
he rushed to and fro, ordering his servants to bring water.   625
Every slave helped in the task but they all labored in vain.°
Imagining that I had escaped, he gave up this toil
and darted into the dark house with his dagger drawn. Then Bromios,
as it seems to me at least, since I speak only my opinion, made a light
in the courtyard.° Chasing eagerly after it, Pentheus rushed forward   630
and tried to stab the shining [image], thinking he was slaying me.
Besides these humiliations, Bacchus outraged him in other ways too.
He smashed the building to the ground. Everything lies shattered
so that now he sees the most bitter consequences of trying to chain me.
From weariness he has dropped his sword and lies exhausted.   635
Though only a man, he dared to fight a god. Calmly leaving the palace,
I have come to you, giving no thought to Pentheus.

Hush! I hear a trampling of boots in the palace. Soon, I think,
he'll be at the door. What in the world will he say after all this?
No matter. I'll remain calm even if he comes out breathing fury.°   640
For it is the part of a wise man to employ a controlled and gentle temper.

616-37 *Pentheus' failed initiation into the Dionysiac mysteries:* The king's ordeals as he
tries to tie up the bull resemble those of the initiand.

618 *Bull imagery* recurs at 100, 920, 1017, 1159; Dionysus is god of the bull. Compare the
frightening apparition of the bull (symbol of male sexuality) at *Hippolytus* 1214.

626 They labored in vain; the house was *not* on fire; Pentheus only *thought* so.

630 *Why does Pentheus mistake 'a light' for his prisoner?* Because in ancient initiation
ritual the mystic light appearing in the (Hades-like) darkness seems to have been
identified with the god himself. So here Pentheus rushes from the *dark* house to the
courtyard where he sees the *light* created by the god, which light he mistakes for a
man—just as he mistook the bull for a man at 619-22. This young king "embodies
not only the ordeals of the initiand, but also, as the god's enemy, the negation of
the desired ritual process. He rejects and attacks even the light in the darkness,
and persists in his hostile and confused ignorance." (Seaford 1981, 256-57)

640 For the third time in this speech Dionysus' calmness is contrasted with Pentheus'
tempestuousness.

Enter Pentheus from the palace, panting heavily.

PENTHEUS
    I have suffered terribly! The stranger has escaped me
    even though I had just forced him into chains.
    Hey! Hey!
    He is right here. What is this?   645

Turning to the Stranger.

    What are you doing in front of my house? How did you get outside?

THE STRANGER
    Slow down. Calm your anger.

PENTHEUS
    How did you escape those chains? How did you get out here?

THE STRANGER
    Didn't I say, or didn't you hear — that someone will set me free?°

PENTHEUS
    Who? The answers you give are always strange.   650

THE STRANGER
    He who grows the rich-clustering vine for mortals.

PENTHEUS
    ....*[one or several lines missing]*

THE STRANGER
    Look, now you've insulted Dionysus for what he's right to be proud of.

PENTHEUS *[turning to his guards]*
    I command you to lock every gate in the encircling rampart!°

Exit two guards, one down each side-ramp.

THE STRANGER
    But why? Don't gods scale even walls?

PENTHEUS
    Clever, very clever indeed, except in what you should be clever!°   655

THE STRANGER
    In whatever I must be especially clever, in that I am indeed naturally so.
    First, however, listen to this messenger here and learn from him.°

---

649 The Stranger had said at line 498 that "the god himself" would free him.
653 Pentheus' purpose is to prevent the Stranger from joining the Theban maenads
     on Mt. Cithaeron.
655-56 The fourfold repetition of "clever" (*sophos*) highlights the opposing opinions
     about "wisdom."
657 *Plot changes direction:* At this point the first main action, Dionysus' escape and
     liberation, has come to an end and the second action, Dionysus' vengeance on
     Pentheus, begins.

He has come from the mountains to bring you news.°
Don't worry. We will stay right here; we won't try to escape.

Enter the first messenger, a herdsman from Mt. Cithaeron, hastily from stage left.

MESSENGER #1
Pentheus, ruler of this Theban land,   660
I have come from Mt. Cithaeron
where the bright shafts of white snow fell incessantly.

PENTHEUS
What message have you come to deliver with such urgency?

MESSENGER #1
I have just seen the august Bacchae. Stung with frenzy
they shot forth from this land bare-footed.   665
I have come desiring to tell you and the city, my lord,
what strange feats they do, greater than miracles.
But I want to know whether I can speak freely to you
about what happened there or whether I must reef in my report.
For I fear the swiftness of your mind, my lord;   670
it is quick to anger and too much that of a king.

PENTHEUS
Speak openly since you won't be punished by me
no matter what your story. [It isn't fitting to be angry with just men.]
The more frightening your account of the Bacchae
the more severe will be the punishment   675
of the man who taught his wiles to those women.

MESSENGER #1°
Our herds of young cattle were just climbing
towards the upland pastures.
As the sun let loose its rays to warm the earth
I see three bands of female choruses.   680
Autonoe was the leader of one group,
your mother Agave of another, and Ino of a third.
They were all sound asleep, relaxed in their bodies,
some leaning their backs on fir-tree foliage,

---

658 *Dionysus as director within the play:* "How does Dionysus *know* that this is a messenger from the mountains? The hint is sown that Dionysus himself has 'arranged'
this messenger-speech as an opportunity for Pentheus to see the truth, in fact one
of a series of opportunities." (Taplin 57)
677-774 *First Messenger speech:* Laden with an air of mystery, it describes the magical
powers of the Theban Bacchae on the mountain. Its main purpose is to persuade
Pentheus to accept Dionysus and his female devotees (769-74).

others resting their heads on oak leaves,   685
scattered on the ground haphazardly but modestly
and not, as you claim, drunk with wine and flute music,°
and hunting down Aphrodite's delights on solo missions in the forest.
     Then your mother, standing up amidst the Bacchae,
shouted a ritual cry and roused their bodies from sleep   690
after she had heard the bellowing of my horned oxen.
Throwing off the fresh sleep from their eyes
they sprang to their feet, a miracle of discipline to behold,
women young and old, and girls still unmarried.°
First they let their hair flow loose onto their shoulders   695
and tied up their fawnskins — those whose knot fastenings
had come undone — and bound tight the dappled hides
with snakes that licked their cheeks.
Some, holding in their arms a fawn or wild wolf cubs,
offered them white milk — those who had just given birth   700
and whose breasts were still swollen,
having left their new-born at home.
They crowned themselves with wreaths of ivy
and oak and flowering evergreen creepers.
One woman, taking her thyrsus, struck it against a rock°
and from it a spring of fresh water leaps out.   705
Another struck her fennel wand against the ground
and for this woman the god sent forth a stream of wine.
As many as had a desire for white drink,
scraping through the earth with their sharp fingers
they got springing jets of milk. And from the ivy thyrsi   710
sweet streams of honey dripped.
So that if you had been present to see these things,
the very god you now censure you would have pursued with prayers.
     We came together, cowherds and shepherds,
to wrangle with one another in our accounts   715
[debating their uncanny and miraculous deeds.]
Then some wanderer from the city with a knack for words
spoke to us all:

---

687 Pentheus had made his claims about the drunkenness and lechery of the Bacchae
     at 221-25 (cp. 236-38); the messenger will correct Pentheus again at 712-13.
694 These are the women whom Dionysus had earlier (35-38) driven mad and onto
     Mt. Cithaeron.
704-11 *Dionysus as god of liquid nature*: "Dionysus is a miraculous wine-maker and his
     power is transmitted to those possessed by him when they wield his magic rod."
     (Dodds 163). The miracle of water, wine, milk, and honey was foreshadowed at
     141-43.

"O you who dwell in the holy uplands
of the mountains, do you wish to hunt Agave,
Pentheus' mother, out from her bacchic revelry   720
and gain the king's favor?"
His suggestion seemed reasonable
so we lay in ambush in the thickets, concealing ourselves
in the foliage. At the appointed hour each woman
began to wave her thyrsus in the bacchic dancing,
calling out with multitudinous voice on Bromios as "Iacchus,"°   725
Lord of Cries, the son of Zeus. The whole mountain
     and all its wild creatures
joined the Bacchic revelry and everything was roused to running.
     Agave happens to jump close by me
and I leapt out hoping to seize her,
deserting the thicket where I was hiding myself.   730
But she shrieked:
     "O my running hounds,
     we are being hunted by these men here. Follow me!
     Follow me, armed like soldiers with your thyrsi at hand!"
Only by fleeing did we avoid
being torn to pieces by the Bacchae;°   735
but they attacked our grazing calves and not with swords in their hands.
You could have seen one of them, apart from the others, mauling with
     both hands
a young heifer with swelling udders, bellowing all the while;
and other women were ripping apart mature cows, shredding them up.
You could have seen ribs or a cleft hoof   740
being tossed up and down. Hanging from the fir trees
the ribs and hooves dripped bloody gore.
Bulls previously aggressive and tossing their horns in rage
now tumbled to the ground, their bodies dragged down
by the myriad hands of young women.   745
Their garments of flesh were ripped off
faster than you could have winked your royal eyes.
Like birds the women rose, racing in rapid flight
over the outstretched plains where Thebes' fruitful crop grows
along the streams of the Asopus river.°   750

725 Iacchus: A mystic name of Dionysus at Athens and Eleusis.
735 *"Being torn to pieces"* (*sparagmos*): The appearance of this important noun here (735, 739) foreshadows a much more gruesome *sparagmos* (cp. 1127, 1135, 1220).
750 Asopus: A small river in Boeotia originating on Cithaeron near Plataea and flowing into the Gulf of Euboea.

Attacking Hysiae and Erythrae,°
nestled in the low hill country of Cithaeron,
like enemy soldiers they scattered things in every direction,
turning it all upside down. They snatched children from their homes.
And whatever they carried on their shoulders   755
was held fast without being fastened and didn't fall [to the black earth,
not bronze, not iron.] On their locks of hair
they carried fire but it did not burn them. And the villagers,
enraged at being plundered by the Bacchae, took to arms.
That was indeed a dreadful spectacle to behold, my lord.   760
For the men's sharp-pointed spears drew no blood from the maenads,
neither bronze nor iron [...], but the women, hurling thyrsi from their
     hands,
were wounding the villagers and turning them to flight.°
Women routed men, though not without some god's help.
Back to that spot whence they had set out the Bacchae returned,   765
I mean to the very streams that the god had made spring up for them.
They washed off the blood while the snakes with their tongues
were licking from their skin the drops on their cheeks.
     So this god — whoever he is — receive him, master,°
into our city since in other matters, too, they say   770
he is great but especially in this, so I hear,
because he gave to mortals the vine that stops pain.
If there were no more wine, then there is no more Aphrodite
nor any other pleasure for mankind.
Exit messenger, stage left.

CHORUS LEADER
     I am afraid to speak freely to the tyrant   775
     but still it shall be said once and for all.
     Dionysus is inferior to none of the gods!

PENTHEUS
     Already it blazes up nearby like fire,
     this insolent hybris of the Bacchae, a huge humiliation to Greeks.
     But I must not hesitate.°   780

---

751 Hysiae and Erythrae: Boeotian villages in the Asopus river valley.
763 *Thyrsus as offensive weapon*: Once an instrument of worship, it here becomes an
     instrument of war. This duality expresses well the ambiguity of Dionysus' cult
     as practiced by the maenads.
769 The messenger's third and final warning to Pentheus to accept the god.
780 *Effect of messenger speech on Pentheus*: It shifts his wrath to the Theban maenads
     whereas before it was focused on the Stranger (674-76).

Turning to an attendant.

You there, go to the Electran gates.
Order all the shield-bearing foot-soldiers
and riders of swift-footed horses to meet me there.
Call up my light infantry, too, and the archers.
We're going to march against the Bacchae
since this is too much to bear, that we suffer   785
what we suffer at the hands of women.°

Exit attendant, stage right.

THE STRANGER

You do not obey me at all, Pentheus, even though you have heard my
    words.°
I have suffered badly at your hands
but still I say you ought not take up arms against a god.
Keep calm. Bromios will not endure any attempts to drive
    his Bacchae   790
from the mountains that ring out with cries of joy for him.

PENTHEUS

Don't lecture me! Since you've escaped despite being bound
won't you guard your freedom? Or shall I punish you again?

THE STRANGER

I would sacrifice to him rather than rage on,°
kicking against the pricks, a man at war with god.   795

PENTHEUS

Yes, I'll sacrifice but it will be the women's slaughter.° That's what they
    deserve.
I'll stir up plenty of it in the valleys of Cithaeron.

THE STRANGER

You will be the ones fleeing, each and every one of you. And what a
    disgrace,
to turn your bronze-forged shields before the wands of women.

---

786 *Humiliation by women*: A common fear of males in tragedy (*Antigone* 484-85). It is
    Pentheus' masculine pride that provokes his call to arms.
787 *The Stranger's various "proofs" of Dionysus' divinity*: Thus far Pentheus remains
    unpersuaded. At 789-809 the Stranger presents one last chance by offering to bring
    the maenads peacefully from Cithaeron to Thebes.
794 *Perils of anger*: Pentheus is being warned about the dangers of his anger (*thumos*).
    Earlier the messenger had feared the suddenness of Pentheus' *thumos* (671). This
    problem of reason being blinded by emotion occurs elsewhere in Euripides. It
    is mainly because of her fierce *thumos* that Medea murders her two sons (*Medea*
    1079-80).
796 It will indeed be "the women's slaughter," but *by* them, not *of* them (see 1114).

PENTHEUS

> Troublesome indeed is this stranger with whom we're entangled.   800
> Whether tied up or not, he just won't keep quiet.

THE STRANGER

> Sir, it is still possible to arrange these things well.°

PENTHEUS

> By doing what? Being a slave to my slaves?

THE STRANGER

> I'll bring the women here without using the force of weapons.

PENTHEUS

> Alas! Now you're devising some trick against me!   805

THE STRANGER

> What sort of trick, if I want to save you by my wiles?

PENTHEUS

> You've made this compact with the Bacchae so you can revel with them
> forever.

THE STRANGER

> I have indeed made a compact — you can be sure of that — but it is with
> the god.

PENTHEUS (*turning to one of his guards*)

> You there, bring my weapons out here.°

Exit guard into palace; Pentheus turns to the Stranger.

And you, stop talking!

THE STRANGER

> Ah! °   810
>
> Do you want to see those women sitting together in the mountains?°

PENTHEUS

> Indeed I would. I'd give a vast weight of gold for that.

---

802 Is Dionysus' offer to resolve the conflict genuine or a sinister mockery? If genuine,
it emphasizes Pentheus' stubbornness.

809 Pentheus, frustrated, breaks off negotiations and again turns to force as a solution
(similarly 503, 653).

810 *"Ah": The play's "monosyllabic turning point"* (Taplin 158). This uncanny moment
marks the beginning of the end for Pentheus who now comes under the god's
power and loses much of his ability to reason. Pentheus' obstinacy has forced Dionysus to shift gears and, as line 811 indicates, to initiate a new strategy, outlined
more fully at 847-61.

811-48 *Dionysus' new plan:* He initiates now a second "device" to prove his divinity; the
first (driving the Theban women into a frenzy) has failed to convince Pentheus.
The second will be to punish Pentheus by driving him into a frenzy. The scheme
has two parts: a) getting Pentheus to go to the mountain and *look at* the maenads
(811, 819); b) agreeing to lead Pentheus to the mountain, if he will *dress up* as a
maenad (821 ff).

THE STRANGER
But why have you fallen into so great a passion for seeing them?°

PENTHEUS
I would be pained to see them drunk with wine.

THE STRANGER
But still you would see with pleasure things that are bitter to you?   815

PENTHEUS
Certainly I would — but in silence and sitting under the fir trees.

THE STRANGER
But they will track you down even if you go secretly.

PENTHEUS
Good point. I'd better go openly.

THE STRANGER
Shall we lead you then? Will you really venture on the journey?

PENTHEUS
Lead me as quickly as possible. I begrudge the time you're wasting.   820

THE STRANGER
Then put on this long dress of fine oriental linen.

PENTHEUS
What are you saying? Instead of being a man shall I join the ranks of
women?

THE STRANGER
Yes. I fear they would kill you if you were seen as a man there.°

PENTHEUS
Another good point. You're a pretty clever fellow and have been right
along.°

THE STRANGER
Dionysus instructed us fully in these matters.   825

PENTHEUS
How could your advice be successfully carried out?

THE STRANGER
I myself will dress you up once we've gone into the house.

PENTHEUS
In what kind of costume? A woman's? But I would be ashamed.

---

813 *Pentheus' **passion** to see the maenads:* The word for "passion" here is *eros*, the strong-
est Greek noun for sexual desire.

823-24 *Why does Pentheus disguise himself as a woman?* Here the primary reason is physical safety; he must look like a maenad lest he be killed.

824 *Pentheus' sudden change of mind:* In the space of just fourteen verses (811-824) the
Stranger virtually transforms Pentheus from a man into a woman.

THE STRANGER

Are you no longer so eager to be a spectator of the maenads?

PENTHEUS

This costume — what exactly do you propose to dress me in?   830

THE STRANGER

First I'll stretch out long the hair on your head.

PENTHEUS

And the second feature of my adornment, what is that?

THE STRANGER

A dress down to your feet. And for your hair we have a headband.°

PENTHEUS

Will you add anything else to my outfit?

THE STRANGER

Yes, a thyrsus for your hand and a spotted fawnskin.   835

PENTHEUS

I couldn't bear to put on a female costume.

THE STRANGER

But you will spill blood if you engage the Bacchae in battle.

PENTHEUS

Good point. I must first go and spy them out.°

THE STRANGER

That is certainly wiser than to hunt down evil by means of evil.

PENTHEUS

But how will I avoid the notice of the Cadmeans as I pass through the
    city?   840

THE STRANGER

We will take the deserted streets. I'll lead you.

PENTHEUS

Anything is better than being laughed at by the Bacchae.

THE STRANGER

Once we've gone into the house, [we'll make the necessary arrangments.]

---

833 The headband, associated with Lydia and usually worn by women to bind their
hair, consisted of a piece of cloth wrapped around the head. It seems to have been
part of Dionysiac ritual dress, possibly a sign of dedication to the god's service.
(Dodds 177)

838 *Pentheus' change of mind:* Pentheus had intended to spill the blood of the Bacchae
(796, 809) but now he will *spy* on them instead. As Seaford (1996, 215) notes, "it is
psychologically apt that it is by a military intention that Pentheus overcomes his
reluctance to wear female dress."

PENTHEUS

[Hold on!] I'll do the deciding about what seems best.

THE STRANGER

Very well. Whatever you decide, *my* course of action is prepared.

PENTHEUS

I think I'll go in. For either I will march with weapons°   845
or I'll obey your advice.

Exit Pentheus into palace.

THE STRANGER°

Women, the man stands within the cast of our net.
He will come to the Bacchae and pay the penalty of death!
Dionysus, now the deed is yours — for you are not far off.
Let us punish him! First put him outside his mind.   850
Instill a light-headed frenzy. Since, if he reasons well,
he definitely won't be willing to dress in a woman's costume.
But if he drives off the road of reason, he will dress up.
I want the Thebans to mock him°
as we parade him through the city in his dainty disguise,°   855
after those terrifying threats of his.
I'll go and dress Pentheus up in the very adornments
he'll wear to Hades after being slain by his mother's hands.
He will come to know Dionysus, the son of Zeus,
that he is, in the ritual of initiation,° a god most terrifying,   860
but for mankind a god most gentle.°

Exit the Stranger into the palace.

---

845 Pentheus' third and final threat to take by force the maenads on Mt. Cithaeron.

847-61 *Thematic prologue to second half of play.* This fifteen line speech summarizes the god's plan of revenge — a plan that will drive the rest of the action.

854 *Laughter as a weapon:* Greek "shame culture" dictated that one man's victory came at another's expense. Being mocked meant "losing face" and was to be avoided at all costs.

855 *Pentheus' female disguise:* Why does he cross-dress? For reasons of safety (821-23) and because transvestism is a well-known feature of initiation rites, depriving the initiand of his previous identity so he can assume a new one.

856 Earlier Pentheus had mocked Dionysus' "girlish shape" (353); now Dionysus returns the favor, mocking Pentheus' "womanly shape."

860 *The terror of Dionysus in ritual initiation.* Dionysus is for mankind "most gentle" but for his initiands "most terrifying" because they must undergo the terrors of ritual death that preceded the spiritual rebirth of the Dionysiac mysteries. [I have translated the important and controversial phrase *en telei* in 860 as "in the ritual of initiation." (Seaford 1996, 217)].

860-61 *The god's elusive doubleness:* This powerful conclusion to Act III underscores the god's frightening ambiguity (i.e., gentility *and* terror).

CHORUS OF ASIAN BACCHAE°

STROPHE 1

Shall I ever move
my white feet in the all-night dances
breaking forth into Bacchic frenzy
tossing my neck back   865
into the night's dewy air
like a fawn sporting amid the green delights of the meadow
when it has escaped the fearful hunt
eluding the ring of watchmen
beyond their well-woven nets   870
as the shouting hunter ˙
incites his speedy hounds?
Swift as a storm-wind the fawn toils, races,
bounds toward the plain alongside the river
delighting in the wilderness devoid of men   875
delighting in the young shoots of the leaf-shaded forest.

REFRAIN

What good is mere cleverness? Or, rather, what god-given gift
brings more honor to mortals
than to hold the hand of mastery
over the head of the enemy?°   880
Whatever is honorable is dear always.°

ANTISTROPHE 1

It starts out slowly
but still the strength of the gods
is trustworthy. And it punishes
those mortals who honor foolish arrogance   885
and those who, in the madness

FOURTH CHORAL SONG (862-911): This passionate ode expresses the chorus'
    restored hope that, as a result of the palace miracles, they will be free to honor
    Dionysus without fear of Pentheus, who must be punished. The hymn separates
    the Stranger's preceding prediction of victory from the victory itself.

879-80 The head of the enemy: Foreshadows Pentheus' fate and also alludes to the main
    tenet of Greek moral thought, namely "to help one's friends and harm one's
    enemies."

881 "What is honorable is dear always." An old proverb; here it bitterly affirms the
    validity of Dionysus' vengeance on Pentheus. The chorus' delight in this revenge
    becomes ever stronger as the play proceeds (cf. 991-96 = 1011-16, 1020-23, 1156-68).
    For a different version of what is honorable see 1150-52.

of their opinions, do not extol things divine.
The gods cunningly conceal
the long foot of time
and hunt down the impious man.   890
One must never, in thought and deed,°
rise above the laws.
For it is a light expense to believe
that these things have power: first, the divine, whatever that
may be; and second, the laws which the long stretch of time   895
has codified forever and which are grounded in nature.

REFRAIN

What good is mere cleverness? Or, rather, what god-given gift
brings more honor to mortals
than to hold the hand of mastery
over the head of the enemy?   900
Whatever is honorable is dear always.

EPODE

Happy the man° who escapes
the storm at sea and reaches harbor.
Happy, too, is he who overcomes
his toils. And in different ways one man   905
surpasses another in prosperity and power.
Besides, countless are the hopes
of countless men. Some of those hopes
end in prosperity for mortals, others vanish.
But I count him blessed whose life,   910
from day to day, is happy.

891-96 *Reconciliation of man-made law (**nomos**) and natural law (**physis**):* Whatever exists
"over the long ages" is not just human law (*nomos*) but natural law (*physis*) since
the former is grounded in the latter. The target of this choral wisdom is Pentheus
who, they imply, violates the unwritten law of worshipping the gods. But Pentheus
nowhere professes atheism; he just does not see that this new god *is* a god. (Kirk
99, Leinieks 248-51)

902-11 *"Happy the man":* This "pronouncement of happiness" gradually builds to an
impressive climax: Happy is he who a) escapes danger; b) overcomes toils; c)
prospers materially; d) nourishes hopes. But most blessed is he who e) enjoys
happiness in the here and now of daily life.

ACT IV°

Enter the Stranger from the palace.°

THE STRANGER

    You there — the one eager to see what you ought not to see°
and seeking things not to be sought, I mean you Pentheus —
come out in front of the house. Be seen by me
wearing your costume of a woman, a maenad, a bacchant,°   915
spying on your mother and her troop.

Enter Pentheus from the palace; his new costume resembles the Stranger's.

    Well, you look very much like one of Cadmus' daughters.°

PENTHEUS

    And truly I seem to myself to see two suns°
and a double Thebes, that fortress of seven mouths.
And you seem to be a bull leading us in front   920
and horns seem to have sprouted on your head.
But *were* you a beast before? Because certainly you are a bull now.

THE STRANGER

    The god accompanies me. Although initially ill-disposed
he is in alliance with us. So now, at last, you see what you ought to see.°

ACT IV, mirror of Act II: In Act II (434-518 = 85 lines) the Stranger (physically bound) is
    ushered in and out by Pentheus. Act IV (912-76 = 65 lines) reverses the situation of
    Act II; now Pentheus (mentally bound) is ushered in and out by the Stranger. Act
    IV can be divided structurally according to the several manifestations of Pentheus'
    delusion, moving from the physical (the changed perceptions of his eyes) to the
    psychological (the changed perceptions of his mind).

912: Why does Dionysus enter before Pentheus? "It is dramatically more effective but
    also because he is acting as his mystagogue," i.e. his initiator into the Dionysiac
    mysteries. (Seaford 1996, 223)

912: *Pentheus as "Peeping Tom"?* To describe him as such (Dodds xliii) is to suggest that
    his behavior is sexually perverted. That is too strong.

915 *The physical resemblance between the Stranger and Pentheus.* Both have long hair (235,
    455, 493; 831), both look like maenads (491; 835-36, 915), and both carry a thyrsus
    (495; 835, 941). All of which means that Pentheus looks like his mother too.

917 *Clothes and power:* Pentheus' act of disrobing divests him not only of his regalia
    but symbolizes the physical dissolution of his kingship and the psychological
    dissolution of his identity.

918-19 *Two suns and two cities:* Why does Pentheus see two suns and two seven-gated
    cities of Thebes? At least two reasons, one physical, one religious. Dionysus has
    sent "a light-headed frenzy" (851) upon him which may well have caused distorted
    vision. Furthermore, Pentheus, as a new initiand into the Dionysiac cult group
    (*thiasos*), is assuming a new identity.

924 An allusion to 502 where the Stranger told Pentheus that his impiety prevented
    his *seeing* Dionysus.

PENTHEUS

How do I look, then? Don't I carry myself like Ino°   925
or like Agave, my mother?

THE STRANGER

Seeing you I seem to see those very women.
But this braid of hair here is out of place,
not as I had arranged it under your headband.

PENTHEUS

While I was inside the palace I shook my head forward°   930
and shook it back, revelling like a bacchant, and jostled it out of place.

THE STRANGER

Well, we'll set it back in place since it is our concern
to serve you. Now, then, straighten up your head.

PENTHEUS

There — you fix it since I give myself up to you.

THE STRANGER

Your girdle, too, is loose and the pleats of your dress   935
hang crooked below your ankles.

PENTHEUS

Yes, at least around the right foot they do indeed seem out of order.°

Checking over his shoulder at the situation in the rear.

But on the left side my dress holds straight along the heel.

THE STRANGER

Surely you will consider me the first of your friends
when, contrary to expectation, you see the Bacchae chaste and sober. 940

PENTHEUS

Will I look more like a bacchant if I hold the thyrsus
in my right hand or here, in my left?

THE STRANGER

You must lift it in your right hand to keep time with the right foot.
I congratulate you that you've changed your mind.

925-44 *Transvestite scene as* **meta-theater** (i.e. theater conscious of itself as theater). The
costume items mentioned at 830-36 are now being proudly worn by Pentheus as
instructed by his fashion designer. Wolff (1982, 263) notes that Dionysus "plays
the part, within his play, of the play's director making backstage preparations
and conducting a rehearsal. The theatrical process itself... has become part ot the
play's subject. This is a mark of a late, self-conscious stage in the history of an
art form."

930-33 These lines reverse the situation of 492-94 where it was Dionysus' hair that was
the center of attention.

937-38 *Tragic comedy.* The sight of the maenads' arch-enemy, himself dressed as a
maenad intently adjusting his feminine costume, has a comic element.

PENTHEUS

    Could I carry the glens of Mt. Cithaeron,   945
    Bacchae and all, on my shoulders?

THE STRANGER

    You could if you wanted. Before you had a mind that was unhealthy
    but now you have just the one you need.

PENTHEUS

    Shall we bring levers? Or should I tear the glens up with my own two
        hands,
    jacking the peaks up with my shoulders or arms?   950

THE STRANGER

    No, please don't destroy the shrines of the Nymphs
    and the haunts of Pan where he plays his pipes.

PENTHEUS

    Good point. Our victory over the women must come not by strength.
    I'll hide my body among the fir trees.

THE STRANGER

    You will be hidden in a hiding place perfect for hiding!°   955
    From there you can do your crafty spying on the maenads.

PENTHEUS

    Yes indeed. Like birds in a bush, I reckon they are in the thickets
    held fast in the sweetest snares of love-making.°

THE STRANGER

    Isn't this the very thing you're being sent to guard against?
    You will catch them perhaps unless you are caught first.   960

PENTHEUS

    Escort me through the main streets of Thebes.
    For I am the only man of all the Thebans to dare this.

THE STRANGER

    Indeed you are the only one who toils for this city, the only one!
    Therefore the contests you deserve await you.
    So follow me. I will go as the escort who brings you salvation   965
    but another will lead you back from there.

PENTHEUS

                        Yes, my mother.

THE STRANGER

    You will be conspicuous to all.°

---

955 The repetition "hidden...hiding...hiding" highlights the secretive nature of Pen-
    theus' activity and foreshadows the ominous events at this "hiding" place.
958 Pentheus returns to his notion of the maenads as obsessed with sex (cp. 223).
967 Pentheus will indeed be conspicuous. See 1139-43.

PENTHEUS

For this very reason I am going.

THE STRANGER

You will be *carried* home.

PENTHEUS

You mean in the lap of luxury.°

THE STRANGER

You will indeed be in your mother's arms.

PENTHEUS

You'll actually force me to be broken by pampering!

THE STRANGER

And *what* a pampering it will be!   970

PENTHEUS

I am taking hold of what I deserve.

THE STRANGER

You are wondrous, wondrous and you are going to wondrous sufferings
so that you will find your fame towering as high as heaven.

Turning toward distant Cithaeron to address the Bacchae there.

Stretch out your hands, Agave, and you, her sisters,
daughters of Cadmus. I am leading this young man here
into a great contest and the victor will be myself and Bromios.°   975
The event itself will show the rest.°

The Stranger escorts Pentheus off, stage left, towards Cithaeron.

CHORUS OF ASIAN BACCHAE°

STROPHE 1

Go forth, swift hounds of Frenzy,° go to the mountain
where the daughters of Cadmus convene their congregation.

---

968 Pentheus proudly imagines he will be carried home in a chariot.
975 *The distinction between the Stranger and Dionysus is dissolved here.* The expression
     "the victor will be" is emphatically singular and so points to just one victor. This
     indicates that "the fiction that the Stranger and Dionysus are different entities,
     which they still were at line 849, has finally been given up." (Rijksbaron 123;
     Seaford 1996, 227).
976 *"The tying of the plot is now complete, the untying about to begin."* (Dodds 197) See
     Aristotle *Poetics* 1455 b24-32.
FIFTH CHORAL SONG (977-1023): Inspired by the Stranger's preceding words, this
     excited song of revenge covers an imagined interval of many hours—the time
     needed for the disastrous offstage action to transpire (i.e. Pentheus' ten mile trip
     to Cithaeron, his death, and the messenger's return to Thebes).
977 *The goddess Frenzy (Lyssa):* The chorus here picks up the Stranger's injunction to
     them at 851 about frenzy (*lyssa*).

Sting them with frenzy
against the man in his woman-miming costume,   980
the deluded spy of the maenads.
First his mother, unseen, from a smooth rock
will see him playing the spy
and call out to the maenads:
    "O Bacchae, who is this searcher   985
    of the mountain-running daughters of Cadmus
    who has come, has come to the mountain, to the mountain?
    Who gave him birth? For he was not born
    from the blood of women. No, his birth was from some lioness
    or from the Libyan Gorgons." °   990

REFRAIN

Let justice go openly!
Let sword-bearing justice go forth,
slaying him
right through the throat —
the godless, lawless, unjust,   995
earth-born offspring of Echion.

ANTISTROPHE 1

Since he, with unjust thought and unlawful rage
concerning your secret rites, Bacchus,
and those of your mother,
sets forth with a maddened mind and insane purpose   1000
believing he will overpower by force the unconquerable,
that is to say, sensible judgment.
But death is unhesitating where divine things are concerned
and to behave as a mortal entails a life free of pain.
    I do not begrudge cleverness. But I rejoice   1005
    in hunting down these other things that are great and manifest
    — for they lead a man's life towards the good —
    namely to be pure and reverent throughout the day and
    into the night and, by rejecting customs
    outside the sphere of justice, to honor the gods.   1010

---

990 Gorgons: three monstrous sisters with snakes in their hair (like the Bacchae). Their
    gaze turned any lookers to stone. Medusa, the most famous Gorgon, suffered a
    fate similar to Pentheus, i. e. decapitation.

R<small>EFRAIN</small>

Let justice go openly!
Let sword-bearing justice go forth,
slaying him
right through the throat —
the godless, lawless, unjust,   1015
earth-born offspring of Echion.

E<small>PODE</small>

Appear as a bull
or a many-headed snake
or a fire-blazing lion to behold.
Go, Bacchus, beast, and with a laughing face   1020
cast the noose of death
on the hunter of the Bacchae
as he falls under the herd of maenads.

ACT V°

Enter Messenger #2, stage left; he is Pentheus' personal attendant.

MESSENGER **#2**
O house, you that once were fortunate throughout Greece,
[house of the old man from Sidon° who sowed in the soil   1025
the earth-born crop of the serpent-dragon]
how I lament for you!
Though I am only a slave, still I lament.

CHORUS **L**EADER
What is the matter? Have you some news to reveal from the Bacchae?

MESSENGER **#2**
Pentheus is dead — the son of Echion, his father.   1030

CHORUS **L**EADER *(singing)*
O lord Bromios, you have revealed yourself a mighty god!

MESSENGER **#2**
What do you mean? Why do you say this? Do you truly rejoice,
woman, in the misfortunes of one who was my master?

CHORUS **L**EADER
I am a foreigner. I cry "euoi" in ecstasy with my barbarian songs.
No longer do I cower under the fear of chains.   1035

Act V (1024-1152) has two sections: a) 1024-1042 = lyric dialogue #2 = announcement
   of, and choral reaction to, Pentheus' death; b) 1043-1152 = narrative description
   of Pentheus' death at hands of Bacchae.
1025 The old man from Sidon, capital of Phoenicia, is Cadmus.

MESSENGER #2

Do you deem Thebes so devoid of men
[that you will go unpunished for rejoicing in Pentheus' death]?

CHORUS LEADER

Dionysus, it is Dionysus, not Thebes
who has power over me.

MESSENGER #2

That, indeed, is pardonable but it is not honorable, women,
to rejoice at the evils that have been done.   1040

CHORUS LEADER

Tell me, speak! By what doom did he die,
the unjust man, contriver of unjust deeds?

MESSENGER #2°

When we had left behind the last settlements of this Theban land
and gone beyond the streams of Asopus°
we were striking into the hill country of Cithaeron   1045
both Pentheus and I, for I was following my master
and the stranger who was our escort for the viewing.°

    First, then, we stop and sit in a grassy glen
silencing the sounds of our feet and tongues
so as to see but not be seen.°   1050
There was a hollow, surrounded by high cliffs,
watered by streams, thickly shaded by pines.
In that very spot the maenads sat plying their hands in tasks of delight.
For some of them were crowning anew their worn-out thyrsi
making them long-haired with ivy.   1055
Others, like fillies set free from their painted yokes,
were singing bacchic songs to one another.

1043-1152 *SECOND MESSENGER SPEECH* (110 lines): In the first messenger speech
(677-774) a herdsman (714) had described the miracles of the Theban Bacchae
on Mt. Cithaeron, including the tearing apart (*sparagmos*) of bulls. In the present
speech one of Pentheus' slaves (1028, 1046), who was apparently on stage with
Pentheus earlier (cp. 1043-47) and departed with him and the Stranger at 965-76,
describes the tearing apart of his master.

1044 The Asopus River separated Thebes from Mt. Cithaeron (cp. 750n.).

1047 *Pentheus as Olympic victor:* The messenger refers to the Cithaeron mission as a
theoria ("a viewing"), i.e. a sending of state ambassadors to the games. In this
part of the play Pentheus is thought of as Thebes' champion competitor (963),
her ace horse jockey (1074, 1108) who is going to a contest (*agon*, 964) to achieve
fame (*kleos*, 972). But Dionysus, his official escort (*pompos*, 965, 1047), will end up
as "the triumphant victor" (1146). (Leinieks 172-75)

1050 This messenger, like the first one, emphasizes three times (1050, 1063, 1077) that
he was an eye-witness to the events he is reporting.

But the wretched Pentheus, not seeing the mob of women,
spoke the following words:
> "Stranger, from where we stand
> my eyes cannot discern the maenads in their sick frenzy.   1060
> But on the banks of the ravine, by climbing a high-necked fir,
> I could see more clearly the shameful deeds of the maenads."

Just then I see miraculous deeds from the stranger.
Seizing hold of the sky-high branch of a fir tree
he kept tugging, tugging, tugging it down to the black ground.°   1065
The fir was arched like a bow being strung
or like a bulging wheel being chiselled on a revolving lathe.
In this way the stranger, tugging on this mountain branch
with both hands, was bending it to the earth, doing deeds not mortal.
And seating Pentheus on the fir's branches   1070
he lets the sapling go straight up through his hands
without shaking it, taking care not to throw the rider.
High up into the high sky the fir towered,°
my master saddled on its back.°
But rather than seeing the maenads from above he was seen by them.
For he was just becoming visible on his lofty perch   1076
when the stranger completely vanished from sight
and some voice from the air— I would guess Dionysus' —
shouted out:
> "Young women, I bring him
> who made you and me and my holy rites   1080
> a laughing-stock. But take revenge on him!"

And while he was speaking these words
a light of holy fire was towering up between heaven and earth.
The high air fell silent, and silent, too, were the leaves
of the forest meadow; nor could you hear the cry of beasts.   1085
Not hearing the voice clearly with their ears
the Bacchae bolted straight up and cast their heads about.
Again he commanded them. And when the daughters of Cadmus

1065 "tugging, tugging, tugging": "The threefold repetition, unique in tragic dialogue, suggests the slow descent of the tree-top." (Dodds 210)

1073 Dionysus' prophecy that Pentheus would find his fame *rising to the sky* (972) has now come true.

1074 *Fir tree as phallic symbol of Dionysus:* "The fir tree has become a thyrsus with Pentheus in maenadic attire crowning its tip as the ivy does the narthex [fennel stalk].... Dionysus has manifested himself in this enormous symbol of his power, the tree-thyrsus.... The scene may represent an erection, not of Pentheus, but of the god himself and therefore a manifestation of his power, just as phalli are raised in the Dionysiac procession as symbols of his power of fertility." (Kalke 416-17)

recognized clearly the command of Bacchus they darted forth
with the speed of a dove [their swift feet impetuously
    carrying them —   1090
his mother Agave and her kindred sisters] and all the Bacchae.
They were leaping through the valleys
swollen by winter torrents and over jagged cliffs,
frenzied by the god's breath.°
But when they saw my master sitting on the fir tree   1095
first they kept hurling hard-hitting stones at him,°
climbing upon a rock that towered on the opposite ravine
and he was bombarded by their javelins of fir.
Others sent their thyrsi through the air at Pentheus.
Theirs was a cruel targeting but they missed the mark.   1100
For the poor wretch sat too high, beyond the reach
of their zeal, though still captive to helplessness.
Finally, blasting some branches of oak with the force of a thunderbolt,
the Bacchae set about tearing up the tree's roots with these unforged
    levers.
But when they failed to accomplish the goals of their toiling   1105
Agave spoke:
    "Come, stand round in a circle, maenads,
    and let each of us take hold of a branch
    so we can capture the mounted beast °
    lest he report the god's secret dances."
And the women put a thousand hands to the fir tree and tore it   1110
out of the earth. High up Pentheus sat and from that height
he falls, crashing to the ground with a thousand wailing cries.
He understood that he was near evil.
It was his own mother who first, as sacred priestess, began the
    slaughter
and falls upon him. He threw the headband from his hair   1115
hoping that the wretched Agave, recognizing her son, might not kill him.

1094 *The god's breath:* Dionysus breathes upon the soul of each member in the cult group
    and thereby controls them; thus each "becomes part of the cult group (*thiasos*) in his
    soul (*psyche*)" (75). "The divine breathing upon not only results in divine control
    of the human subject, but it also makes the human subject divinely empowered
    (*en-theos*).... That does not mean that one has a god within him, but rather that one
    has within him power originating from a god." (Leinieks 92-97).
1096 Earlier in the play (356-57), Pentheus had imagined that Dionysus would be
    brought to justice by being stoned to death at Pentheus' command. Now the
    tables have turned.
1108 *First indication of Agave's delusion about her son:* At 1215 and 1278 the "beast" of
    1108 becomes further defined as a "lion" (cp. chorus at 989-90).

Touching her cheek, he spoke:
   "It is I, mother, your son
   Pentheus to whom you gave birth in the house of Echion.
   Take pity, mother, and do not,   1120
   because of my errors,° kill your son."
But Agave, foaming at the mouth and rolling her protruding eyeballs,°
not thinking what she ought to think,
was held fast by the Bacchic god nor was Pentheus persuading her.
Seizing his left arm with her forearms   1125
and pressing her foot against the doomed man's ribs
she tore off his shoulder, not by her own strength —
no, the god gave a special ease to her hands.
Ino completed the job, tearing off his other shoulder,
ripping pieces of flesh while Autonoe and the entire mob of Bacchae 1130
continued to press upon him. Every kind of shout was mingled together,
and for as long as he had breath he screamed in pain
while the maenads were crying out in triumph. One was carrying an
   arm,
another a foot still in its hunting boot. The ribs were laid bare
by the tearing apart. All the women, with blood-spattered hands,   1135
were playing ball with Pentheus' flesh.
   His body lies scattered, one part beneath rugged rocks,
another in the thick foliage of the forest,
not easily sought out. But the pitiful head, the very one
which his mother just then happened to take with her hands,   1140
she impales on the tip of her thyrsus and carries it,°
as if it were the head of a mountain lion,° through the middle of
   Cithaeron,
leaving behind her sisters in the choruses of dancing maenads.
Rejoicing in her ill-fated prey she comes inside these city walls

1121: *Pentheus' recognition of the truth?* For the first time he confesses to "errors" but what he means, beyond the fact of his physical danger, is unclear.

1122 *Agave's foaming mouth and protruding eyeballs*: Well-known symptoms of abnormal mental states and, in particular, of epilepsy. Mother becomes like son to the degree that she confuses "what she ought to think" just as Pentheus had confused "what he ought to see" (924).

1141 *Impaling of Pentheus' head*: The second climax of this speech, even more harrowing than the first (cp. 1114). "Euripides creates a Pentheus who is transformed visually into a symbol of Dionysus. Pentheus becomes the thyrsus of the god: first he is crowned with long hair and a *mitra* [headband], then he himself crowns the tip of a fir tree raised by the maenads on the mountain, and finally he becomes the literal crown of the thyrsus carried by his mother." (Kalke 410)

1142 *Pentheus' head as that of a lion* (another one of Dionysus' animal manifestations): Such is Agave's consistent perception: 1196, 1215, 1278; cp. 1142, 1183, 1210, 1237.

calling upon the Bacchic god as her 'fellow huntsman,'   1145
her 'comrade in the chase,' the 'triumphant victor'
in whose honor she carries off tears as a victory-prize.
　　So I will depart out of the way of this disaster
before Agave returns to the palace.
Moderation and reverence for things divine,   1150
this is the best course. And it is also, I think,
the wisest possession for those mortals who use it.°

Exit Messenger #2, stage right.

CHORUS OF ASIAN BACCHAE°
Let us lift up our feet and dance for Bacchus!
Let us lift up our voices and shout for the doom of Pentheus,
descendant of the serpent.   1155
He took the clothes of a woman°
and the fennel-rod fashioned into a beautiful thyrsus,
a sure warranty of death in Hades,
having a bull as his leader to doom.°
Cadmean Bacchae, you have made your victory hymn renowned,   1160
but it ends in a dirge of wailing, of tears.
A fine contest — to plunge your hands
in the blood of your child so that they drip with his blood!

1150-52 *Moral of messenger's story:* "Moderation and piety toward the gods are man's
　　wisest possessions." This traditional but powerful platitude restates the answer
　　to the crucial question asked by the chorus twice earlier (877-81 = 897-901) about
　　the nature of wisdom. (Dodds 219)

SIXTH CHORAL ODE (1153-64): A celebration of Pentheus' death and Agave's
　　homecoming, as if she was a victor returning from the Olympic games (1160). It
　　is the play's only astrophic ode (a single stanza with no metrically responding
　　counterpart) and is sung in an excited meter. This last ode is the play's shortest
　　because "as the action hurries to its climax there is time only for a brief song of
　　triumph.... The opening words suggest a joyful accompanying dance; but as the
　　thoughts of the singers turn from Pentheus to Agave horror, if not pity, creeps in.
　　The last lines prepare the audience for what their eyes must now meet." (Dodds
　　219; cp. Leinieks 278)

1156-58 *Hades and Dionysus:* By dressing like the maenads and taking up their main
　　instrument, the thyrsus, Pentheus assured his own death (cp. 857-59, 1141). The
　　irony, then, is that what should have been Pentheus' means of initiation into Dio-
　　nysus' cult group has become instead his means of initiation into Hades' house.
　　Hence the apparent opposites, Hades (death) and Dionysus (exuberant life) turn
　　out to be one and the same.

1159 The chorus is referring to Pentheus' vision of Dionysus as a bull at 920-22.

Exodus°

Chorus Leader (*interrupting the song, addressing her companions*)
Stop! I see Pentheus' mother, Agave,   1165
rushing toward the house, her eyes rolling wildly.
Receive this reveler of the god of ecstasy!

*Enter Agave alone, stage left, excitedly dancing (cp. 1230-31) in her maenad costume;
she carries Pentheus' blood-stained head (i.e. mask) atop her thyrsus.*

Lyric Dialogue°

Strophe 1

Agave
Asian Bacchae...

Chorus Leader
                    Why do you call out on me, woman?

Agave
We bring from the mountains to the palace
a freshly cut tendril,   1170
a blessed prey!

Chorus Leader
I see it and will accept you as a fellow-reveller.

Agave
I captured him without any snares,
this young whelp [of a mountain lion]
as you can see for yourself.   1175

Chorus Leader
Where in the wilderness did you capture him?

Agave
Cithaeron...

Chorus Leader
                    Cithaeron?

Agave
                    ...slaughtered him.

EXODOS ("a going out," with reference to the chorus' departure, as at the end of most
    Greek tragedies). This epilogue presents the play's tragic "reversal" which Aristotle
    defined as "a change of the action to its opposite...which must conform to prob-
    ability or necessity." (*Poetics* 1452a 22-24). That reversal had been foreshadowed at
    1147 where the messenger told of "she who carries off tears as a victory-prize."
1168-99 *Lyric Dialogue #3:* (cp. 576-603, 1024-42). The singing here continues the swift
    and excited choreography of the preceding song. There are two stanzas which re-
    spond to one another metrically: *strophe* (1168-83): chorus asks Agave about her
    hunting of a lion cub (= Pentheus) on Cithaeron; *antistrophe* (1184-99): Agave, in
    her frenzy, invites the chorus to share in a feast of her "catch."

Chorus Leader
Who was the woman who struck him?

Agave
                              First honors belong to me.
'Blessed Agave' is what the worshippers call me.°   1180

Chorus Leader
Who else struck him?

Agave
                              Cadmus'...

Chorus Leader
Cadmus' what?

Agave
                              His daughters,
but only after me. Only after me did they lay their hands
on this beast here. Lucky indeed is this catch!

Antistrophe 1

Agave *(gently caressing Pentheus' head)*
Share in the feast, then.

Chorus Leader
                    What? Am I to share in this, wretched woman?°

Agave
The bull is still young:°   1185
beneath his crest of soft hair
his cheeks are just now blooming with down.

Chorus Leader
Yes, with his mane he resembles a beast of the wild country.

Agave
The Bacchic god, being a clever hunter,
cleverly urged his maenads   1190
against this beast.

1180 One of the play's most bitter ironies—that Agave should call herself "blessed" (*makar*) when she is carrying the head of Pentheus whose name ("Man of Pain") means the opposite of "blessed."

1184 *Agave as cannibal:* She still thinks Pentheus' head is the head of a lion, hence she suggests feasting on it. The idea of eating Pentheus' remains raw (= *omophagia*, see 135-39n.) repels even Dionysus' most ardent worshippers. Animals might eat humans, as did Actaeon's dogs (see 337-41n.), but humans eating humans goes beyond the pale. Agave, in her delusion, ignores their reaction of pity (cp. 1200-1). She will reiterate her invitation to Cadmus at 1242 and will receive a similar response.

1185 *Agave's changing perception of Pentheus:* Her most consistent delusion is that he is a young lion (1142, 1196, 1215, 1278); at 1170 he seems like a shoot of ivy; here, at 1185, a young bull.

CHORUS LEADER

For our king is a hunter.

AGAVE

Do you praise me?

CHORUS LEADER

I do praise you.

AGAVE

And soon the Cadmeans...

CHORUS LEADER

and your son Pentheus, too, ...   1195

AGAVE

will praise his mother

for capturing this lion-like prey.

CHORUS LEADER

So extraordinary a catch!

AGAVE

Caught in such an extraordinary way!

CHORUS LEADER

Do you exult in him?

AGAVE

I do indeed rejoice

since, in capturing this prey, I have accomplished
a great deed, a great deed for all to see.

CHORUS LEADER

Show, then, poor wretch, show to the citizens the prey   1200
that brought you victory and that now you have brought to us.

AGAVE

O you dwellers of Thebes, city of beautiful ramparts,
come so you can see this prey of a beast that we,
the daughters of Cadmus, have hunted down
not with thonged Thessalian javelins,   1205
not with nets, but with the sharp white blades
of our hands. So who would brag
that he owns the weapons of spear-makers? They are useless!
With our very own hands we captured this one here
and piece by piece tore to shreds the limbs of the beast.   1210
     Where is my father, the old man? Let him come near!
And Pentheus, my son, where is he? Let him take and raise
a sturdy ladder against the palace

so he can climb up and nail to the triglyphs°
this lion's head that I have hunted and brought here.   1215

Enter Cadmus, stage left, followed down the side entry ramp by a slow procession of
mute pallbearers carrying a bier with the covered remains of Pentheus' corpse.

CADMUS°
Follow me as you carry the sad weight of Pentheus.
Follow me, attendants, in front of the house.
I bring this body here after toiling in a thousand searches,
having found him in the folds of Cithaeron,
torn to pieces, [taking] not one limb in the same part   1220
of the ground [lying in that impenetrable forest].
    For I heard from someone the daring deeds of my daughters
just as I got back inside the city walls.
With the old man, Tiresias, I was returning from the Bacchae.°
So I bent my way back to the mountain   1225
where I recovered the child slain by the maenads.
I saw Autonoe, who once mothered Actaeon to Aristaeus,°
and Ino with her, still in the thickets,
poor wretches, and still stung with madness.
But the other, Agave, was said to be returning home   1230
with the frenzied step of a Bacchic dancer. Nor was this idle gossip
since I see her now and she is not a happy sight.

AGAVE *(who has, by now, taken Pentheus' head from her thyrsus and cradles it in*
her arms)
Father, now you can boast most proudly
that you, of all mortals, have sown by far the best daughters.
I mean all your daughters but especially me.   1235
For it was I who left behind the spindles at the loom
to come to greater tasks, the hunting of wild beasts with my own hands.°

1214 Triglyph: a slightly projecting, three-grooved rectangular block occurring at
    regular intervals in a Doric frieze; between each triglyph was a plain square area
    called a metope.
1216 Cadmus' entrance answers Agave's question (1211). His final words before his
    last previous exit (369) had been a warning to Pentheus lest he suffer Actaeon's
    fate of being ripped apart by his own hounds (338-41). Now, ironically, Cadmus
    must relate how Pentheus has been ripped apart by his own mother.
1224 Earlier Cadmus had accompanied Tiresias to Mt. Cithaeron to celebrate Bacchus'
    rites (cp. 360 ff.).
1227 Aristaeus was the son of Apollo and the nymph Cyrene.
1236-37 Sex role reversal: Agave abandons her domestic role (as weaver; cp. 118) in the
    house (the female's normal place in Greek society) to pursue the "greater task" of
    being a hunter in the wild.

I carry here in my arms, as you see, this prize of valor°
that I captured to be hung up as a dedication
in your house. Receive it, father, in your hands!   1240

Offering the head to him.

Rejoice in the spoils I captured in the hunt!
Invite your friends to a feast! For you are blessed,
blessed by the deeds we have done!

CADMUS

[O sorrow beyond measure nor able to see.
Murder — that's what you've done with those pitiable hands.]   1245
A fine victim is this you have struck down as a sacrifice for the gods.
And now you invite this Thebes here and me to a feast.
Alas the pain of these evils, first yours, then mine.
How the god has destroyed us — justly, yes, but too severely
given that lord Bromios was born within our family.°   1250

AGAVE

How crabbed is old age for men!
How it scowls in the eyes!
Would that my son were a skilled hunter, resembling the ways
of his mother whenever he joined the young Theban men
and aimed at the beasts! But all that boy can do   1255
is fight against the gods. He must be scolded, father, by you.
Who will call him here before me
so that he might see my blessed state?

CADMUS

Alas, alas! When you come to your senses and realize
what you have done you will feel pain, terrible pain.   1260
But if you remain forever in your present state
you will imagine yourself fortunate, though in reality you are most
    unfortunate.

AGAVE

But in all this, what is not well? What is so painful?°

1238-40 *Pentheus' death as an animal sacrifice:* The climax of a long series of details in the
    play's second half which suggest that Euripides saw Pentheus' death as following
    the pattern of a Greek *animal* sacrifice.
1250 As the son of Semele, Dionysus was Cadmus' grandson.
1263-1300 *Famous "psychotherapy scene" and its historical importance:* The alternating
    single line dialogue allows Cadmus, by the healing art of persuasion, to coax his
    daughter out of her delusion. Here we have "an important document in the history
    of human culture...the first surviving account of an insight-and-recall oriented
    psychotherapy.... Such an innovation is the natural consequence of the basic outlook
    of a poet who...systematically substituted psychological explanations of human
    motivation for traditionally supernatural ones." (Devereux 42)

CADMUS

First turn your eyes this way, up toward the sky.

AGAVE *(looking skyward)*

There. But why did you advise me to look at the sky?   1265

CADMUS

Does it still appear the same to you or has it undergone a change?

AGAVE

It is brighter than before and more translucent.

CADMUS

Is this fluttering sensation still in your soul?

AGAVE

I don't understand your question. But somehow...

(pausing for a moment)

somehow I am coming to my senses, changed from my previous state of
    mind.   1270

CADMUS

Could you, then, hear a question? And could you answer it clearly?

AGAVE

Yes, but I have completely forgotten what we just said, father.

CADMUS

To whose house did you come when you got married?°

AGAVE

You gave me to Echion, one of the Spartoi, the Sown Men, as they call
    them.

CADMUS

And who in this house is the son of your husband?   1275

AGAVE

Pentheus, by my union with his father.

CADMUS

Well then, whose face do you hold folded in your arms?°

1273-84 *Role of memory in Agave's recognition:* "Cadmus skillfully leads up to the *anag-
    norisis* (recognition), appealing to the older memories that have not been repressed.
    She remembers her husband? Her son? Then at 1277 he shoots the crucial question
    at her. With averted eyes she answers 'A lion's—*or so they told me* in the hunt.'
    Gently but relentlessly he forces her from this last refuge: 'Come, you must look
    properly: it is only a moment's effort.' Then she knows; but she will not or cannot
    speak the name until he drags it from her. The whole dialogue is magnificently
    imagined." (Dodds 230)

1277 The word for "face" here (*prosopon*) might also mean "mask"; it is Pentheus' mask,
    of course, that Agave is carrying. The mother's dance with her son's severed head,
    her ritual rejoicing over her "bestial" victim, must have been a shocking spectacle
    for Euripides' audience.

AGAVE

A lion's head — at least that's what the women hunters told me.

CADMUS

Look again, straight at it. The toil of looking is brief.

AGAVE

Ah! What do I see? What is this I am carrying in my hands?   1280

CADMUS

Look again closely so you can learn more clearly.

AGAVE

I see the greatest pain, wretched woman that I am.

CADMUS

Surely it doesn't resemble a lion, does it?

AGAVE

No. Wretch that I am, this is Pentheus' head that I am holding!°

CADMUS

Much lamented by me long before you recognized him.   1285

AGAVE

Who killed him? How did he come into my hands?

CADMUS

Cruel truth, how untimely is your presence!°

AGAVE

Speak! How my heart leaps in fear about what is coming.

CADMUS

You killed him, you and your sisters.

AGAVE

But where did he die? In the house? Tell me, where?   1290

CADMUS

In the very place where the hounds once tore Actaeon to pieces.°

AGAVE

Why did he go to Cithaeron, this doomed boy?

CADMUS

He went to mock the god and your Bacchic rites.

AGAVE

And in what manner did *we* get there?

1282-84 *Agave's moment of truth:* She finally realizes that the head she holds does not belong to a lion. Her recognition induces her to begin to ask the questions, thereby switching roles with Cadmus.

1287 The first and only time in the play that the word "truth" (*aletheia*) occurs.

1291 Actaeon, the son of Autonoe, was Pentheus' first cousin; 337-40n.

CADMUS

You all were mad and the entire city was frantic with Bacchic
   frenzy.   1295

AGAVE

Dionysus has destroyed us. Only now do I realize this.°

CADMUS

Yes, he was insulted by our insolent hybris. For you all refused to believe
   he was a god.

AGAVE

And the most beloved body of my son, father, where is it?

CADMUS

With great difficulty I searched it out and am carrying it here.

AGAVE

Have all the limbs been fitted into their sockets in a decent way?   1300

CADMUS

No, not all the limbs have been reassembled; the head is still missing.°

AGAVE

Who is this one whom I hold in my hands as a corpse?°
And how shall I, wretch that I am, tenderly
hold him to my breast? In what manner shall I sing a dirge?
Would that I might embrace every limb, son,
kissing the pieces of flesh, the very ones which I myself nourished.
In what kind of grave could I bury your body
and with what shrouds shall I cover your corpse?
And how shall I sing the native songs for you?
Come, old man, let us put back the head of the thrice-blessed boy
in a proper way and make the whole well-fitting.
Let us arrange the body as best we can.
O dearest face, o youthful cheek,
behold, with this veil I cover your head.

1296 Agave, like Pentheus (cp. 1113, 1121), understands her error.

Text in italics: Cadmus' reply to Agave as well as most of Agave's subsequent speech
   and other portions of the dialogue in this part of the Greek manuscript are lost
   and have been reconstructed from various sources; the reconstructed portions
   are printed here in italics.

Agave's lament over Pentheus: "The enactment of a funerary ritual at this point...moves
   the violent and disturbing action toward closure and also helps the audience
   achieve a cathartic experience of the horror they had seen. But it is, of course, a
   grotesquely intensified version of a normal ritual. Instead of a mother washing,
   laying out, and caressing the body of a son...this mourning mother actually has
   to handle and position the pieces of her son's body— a body that she herself dis-
   membered. Thus this most intimate role of the mother in the last offices to a child
   here appears in this ugly and horrible form." (Segal 1994, 15-16)

Your blood-stained and furrowed limbs
and parts I cover with new shrouds,
and your ribs, too, all pierced and bloody.

AGAVE

And what share had Pentheus in my folly?   1301

CADMUS

He proved himself like all of you, showing no reverence to the god.
Therefore the god joined everyone together in one ruin,
all of you and Pentheus here, so as to destroy my house and me.
And I am indeed destroyed since I was born childless, without any male
    offspring.   1305
So now, wretched woman, I look upon this young shoot of your womb,
he who has been slain so shamefully and so evilly.
Through him the house was recovering its sight.°

Turning to Pentheus' corpse.°

It was you, child, who held my palace together, you, my daughter's son,
who were such a terror to the city. No one was willing   1310
to commit hybris against the old man, at least not in your presence;
for you would have exacted the proper penalty.
But now I will be thrown out of my palace, dishonored,
Cadmus the great who sowed the race of Thebans
and reaped a most beautiful harvest.   1315
O most beloved of men — for though you are dead
still you will be counted, child, among those I love most —
no more will you touch this chin of mine with your hand,
no more will you call me "grandfather" as you embrace me, son —
no more will you ask,   1320
    "Who wrongs you, old man, who dishonors you?
    Who upsets your heart and causes you pain?
    Speak up so I can punish whoever wrongs you, father."
But now I am wretched and you are miserable
and your mother pitiful and your sisters miserable.
So if there is anyone who disdains the gods   1325
let him look at the death of this man here and let him believe that gods
    exist.°

1308 Since Cadmus had no sons (1305), his grandson was the only hope for the future,
    his shining light.

1309-22 *Cadmus' funeral oration*: "Cadmus' lament is almost a parody of a funeral oration.
    It is delivered in private rather than in public and has more praise for Pentheus'
    domestic than civic actions.... Nor does Cadmus mention the traditional topic of
    fame or lasting memory." (Segal 1994, 16)

1326 Pentheus had refused to believe any of Dionysus' series of proofs of his existence.
    In retribution the god has made the death of the unbeliever himself the crowning
    proof of his divinity.

CHORUS LEADER

I am pained by your fate, Cadmus. But your grandson,
he has received just punishment, though painful to you.

AGAVE

Father, since you see how greatly my fortunes have changed   1329
and how wretched I am who exulted proudly just moments ago,
what hands, child, will bury you?
Would that I had not taken my own pollution into my own hands!°

CADMUS

Take courage. Though the labor is painful
be assured that I will carry Pentheus' furrowed and blood-stained limbs
from this place and give them a proper burial.

[Enter Dionysus as a god atop the palace roof.°]

DIONYSUS°

Whoever of mortals has seen these things
let him be taught very well:
Zeus is the one who sowed the god Dionysus.
In light of the deeds done,
know clearly that he is a god....
The Cadmeians spoke indecent words about me
that [Semele] was born from some mortal; all of them said this
[but Pentheus here is especially culpable.]
And it was not enough for me to be treated with hybris in these things alone
[but he himself, though a mortal, stood against us.]
He tried to chain and abuse me.
[And then, mounted on disaster, he went to the mountain
and dared to spy upon the secret rites of the maenads.]
Accordingly he died at the hands of those who least of all should have murdered
*   him.*

Text in italics. Again, as at 1301 ff., the text has been reconstructed from various sources.
    The reconstructed portions are printed here in italics. Brackets indicate lines that
    have been made up by C. Willink for the purpose of suggesting the kind of verse
    that would have made sense in the particular context.

Dionysus' epiphany: For the first time the god appears in his divine form (*deus ex machina*,
    "god out of the machine"). Earlier he was, like a Homeric god, disguised. The ancient
    hypothesis (plot summary) is our main evidence for the missing part of the god's
    speech: "Dionysus, having appeared, announced [initiation rituals?] to everyone.
    To each one he made clear what would happen in deeds so that he would not be
    despised in words as a man by one of those outside [Dionysiac religion]."

Dionysus' physical appearance: The actor probably did not change his mask; no firm
    evidence exists for mask changing. Costume changing is also not common. It
    would be the place of his entry (i.e. atop the palace) which would immediately
    signal that 'the Stranger' was now revealing himself as a god.

And he suffered these things [justly].
Furthermore I will not conceal the evil sufferings which the people must endure,
for you will learn that you have come upon the suffering that you deserve.
You must yield your city to foreigners after it has been sacked by the spear,
and endure many evils,
and visit many cities submitting to the yoke of slavery at the hands of the
     Argives.
[It is not at all necessary to exile this man in dishonor,
but as for the daughters of Cadmus, who killed him]
Ino and Agave who gave him birth
and Autonoe, the mother of Actaeon,
I say that they must leave the city, by their exile paying
the penalty for their unholy pollution of the man whom they killed
and no longer look upon their fatherland.
For it is impious for them to remain as sacrificers at the graves of the slain.
And you, wretched Agave, last of all on this day,
holding in your hands the most miserable corpse,
in your madness, Agave, you planned these things.
I save those who are pure but I hate those who dishonor me,
and as a doer of the most impious murder
your blood pollution prevents you from seeing
the day of homecoming.
What calamities you are destined to fulfill I will tell.
You, Cadmus, will be changed into a serpent and your wife,   1330
turned into a beast, will take the form of a snake, I mean Harmonia,°
Ares' daughter, whom you, though a mortal, took as your wife.
And as the oracle of Zeus says, you and your wife
will drive a wagon of oxen, leading foreigners.
You will sack many cities with your army of countless men.   1335
But when they plunder the oracle of Apollo
your foreigners will get a disastrous homecoming.
But Ares will rescue you and Harmonia
and in the land of the blessed° establish your life.

     I say these things as Dionysus, born not from a mortal father   1340
but from Zeus. If you had known how to behave wisely

1331 Harmonia: the idealized personification of marriage, uniting the opposite prin-
     ciples of her father and mother, namely Ares (War) and Aphrodite (Sex); she was
     the mother of Agave, Semele, Autonoe, and Ino. All the gods attended the wedding
     of Cadmus and Harmonia at Thebes.
1339 *The land of the blessed:* a Greek version of paradise. Located at the ends of the earth,
     it was an Olympus-like place of afterlife which Zeus reserved for a very few select
     heroes (Menelaus; Helen; Cadmus).

when you chose otherwise, you would now be happy
and have the son of Zeus as an ally.

CADMUS

Dionysus, we beg you, we have wronged you.

DIONYSUS

You were late to understand us.° When you ought to have known us,
   you did not.   1345

CADMUS

We have realized our mistakes now. But your punishment is too severe.

DIONYSUS

Yes, but I am a god and was treated with hybris by you.

CADMUS

Gods ought not be like mortals in their passions.°

DIONYSUS

Long ago Zeus, my father, assented to these things.°

AGAVE

Alas, old man, it has been decreed — miserable exile.   1350

DIONYSUS

Why, then, do you delay what necessity mandates?

Dionysus probably disappears from the palace roof at this point.°

CADMUS

O child, what a dreadful evil we have come to,
all of us — you in your misery, and your sisters,
and I in my misery. I will arrive among foreigners

1345 *Theme of late learning:* The relationship between time and knowledge is important
   in tragedy; often, characters only "learn by suffering" (*Agamemnon* 177).

1348 *The passions and wrath of the gods.*"Cadmus pleads with Dionysus, as the old servant in the *Hippolytus* with Aphrodite (*Hipp.* 120)—"'The gods ought to be wiser
   than mortals.' And both plead in vain: for such gods as these the human 'ought'
   has no meaning. We need not conclude that the poet denies their title to worship;
   to do so is to confuse the Greek with the Christian conception of deity." (Dodds
   238) For the thought compare Virgil *Aeneid* 1.11: "Can wrath so grievous dwell in
   the minds of the gods?"

1349 *Is this a weak evasion of responsibility by Dionysus?* Only "so long as we think of gods
   as personal agents having moral responsibility for their acts. Other Euripidean
   gods fall back in the same manner upon 'Destiny' or 'the Father's will' to justify
   their own actions and the fate of the human characters. 'The appeal to Zeus is
   an appeal to ultimate mystery, to a world structure in which the forces Dionysus
   represents are an inescapable element. With that there is no quarrelling, and Agave
   recognizes that this word is final.' [Winnington-Ingram]." (Dodds 238)

1351 *Does Dionysus exit now?* It seems unlikely that he would remain a silent spectator
   for the last 40 lines of the play. The focus now is on the two humans and their
   compassion toward each other.

as an old and alien settler. And still for me there is an oracle   1355
that I must lead into Greece a motley army of foreigners.
Against the altars and tombs of the Greeks
I will lead Harmonia, Ares' daughter and my wife —
both of us as savage snakes — and I will lead the way
with my troop of spearmen. Nor will I have any respite from evils,   1360
miserable man that I am, nor will I come to peace and quiet
when I sail across the downward-plunging Acheron.°

AGAVE (*embracing Cadmus*)
O father, I will go into exile and be deprived of you.

CADMUS
Why do you embrace me with your hands, wretched child,
like a swan protecting its white-haired, helpless drone of a parent?   1365

AGAVE
Where shall I turn after having been banished from my fatherland?

CADMUS
I do not know, child. Your father is a weak ally.

AGAVE°
Farewell, O palace, farewell, O city of my fathers.
I leave you in misfortune
an exile from my own bed-chambers.   1370

CADMUS
Go, then, child, to Aristaeus' [house...]
[*one line is missing from the text*]

AGAVE (*slowly beginning to exit*)
I mourn for you, father.

CADMUS
                              And I mourn for you, child,
and I weep for your sisters.

AGAVE
For lord Dionysus has brought
this terrible brutality   1375
into your house.

CADMUS
Yes, because he suffered terribly at your hands:
his name received no honor in Thebes.°

1362 Acheron (literally = "flowing with sorrow"): a river in northwest Greece said to
flow into the underworld.
1368-92 The meter changes to marching anapests, appropriate for departures.
1378 This theme of being punished for not honoring the god is emphasized by Cadmus
throughout the end of the play; but he also stresses the excessiveness of the god's
punishment.

AGAVE

Farewell, my father.

CADMUS

Farewell, my sorrowing daughter,
though only with difficulty could you fare well.   1380

AGAVE

Escort me, O friends, to where we will gather
my sisters, companions in exile and in sadness.
May I go to where
neither polluted Cithaeron [can see me]
nor I polluted Cithaeron,   1385
nor where any memorial of the thyrsus is dedicated.
Let these — Cithaeron and the thyrsus — be the care of other Bacchae.°

Exit Cadmus and his attendants, stage right, carrying the bier of Pentheus; exit Agave, stage left, into exile.°

CHORUS

Many are the shapes of divinity,
many the things the gods accomplish against our expectation.
What seems probable is not brought to pass,   1390
whereas for the improbable god finds a way.
Such was the outcome of this story.°

1387 Future maenadism at Thebes will be left to others. Agave's rejection of Dionysus
        and his devotees could not be more emphatic and in this final rejection she carries
        on the spirit of her son.
"*The play ends with the heavy departures, in opposite directions,* of Cadmus, the heroic
        founder of a great city, and of Agave, daughter and mother of kings—departures
        away from the palace, scene of their greatness, and off into the empty, friendless
        outside. One only has to contrast the end of *Ion.* We see here the dispersal of a
        great house, a house great enough to breed a god: so dangerous is it to be mortal
        kin to the immortals. Thus Euripides uses the necessary clearance of the stage to
        demonstrate the frailty of human exaltation." (Taplin 56-57)
1388-92: *Are these final five lines genuine?* Scholars are sharply divided. If they are spuri-
        ous, the chorus could have exited silently after 1387 or even after 1351, with their
        god Dionysus, if (as seems probable) he exited then. (Seaford 1996, 258)

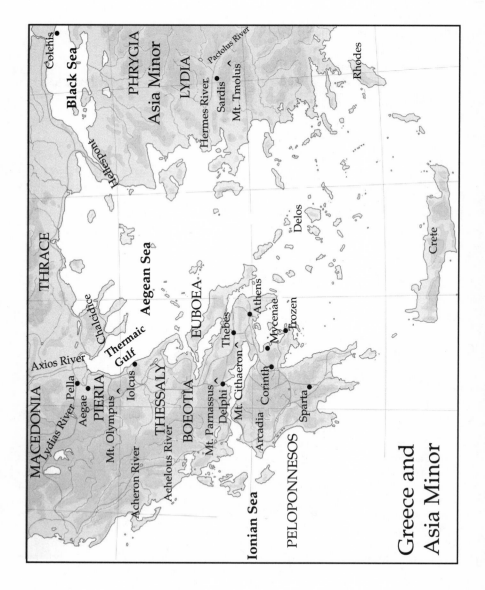

Greece and Asia Minor

Colchis

Black Sea

PHRYGIA

Asia Minor

LYDIA

Pactolus River

Rhodes

Hermes River

Sardis

Mt. Tmolus

Hellespont

THRACE

Aegean Sea

Delos

Crete

Chalcidice

Thermaic Gulf

EUBOEA

Athens

Axios River

Iolcus

Mycenae

Trozen

MACEDONIA

Lydias River Pella

THESSALY

Thebes

Mt. Cithaeron

Corinth

Aegae

PIERIA

Mt. Parnassus

Mt. Olympus

BOEOTIA

Delphi

Arcadia

Acheron River

Achelous River

PELOPONNESOS

Sparta

Ionian Sea

Appendix One

The *Hippolytus*: An Interpretation

By Michael R. Halleran

No one has ever challenged the assessment of the *Hippolytus* pronounced by Aristophanes of Byzantium—"this play is among the best." It displays some of Euripides' finest poetry and a fascinating portrayal of many of life's basic emotions and concerns—passion, honor, family, reputation, virtue, and death. Working with traditional material, the playwright crafted a nuanced and intricate exploration of these issues, embedding them within a powerful dramatic structure. In this essay, I look at various aspects of the drama, trying to tease out some of the richness of its themes, patterns and meanings.

HIPPOLYTUS IN MYTH AND THE FIRST HIPPOLYTUS

The basic story pattern is an old and common one: a young man becomes the object of a married woman's desire, rebuffs her sexual overtures, and is then falsely accused to the woman's husband of rape. With variations, Greek mythology told this tale about Bellerophon and Stheneboea, Phoenix and his father's concubine, Peleus and Astydamia, and versions of it are found in many cultures.[1] This common mythological pattern developed also around Hippolytus and Phaedra, only in this case the situation is further complicated by the woman being the wife of the young man's father, Theseus. Although in some form the story with these three figures may stem from the archaic period (or beyond), it does not come into prominence until given shape by fifth-century tragedy.

Hippolytus is the earliest extant full-length treatment of the story, as this mythological character leaves little trace of any sort before the fifth century. His very name is elusive. It suggests something about horses and loosing, and may very well refer to the circumstances of his death—"loosed by horses." The ancient mythographer Apollodorus (3.10.3) reports that in the epic *Naupactia* (composed perhaps in the sixth century) Asclepius raises him from the dead, a story which Pindar tells allusively (Pythian 3.54ff.). Hippolytus does not

---

1   This common motif is often named after Potiphar's wife from the version of the story in Genesis 39. In general see S. Thompson, *Motif-Index of Folk-Literature*, rev. ed. (Bloomington 1955-8), 4.474-5 ("Potiphar's Wife") and 5.386, ("Lustful Stepmother").

appear in Greek art until the following century, the earliest representations being on Italian vases showing his death by his horses.

The only mention of Phaedra before the fifth century occurs in the Nekuia ("calling up of the dead") in Homer's *Odyssey* (11.321), where she is named, along with Procris and Ariadne, among the women in the underworld. The association with Procris, the daughter of the Athenian king Erechtheus, and the Cretan Ariadne, who is commonly represented as Phaedra's sister, indicates a presumed association with both Athens and Crete. Phaedra is the daughter of Minos and Pasiphaë and much is made in Hippolytus of her Cretan past. Because, according to most accounts, Minos refused to sacrifice a certain bull to Poseidon, the god took vengeance by making his wife enamored of the bull.[2] Assisted by the disguise of a wooden cow fashioned by Daedalus, Pasiphaë satisfied her desire and produced a hybrid bull-child, the Minotaur (cf. *Hipp.* 337-8). When Theseus came to Crete in order to stop the Athenian tribute of young men and women to the Minotaur, he was aided by Ariadne, who had fallen in love with him. About what happened after Theseus killed the Minotaur our sources differ: at some point Dionysus becomes Ariadne's husband and in some accounts (see esp. *Od.* 11.324-5) this ends unhappily (cf. *Hipp.* 339). Phaedra has virtually no mythology apart from her Cretan associations and the tale linking her with Hippolytus; the circumstances leading up to her wedding to Theseus are not known.

By the sixth century Theseus became the major figure in Athenian mythology, a character modeled on the great pan-Hellenic hero Heracles. He had close associations with both Athens and Trozen. Like many heroes (Heracles being the most notable example), Theseus had a mortal and an immortal father, his mortal father Aegeus being king of Athens, his immortal father Poseidon worshipped as king in Trozen. His mother, Aethra, was Trozenian. His adventure with the Amazons is confusing in many details, but clear in linking him amorously with one of the Amazons, whom he abducts in most, especially early, versions of the tale. This woman's name is most commonly (and on sixth-century vases exclusively) Antiope, and she becomes the mother of Hippolytus. In Hippolytus, she is simply referred to as "the Amazon," and great stress is laid on Hippolytus' bastard status.[3] Accounts of how her liaison with Theseus ended vary (most commonly she is killed in battle either against or on the side of Theseus), and sometime after this union, Theseus marries Phaedra and has children by her.

---

2 Bulls play a prominent role in the mythology relevant to the Hippolytus story. Minos is the child of Europa and Zeus in the form of a bull; Poseidon has a special association with bulls, as seen here and in his sending a bull against Hippolytus' horses; Pasiphaë, too, has an obvious involvement with bulls; Theseus, in addition to slaying the Minotaur, also, shortly after his arrival in Athens, captures the dangerous bull of Marathon.

3 It is possible that in versions prior to this play, Hippolytus was in fact the legitimate offspring of Theseus and Antiope. The issue of legitimacy would resonate deeply among the Athenians, who in 451/0 passed a highly restrictive citizenship law, limiting full rights to those with two citizen parents.

In watching this play in 428 BCE, spectators at the City Dionysia in Athens witnessed a remarkable event: Euripides' *Hippolytus* was the second treatment the playwright had given to the myth, the only certain instance of an Athenian tragedian rewriting a play.[4] Earlier he had produced a different play on this topic, a play which, we are informed, was a failure, while *Hippolytus* and the other plays produced by Euripides in 428 were awarded first prize in the dramatic competition.

Aristophanes of Byzantium, a scholar of the late third and early second century BCE, explained that the surviving play must have been second because it "corrected" what was "unseemly and worthy of condemnation" in the first. From that first play, at times called *Hippolytos (Kata)kaluptomenos* ("Hippolytus Veiled"), we have some twenty (short) fragments and a few late sources that might inform us about the first play. What Aristophanes of Byzantium meant by "corrected" is probably indicated in an ancient Life of Euripides and the comic playwright Aristophanes' *Frogs* (1043, 1052-4), which both suggest a Phaedra intent upon adultery. Such a Phaedra must come from *Hippolytus I* and would conform to the mythological stereotype of "Potiphar's wife" and contrast sharply with the virtuous and discreet Phaedra of *Hippolytus*. The following sketch of *Hippolytus I* offers a reasonably likely account of the first play. Much, however, remains unknown or uncertain.[5]

Like all extant Euripidean plays, *Hippolytus I* began with an expository prologue, which was spoken by Phaedra. We now know that the play was very likely set in Trozen. Phaedra's Nurse, a staple of the story, must have been a character in this play, even though she left no definite traces in the fragments. We can say very little about the chorus, who would have entered after the opening scene, except that, like the chorus in *Hippolytus*, they were female and probably Trozenian. Either in the prologue scene, or in the first episode, Phaedra and the Nurse had a scene in which they discuss Phaedra's passion. Several of the surviving fragments seem to come from this scene. Certainly, in typical Euripidean fashion, Hippolytus was depicted in a scene before his encounter with Phaedra. A line giving advice not to be unbending in chastity might come from that scene, which may have included a servant (or comrade) of Hippolytus. A direct confrontation between Phaedra and Hippolytus is assumed universally, and suggested by a number of the fragments. In this confrontation, Phaedra would have most likely tried to seduce Hippolytus with the lure of Theseus' throne. An oath from Hippolytus was probably secured in this scene, as a line referring to the consequences of violating a supplication seems to indicate.

The distinguishing epithet sometimes given to the title of the first play, *(Kata)kaluptomenos*, very plausibly stems from a scene in which the shocked

---

4   While we do not know for certain that the extant play is the later of the two, with almost all scholars, I accept this relative dating and refer to the two plays as Hippolytus I (the first one) and simply Hippolytus (the extant play).

5   A fuller account of these fragments and the reconstruction of the first Hippolytus can be found in my 1995 commentary.

Hippolytus covered himself with his cloak in response to Phaedra's overtures. At some point thereafter (perhaps in the following scene), Phaedra falsely accused Hippolytus to Theseus, who has been conveniently out of the picture. How the false allegation of rape was made (Phaedra directly? by falsified evidence?) is unclear, but it obviously must occur before the confrontation between Theseus and Hippolytus. Like most Euripidean plays (including *Hippolytus*), this play probably had an *agon* (a balanced set of opposing speeches) between Theseus and Hippolytus, and several fragments, including one lamenting clever rhetoric, suggest it. At some point Theseus must pronounce his curse against Hippolytus, most likely after the *agon*. Hippolytus might have also been banished with exile, but his departure could equally be an (understandable) response to his father's curse.

There can be no doubt that this play had a messenger scene describing Hippolytus' disastrous chariot ride, and one fragment comes from that speech. The fragments are completely silent about Phaedra's suicide, which most probably occurred after Hippolytus' death. (Hippolytus' death would itself have happened off-stage; the scene in the second play of his final pain-wracked moments and his reconciliation with his father seems very much unique to it.) Perhaps Phaedra responds to the news of Hippolytus' death with (an off-stage) suicide, which could then have been reported by the Nurse. It is improbable that Phaedra reveals the truth to Theseus; the Nurse or the divinity appearing at the end of the play most likely performed this function. The play concluded with a divine appearance. A four-line choral tag that survives, referring to Hippolytus' future cult, allows one to infer that the play conformed to many other Euripidean dramas in having a divinity who appeared on high and who, among other things, predicted Hippolytus' future cult. The most likely candidate for this divine appearance is Artemis, Hippolytus' patron.

PLOT, STRUCTURE, AND DESIGN

While the fundamental story of the play conforms to the motif of "Potiphar's Wife," another story pattern is grafted onto this one, that of revenge. What drives this play is not simply Phaedra's passion for Hippolytus, but also Aphrodite's revenge against him. The two patterns are clearly joined in Aphrodite's prologue speech when she explains that she will punish Hippolytus by having his stepmother fall in love with him. Many have observed that the actions of the play are credible without the divinities' direct participation—the destructive force of illicit passion is readily understandable. But with their active involvement it is a very different drama. Phaedra's passion becomes in a sense secondary; Hippolytus' violent rejection is seen as a rebuff not only of his stepmother, but of a divinity; and human actions are subject to a different kind of moral calculus. And, of course, dramatic irony permeates the whole play to a degree that would be impossible without Aphrodite's speech explaining her intervention. It is possible that the deities were added directly to this play as part of the decision to rewrite the earlier one; that is, the role of Aphrodite was introduced to mitigate Phaedra's culpability. Whatever the motivation, such a prologue alters the prism through which we view the play. The added dimension of the divine does not displace the mortal one but rather complicates it.

The formal excellence of Hippolytus is universally accepted. Part of that excellence is its artful structure, one which, while dealing with two disparate motifs, joins them in a balanced whole. The play seems to fall into two roughly even halves, the first (1-775) devoted chiefly, although not exclusively, to Phaedra (and Hippolytus), the second (776-1466), chiefly to Hippolytus (and Theseus). With the conclusion of the second stasimon (775), Phaedra is dead, her brave fight against her passion and for her good name over, and the action turns to Hippolytus' combat against the false charge of rape and for his reputation before his father's eyes. A long episode of roughly equal length dominates each of the play's halves (170-524 [355 lines] and 776-1101 [326 lines, or, with some likely deletions, 322]). In the first one, the Nurse extracts from a silent and reluctant Phaedra the truth about her sexual passion for Hippolytus and engages her in debate about it. In the second, Theseus believes Phaedra's lying note about Hippolytus' (alleged) sexual violation of his wife and then, after condemning him, debates with Hippolytus about this charge (902-1101).

The play offers a "divine frame:" Artemis' appearance at the end balances Aphrodite's at the beginning. Although Euripides very frequently introduced gods into the beginnings and ends of his dramas, this is only one of three plays (Ion and Bacchae being the other two) in which gods appear both at the beginning and at the end. While these two goddesses stand on opposite sides (against and for Hippolytus), and can be read symbolically as representing different aspects of the world (e.g., sexuality and chastity), they have much in common in their motives and language, and these similarities underscore the play's symmetrical structure. A brief astrophic song to Artemis follows immediately Aphrodite's departure; a brief astrophic song to Aphrodite precedes Artemis' entrance.

Other structural and visual parallels give shape to the drama. When Phaedra first arrives on stage, she is half-dead, carried by attendants and giving lyric expression to her woes. Later in the play Hippolytus arrives half-dead, supported by attendants and speaking initially in lyrics. Upon Phaedra's arrival, the chorus and Nurse in ignorance ask about the cause of her plight. When Hippolytus returns to the stage (901), he is ignorant of and inquires about Theseus' situation. Two acts of supplication, from sequential scenes, also provide parallel structures. Phaedra's refusal to tell her Nurse what afflicts her is met with the extreme (and successful) act of supplication, which ultimately breaks Phaedra's silence. In the following scene, the Nurse attempts another act of supplication, this time of Hippolytus, to obtain not his speech, but his silence. This time, the supplication itself fails (although a previously extracted oath holds).

HUMAN CHARACTERS AND THE GODS

Few among the surviving Greek tragedies have attracted as much interest in their characters as Hippolytus. The chaste and tortured Phaedra, the religiously dedicated and proud Hippolytus have been the subject of many studies. Theseus and the Nurse do not demand the same sort of attention, but interestingly among these four characters there is no huge difference in the number of lines spoken by each. While this play is not primarily a psychological drama, the characters are drawn carefully, in relation both to each other and to the gods.

Aphrodite offers the first portrait of Hippolytus: he is an arrogant young man who should be punished for his contempt for her world. Hippolytus presents himself as a devoted follower of Artemis. His opening address to her (73-87) reflects a pious and committed soul. Yet these same words also reflect an exclusivity and narrowness. These traits, already observed by Aphrodite, are revealed again in the scene between Hippolytus and his servant, as he expresses his reservations about gods "worshipped at night" (106) and his disrespect for Aphrodite (113). His response to the Nurse's proposition is extraordinary, leading him not only to condemn all women, but even to wish for a world in which there were no women at all (616-24). Yet in this furious attack, he vows to maintain his oath of silence, a vow that he will keep, even at the cost of his own life. His fury, moreover, makes some sense in the context of the Nurse's falsely asserting that her mistress seeks a sexual union with him. Those who fault Hippolytus for his outrageous conduct here also condemn what they see as his frigid and self-righteous behavior towards his father later on and his proud self-proclamations of virtue then and in the concluding scene. Hippolytus has, to be sure, no small opinion of himself and follows a rigid and exclusive adherence to one divinity, but he also possesses an impressive piety and religious devotion. His pious devotion and his ruin are part of the same cloth (see 1402).

Phaedra in this play is no longer the brazen and intemperate woman of *Hippolytus I*, but rather is presented as virtuous and intent on doing the right thing. Her virtue is proclaimed by Aphrodite (47-8) and Artemis (1300-6) alike; the Nurse, at the very moment when she learns of her mistress' passion for Hippolytus, includes her among the chaste (358-9); and even Hippolytus has grudging admiration for her (1034-5). The early part of the play especially shows her deep struggle against her passion and her valiant attempts to retain her virtue.

A different Phaedra requires a different Hippolytus; the new Phaedra of the second *Hippolytus* needs a more subtle and ambiguous figure to play against. Hippolytus is now presented as one in comparison to whom the suffering Phaedra appears the more sympathetic, and against whom her false accusations seem less reprehensible. Writing the lying tablet cannot—and should not—be dismissed; it is (at least in part) vindictive and destructive. But the characterization of Hippolytus leavens judgment against Phaedra. Several other factors also militate against viewing her behavior in an unfavorable light: Aphrodite, a powerful and external force, is seen as the cause of her passion; Phaedra herself has tried greatly to master this illicit desire; the Nurse, not Phaedra, brings about her confession of this desire and the conveying of it to Hippolytus. Another important aspect is Phaedra's Cretan past. Her mother

Pasiphaë was afflicted with passion for a bull, her sister is said to be ill-fated in love, and throughout the play we are reminded of this Cretan background (esp. 337-41, and cf. 372, 719 and 752ff.). In fighting against her passion, Phaedra is trying to overcome her family lineage, while also contrasting with her literary predecessor of the earlier play.

Conveniently absent from the first part of the play, Theseus, on his return, immediately following Phaedra's death, is confronted with his wife's corpse and lying note. He responds with grief and outrage, condemning his son and punishing him with a curse and exile. Like Hippolytus, Theseus himself comes from an illegitimate union (between Aethra and Aegeus—or Poseidon), and he is unsure of his paternity. (For him the efficacy of the curse establishes Poseidon as his father, 1169-70.) His reaction is rash, as the chorus (891-2), Hippolytus (1051-2) and Artemis (1321-4) all claim. But this rashness is needed for the plot and is in keeping with his character as a man of action. At the end of the play, he reveals his remorse and his eagerness to be reconciled with his son.

Euripides, famed for "domesticating" tragedy, nowhere else developed so fully a non-aristocratic character like Phaedra's Nurse. She is essential not only as a catalyst for the plot (without her, Phaedra would die and Aphrodite's revenge fizzle), but also in serving as an interlocutor and foil for Phaedra. Phaedra's passion could be explored in a monologue (by Phaedra) only so far; the Nurse, with her persistent questions, forceful supplication, and opposing views, allows for an extended examination of it. She contrasts with Phaedra at almost every turn. She is ignorant when Phaedra is tormented by knowledge of her passion; she is eager for speech when Phaedra is for silence; she is stunned while Phaedra talks; she wants action while Phaedra wants a good name; she wants Phaedra's life when Phaedra has already chosen death. Her chief motivating force is her interest in Phaedra's life. Unlike Phaedra, however, she has no concern for other moral standards and judges things only with a pragmatist's interest in results (700-1). Her role in the plot should not be undervalued, but to think of her as an agent of Aphrodite is to overstate the case and to misread the gods' role in the drama.

The goddesses, appearing at the play's beginning and end, have much to do with its outcome, but, as often in Greek literature, they rely very much on human behavior to effect it. Aphrodite causes Phaedra to fall in love with her stepson, but she does not compel her response to this passion or the other responses that ripple from it. She predicts most of the major events of the play, but that is not the same as causing them. Phaedra, the Nurse, Hippolytus, and Theseus all respond as autonomous individuals under the circumstances created by the divinity. It is true that vital decisions are made under misconceptions and in ignorance, but these are made by the mortals, not the gods. Not only Aphrodite, but many mortals contribute to the play's tragic outcome. Phaedra's intense desire for her good name; the Nurse's relaying Phaedra's passion to Hippolytus; Hippolytus' own savage response; Theseus' rashness in punishing his son—these all contribute to Hippolytus' and Phaedra's deaths and Theseus' desolation. Poseidon, to be sure, also contributes by sending the bull from the sea, but, as Artemis says (1318-9), he did only what he had to, fulfilling one of the prayers he promised to Theseus, and Hippolytus is traveling along the shore, where the bull attacks, because he has been exiled by Theseus. Artemis, in explaining matters to Theseus and Hippolytus, lays the primary blame on her fellow divinity (1301-3, 1325-8, 1400, 1416-22), but she also finds fault with Phaedra (1310-2), the Nurse (1305-6), and especially Theseus (1285-95, 1297, 1316-7, 1321-4, 1325). There is plenty of blame to go around.

The gods' power is clear; the rightness of it is not. Hippolytus' servant remarks that gods should be wiser than mortals and forgive someone like Hippolytus (114-20). There is no reason to regard this as privileged discourse, the "voice of the poet," but it does offer the suggestion that Aphrodite's planned punishment is excessive, at least from a mortal perspective. Artemis, in sharing many traits with Aphrodite, is open to the same criticisms. She could not prevent Aphrodite's vengeance, but will in return exact vengeance from a mortal, one of Aphrodite's favorites (1420-2). The play's violence, triggered by a goddess's vengeance, will thus continue against another mortal. Artemis does assist in reconciling father and son (1435), but she does not stay with Hippolytus as he dies (1437-8). Hippolytus' response, "Easily you leave a long companionship" (1441) is difficult to interpret neutrally. His entire relationship with Artemis, although special, is asymmetrical: he cannot see her (85-6; cf. 1391-2), and her concern for him has real limits. The divine frame is only partial. Artemis is gone before the play ends. Its final moments show Theseus embracing his son, Hippolytus forgiving his father. Aphrodite's evils will not be forgotten (1461), but neither will the human actions that dominate the drama. The concluding choral tag (1462-6) ignores the gods and focuses entirely on the grief for Hippolytus and the fame born of great men.

SPEECH, SILENCE, AND DECEPTION

It has long been recognized that this play is deeply concerned with speech, silence, and their consequences. Words for speech and silence permeate the play, and each character makes important decisions about speech and silence; the consequences of these decisions give the drama much of its shape. The importance of silence is announced in Aphrodite's prologue when she explains that Phaedra is dying in silence (40). Phaedra breaks this silence in a series of lyric outbursts (198ff.), only to return to silence in shame at what she has said (244). The Nurse then deliberately seeks to break through this silence, succeeding finally through supplication, and only gradually and partially does Phaedra bring herself to speak out about her passion. Hearing of this passion functionally silences the Nurse, while Phaedra gives a *rhesis* in which she explains that her first effort at combating her passion was silence and concealment (394). Phaedra is soon afraid that the Nurse will succeed in using "overly fine words" (487) that prove destructive; she wants the Nurse to be silent (498-9). The Nurse will not be silent and reveals to Hippolytus her mistress's desire for him. This is the first of several important misrepresentations in the play. The Nurse, acting from a brand of pragmatism and taking advantage of many verbal ambiguities (see 486-524n.), presents Phaedra as other than she wants—or intends—to be. Without this misrepresentation the play's disastrous actions would not proceed. But the resourceful Nurse does, in advance of making her case to Hippolytus, secure from him an oath of silence. Although the young man will implicitly threaten to break this oath (612), he will ultimately abide by it and keep silent because of his piety. Shocked, however, by the Nurse's proposal, he issues a long and violent speech against women, which includes the wish that women had only voiceless beasts as attendants (646). This speech proves destructive, since in response to it Phaedra fears that he will in fact reveal her passion (689-92) and wants to punish him for his arrogance (728-31). The chorus's complicity in her plotting is secured by their own oath of silence (710-4). However one imagines Phaedra's location during Hippolytus' speech (see 600n.), the two main characters never address one another in this play of many miscommunications.

In going to her death, Phaedra explains that she needs "new words" (688). These words prove to be the written tablet she leaves for Theseus in which she falsely accuses Hippolytus of rape. This tablet "speaks" for her and in Theseus' description it is repeatedly personified (see 856n.). Phaedra has created a false but persuasive representation of Hippolytus, to which Theseus responds with two speech acts of his own: a curse on his son (to be fulfilled by Poseidon) and a proclamation of exile. When Hippolytus returns to the stage, Theseus is initially silent and Hippolytus tries to elicit speech from him (911), but at the end of this scene it is Hippolytus who becomes silent because of his oath (1060-3), and wishes for mute witnesses to his character (1074-5). Also in this scene Theseus wishes for a world in which everyone would have two voices, one of which could refute the lying one (928-31). Words that break through the lies and misrepresentations come from Artemis, who explains Aphrodite's role, Phaedra's lying words, and the Nurse's tricks, while condemning Theseus' own hasty actions. Two important speech acts remain, one promised, the other enacted. Hippolytus will be commemorated in a cult in which his name will not pass into oblivion and Phaedra's passion for him will not grow silent (1429-30). Finally, Hippolytus forgives his father in words that, unlike most in the play, effect reconciliation and not destruction.

REPUTATION, SHAME, AND HONOR

Phaedra's desire for a good reputation (*eukleia*) ranks high among her many motivations. In sharp contrast to her counterpart in *Hippolytus I*, this Phaedra is determined to act virtuously, to preserve her good name at all costs. It is important to remember that fifth-century Athens was still predominantly a "shame culture," that is, one in which excellence and its opposite were measured by external standards and one's worth was not easily distinguished from one's reputation. Accordingly, one often finds expressions such as "may I not be seen doing X" where we might say "may I not do X." In her prologue, Aphrodite predicts that even in death Phaedra will have a good reputation (47). Phaedra herself emphasizes the importance of this reputation explicitly by using the word *euklees* (the adjectival form of *eukleia*) and its opposite several times of herself and her children. When the play opens she has already determined to take her own life, knowing that illicit passion brought a bad reputation (405) and being unwilling to compromise her children's good reputation coming from their mother (419-23); after the Nurse's revelation to Hippolytus, Phaedra fears that she will no longer die with such a reputation (687-8); but then she finds a remedy to ensure her children's good name after all (717). The chorus confirms the importance of her good name in the song that follows her exit to her death (772-3). Hippolytus, when he is faced with exile, prays that he die without fame (1028) if he is evil, and Artemis, at the end of the play, acknowledges Phaedra's "nobility" (1301), but explains that she has come so that Hippolytus may die in good repute (1299).

In order to ensure her good reputation, Phaedra seeks to avoid anything that might cause disgrace. She cannot bear the thought of disgracing her husband (420, 720-1) or her Cretan home (719). In these cases the word used for "disgrace" is the verb *aischuno* or its related adjective. After expressing her desire for the mountains and horses, she checks herself out of shame at her words (244). The word used to express shame here is *aidos*. *Aidos*, prominent in the play, refers to a complex set of emotions which include the feeling that inhibits one from improper action; it is "that which renders one sensitive to the general values of society and inhibits departure from them."[6] In part, it keeps one from conduct that would jeopardize one's good name. It is also what one feels having committed such action; thus it suggests "shame" as well as "reverence, respect." At the crucial juncture where Phaedra yields to the Nurse's supplication, she explains, "I respect [feel *aidos* before] your supplication" (335). Later, after this respect for the Nurse's supplication leads to what she feels will be certain disgrace, she kills herself, feeling, the chorus imagine, shame (*aidos*) at her misfortune (772). *Aidos* is also significantly placed in her major speech explaining the motives of her actions (385-6). For Hippolytus, a personified *aidos* tends his exclusive, inviolate meadow (78). It is the feeling that operates in those he would consider his friends (998). While the word appears in connection with Theseus only in explaining his curtailed joy at his son's death (1258), he implicitly refers to this concept when he imagines that if he does not punish his son he will seem inferior in the eyes of the brigands he has already punished (976-80).

The reference to another's gaze, fundamental to the dynamics of a "shame culture," appears several times in this play. It is reflected in the words of all three main characters: Phaedra wonders how adulterers can look their husbands in the eye (415-6), and explains that she will never come before Theseus after doing disgraceful deeds (721); Hippolytus threatens that when he returns he will observe how Phaedra and her Nurse can look at Theseus (661-2); Theseus commands Hippolytus to show his face to his father (946-7), and hopes to refute his son face to face (1265).

Honor forms another part of this matrix. Honor is an outward manifesta-

---

6   D. Cairns *Aidos: The Psychology and Ethics of Honour and Shame in Ancient Greek Literature* (1993) 154.

tion of one's worth, and gods and mortals display a keen interest in it. Aphrodite in her prologue explains the role of honor as a general principle—gods like being honored (8). Hippolytus honors Artemis (16; cf. 55), not Aphrodite, who will punish Hippolytus for her perceived lack of it from him (21). The word for "punish" which Aphrodite uses at 21 is etymologically related to words for "honor" (the root is *tim-*), punishment being a way of establishing or protecting one's worth, one's honor. Hippolytus' refusal to honor Aphrodite lies at the center of his tragedy, and this refusal is underscored in his exchange with his servant (88ff., esp. 107 and 104) and confirmed by Artemis (1402). Phaedra's intended suicide will, she feels, bring her honor (329). And in writing the lying tablet she will punish Hippolytus (see esp. 728-31, although no word from the root *tim-* is used). Theseus mocks Hippolytus' (seemingly) feigned honoring of mystic texts (954). After learning of Hippolytus' destruction, the chorus sing of Aphrodite's extraordinary "power" (1281), another sense of the word *time*. At the end of the play Artemis declares that Aphrodite's anger against her favorite will not be "unavenged" (*atimoi*, 1417), but, like Aphrodite, she will herself both take vengeance (*timoresomai*, 1422; cf. 21) and establish a Trozenian cult in which Hippolytus will receive honors (*timai*, 1424).

SOPHROSUNE

No word is more fundamental to any Greek play than *sophrosune* is to this one, and in no other play do words from this root appear so often (eighteen times—*Bacchae* with twelve occurrences is the next highest). In its most radical sense the word means "safe-mindedness," the quality which allows one to act sensibly. In Plato's *Symposium* (196c) it is defined by Agathon as "being in control of pleasures and desires," while Antiphon (frag. 59 D-K) sees its essence in not merely not desiring what is evil, but in overcoming temptation. Its semantic sphere came to include various senses, including the several found in this play—good sense, self-control, sexual self-control, i.e., chastity, and virtue (in general).[7] In the play Hippolytus himself claims several times that no one is more *sophron* (the adjective of the noun) than he (995, 1100, 1365), condemns women who are not *sophron* (see esp. 667), wishes that his being sophron could persuade his father of his innocence (1007), and realizes that Phaedra was in some sense better able to use *sophrosune* than he (1034-5 and note). He also defends himself to his father with an argument about those who are, like him, *sophron* (1013), while Artemis defends him as being *sophron* (1402). Phaedra tries to conquer her passion by being *sophron* (399), hates those who are *sophron* only in words (413), and dies hoping that Hippolytus will learn to be *sophron* (731). From the Nurse's perspective, Phaedra is not *sophron* (358, 494), nor is she herself, she admits, in telling Hippolytus about Phaedra's passion (704), and, from Theseus' point of view, neither is Hippolytus (949). The chorus voices the commonplace that *sophrosune* is a good

---

7   In the translation, I have rendered this word, and its cognates, as "moderation, moderate," "virtue, virtuous," "chastity, chaste," "sensible" depending on the context, but its full semantic range should be borne in mind.

thing (431-2). The different claims about *sophrosune* and its varying shades of meaning conform with and help to create the ambiguities, paradoxes, and failures of understanding which permeate and animate the drama.

Hippolytus' assertion that he is *sophron* is matched by his assertion that he is *semnos*: "Here I am the reverent (*semnos*) and god-revering,/ here I am the one who surpassed everyone in *sophrosune*" (1364-5). But the word *semnos* is ambiguous and charged. It is used in both negative ("arrogant," "proud") and positive ("august," "revered," "pious") senses. In a telling scene with his servant, this word appears three times in shifting senses. This dialogue suggests that it is one thing for a god to be *semnos* (in its positive sense), another for a mortal to be *semnos* (in its negative sense) (88-105; see 93n.). Aphrodite has already made clear that Hippolytus will be punished for his refusal to reverence her. Hence his claim to being *semnos*, juxtaposed to the paradoxical claim of surpassing everyone in *sophrosune*, rings ominously.

PASSION AND REASON

Sexual passion, refused by Hippolytus and combated by Phaedra, drives the play's action, and much of the play can be read as a discourse on passion. Aphrodite faults Hippolytus for reviling her (12-3; and cf. 113) and also, strikingly, not for neglecting her altar but for refusing her realm, the realm of marriage and sex (14). But what she wants from him is impossible if he is going to continue as a virgin follower of Artemis. And this impossibility is the essence of his tragedy. Artemis explains the situation concisely: "She [Aphrodite] found fault with your homage, and she was vexed at your virtue" (1402). Hippolytus has no place in his world for sex. In his extraordinary response to the Nurse's proposition (616-68), his world has no place for women at all, and he even thinks he has been sullied by the Nurse's words (654-5). He consistently (and futilely) asserts his chastity and purity in his debate with his father (esp. 1003-6). For Phaedra, not passion per se, but an illicit passion for her stepson is at issue. This passion is imagined as a disease. The word *nosos* is used frequently both of the passion itself and of the effects it has on Phaedra. It is a sickness because it is illicit and too strong; it threatens the good name that is so important to her.

The Nurse, on the other hand, sees sexual passion, of whatever sort, simply as part of life, something sent from the Aphrodite (437-40) that afflicts the gods as well as mortals (451-61). When it leads to illicit acts, it is best to ignore them (462-9). She recognizes the important role Aphrodite plays throughout the universe (447-50) and even sees her as something greater than divinity (359-60). She argues that the one who opposes Aphrodite is struck that much harder by the goddess (443-6), and that it is even hubris to try to fight passion (473-6). Theseus, like the Nurse, responds to the effects of passion, but, unlike the Nurse, responds to a distorted version of those effects. He readily accepts Phaedra's version of what happened, not only because of the damning evidence of the corpse and the lying note, but because the false tale she created conforms to his belief about young men (966-70).

The choral songs, especially the first stasimon, contribute to the play's exploration of passion. The *parodos* ironically considers Theseus' infidelity as a possible cause of Phaedra's distress (151-4). The next choral song (525-64), sung after the revelation of Phaedra's desire for Hippolytus and while the Nurse approaches the young man within, offers the play's most extended reflection on passion. The chorus describe Eros as a warrior, yet, paradoxically, one who brings "sweet delight" to those he attacks, echoing the motif of Eros the bittersweet already introduced by the Nurse (348). These women of Trozen pray that this god not come to them with evil intent or "out of measure," recognizing that it is under such circumstances that Eros is intolerable. This prayer reflects the dynamics of the play: passion under "proper" circumstances is (implicitly) welcome and benign; otherwise it can be ruinous. The rest of the song focuses on the destructive power of desire, proclaiming the lack of ritual observance Eros receives and then recounting the specific examples of destructive passion in the cases of Zeus and Semele and Heracles and Iole. Permeating the second half of the song are terms and images associated with weddings, used so as to suggest the perversion of wedding rituals. Broadly the song points to the destructiveness of passion, which brings down, directly or indirectly, all three of the play's main characters. More specifically, it hints that the perversion of these rituals leads to these characters' ruin. Phaedra does not violate her marriage, but it is the fear that she might that leads her to her death. Hippolytus' violation of marital norms is in his extraordinary refusal to participate in them, announced by Aphrodite and obliquely echoed in this song's concern with the lack of observance paid to Eros. Theseus' "violation" of these norms is oblique. His sexual transgressions were notorious, but what draws attention in this play is the bastardy of Hippolytus. Repeatedly we are reminded that the unstable familial situation (a bastard child who poses a sexual temptation to Theseus' wife) stems from his sexual transgression. And, as already noted, his ready assumptions about a male's sexual behavior lead him to condemn his son precipitously.

Following Phaedra's exit to her death, the chorus wish to escape from their present plight and revert, in the second half of the song, to Phaedra's ill-omened wedding voyage from Crete to Athens. They connect this directly with her suffering and her current illicit passion, caused by Aphrodite, which is leading to her death. At Hippolytus' departure, the chorus laments the loss of Hippolytus, including the loss to maidens of a contest for his hand (1140-1). The invocation of the "yoked Graces" (1148) might evoke images of a wedding. The brief choral song preceding the exodos is devoted fully to the overwhelming force of passion, hymning the power of Eros and Aphrodite. Here, near the play's conclusion, the song emphasizes the universal, procreative, and overwhelming power of these gods or forces, rather than their destructiveness. In her final speech, Artemis establishes Hippolytus' paradoxical connection with marriage rites, promising that Trozenian maidens before their weddings will honor him in cult and will remember Phaedra's passion for him in song.

Passion has several forces opposing it in this play. Moderation and reason in particular are imagined in opposition to it (ultimately without success).

Sophrosune, as discussed above, although frequently approximating English "virtue" or "moderation," literally refers to one's intellect ("safe-mindedness"). So even *sophrosune's* opposition to passion can be viewed as part of a larger opposition of reason and passion. Phaedra clearly imagines her struggle in terms of intellection. Words for intellection dominate the entire speech in which she explains her course of actions. She describes her struggle against her passion for Hippolytus in cerebral terms, concluding that, since she could not subjugate it, she must choose death. The chorus, as they conclude their song in response to her presumed death, describe it, using the same opposition, as Phaedra's attempt to rid this passion from her mind (774-5). Earlier Phaedra attributed her expressions of desire (198ff.) to madness and ruin (241), which led her away from the course of good thinking (240). And the Nurse, after recovering from her initial shock at the object of Phaedra's passion, tells her that she suffers nothing "unaccountable" (literally "beyond reason," 438). For Hippolytus there is no comparable internal conflict. His *sophrosune* brings about his ruin, and his power of speech, curtailed by his sworn oath, and his argumentation are unable to save him. Sexual passion overcomes him, but only indirectly. Theseus acts rashly, his powers of reflection and considered judgment overtaken by the anger induced by Phaedra's lying note (1310-2, 1336-7; and cf. 1413). In the play as a whole, speech is typically portrayed as destructive, while reason is shown to be unable to cope with the forces of passion.

IGNORANCE

Aphrodite's opening speech creates at once a fundamental dramatic irony—we know (more or less) what is going to transpire, while the play's characters do not. Such dramatic irony is not uncommon, especially in plays in which a god delivers the prologue, but ignorance, real and feigned, resonates throughout this play, in big ways and small. Aphrodite explains that none of the servants knows Phaedra's malady (40), and that Hippolytus does not know that the gates of Hades lie open for him (56-7). The servant introduces his exchange with Hippolytus with a question about his master's knowledge (91); the chorus's first words when the Nurse enters reflect their ignorance about Phaedra's condition (173-5; and cf. 270 and 282-3), and the Nurse herself is ignorant of the cause of Phaedra's illness (271), and shows her confusion in response to Phaedra's "delirium." The Nurse does evoke a response from a silent Phaedra when she mentions the name of Hippolytus, whom, she says, "you know well" (309), but only gradually does she learn what she wishes to know (see 344, 346). Phaedra's speech on knowledge and our limitations in carrying out the good forms another part of this matrix. The Nurse does not so much persuade Phaedra as dupe her, resorting to an evasive claim of ignorance about her own plans (517). When she learns Hippolytus' response to what the Nurse has actually done, Phaedra says, "I don't know, except one thing—to die as quickly as possible" (599). Hippolytus himself is ignorant of the full import of his oath to the Nurse. And this oath compels him to feign ignorance in the confrontation with his father (1033), after an initial honest claim of ignorance about the cause of Theseus' alarm (903-4). At the end of the scene with his father, he refers enigmatically to the constraints of this oath, "I know these things, but I don't know how to reveal them" (1091). The chorus's oath to Phaedra also constrains them to lie about their knowledge in response to Theseus' question about her death (804-5). Theseus laments that mortals do not yet know how to teach good sense (919-20); he does, however, claim to know how young men are affected by passion (967-70), a general statement which does not apply to his son. Hippolytus, in this debate with his father, asserts his knowledge of proper behavior (996ff.) and his ignorance of sex (1004-5), an ignorance that has ignited Aphrodite's wrath.

Because of the lying tablet and the sworn oaths, Theseus acts in the most profound and destructive ignorance. Yet this very ignorance acquits him, in Artemis' view, from the charge of wickedness (1334-5). Ignorance, as much as anything else, separates mortals from the gods and defines the human condition. Human characters make crucial choices—for speech, for silence, for vengeance—in ignorance. Phaedra claims that mortals know what is right but cannot carry it out. The play, however, strongly suggests that mortals too often do not know enough even to begin to make the right decisions, and do not seek out further information. Passion is an overwhelming force in mortals' lives, and so is ignorance. Both forces act on mortals to bring about the play's multiple acts of destruction.

Appendix Two

The *Heracles*: An Interpretation

By Michael R. Halleran

THE MYTH OF HERACLES

Stories about Heracles were many and varied, showing his great importance and popularity in Greek culture. It will be useful to summarize the basic facts of his myths. Heracles was the child of the chief Olympian, the sky god, Zeus, and a mortal woman, Alcmene, the wife of Amphitryon. Hera, Zeus' wife, was outraged at this adultery and persecuted Heracles even before he was born. On the day Heracles was due to come into the world, Hera tricked Zeus into proclaiming that one born of his blood on that day would rule over those around him (cf. Homer, *Iliad* 19.95ff.). Zeus meant Heracles, but Hera brought it about that Eurystheus, Zeus' great-grandson, was born that day (prematurely), and thus from Tiryns lords it over Heracles in nearby Thebes. Heracles' persecution at the hands of Hera and his subservience to Eurystheus are two of the major features of his stories. He is forced to undertake various tasks, eventually canonized as his "twelve labors", at Eurystheus' orders. These adventures provide much of the material for the Heracles myth since they bring him into contact with various peoples and places throughout the Greek world. These exploits show Heracles subduing wild creatures, capturing miraculous objects, and even going to and returning from the underworld. Heracles also is involved in numerous other events and places independent of the labors. After the completion of his labors, Heracles eventually undergoes an apotheosis and becomes a full-fledged Olympian god.

Our sources for Heracles' myths are disparate: some are archaic epic poetry from the eighth century BCE, others are passing references in authors a thousand years later. The pre-Euripidean tradition, i.e. what Euripides had to work with and what he would assume his audience knew, is difficult to determine with precision. But an attempt can be made to reconstruct the pre-Euripidean tradition of the aspects of the Heracles myth most relevant to Euripides' play.

In viewing the *Heracles* the audience would have recognized several familiar features of the story and have been struck by some innovations. Amphitryon, who delivers the prologue speech, first relates some historical and genealogical information, including his own exile from his native Argos because of his unintentional murder of his wife's father, Electryon. He then explains that Heracles is in Hades, finishing the last of his labors, while a man named Lycus has staged a coup and now threatens Heracles' family with death. The most striking departure from the pre-existing tradition is the sequence of events. According to a likely reconstruction of this earlier version, the murder of the children *preceded* the labors and may have provided the motivation for them, as Heracles performed these deeds in service to Eurystheus as purification for the murders. In Euripides' version, the murders *follow* the labors; thus the hero is struck with madness and commits the murders at the moment of his greatest triumph, the completion of the labors and return from Hades. Euripides' account of the story also necessitates a different motivation for the labors. Amphitryon explains (17-21) that since he himself is in exile from his native Argos, Heracles acts to "ease [these] misfortunes" as well as to win his own return to his fatherland. Filial piety has replaced purification for kindred murder. The audience would be unsurprised to hear Amphitryon add that this "great price for the return" is paid to Eurystheus, Heracles' mortal persecutor, and that Hera is also involved in causing his labors, since these two, as we have seen, were very much part of the tradition. Theseus' later appearance and his involvement in this stage of the story must also be novel, since it hinges on his rescue by Heracles from the underworld, i.e. during the completion of his labors. Amphitryon's speech introduces one other new element: Lycus and his usurpation of power and his threat to the family. This Lycus, it seems, is a Euripidean invention and found nowhere in Greek literature before this play and nowhere afterwards independent of the play's influence. This new character is of obvious importance for the threat he poses to the family, since this motivates the first section of the play.

An interesting question which cannot be answered with any certitude suggests itself: did the audience, aware of the apparent shift in the traditional sequence of events, know or suspect that Heracles at some point in the play would kill his children? What did they think would be the consequences of Euripides' innovation? Some might have suspected or wondered about the possibility of the children's murder, but at the point of Heracles' return Euripides stresses the success of Heracles' homecoming and his subsequent victory over Lycus. If the audience did think at all of the gruesome possibility of the children's murder, that added a finer dimension to the experience of viewing the play, as it would create a tension between what the play suggests and the viewer fears.

THE *HERACLES*: AN INTERPRETATION

About the *Heracles* critical opinion has never been tepid. The verdicts issued both for and against the play have been forceful and some have become almost as famous as their authors. The poet Robert Browning referred to the play as "the perfect piece" while his younger contemporary Swinburne, in a graphic and memorable phrase, called it a "grotesque abortion". The most important classical scholar of the late nineteenth and early twentieth century,

Wilamowitz, devoted his masterly study of Greek tragedy to this play, but earlier in this century the influential British classicist Gilbert Murray pronounced it "broken-backed". These critics, and the many others who have shared their views, were responding to the same play, and at times even to the same features of the play. The play is bold in its handling of the myth, ambitious in design, and arresting in its many reversals of fortune. While its supporters have seen it as a superb example of Greek tragedy's potential to delineate the tragic and the humane in life, its critics have been disturbed by its alleged lack of unity, specifically the absence of a clear causal link between the events of the first half of the play and those of the second. Anyone coming to the *Heracles* expecting the tight structure of Sophocles' *Oedipus the King* or Euripides' *Hippolytus* will, doubtless, be disappointed in this regard, but such a narrow notion of unity ill serves a study of Greek tragedy. Every play has its own patterns and rhythm, and a seeming disjuncture may very well be part of its design.

The play's opening suggests to the audience the dire straits of the characters. A group, an old man, a woman, and three young boys, sits at an altar in supplication. The altar, this opening tableau reveals to us, is their only hope of refuge: they are passive and helpless and their leaving the altar will signify their rescue or their doom. The play's first speech, the prologue delivered by Amphitryon, verbally confirms this visual impression of helplessness, as the old man explains that with Heracles away in Hades Lycus has staged a coup in Thebes and now threatens the family of Heracles with death. Amphitryon and the family have accordingly taken refuge at the altar of Zeus the Rescuer, and seek his help since their own true friends are too weak to aid, while others have proven to be not true friends at all. Euripides commonly begins his plays with such expositions, which not only provides the basic background information to the drama's action but helps to establish the play's themes and mood. Here, for instance, we notice that Amphitryon's opening self-identification (necessary in a theater without playbills) links him with Zeus: "What mortal does not know of the man who shared his marriage bed with Zeus,/Amphitryon of Argos—the father of Heracles? "(1-3). The opening reference to Zeus has double point: it initiates the thematic issue of Heracles' paternity (is Zeus or Amphitryon his father?) which is developed throughout the play (see, e. g., 1-3, 148-49, 170-71, 339-47, 353-54, 798-804, 1263-65) and it suggests that Zeus, at whose altar these suppliants sit, has special reason to offer them protection, since he has a share in Amphitryon's marriage bed and Heracles' birth.

In providing background information for the play's action, Amphitryon's speech also gives some indication to the audience of the play's assumptions. Euripides made several innovations in this play, the most important of which Amphitryon makes clear in this speech: the labors are not preceded by the murder of the children. What will happen to them, the audience must wonder? Amphitryon also introduces Lycus and his threat with special care, since he too is new to the tale and is essential for the first half of the action. Not only does he, by threatening the family, motivate the first third of the play, but consequently also allows Heracles to dispatch the wicked tyrant and show his deep concern for his family, all of which leads up to the shocking reversal in the next act.

Amphitryon also announces in his opening speech a theme which proves central to the drama: friendship. The family is in its current plight because, "Some of our friends I realize are not reliable friends,/while others who truly are cannot help." (55-56) The word translated as friend, *philos*, had, as discussed in the notes (see on line 266), a wider range than English "friend": it referred to anyone who was near and dear, including non-family members, as well as those related by blood or marriage. The *philos* whom the family most needs, the one who could readily set things straight, is Heracles, but the first third of the drama assumes that he cannot return from Hades (cf., e. g., 80ff.,145-46, 296-97). Heracles cannot, it seems, save his family, but the dramatic situation demands that he do just that, and this paradox animates the first part of the play.

In her initial response to Amphitryon (60-86), Megara offers a different view of their situation. Whereas Amphitryon explained the general background of their situation, Megara gives a more personal account. In her view her own plight shows the uncertainty of human fortune (62ff.): she has gone from the acme of mortal prosperity to the verge of death. She also paints a vivid picture of the children's anxiety as they expectantly await their father's return. She has abandoned hope, since death, she believes, is inevitable, and she turns to Amphitryon to provide some means of rescue; their safety is in his hands. Amphitryon, by contrast, will not despair: "This man is the best, the one who always/trusts in hope." (105-06).

At this point the chorus of sympathetic old Theban men arrives in the orchestra, just as in Euripides' other so-called "suppliant" plays a chorus concerned with the well-being of the suppliants enters after the opening scene. The identity of the chorus is very well chosen: they are as well-intentioned as they are impotent. Singing their first song, these men of Thebes make clear their infirm condition ("We are mere words, the nocturnal semblance/of nighttime dreams" [111-12], and see 108-110, and 119-130), and their sympathies ("We come feeble, but eager still" [114]). At the end of the song they focus on the children and what their loss will mean to Greece, thereby providing a link to the following scene, as they immediately announce the arrival of the man who will cause Greece to lose them, Lycus.

The scene between Lycus and the suppliants is instrumental to the depiction of these characters, to the plot and to the themes of the drama. Attempts to criticize it have been wide of the mark. Lycus offers an unabashed pragmatism: he now holds power (cf. 141-42) and seeks to rid himself of possible avengers for his murder of Megara's father (165-69). To him this is not shamelessness, but prudence (165-66). As for Heracles, Lycus adds his voice to the belief that having gone down to Hades, he cannot return to rescue his suppliant family. And he ridicules the hero's achievements: his reputation rests on exaggerated victories over mere beasts; using the bow, he is a coward, not facing men in battle face to face; the children deserve no special consideration for such deeds of their father. He shows no respect for the altar's sanctuary: when Amphitryon does not yield, but meets and defeats his arguments with his own (170-235), Lycus will resort to force, ordering men to bring wood so he can burn them at the altar (240-46).

Amphitryon tries to maintain his hope. First he launches a long defense of Heracles and his use of the bow. He vindicates Heracles' labors and explains the cleverness of the bow. This latter argument, as has been suggested, may reflect contemporary interest in military strategy, but more importantly, in addition to giving Amphitryon the chance to defeat Lycus in words and pro- claim Heracles' bravery, it has a key thematic role in the drama, as the bow is used in the murder of the children and at the end of the play will take on a symbolic value in Heracles' decision to continue with his life. Amphitryon also criticizes Lycus' cowardice, as well as that of Thebes and Greece, for not coming to the family's rescue. He concludes with a feeble threat against Lycus, saying what he would do if he had the strength of his youth (232-35). Like the chorus, he can offer nothing more than words, as Lycus well recognizes (cf. 238-39). Megara, in viewing the situation, displays again her resignation (275-311). She loves her children, of course, but there is no hope of Heracles' return. Death is inevitable and exile, even if offered, would be wretched. Since such is the case, they should seek a death with honor, not burned at the altar, the object of their enemies' ridicule. "Whoever struggles against the fortunes of the gods/he is eager, but his eagerness is senseless./For what must happen no one will ever make not happen" (309-11).

The cumulative effect of Lycus' threats and Megara's persuasion suc- ceeds in convincing Amphitryon to abandon the altar. He had wanted to save Heracles' children, but he concludes that he seemed "to desire the impossible" (318; cf. 92). He leaves the altar and offers himself to Lycus; Megara follows and asks only for one favor: to enter the house and dress the children in the garments of the dead. Lycus agrees and departs, and Megara goes into the house with the children, while Amphitryon remains to address final words to Zeus. His attack on Zeus seems an appropriate conclusion to this preceding scene. Zeus has proved uncaring ("You were after all less of a friend [*philos*] than you seemed." [341]) and useless ("But you do not know how to save your friends [*philoi*]." [346]) His special connection with the family, being "partner in my child" (340), has, Amphitryon concludes, been of no value. These final words of Amphitryon not only highlight the issue of Heracles' paternity but underscore the question of divine justice, which already has been raised (cf. 212). Zeus seems not to care for justice: Heracles' family is going to die.

The chorus' responds to these events by singing of Heracles' labors. They assume he is dead ("Excellent glory achieved with noble toil/are glory for the dead." [356-66]) and sing a type of lament (*threnos*) in his honor. The song has several purposes. First, it offers another response to Lycus' shallow attack on Heracles' heroism. Second, it shows Heracles as a civilizing, ben- eficial force, subduing the Centaurs who terrorized the Thessalians (364-74), taming the mares of Diomedes who feasted on human flesh (380-86), calming the seas for mortals (400-02). It concludes with the present situation: Heracles is finishing his life in Hades, while the family looks to him in his absence. The chorus cannot help; they lack their "blessed youth". The tension of the play's first section is experienced in miniature in this song: by singing the praises of Heracles, the chorus makes clear how easily he could save his family, while the form of the song, a *threnos*, reminds us that he is, it appears, dead.

Lycus had said (334-35) that he would return after the family had donned their robes of death. At this juncture, then, we should expect his return, but it is delayed while the pathetic picture of the family, sketched in the previous scene, is painted with full, affecting strokes. Megara turns to the children and describes the games Heracles used to play with them, as he promised them future rule, and she recounts her own choosing of brides for her sons. She concludes with a despairing appeal to Heracles: "Help! Come! Appear even as a shadow!" (494) Amphitryon then continues the attack on Zeus which he began at the close of the previous scene, calling upon him, but thinking it a vain appeal. Having been won over to Megara's position, he elaborates on the vicissitudes of life, as seen in his own case; hope he has finally abandoned.

At this moment of despairing resignation to death, Euripides presents the play's first reversal. Heracles is seen approaching. The hero whose return was repeatedly denied as impossible, whose return was the only thing that could save the threatened family, arrives, as if in answer to Megara's appeal, at the critical moment to save his family and punish the tyrant. Euripides exploits the dramatic possibilities of this entrance by drawing it out, displaying Megara's confusion, disbelief and joy. Zeus did not save them, but Heracles will: as Megara explains to the children, to them he is "not at all second to Zeus Soter" (522). Shocked at what he sees and angered when he learns the situation and the threat to his family, Heracles vows revenge (565-73). The strong language in which he describes his vengeance has disturbed some critics, leading them to think that Heracles is either already showing signs of his incipient madness or that he is guilty of some sort of excess. Neither is the case. Nothing in the play prior to the arrival of Iris and Lyssa suggests his madness (in fact Euripides lays great stress on the madness as sudden and external) and Heracles' threatened vengeance, although it reminds us of the type of violent deeds he can perform, is not out of line with the code of helping your friends and hurting your enemies (cf. n.266). The prime target of his destruction is the man who threatens his own family and the others are those who tolerated this treatment, when they themselves had benefited from him. The labors have been greatly emphasized in part so Heracles can here disown them in favor of something he values more dearly. "Farewell, labors!" (575). His subduing the Nemean lion and all the other wondrous deeds pale in comparison to his defense of his family. Now his defense of them will become the new test of his heroism (cf. 580-82).

After discussing strategy with Amphitryon, and revealing that he rescued Theseus while he was in Hades (a fact that becomes important later), Heracles calls to his children to enter the house with him. Here we experience visually the reversal presented in this scene, which began with the announced entrance of the children with Megara and Amphitryon (445-47): "and his loving wife,/pulling [*helkousan*] beside her their children/who cling to her feet which guide them". Heracles now proclaims, "Taking them [his children who are clinging to his robes] in hand I will lead [*ephelxo*] these little boats/and like a ship I will pull them in tow" (631-32). Tears also connect the two stage actions (cf. 449-50, 625). Finally, Heracles himself contrasts their exit from to their entrance into the house: "So your entrances into it are fairer/than your exits from it, right?" (623-24). The exit from the house at the beginning of the scene seemed to mark the family's imminent death, but did not, while the entrance into it seems to signal their safety, but this too is only temporary and illusory. Heracles delivers the scene's final words, just as we see what proves to be the last of the children and Megara: "Everyone loves his children" (636).

Heracles' successful return inspires the chorus to sing in celebration (637-700). The previous song was a lamentation over the presumed dead Heracles; this one is a type of victory song, an epinician, praising, indirectly and directly, the living and successful hero. The two songs frame the scene in which the first reversal of fortune, marked by Heracles' return, occurs. Youth, which the chorus has constantly made clear it sorely lacks, is dear to them, old age a burden; wealth, a conventional measure of excellence, is not to be preferred to youth. The gods should give a double youth to those who excel as a clear sign of their excellence. This odd-seeming wish pertains indirectly to Heracles, since having just returned from Hades, he has experienced a type of rebirth and has come to possess a second youth. Following a common pattern, the first half of this song (the first two stanzas) is general, while the second half is particular, as the chorus turns specifically to their praise of Heracles. They will never stop singing his praises. He is the child of Zeus and is "surpassing in excellence (*arete*) more than in birth" (696-97).

Once Heracles has arrived, the death of Lycus is a foregone conclusion, and Euripides wastes little time on it. Lycus returns at the start of the next scene, looking for the family he intends to kill. He is tricked, however, by Amphitryon into entering the house, where Heracles lies in ambush (this is an intrigue pattern which Euripides employs elsewhere, e.g. in *Hecuba, Electra, Antiope*). His death screams are interspersed with the chorus' cries of joy at the return of the old ruler and the punishment of the wicked new one. For them this death is proof of divine justice. As they sing in their following song, "The gods, the gods/take care to heed/the unjust and the holy" (772-73). The previous ode not only looked backwards, commenting on the successful return of Heracles and framing with the first stasimon that return, it also with the present song marks the final stage of Heracles' victory, the killing of Lycus. Together these two songs surrounding the brief scene of Lycus' death create an impressive mood of joy and celebration. This change of fortune is proof of a theodicy, and Thebes celebrates with dancing, festival, and song. For the chorus Heracles' success is proof not only of a theodicy but also of his divine birth. Zeus is indeed his father. The serious doubts suggested by Amphitryon's stinging words are forgotten in the joy of this victory. Heracles is Zeus' son and the gods care for justice. The conclusion of the song is confident: "You [Heracles] were a better lord to me/than the ignoble lord,/who now makes clear to anyone/looking at the contest of swords/whether justice/still pleases the gods." (809-14)

At once Iris and Lyssa, the personification of madness, appear on high to madden Heracles into killing his family. The joy of the ode and Heracles' success are short-lived. This juxtaposition of joyous song and destructive action could not be more sudden or arresting. And the appearance of gods in mid-play is unique in Euripides. Elsewhere they appear only at the beginnings and ends of the dramas, and nowhere else do two superhuman characters appear with speaking parts. This unusual and sudden appearance underscores the reversal which it signals. Iris explains that they mean no harm to the city; only against one man, Heracles, do they come. Ironically Lyssa, the personification of madness, does not wish to madden the intended victim. (Note the similarity between this scene and the opening of *Prometheus Bound*, where another pair of divinities argues about the justice of punishing a mortal who has benefited others and where Hephaestus, the one who ought to be interested in persecuting the mortal, demurs.) She argues (847-54) that Heracles has performed many noble deeds and explains that "he alone of mortal men set up the honors/Of the gods which had fallen at the hands of impious men" (852-53). Iris, her superior, demands that she perform her duty and Lyssa does so, forecasting the madness she will bring upon Heracles and his murder of the children.

Why is this madness sent upon Heracles? This question, as much as any other, has disturbed and puzzled critics of the play. Iris gives no long explanation. While Heracles was performing his labors, Necessity and Zeus did not allow Hera or Iris to harm him. Now that he has completed them, they may drive him to kill his children so "he may recognize what sort is Hera's anger against him/and learn mine. Otherwise the gods are nowhere/and mortal things will be great, if he doesn't pay the penalty" (840-42). The cause of Hera's anger, unspecified here, is mentioned later in the play (cf. especially 1307-10): Zeus' illicit union with Alcmene and the resulting offspring, Heracles. Even before hearing this expressly, the audience would assume that this is the reason for Hera's anger, since it was well known and already found in Homer's *Iliad* (19. 95ff.). The thematic issue of Heracles' paternity ("Is Zeus or Amphitryon his father?") has, it is seen in this regard, an extra point: to keep before the audience's mind the illicit union which produced him. Iris' anger is perhaps somewhat more puzzling. It has been suggested that she acts as a stand-in for Hera in this scene. It would be inappropriate and distracting for the queen of heaven to make such an appearance, and Iris, on a more equal footing with Lyssa, allows for a better contrast between the two opposing characters. She is little more than an alter-Hera and her anger is simply Hera's transferred. In any case, Iris' anger receives little dramatic attention; the focus is on Hera.

Iris' reference to Heracles' "paying the penalty" raises another question: penalty for what? Heracles, many have assumed, must have done something wrong. Various theories have been spun, focusing chiefly on Heracles' alleged *hybris*, his offense of excess, perhaps in coming back from the "dead" in Hades, perhaps by performing his many great deeds. Others have glided over this passage and found the madness in the hero himself, the divine apparatus being a mere symbol of his internal state. Such theories founder, however, on the evidence of the play. Throughout the drama Euripides underscores the external nature of the madness, and nowhere is it suggested that Heracles is guilty of arrogant or excessive behavior. In fact Euripides strives to show the opposite: Heracles has helped the gods in combat (177ff., 1190ff.), restored their honors (852-53), and been a great benefactor to man (cf., especially, the description of the labors in the first stasimon). The gods, however, do not need to satisfy mortal curiosity about the motivation for their actions. From the point of view of Hera (and Iris) Heracles must be "punished", punished for deeds left unspecified. The gods here appropriate language used elsewhere in this play to describe Lycus' punishment (especially in the previous choral celebration, e.g. at 740 and 756). The audience is left to decide whether this conforms to their own notions of justice. Euripides helps them in forming their judgment by offering no evidence of Heracles' "crime" but, on the contrary, much to suggest his piety. The appearance of Iris and Lyssa is meant as a sharp rupture, a sudden and fierce overturning of the previous action. The dramatic rupture underlines the causal one: the drama's action does not suggest a reason for Heracles' "punishment" and madness other than the will and power of the gods.

Iris' and Lyssa's appearance occurs roughly at the halfway point of the play, and since it so radically changes the play's direction, many have viewed the drama as having two sections, the first consisting of lines 1-814, the second lines 815-end. Others have preferred to see the play as tripartite: the same first part (lines 1-814), a second part (815-1162), and a third, punctuated by Theseus' arrival, extending from 1163-end. Those who argue for a three-fold division can find support in the surprising entrances of the divinities at 815 and of Theseus at 1163 as signalling the second and third parts respectively. Both sides of the debate are in a way correct. The play does seem to have three divisions, neatly punctuated by the surprise entrances which move the action in new directions (one might argue that Heracles' arrival at 514 constitutes yet another division), yet the actions are fundamentally two, each one of which is then reversed. The first action, the "suppliant" drama, is marked by the surprising rescue by Heracles. After this action is completed, the gods arrive, introducing the second action, the one in which Heracles is "rescued", and in which several reversals of the first action occur.

We experience Heracles' madness and the murder of his children in several stages. It is first announced by Iris and Lyssa, then predicted by the chorus in lyrics, and followed by Amphitryon's cries from within confirming the bloodshed, interspersed with choral lamentation; a messenger then enters from the palace to narrate the sorry deeds, and finally the corpses and the subdued Heracles are wheeled out on the *ekkyklema* offering visual proof of the events. The messenger's description of the murders is chilling. As Heracles and his family stands around the altar where he is in the process of performing expiatory sacrifice for his murder of Lycus, the madness strikes ("He was no longer himself" [931]). He imagines that he will go after Eurystheus, but in his frenzy he takes his own children for those of Eurystheus; the children's rescuer now becomes their slayer. In Megara's speech almost immediately before Heracles' return from Hades, she described how the boys' father had given one his club to play with (470-71), while to another he promised rule over Oechalia, "which he had once sacked with his well-aimed arrows" (473). The messenger relates how with these very weapons he killed his sons and wife (977ff.). The third child is killed as his mother tries to protect him (996-1000), a grim echo of Megara's own words in her first speech (71-72).

Before the carnage is presented visually to the audience, the chorus sings a brief song commenting on the events within. Referring to other examples of kindred murder, the slaying of husbands by the daughters of Danaus and the filicide committed by Procne, they conclude that Heracles' murder of his children surpasses these. The doors then open and the *ekkyklema* reveals the corpses of the three children and Megara, and Heracles tied to a broken pillar. This tableau presents a visual echo of the original scene of supplication. The play opened with the children, Megara and Amphitryon gathered around the altar; now we see the corpses of Megara and the children surrounding Heracles tied to a pillar, which, like the altar, is an impressive stage property. The stage now holds two striking reminders of failure. The rescue by Heracles failed, just as the altar of Zeus failed, to protect the family. The now-deserted altar has nearby the scene of divinely-caused slaughter.

Heracles' maddened slaughter was stopped only by the intervention of Athena, who subdued Heracles into sleep by striking him with a rock. Will he be mad when he awakes? Amphitryon's and the chorus' vivid discussion about Heracles and his mental state enlivens the scene. When Heracles does waken, he only gradually realizes what he has done; like Agave in the Bacchae, he learns the full horror of his actions in stages. Fully informed of his horrific deeds, Heracles decides on suicide (1146-1152). By this means he will be able "to thrust away my life's infamy which remains" (1152). A fuller notion of what he means by this infamy he describes later (1281-90). Just as Megara was motivated to abandon the altar by thoughts of the family's reputation (see, e.g., 284-93), Heracles is driven to death by the same considerations. Heracles has now arrived at the point reached first by Megara and then by Amphitryon. He sees no reason for living; he is resigned to death. Like Ajax in Sophocles' play, Heracles is driven to contemplate suicide by the disgrace he feels at his acts. But unlike Ajax, Heracles has someone who will come to save him and help him to live in his wretched circumstances. No sooner does Heracles finish declaring his plans for suicide than he spots and announces the arrival of Theseus, "interrupting my thoughts of suicide" (1153), whom he describes as his friend (1154, 1156). Ashamed of what he has done and wishing not to pollute Theseus with blood guilt, he covers himself. As mentioned above, the play's three reversals are each marked by a surprise entrance: Heracles, Iris and Lyssa, and now Theseus. We had learned before of Theseus' rescue by Heracles from Hades and his return to Athens (619-21), but we have no reason to expect his arrival here.

This arrival is not only timely in thwarting Heracles' plans of suicide, it also sets in motion the final act of the play. He explains at once that, having learned of political troubles in Thebes, he has come with troops to aid Heracles;

he does so in return for Heracles' rescuing him from Hades. The impulse of succor stems from the traditional code of helping friends and harming enemies; this would dictate, as Theseus implies, a return of beneficial action. But Theseus in this scene is depicted as extraordinary. Nothing, not even the threat of pollution will deter Theseus from befriending Heracles ("But if I come to share the pain? Uncover him" [1202]; "There is no avenging spirit from friend to friend." [1234]). In fact what dominates this final scene is the theme of friendship (cf., e.g., 1154-56, 1169-70, 1200, 1202, 1221-25, 1234, 1336-37, 1403-04). Theseus is adamant in his insistence on helping Heracles. Even at the risk of pollution, even if it means faring poorly (cf. 1220-21), he wants Heracles to unveil himself and to speak with him face to face. He acknowledges that Heracles' ills are great ("For no darkness holds so dark a cloud/that it could hide your misfortune and ills" [1216-17]). But we must endure what comes from the gods ("Whoever of mortals is noble/bears what falls from the gods, and does not refuse them" [1227-28]). Endurance, especially of what comes from the gods, was a time-honored virtue (cf. especially the example of Odysseus), but Heracles seems to have taken it to a new extreme, one which he feels must have an end

"Toiling must have its limits." (1251). Theseus must not only offer his friendship, but remind Heracles of his heroism: in response to Heracles' threat of suicide, Theseus retorts, "You've spoken the words of a common man" (1248).

The initial exchange between the two men leads to a debate on Heracles' life and suffering, which deserves special attention because it shows how the stricken Heracles, brought from the acme of success to the lowest point of ruin and disgrace, overcomes the blows of fortune, and it also touches on critical thematic issues. Three long speeches form the core of this debate. First Heracles recounts a life of unremitting persecution at the hands of Hera, beginning with the circumstances of his engendering ("Zeus... begot me as an enemy/to Hera" [1263-64]). The arduous labors led to his murder of the children ("This final labor I, the sufferer, endured/in killing my children, to cope the house with ills" [1279-80]). Because of the blood pollution, he can no longer live in Thebes. And where else could he turn? What city would receive him? Where would he not be the object of reproach? Even the earth and the sea, he imagines, will cry out that he not touch them. A sufferer since birth, the murderer of his children, cut off from his community in Thebes and any other community, Heracles concludes that his life is not worth living. In his final words he displays his resignation to Hera's power: "Let the famous wife of Zeus dance... For she has achieved the purpose she wished/turning upside down the first man of Greece/roots and all. Who would pray/to such a goddess? One who because of a woman/in jealousy over Zeus' marriage bed destroyed/Greece's benefactor, who was not at all blameworthy" (1303; 1305-10).

Theseus makes a kind of argument not unfamiliar to the audience, an *a fortiori* argument based on divine behavior: the gods err and go on living, will you ,a mortal, not do so too? (1314-21) He follows this up with a generous offer of purification of the pollution, a home, gifts,and eventually honorific burial in Athens. All this is repayment for Heracles saving him from the underworld (1336-7). In his initial argument, Theseus with good intentions blurs a distinction between the divine examples and Heracles' situation, a blurring which points to an essential difference. The gods in Theseus' examples deliberately err and endure, while Heracles has erred unwillingly; he has, in fact, been erred against. Accordingly, in making his comparison Theseus employs the neutral word, fortune (*tuche*), to cover both cases.

The opening of Heracles' reply has generated much discussion, for in these words he raises fundamental questions about divinity and divine justice, and to many he seems to be speaking out of character, mouthing the views of the poet himself. But the words have a clear and precise context and are integral to the play, touching upon one of its central concerns. Theseus in his argument had maintained that if, as he assumed, the tales of the poets are true, the gods have engaged in illicit unions and bound their fathers in chains for the sake of rule. Heracles' reply meets his friend's argument point for point, meets it and dismisses its value for his own situation (1340-46):

> *Oimoi*. These things are incidental to my ills;
> for I don't believe that the gods put up with
> illicit unions and binding hands with chains—
> neither did I ever think this proper nor will I be persuaded—
> nor that one is by nature master of another.
> For god, if he is truly god, needs
> nothing; these are the wretched stories of poets.

Heracles dismisses Theseus' argument by denying its premise: gods do not behave like that. He does decide to live, but it is because he wishes to avoid the charge of cowardice for taking his own life (1347-48). As he describes it, "For whoever cannot withstand the blows of fortune,/he would not be able to withstand a man's weapon./ I will brave death." (1349-51) He will accept Theseus ' gifts and follow him to Athens. Heracles' reply makes clear that his decision to live is based on his own consideration of the cowardice of suicide; his own sense of heroism (*arete*) will not allow him to take his own life. (Contrast, as the original audience must have, the situation of Sophocles' Ajax, whose sense of shame leads him to that very act of self-destruction.) He will even take up the bow, the murder weapon and a harsh reminder of his heinous act, a symbol of his renewed heroism.

The opening of Heracles' reply, although it has a definite context and narrow dramatic purpose, to reply to and dismiss Theseus' argument, has a larger dramatic function as well. Some critics have tried to make these lines the cornerstone of the play, while others have tried to dismiss them as merely the obtrusive opinion of the poet. Still others, while acknowledging their relevance to the immediate context and debate, deny them any value outside of that context. But in a play in which the question of divine justice and Heracles' paternity are both at issue, it is impossible to deny these lines a significance beyond their narrow context. We have already observed the traditional account

of Hera's anger and persecution of Heracles, the account referred to in Heracles' first speech to Theseus (1255-1310), the account assumed and nowhere
denied throughout the drama. Heracles' pronouncement on the gods echoes
these earlier statements and assumptions. His words also gain a resonance
from their clear echo of an earlier poet-philosopher's criticism of the poets'
accounts of divine behavior. Writing in the late sixth and early fifth centuries,
Xenophanes faulted the poets for wrongly ascribing to the gods rule over one
another, adultery, theft, and deception. Heracles, then, is drawing attention
to and criticizing the poets (among whom, of course, Euripides is numbered)
for their accounts of divine behavior, the type of behavior on which the entire
dramatic action, stemming from Zeus' illicit union with Alcmene, is based.

Heracles' words are in opposition not only to what we have heard
earlier in the play but also to what Heracles himself says at the end of this
speech: "We are all completely ruined/miserable, struck down by one blow
of fortune from Hera." (1392-93) At the end of this speech, which is framed
by these statements on divine malfeasance, Heracles returns to the traditional
assumptions about the cause of his sufferings and, implicitly, about his paternity. Earlier in this same speech Heracles had said, "We must be a slave to
fortune." (1357) Fortune (*tuche*) has not replaced Hera, although that argument
has been made. Rather Heracles recognizes that the seemingly random events
of his life, culminating in his overthrow at the moment of his greatest victory,
have behind them the presence of Hera. She, he finally concludes, is indeed
the cause of his suffering.

But his opening words in this final speech, even if he implicitly rejects
them, have a greater significance to the audience. Unlike the character Heracles,
who exists only to the extent that the dramatist creates, the audience, and read-
ers of the play, are free to consider and evaluate the implications of Heracles'
assertion. And the events of the play provide ample motive for doing so, as the
issue of divine justice has been raised from the beginning of the drama. The
altar of Zeus the Rescuer, an altar established by Zeus' own son, seems to offer
no protection to that son's family and the man whose wife Zeus shared. Amphitryon puts the issue of divine justice into sharp focus in his two "challenging
prayers" to Zeus (339ff., 499ff.). And then, when all seems lost, Heracles returns
to save the family, proof to the chorus' mind that the gods do care for justice.
But the appearance of Iris and Lyssa shatter that belief. That scene serves, in
a way, as a counterpart to Heracles' later pronouncement on the gods. The
interruption of the two gods is, we have seen, in several ways extraordinary.
It emphasizes the external causation of Heracles' madness, laying bare the
divine machinery and underscoring the gods' extreme cruelty and injustice,
at least when viewed from the human perspective, the perspective of the
audience which must interpret these events. An irony is thus created in the
play's conclusion, as Heracles accepts one notion of divinity and the audience
is invited to at least consider another, contradictory one.

Our final impression of Heracles is of not a defeated, but a triumphant
hero. He has gone through the worst labor (cf. 1279-80) and survived. He
has survived not because of the gods (although Athena did intervene and

stopped him from killing his father) but in spite of them and because of the human friendship provided by Theseus. Theseus offers his aid and comfort as a return on Heracles' initial act of friendship, a point made several times in the drama. The traditional code of helping your friends has served Heracles well. Although Theseus' arrival and succor are crucial to the plot and Heracles' survival, it is Heracles, the play makes clear, who decides on his own beliefs and code to continue with life. Nor is he fundamentally changed. His painful decision to take up the same bow with which he killed his family (1376-85) helps to demonstrate not so much a new, revised heroism (*arete*), but a revived one, one that is able to flourish because of his friendship with Theseus. He is not self-sufficient: he needs his friend Theseus in order to live.

The play ends with separation and departure. Heracles must leave his family (he is not allowed to bury them) and Amphitryon in Thebes and go to Athens. Parting from Amphitryon is painful and drawn out affectingly. Finally Heracles exits with Theseus. He has made the decision to leave, but his reliance on Theseus' friendship is symbolically shown in the final stage action: "And I, having destroyed my house with shameful deeds,/all ruined, will follow Theseus, a little boat in tow." (1423-24) The echo of his earlier words as he led his children into the house (631-32), especially of the very rare word for "little boat in tow" is clear and important. As discussed above, the exit of the family with Heracles into the house echoed their earlier entrance from it. Now this exit echoes the previous one. These three stage actions, each articulating an important stage of the action, suggest in outline the play's progression. In the first, the former suppliants enter to seemingly certain death, but they are rescued and then exit to apparent safety, where in fact they will be fiercely murdered. The final exit, mirroring the first, provides true safety, as Heracles departs to haven in Athens.

Heracles' closing words continue the theme of friendship: "Whoever wishes to acquire wealth or strength/more than good friends, thinks badly." (1425-26) And the chorus has the play's final words, also on this theme: "We go, pitiable and much lamenting/after losing the greatest of friends." (1427-28) The importance of friendship was announced first in the conclusion of Amphitryon's opening speech and has been repeated throughout the drama. Heracles does not defeat the gods, he does not better Hera. The play suggests the power of the gods, even while suggesting that our comprehension of them might be faulty. The vicissitudes of life, the role of fortune (not Fortune) are nowhere more forcefully seen than in this view of Heracles' life. At the moment of his greatest success, rescuing his family, which he has declared more important than his just-completed labors, Heracles suffers a complete reversal of fortune. He becomes not his family's rescuer, but their murderer. Even the greatest hero is subject to the cruellest and most terrible ruin. The Greeks, from the time of Homer onwards, understood that success was ephemeral, but the turnabout here is as shocking and total as anything in Greek literature. And, as we have seen, Euripides has tailored the traditional version of the myth in order to emphasize this point. The juxtaposition of the two actions is his design, not his failing. Although Heracles cannot control all the elements of his life, he can make some decision within it. Buoyed by the friendship of Theseus, he is able to reject suicide and go on with his life. According to Greek myths, Heracles eventually became a full-fledged deity, a reward for his labors and suffering. Euripides avoids any mention (and, I think, even any allusion) to this later apotheosis in order to focus on the human Heracles, a Heracles who sustained by human friendship can survive in a capricious and harsh world.

Greek Tragedy and Euripides:
A Select Bibliography

REFERENCE BOOKS ON GREEK TRAGEDY

1. Csapo, E. and Slater, W.J. *The Context of Ancient Drama* (Ann Arbor, 1994).
2. Easterling, P.E. (ed.) *The Cambridge Companion to Greek Tragedy* (Cambridge, 1997).
3. Lesky, A. *Greek Tragic Poetry* trans. M. Dillon (New Haven, 1983).
4. Sommerstein, A. *Greek Drama and Dramatists* (London and New York, 2002).

WHAT IS GREEK TRAGEDY?

1. Golden, L. "Toward a definition of tragedy" *Classical Journal* 72 (1976) 21-35.
2. Griffin, J. "The Social Function of Attic Tragedy" *Classical Quarterly* 48 (1998) 39-61.
3. Hall, E. "The Sociology of Athenian Tragedy" in Easterling, P.E. (ed.) *The Cambridge Companion to Greek Tragedy* (Cambridge, 1997) 93-126.
4. Lesky, A. "What is Tragedy?" in Lesky, A. *Greek Tragedy* trans. H.A. Frankfort (London and New York, 1965) 1-26.
5. Seaford, R. "The Social Function of Attic Tragedy: A Response to Jasper Griffin" *Classical Quarterly* 50 (2000) 30-44.

WHAT IS ATHENIAN DEMOCRACY?

1. Finley, M.I. *Democracy Ancient and Modern* (New Brunswick, NJ, 1973).
2. Gomme, A.W. "The Working of the Athenian Democracy" *History* 36 (1951) 12-28 = *More Essays in Greek History and Literature* (ed.) D.A. Campbell (Oxford, 1962).
3. Raaflaub, K. and Morris, I. (eds.) *Democracy 2500? Questions and Challenges* (Dubuque, IA, 1997).
4. Raaflaub, K. and Boedeker, D. *Democracy, Empire, and the Arts in Fifth-Century Athens* (Cambridge and London, 1998).
5. Rahe, P. "The Primacy of Politics in Classical Greece" *American Historical Review* 89 (1984) 265-93.

6. Samons, L.J. (ed.) *Athenian Democracy and Imperialism* (Boston, 1998).

7. Samons, L. J. "Democracy, Empire, and the Search for the Athenian Character" *Arion* (Winter 2001) 128-57.

EURIPIDES: GENERAL ARTICLES

1. Arrowsmith, W. "Euripides' Theater of Ideas" in Segal, E. (ed.) *Euripides: A Collection of Critical Essays* (Englewood Cliffs, NJ, 1968) 13-33.

2. Arrowsmith, W. "Euripides and the Dramaturgy of Crisis" in *Literary Imagination* 1.2 (1999) 201-26.

3. Jaeger, W. "Euripides and His Age" in *Paideia: The Ideals of Greek Culture*[2], vol. I trans. G. Highet (1945) 332-57.

4. Kovacs, D. "Introduction" in *Euripides: Cyclops, Alcestis, Medea* (Loeb Classical Library, Cambridge, Ma. and London, 1994) 1-42.

5. Lefkowitz, M. "Euripides" in *Lives of the Greek Poets* (Baltimore, 1981) 88-104.

6. March, J. "Euripides the Misogynist?" in A. Powell (ed.) *Euripides, Women, and Sexuality* (New York and London, 1990).

7. Rabinowitz, N. *Anxiety Veiled: Euripides and the Traffic of Women* (Ithaca, 1993).

EURIPIDES AND THE PHILOSOPHERS

1. Allan, W. "Euripides and the Sophists: Society and the Theatre of War" in M. Cropp, K. Lee, and D. Sansone (eds.) *Euripides and Tragic Theatre in the Late Fifth Century* (Champaign, 2000) 145-56.

2. Claus, D. "Phaedra and the Socratic paradox" *Yale Classical Studies* 22 (1972) 223-38.

3. Collinge, N. "Medea versus Socrates" *The Durham University Journal* 42 (1950) 41-47.

4. Conacher, D. J. *Euripides and the Sophists: Some Dramatic Treatments of Philosophical Ideas* (London, 1998).

5. Irwin, T. H. "Euripides and Socrates" *Classical Philology* 78 (1983) 183-97.

6. Irwin, T. H. "Socrates and the Tragic Hero" in *Language and the Tragic Hero* (ed.) P. Pucci (Atlanta, 1988) 55-83.

7. Michelini, A. "Socratic Ideology" [in Euripides' *Hippolytos*] in *Euripides and The Tragic Tradition* (Madison, 1987) 297-10.

8. Moline, J. "Euripides, Socrates and Virtue" *Hermes* 103 (1975) 45-67.

9. Sansone, D. "Plato and Euripides" *Illinois Classical Studies* 21 (1996) 35-67.

Euripides and the Gods

1. Knox, B. "Athenian Religion and Literature" in *The Cambridge Ancient History* vol. V (Cambridge, 1992).

2. Lefkowitz, M. "Was Euripides an Atheist?" *Studi Italiani Di Filologia Classica* 5.2 (1987) 149-66.

3. Lefkowitz, M. "Impiety and Atheism in Euripides" *Classical Quarterly* 39 (1989) 70-82.

4. Mikalson, J. *Honor Thy Gods: Popular Religion in Greek Tragedy* (Chapel Hill and London, 1991)

5. Ostwald, M. "Atheism and the religiosity of Euripides" in *Literary Imagination, Ancient and Modern: Essays in Honor of David Grene* (ed.) T. Breyfogle (Chicago and London, 1999)

6. Sansone, D. "Language, Meaning and Reality in Euripides" in *Ultimate Reality and Meaning* 8.2 (1985) 92-104.

Medea

1. Boedeker, D. "Euripides' *Medea* and the Vanity of Logoi" *American Journal of Philology* 86 (1991) 95-112.

2. Clauss, J. and Johnston, S. I. (eds.) *Medea : Essays on Medea in Myth, Literature, Philosophy, and Art* (Princeton, 1997).

3. Corti, L. "Euripides and the Tyranny of Honor" in *The Myth of Medea and the Murder of Children* (Westport, Ct. and London, 1998) 29-58.

4. Hall, E.; Macintosh, F.; Taplin, O. (eds.) *Medea in Performance 1500-2000* (Oakville, 2001).

5. Simon, B. "Euripides' *Medea*" in *Tragic Drama and the Family: Psycholanalytic Studies from Aeschylus to Beckett* (New Haven / London 1988) 69-102.

Hippolytus

1. Gill, C. "The Articulation of the Self in Euripides' *Hippolytus*," in A. Powell (ed.) *Euripides, Women and Sexuality* (London 1990) 76-107.

2. Goldhill, S. *Reading Greek Tragedy* (Cambridge 1986) 107-37.

3. Gregory, J. *Euripides and the Instruction of the Athenians* (Ann Arbor 1991) 51-84.

4. Halleran, M. R. (ed.) *Euripides: Hippolytus, with Introduction, Translation and Commentary* (Warminster 1995).

5. Knox, B. M. W. "The *Hippolytus* of Euripides" in *Word and Action* (Baltimore 1979) 205-30.

6. Segal, C. "The Tragedy of *Hippolytus*: The Waters of Ocean and the Untouched Meadow" in *Interpreting Greek Tragedy: Myth, Poetry, Text* (Ithaca 1986) 165-221.

7. Snell, B. "Passion and Reason: Medea and Phaedra in *Hippolytos* II" in *Scenes from Greek Drama* (Berkeley and Los Angeles 1967) 47-69.

HERACLES

1. Arrowsmith, W. "Introduction to *Heracles*" in *Euripides* vol II (eds.) R. Lattimore and D. Grene (Chicago 1952) 44-59.

2. Burnett, A. *Catastrophe Survived: Euripides' Plays of Mixed Reversal* (Oxford 1971) 157-82.

3. Dunn, F. *Tragedy's End: Closure and Innovation in Euripidean Drama* (Oxford and New York 1996) 115-29.

4. Foley, H. *Ritual Irony. Poetry and Sacrifice in Euripides* (Cornell 1985) 147-204.

5. Gregory, J. *Euripides and the Instruction of the Athenians* (Ann Arbor 1991) 121-54.

6. Halleran, M. *Stagecraft in Euripides* (London 1985) 80-92.

7. Lawrence, S. "The God That is Truly God and the Universe of Euripides' *Heracles*" *Mnemosyne* 51 (1998) 129-46.

8. Pucci, P. "Survival in the *Heracles*" in *The Violence of Pity in Euripides' Medea* (Ithaca and London, 1980) 175-87.

9. Yunis, H. "A New Creed: *Heracles*" in *A New Creed: Fundamental Beliefs in the Athenian Polis and Euripidean Drama* (Gottingen, 1988) 139-71.

BACCHAE

1. Dick, Bernard "*Lord of the Flies* and the *Bacchae*" *Classical Journal* 57 (1964) 145-46.

2. Esposito, S. "Teaching Euripides' *Bacchae*" in *Approaches to Teaching the Dramas of Euripides* ed. R. Mitchell-Boyask (2002) 189-202.

3. Friedrich, R. "Dionysus Among the Dons: The New Ritualism in R. Seaford's Commentary on the *Bacchae*" *Arion* 7.3 (2000) 115-52.

4. Roncace, M. "The *Bacchae* and *Lord of the Flies*: A Few Observations with the Help of E. R. Dodds" in *Classical and Modern Literature* 18 (1997) 37-51.

5. Segal, C. "Lament and Recognition: A Reconsideration of the Ending of the *Bacchae*" in *Euripides and Tragic Theatre in the Late Fifth Century* (eds.) M. Cropp, K. Lee, D. Sansone (2000) 273-91.

BACCHAE: WORKS REFERENCED IN THE FOOTNOTES TO ESPOSITO'S TRANSLATION

1. Devereux, G. "The Psychotherapy Scene in Euripides' *Bacchae*" *Journal of Hellenic Studies* 90 (1970) 35-48.

2. Dodds, E. R. *Euripides: Bacchae*[2] (1960).

3. Kalke, C. "The Making of a Thyrsus: The Transformation of Pentheus in Euripides' *Bacchae*" *American Journal of Philology* 106 (1985) 409-26.

4. Kirk, G. *The Bacchae of Euripides: A Translation with Commentary* (1970).

5. Leinieks, V. *The City of Dionysos: A Study of Euripides' Bakchai* (1996).

6. Rijksbaron, A. *Grammatical Observations on Euripides' Bacchae* (1991).

7. Seaford, R. "Dionysiac Drama and the Dionysiac Mysteries" *Classical Quarterly* 31 (1981) 252-71.

8. Seaford, R. *Euripides' Bacchae with an Introduction, Translation, Commentary* (1996).

9. Segal, C. "Female Mourning and Dionysiac Lament in Euripides' *Bacchae*" in *Orchestra: Drama, Mythos, Bühne* (eds.) A. Bierl and P. von Möllendorff (1994) 12-18.

10. Stanford, W. *Ambiguity in Greek Literature* (1939) 174-79.

11. Taplin, O. *Greek Tragedy in Action* (1978).

12. Willink, C. "Some Problems of Text and Interpretation in the *Bacchae*" *Classical Review* 16 (1966) 27-50.

13. Wolff, C. "Euripides" in *Ancient Writers: Greece and Rome* vol. 1 (ed.) T. Luce (1982) 233-66.

ADDENDUM TO THE BIBLIOGRAPHY OF THE 2002 EDITION

1. Allan, William *Euripides: Medea* [Duckworth Companions to Greek and Roman Tragedy] (2002).

2. Bloom, Harold (ed.) *Bloom's Major Dramatists: Euripides* (2003).

3. Easterling, P. E. and Hall, E. (eds.) *Greek and Roman Actors: Aspects of an Ancient Profession* (2002).

4. Easterling, P. E. "The Infanticide in Euripides' *Medea*" in *Euripides: Oxford Readings in Classical Studies*, ed. J. Mossman (2003) 187-200.

5. Foley, H. "Tragic Wives: Medea's Divided Self" in *Female Acts in Greek Tragedy* (2001) 243-71.

6. Gregory, J. "Euripides as a Social Critic" *Greece and Rome* 49 (2002) 145-62.

7. Halliwell, S. "Nietzsche's 'Daimonic Force' of Tragedy and Its Ancient Traces" *Arion* 11 (2003) 103-23.

8. Humphries, W. Lee *The Tragic Vision and the Hebrew Tradition* (1985).

9. Kaimio, M. "The citizenship of the Theatre-Makers in Athens" in *Wurzburger Jahrbucher fur die Altertumswissenschaft* 23 (1999) 43-61.

10. Kovacs, D. *Euripidea* (1994), esp. pp. 1-141 on sources for Euripides' life (in translation).

11. Kovacs, D. (ed. / trans.) *Euripides: Bacchae, Iphigeneia at Aulis, Rhesus* [Loeb Classical Library] (2002).

12. Lee, K. H. "The Dionysia: instrument of control or platform for critique?" in *Gab es das Griechische Wunder? Griechenland zwishcen dem Ende des 6. und der Mitte des 5. Jahrhunderts v. Chr.* eds. D. Papenfuss and V. Strocka (2001) 77-89.

13. Mastronarde, D. (ed.) *Euripides: Medea* (2002); Greek text and commentary with a comprehensive introduction which is accessible to the general reader.

14. Mills, S. *Euripides: Hippolytus* [Duckworth Companions to Greek and Roman Tragedy] (2002).

15. Morwood, J. *The Plays of Euripides* [Classical World Series] (2002).

16. Rhodes, P.. J. "Nothing to Do with Democracy: Athenian Drama and the Polis" *Journal of Hellenic Studies* 123 (2003) 104-19.

17. Romilly, J. de "The Rejection of Suicide in the *Heracles* of Euripides" in *Euripides: Oxford Readings in Classical Studies*, ed. J. Mossman (2003) 285-94.

18. Scodel, R. "The Poet's Career, The Rise of Tragedy, and Athenian Cultural Hegemony" in *Gab es das Griechische Wunder? Griechenland zwishcen dem Ende des 6. und der Mitte des 5. Jahrhunderts v. Chr.* eds. D. Papenfuss and V. Strocka (Mainz 2001) 215-27.

19. Scott, W. and Steyaert, K. "Musical Disorder in Euripides' *Bacchae*" in *Text and Presentation: Journal of the Comparative Drama Conference* 14 (1993) 87-90.

20. Scullion, S. "'Nothing to Do with Dionysus': Tragedy Misconceived as Ritual" *Classical Quarterly* 52 (2002) 102-37.

21. Scullion, S. "Euripides and Macedon, or the Silence of the Frogs" *Classical Quarterly* 53 (2003) 389-400 who argues provocatively, against the highly unreliable ancient biographical tradition and the consensus of modern scholarship, that Euripides never went to the court of King Archelaus of Macedon at the end of his life (c. 408 BCE) to write his last plays in self-imposed "exile" and furthermore that he probably died in Athens (407/6).

22. Seaford, R. "Dionysos, Money, and Drama" *Arion* 11 (2003) 1-19.

23. Seaford, R. "Tragic Tyranny" in *Popular Tyranny: Sovereignty and Its Discontents in Ancient Greece*, ed. Kathryn Morgan (2003) 95-115.

24. Segal, C. "Introduction" in *Euripides' Bakkhai* trans. R. Gibbons, introduction and notes by C. Segal (2001) 3-32.

25. Winkler, M.M. (ed.) *Classical Myth and Cutlure in the Cinema* (2001).